A-Z NOTTINGHAM

Key to Map Pages	2-3
Large Scale City Centre	4-5
Map Pages	6-81
Postcode Map	82-83

Roa...
Inde...
Villa...
and...

REFERENCE

Motorway	**M1**
A Road	**A46**
B Road	**B682**
Dual Carriageway	
One-way Street Traffic flow on A Roads Is also indicated by a heavy line on the driver's left.	
Road Under Construction Opening dates are correct at the time of publication.	
Proposed Road	
Restricted Access	
Pedestrianized Road	
Track / Footpath	
Residential Walkway	
Railway	Heritage Station — Station — Level Crossing — Tunnel
Nottingham Express Transit (NET) The boarding of NET trams at stops maybe limited to a single direction, indicated by the arrow	Stop
Built-up Area	ORFORD AV.
Local Authority Boundary	
Post Town Boundary	
Postcode Boundary (within Post Town)	
Map Continuation	**40** Large Scale City Centre **4**

Car Park (selected)	**P**
Church or Chapel	†
Cycleway (selected)	☒☒☒
Fire Station	■
Hospital	**H**
House Numbers (A & B Roads only)	37 44
Information Centre	**i**
National Grid Reference	345
Park and Ride	Lace Market **P+R**
Police Station	▲
Post Office	★
Safety Camera with Speed Limit Fixed cameras and long term road works cameras. Symbols do not indicate camera direction.	**30**
Toilet	▽
Educational Establishment	
Hospital or Healthcare Building	
Industrial Building	
Leisure or Recreational Facility	
Place of Interest	
Public Building	
Shopping Centre or Market	
Other Selected Buildings	

SCALE

Large Scale Pages 4-5   1:7,920

0   ⅛   ¼ Mile

0   100   200   300 Metres

8 inches (20.32cm) to 1 Mile   12.63cm to 1km

Map Pages 6-81   1:15,840

0   ¼   ½ Mile

0   250   500   750 Metres

4 inches (10.16cm) to 1 Mile   6.31cm to 1km

A-Z A͞Z AtoZ

registered trade marks of Geographers' A-Z Map Company Ltd

www./az.co.uk

EDITION 8   2019

Copyright © Geographers' A-Z Map Co. Ltd.

© Crown copyright and database rights 2018 OS 100017302.

Safety camera information supplied by www.PocketGPSWorld.com
Speed Camera Location Database Copyright © PocketGPSWorld.com

Every possible care has been taken to ensure that, to the best of our knowledge, the information contained in this atlas is accurate at the date of publication. However, we cannot warrant that our work is entirely error free and whilst we would be grateful to learn of any inaccuracies, we do not accept responsibility for loss or damage resulting from reliance on information contained within this publication.

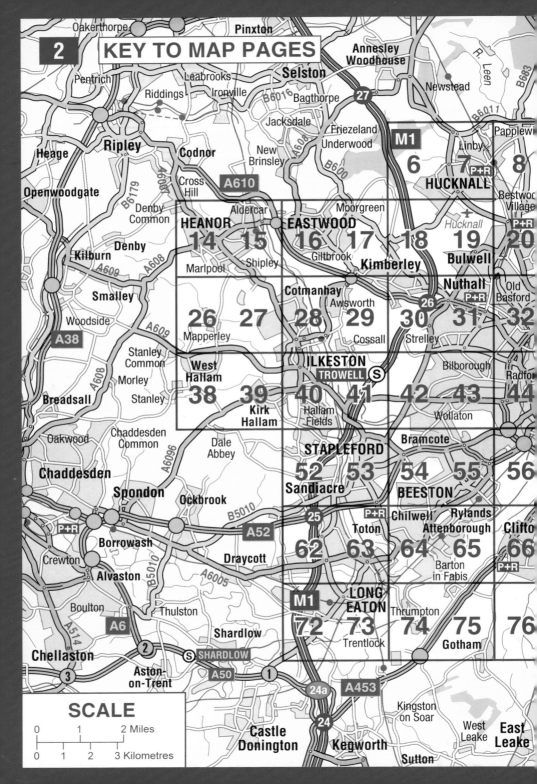

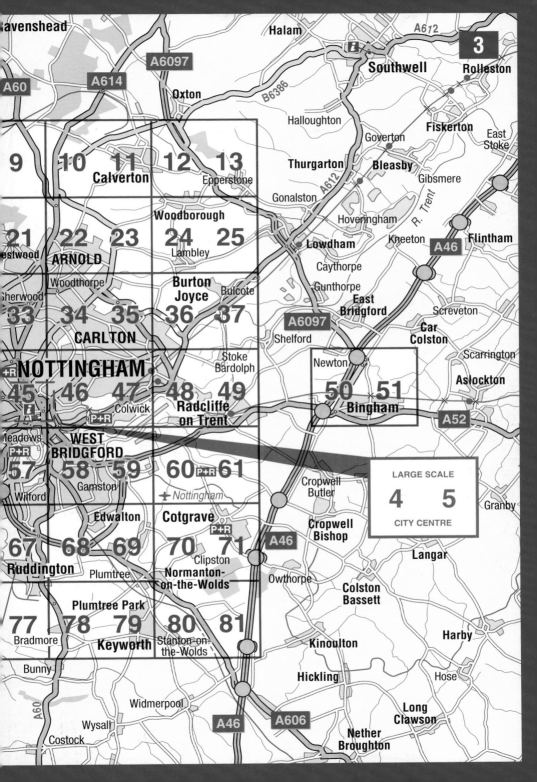

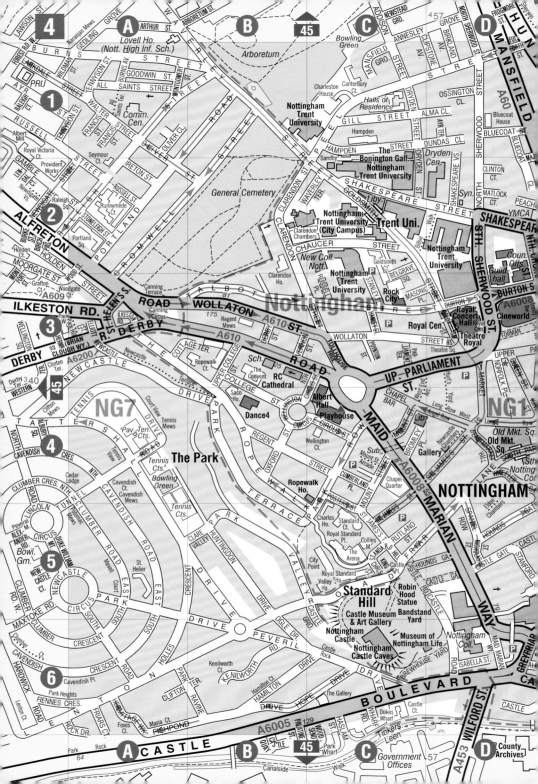

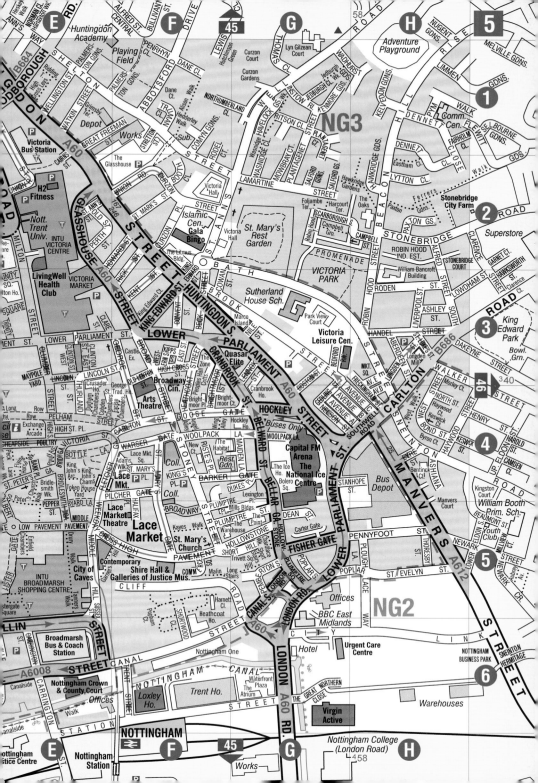

10

Great Burntstump Plantation

4 58

3 51

A Sawpit Plantation

B

C Richmond's Farm 59

D Watchwood Plantation

BURNTSTUMP

Burntstump Plantation

1 The Nursery Beech Wood Spts. Gd.

ntstump ntry Park

Country Park and Walks

Arnold Seely C of E Prim. Sch.

Cockliffe Hill Farm

Cockliffe House

ckliffe ood

Sports Ground

Foxcovert Plantation

Nottingham

2

The Warren

The Knoll

50

Cottage Wood

Round Plantation

Patchings Art Centre

HOLLOW MAIN

3

ike ation

Jubilee Plantation

RAMSDALE PARK GOLF CENTRE

B6386

6

Robin Hood Farm

The Rowans

Greenwood Bonsai Studio

Ramsdale Cottages

Driving Range

Club Ho.

East Hill Plantation

4

Ramper Covert

49

A614

Ramsdale House

NG5

RAMSDALE PARK GOLF CENTRE

Forest Farm

HOLLINWOOD

Hollinwood House

5

MANSFIELD

North Peacock

RAMSDALE PARK

Leila's Plantation

Calverton Hill

Ramsdale Park

Ramsdale Hill

The Belt

South Peacock

50

6

Woodlands

A60

Tophouse Farm

LITTLE LIME LA.

LAMINS

48

LIME LANE

B684

Limelane House

Reservoirs (covered)

CALVERTON

ROAD

G

A 58

B 59

22

C

D Wood Farm

ROAD

GRAVELLY HILL

ROAD

OXTON

LIME LANE

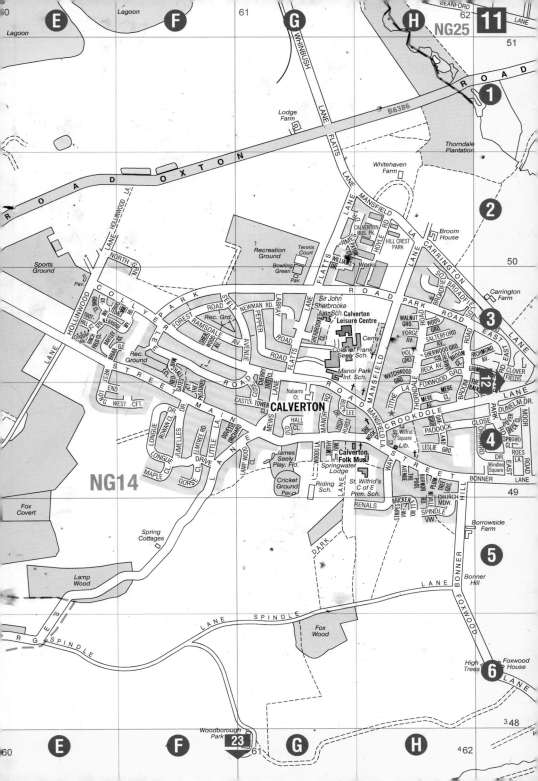

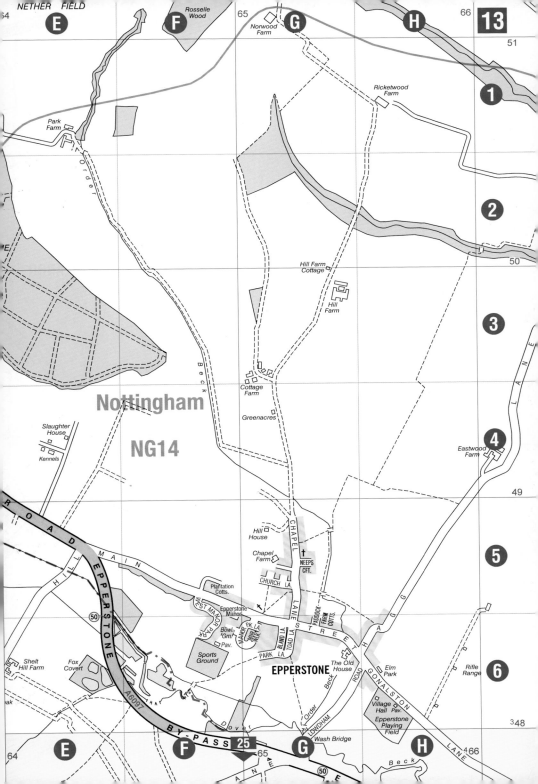

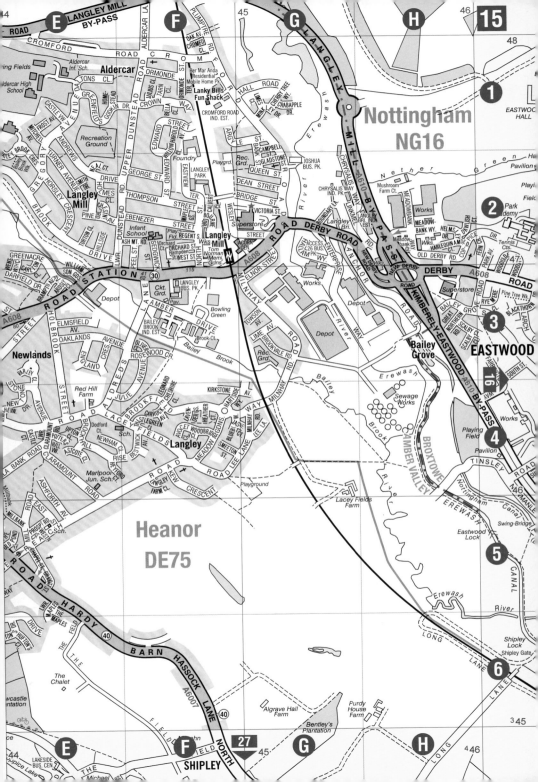

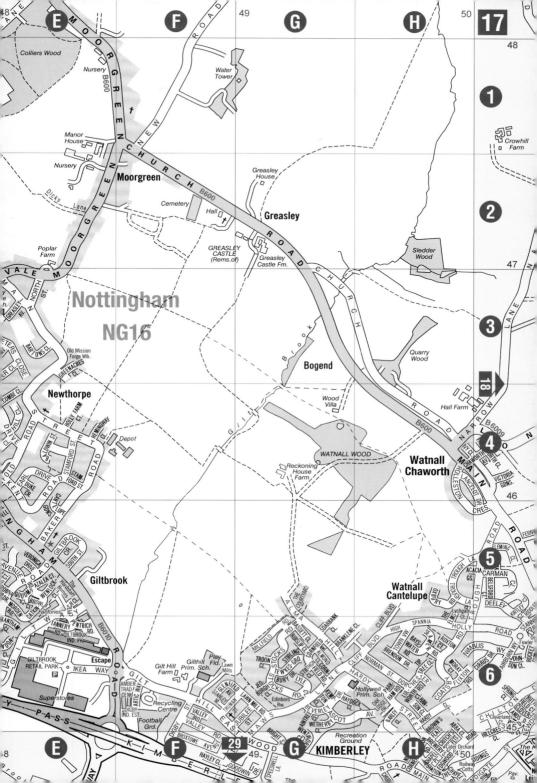

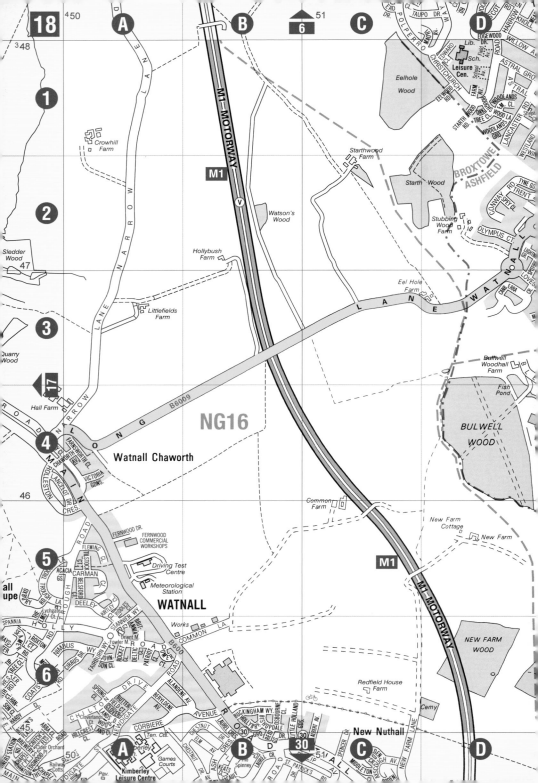

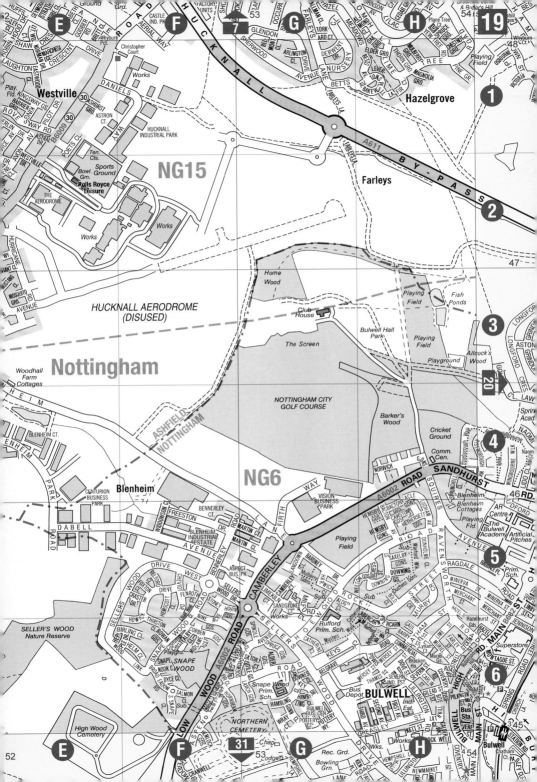

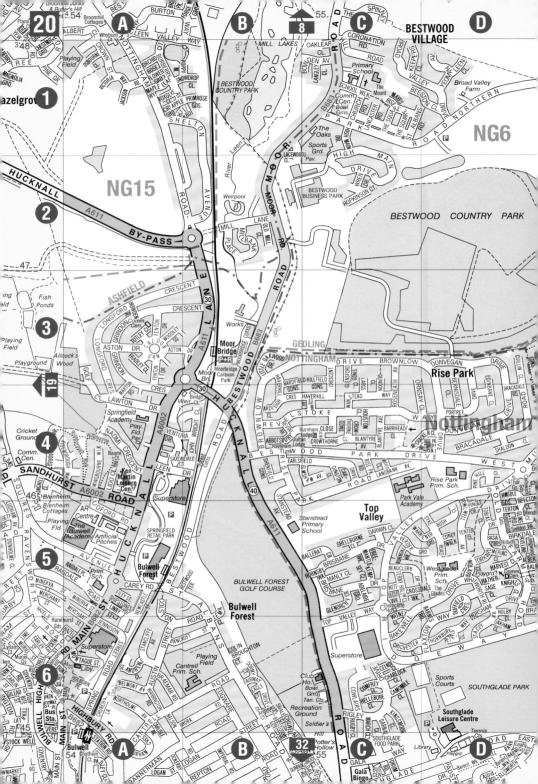

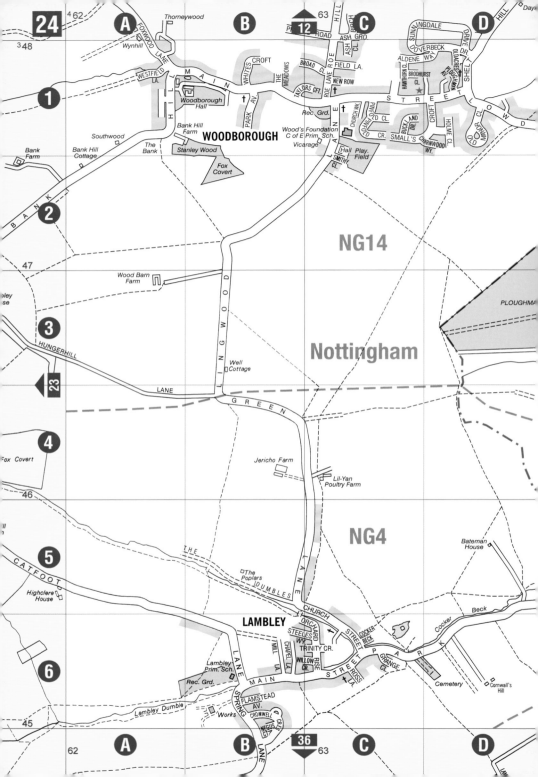

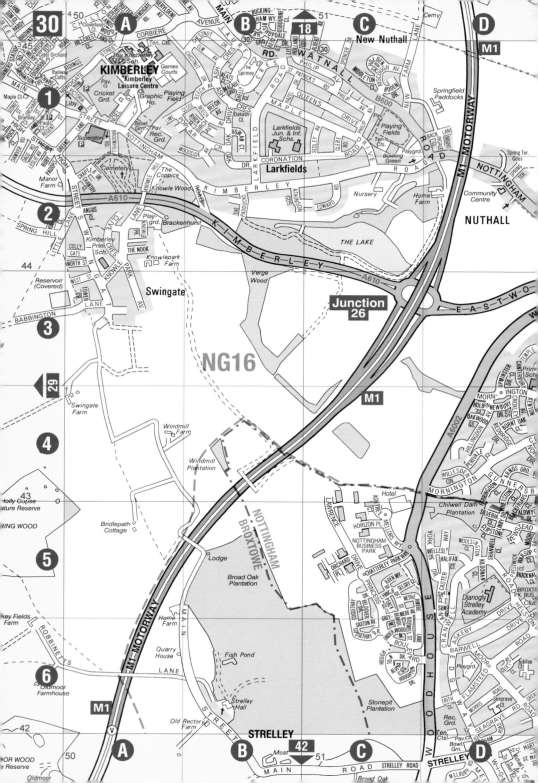

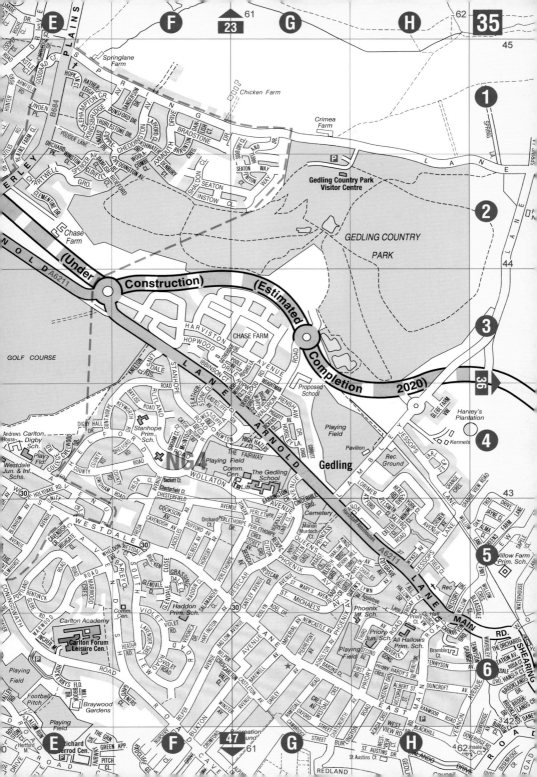

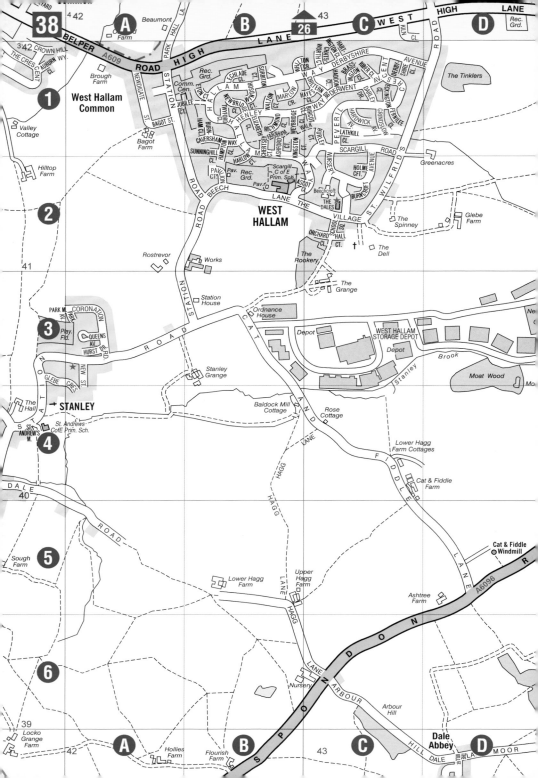

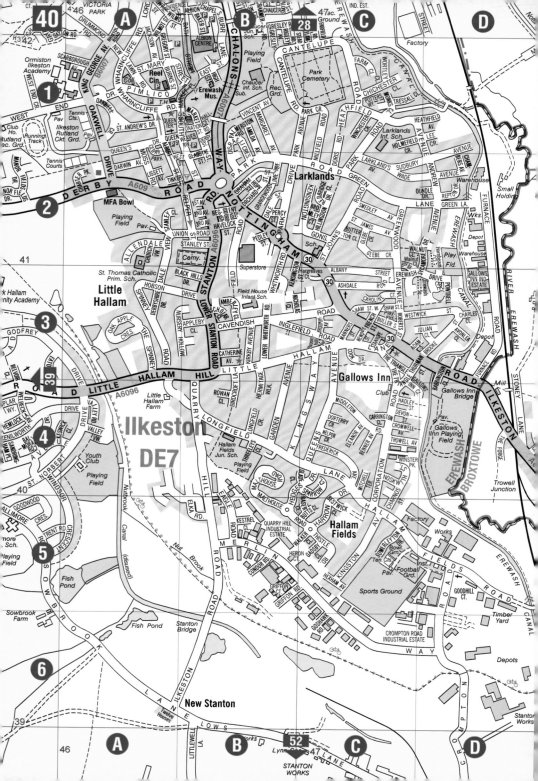

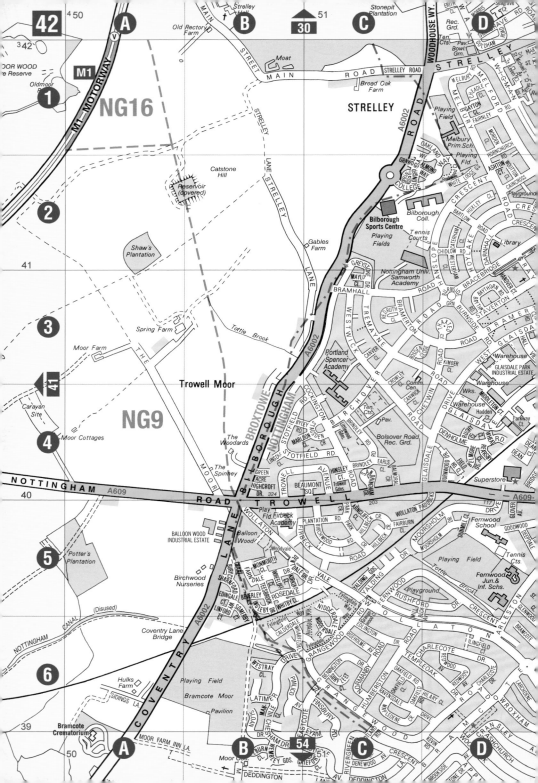

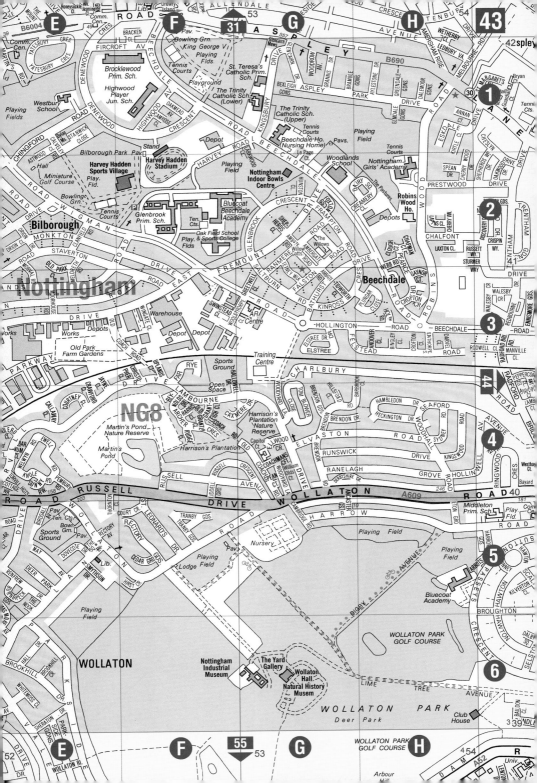

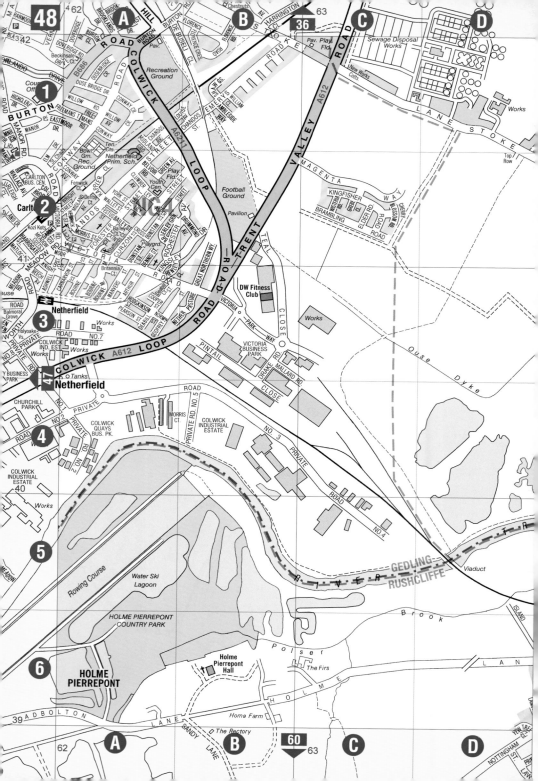

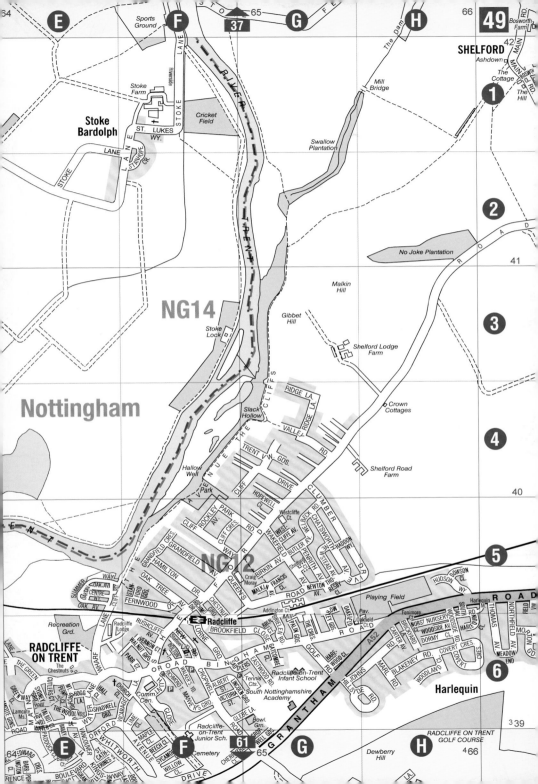

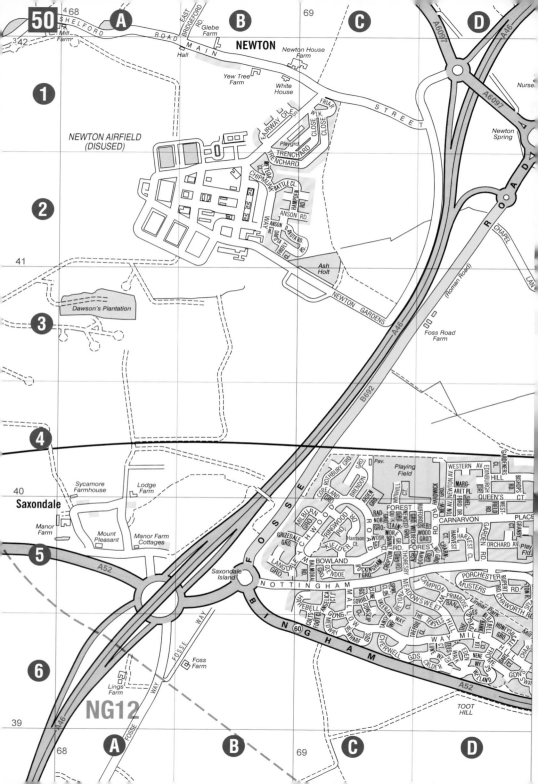

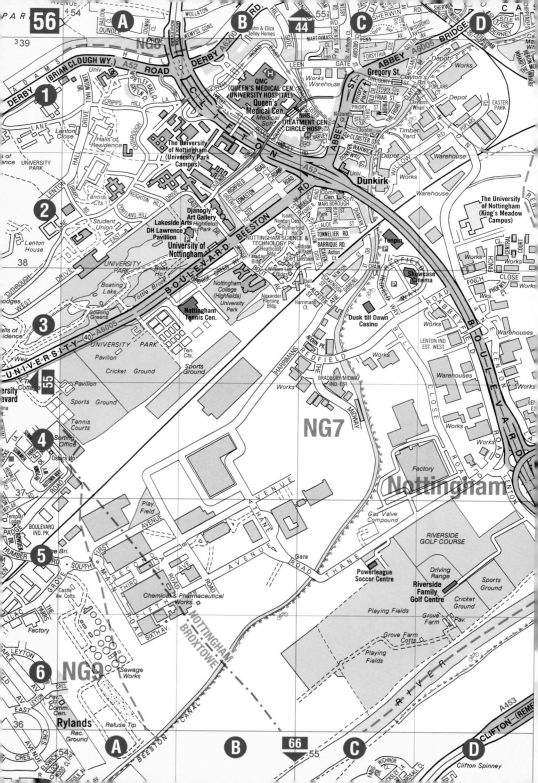

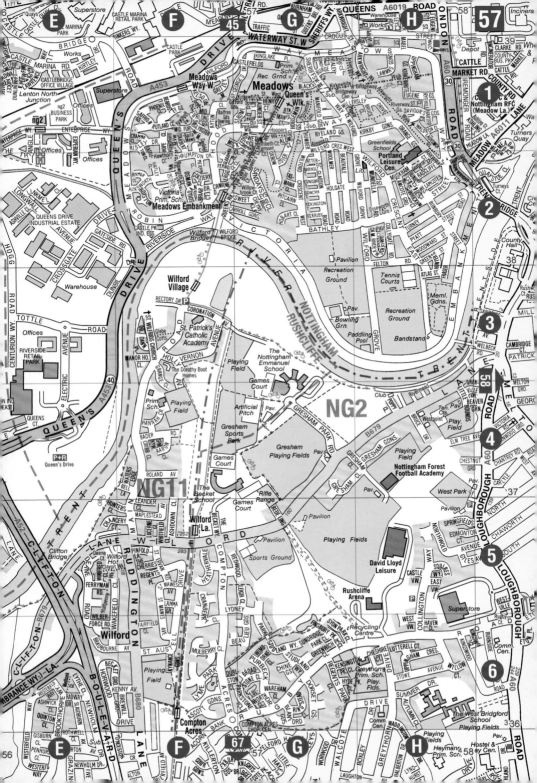

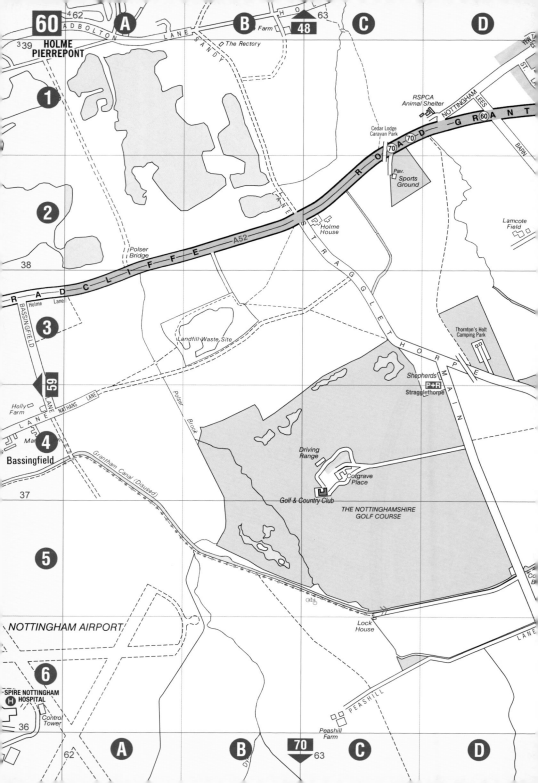

60

HOLME PIERREPONT

A52 RADCLIFFE ROAD · GRANTHAM ROAD

60

The Rectory

Farm

48

RSPCA Animal Shelter

Cedar Lodge Caravan Park

70

Pav. Sports Ground

Lamcote Field

Holme House

Polser Bridge

Holme Lane

Landfill Waste Site

Thornton's Holt Camping Park

Shepherds

P+R

Stragglethorpe

BASSINGFIELD

65

Holly Farm

NATHANS LANE

Driving Range

Cotgrave Place

Golf & Country Club

THE NOTTINGHAMSHIRE GOLF COURSE

Manor Farm

Bassingfield

Grantham Canal (Disused)

Polser Brook

Lock House

NOTTINGHAM AIRPORT

SPIRE NOTTINGHAM HOSPITAL

H

Control Tower

Peashill Farm

PEASHILL

70

38
37
36

62
63
62
63

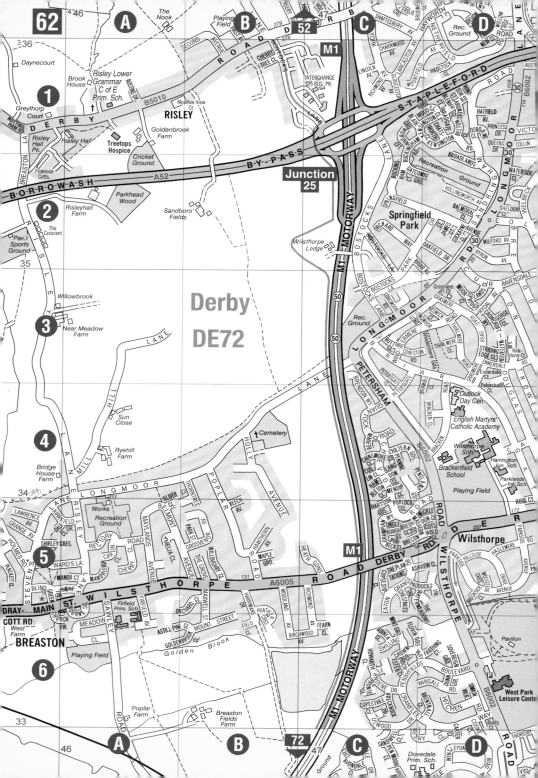

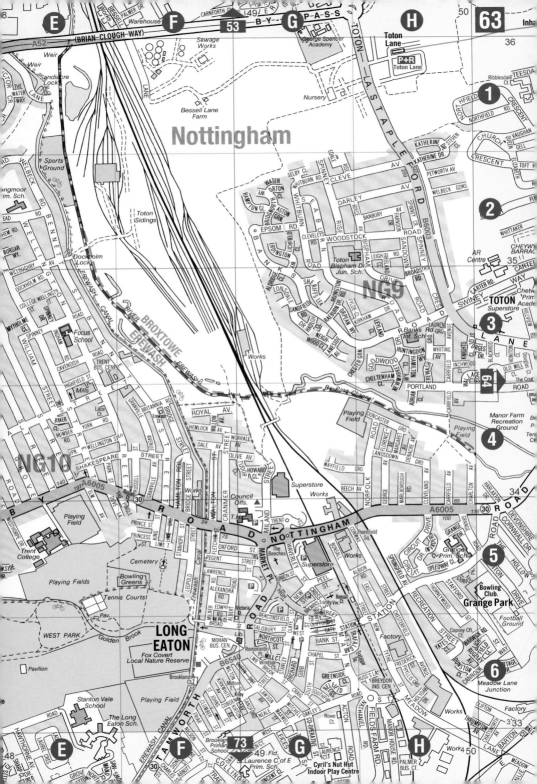

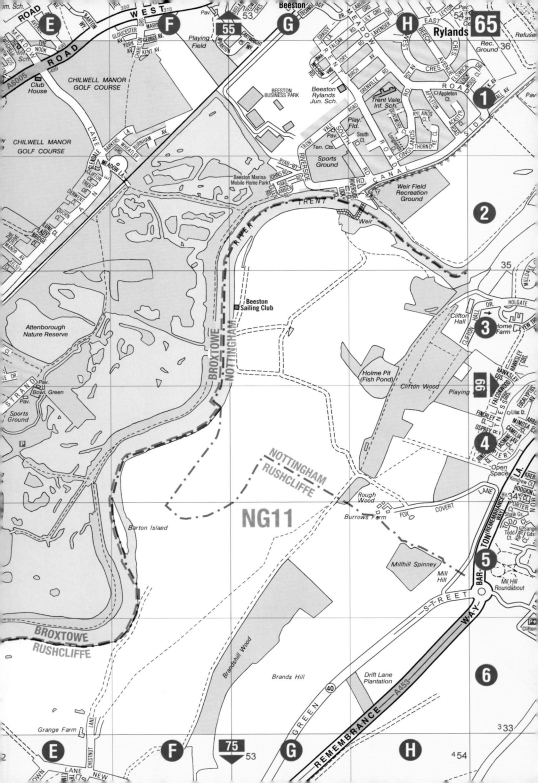

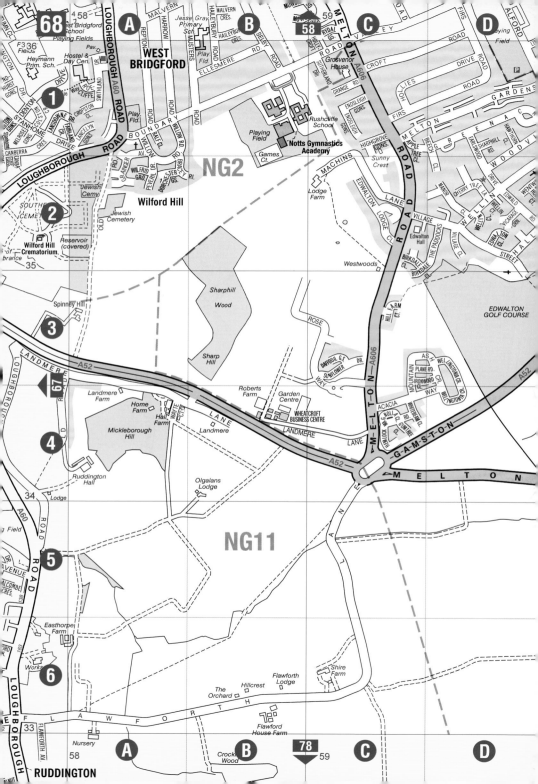

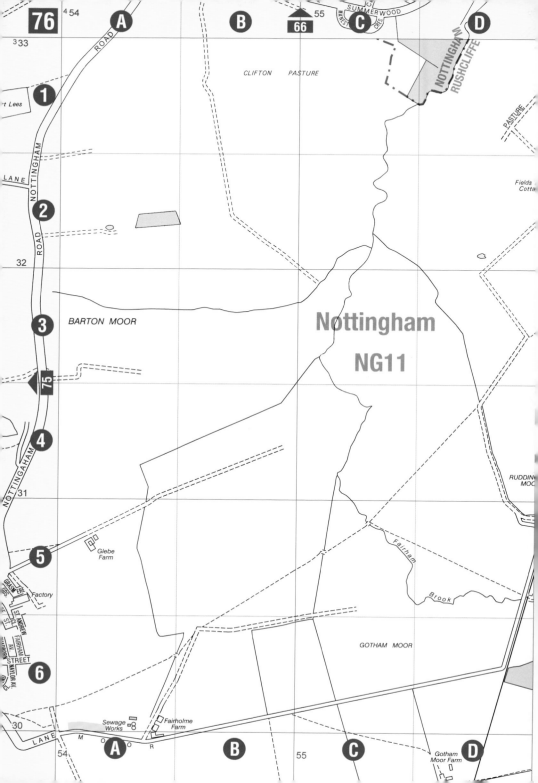

PLUMTREE
Plumtree Sch.
CHURCH LA.
FELLOWS YD.
CHURCH HILL
BRADLEYS YD.
OLD MELTON ROAD
THE POPLARS
STATION ROAD
Cricket Grd.
Pav.
Chestnut Farm
MELTON A606 ROAD
The Lawn
Normanton House
Chapel Yard
BRADMORE LANE
Blackcliffe Hill
Nottingham
NG12
Crossdale Drive Prim. Sch.
Plumtree Park
Field
Pav.
Shelton House
British Geological Survey
PARK ROAD
PARK TER.
PARK AV.
GREEN CL.
Poplars Cl.
PARKSIDE
PLATT LANE
NICKER HILL
BROCKDALE GDS.
BROCKWOOD CR.
BRIAR CL.
ROSE GRO.
VILLA RD.
CROSSDALE DRIVE
FRANKLYN GDS.
ADAMS HILL
CLIFFORD CL.
FEIGNIES CT.
NORMANTON LANE
LOWLANDS DR.
COMBE GDS.
COVERT CL.
PLEASANT
WOLDS RISE
MOUNT
WYNBRECK DR.
HILLCREST RD.
BEAUMONT CL.
DELVILLE AV.
HIGHBURY RD.
HIGHFIELD RD.
BELVEDERE CL.
ABBOT CL.
BISHOPS CL.
SIDMOUTH CL.
RANCLIFFE AV.
DEBDALE LANE
LANE ROAD
CHESTNUT CL.
MANOR ROAD
THELDA AV.
DALE RD.
SPINNEY ROAD
CROFT CT.
GORSE RD.
HAYES RD.
PLANTATION RD.
INTAKE RD.
FAIRHAM RD.
ROSE HILL
BARNT CT.
CHURCH DRIVE
ASHLEY CRES.
ASHLEY RD.
WALTON DRIVE
CRANTOCK GDS.
RANNOCK GDS.
Walton Ct.
CHERRY HILL
HIGH VIEW AV.
MEADOW DR.
THE RIDINGS
PRIVATE RD
PLEASANT
FAIR WAY AVENUE
CROFT RD.
PARK AV. WEST
PARK AV. EAST
HIGH COURT DR.
AVENUE
WEST CL.
CHARNWOOD AV.
Keyworth Prim. Sch.
EAST CL.
LEIGH CL.
WOOD CL.
NOTTINGHAM ROAD
Recreation Grd.
Hall
ELM AV.
ELM CL.
South Wolds Comm. Acdmy.
Lib.
Keyworth Leis. Cen.
Playing Fld.
WINDMILL CT.
WOLDS
BEECH AV.
LAUREL AV.
LIMETREE CL.
ALDER WY.
ASH GRO.
Key VI Fitness
SELBY LANE
Greenhays Farm
Woodfields
Lynwood
Wheatcroft Farm
ROSELAND CL.
BROOK VIEW
HAWTHORN CL.
WRIGHTS ORCHARD
COMMERCIAL RD.
BLIND LA.
The Sq.
STREET
KEYWORTH
HOLMSFIELD DRIVE
BARROW SLADE
FAR PASTURES CL.
Brook Vw. Ct.
FLINDERS ORCHARD
CEDAR DR.
MAIN STREET
Holly Farm Cotts.
Burial Grd.
LANE
Sewage Works
The Bungalow
LINGS LANE
Twyn-Bays
WYSALL LANE
WOLDS LANE
Cotton's Plantation
Crawford House
69
80
E
F
G
H
1
2
3
4
5
6
60
61
62
33
32
31
330
462

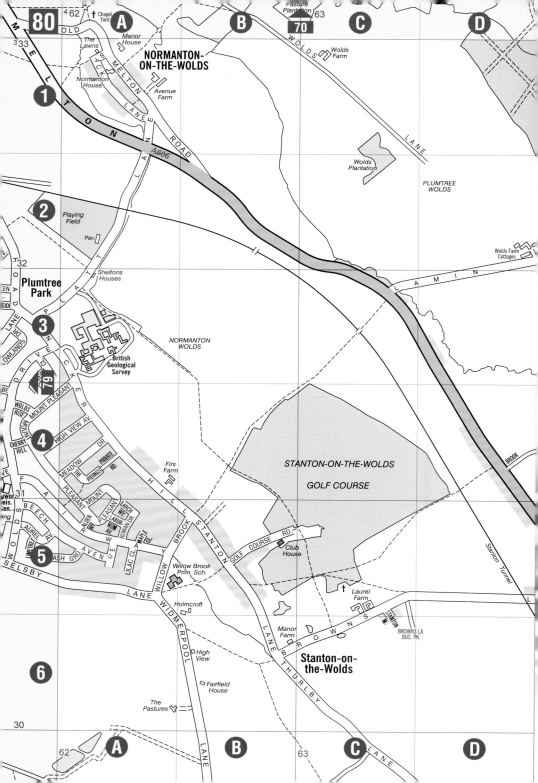

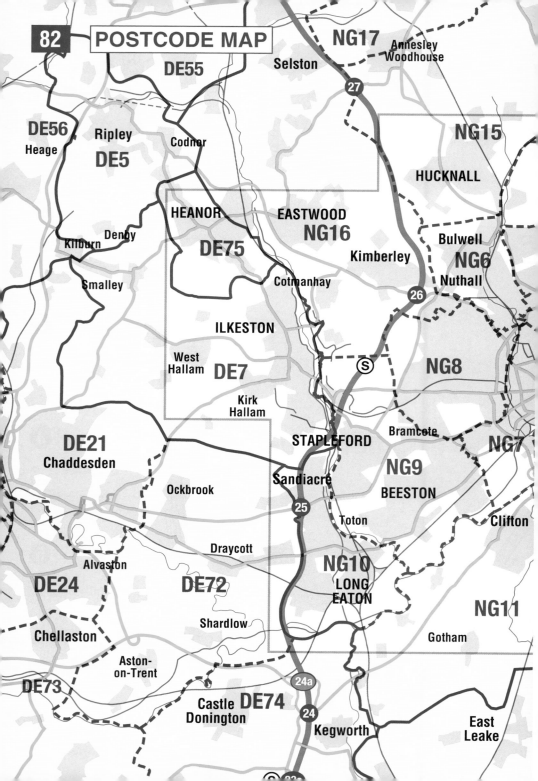

DE55

NG17

Selston

Annesley Woodhouse

27

DE56

Ripley

DE5

Codnor

NG15

Heage

HUCKNALL

Kilburn

Denby

HEANOR

EASTWOOD

NG16

Bulwell

NG6

Smalley

DE75

Kimberley

Nuthall

Cotmanhay

26

ILKESTON

West Hallam

DE7

(S)

NG8

Kirk Hallam

Bramcote

NG7

DE21

Chaddesden

STAPLEFORD

Ockbrook

Sandiacre

NG9

BEESTON

Clifton

25

Toton

Draycott

NG10

Alvaston

DE72

LONG EATON

NG11

DE24

Shardlow

Gotham

Chellaston

Aston-on-Trent

DE73

24a

DE74

Castle Donington

24

Kegworth

East Leake

(S)

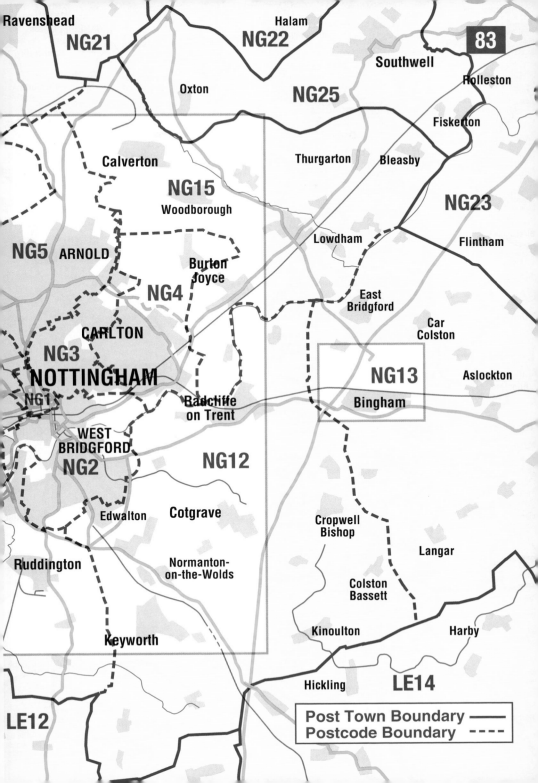

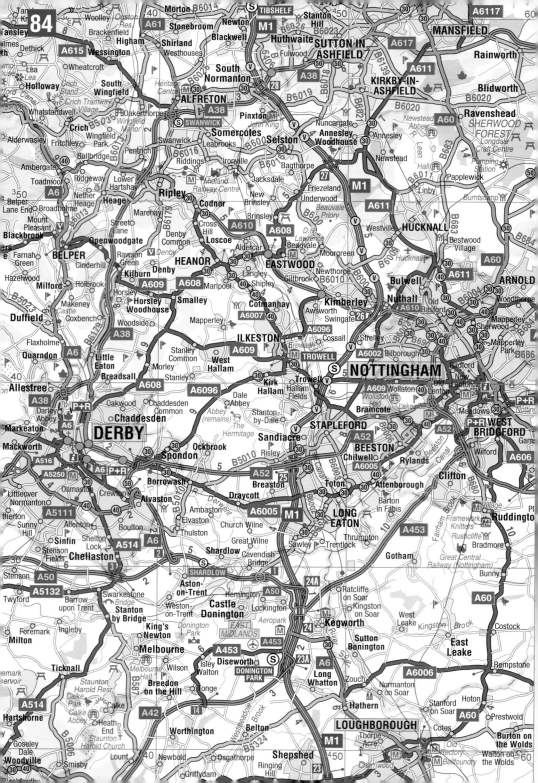

INDEX

Including Streets, Places & Areas, Hospitals etc., Industrial Estates,
Selected Flats & Walkways, Service Areas, Stations and Selected Places of Interest.

HOW TO USE THIS INDEX

1. Each street name is followed by its Postcode District, then by its Locality abbreviation(s) and then by its map reference;
e.g. **Abbey Bri.** NG7: Lent . . . .1C **56** is in the NG7 Postcode District and the Lenton Locality and is to be found in square 1C on page **56**.
The page number is shown in bold type.

2. A strict alphabetical order is followed in which Av., Rd., St., etc. (though abbreviated) are read in full and as part of the street name;
e.g. **Apple Tree Cl.** appears after **Appleton Rd.** but before **Appletree La.**

3. Streets and a selection of flats and walkways that cannot be shown on the mapping, appear in the index with the thoroughfare to which they are connected
shown in brackets; e.g. **Albion Ter.** DE7: Ilk . . . .6B **28** (off Northgate St.)

4. Addresses that are in more than one part are referred to as not continuous.

5. Places and areas are shown in the index in **BLUE TYPE** and the map reference is to the actual map square in which the town centre or area is located and
not to the place name shown on the map; e.g. **ARNOLD** 6B **22**

6. An example of a selected place of interest is **DH Lawrence Birthplace Mus.** 2B **16**

7. Transport hub examples:
Attenborough Station (Rail) . . . .3D **64**; **Basford Stop (NET)** . . . . 4C **32**; **Broadmarsh Bus Station** . . . .6E **5** (6G **45**); **Hucknall Park & Ride** 4A **8**

8. Service Area names are shown in the index in **BOLD CAPITAL TYPE**; e.g. **TROWELL SERVICE AREA** 3G **41**

9. An example of a Hospital, Hospice or selected Healthcare facility is **HEANOR MEMORIAL HOSPITAL** 4D **14**

10. Map references for entries that appear on large scale pages **4** & **5** are shown first, with small scale map references shown in brackets;
e.g. **Abbotsford Dr.** NG3: Nott 1F **5** (3H **45**)

GENERAL ABBREVIATIONS

All. : Alley	**Est.** : Estate	**Pde.** : Parade
App. : Approach	**Fld.** : Field	**Pk.** : Park
Arc. : Arcade	**Flds.** : Fields	**Pas.** : Passage
Av. : Avenue	**Gdn.** : Garden	**Pl.** : Place
Blvd. : Boulevard	**Gdns.** : Gardens	**Pct.** : Precinct
Bri. : Bridge	**Ga.** : Gate	**Prom.** : Promenade
Bldg. : Building	**Gt.** : Great	**Res.** : Residential
Bldgs. : Buildings	**Grn.** : Green	**Ri.** : Rise
Bus. : Business	**Gro.** : Grove	**Rd.** : Road
Cvn. : Caravan	**Hgts.** : Heights	**Rdbt.** : Roundabout
Cen. : Centre	**Ho.** : House	**Shop.** : Shopping
Chu. : Church	**Ind.** : Industrial	**Sth.** : South
Circ. : Circle	**La.** : Lane	**Sq.** : Square
Cir. : Circus	**Lit.** : Little	**St.** : Street
Cl. : Close	**Lwr.** : Lower	**Ter.** : Terrace
Comn. : Common	**Mnr.** : Manor	**Trad.** : Trading
Cotts. : Cottages	**Mkt.** : Market	**Up.** : Upper
Ct. : Court	**Mdw.** : Meadow	**Va.** : Vale
Cres. : Crescent	**Mdws.** : Meadows	**Vw.** : View
Cft. : Croft	**M.** : Mews	**Vs.** : Villas
Dpt. : Depot	**Mt.** : Mount	**Vis.** : Visitors
Dr. : Drive	**Mus.** : Museum	**Wlk.** : Walk
E. : East	**Nth.** : North	**W.** : West
Emb. : Embankment	**No.** : Number	**Yd.** : Yard
Ent. : Enterprise		

LOCALITY ABBREVIATIONS

Annesley: NG15 . . . . .Ann	Cropwell Bishop: NG12 . . . . .Crop Bi	Loscoe: DE75 .Los
Arnold: NG3,NG5 . . . . .Arn	Dale Abbey: DE7 . . . . .D Ab	Lowdham: NG14 . . . . .Lowd
Aslockton: NG13 . . . . .Aslo	Draycott: DE72 . . . . .Dray	Mapperley: DE7,NG3 . . . . .Mapp
Aspley: NG8 . . . . .Aspl	East Bridgford: NG13 . . . . .East B	Mapperley Park: NG3 . . . . .Mapp P
Attenborough: NG9 . . . . .Atten	Eastwood: NG16 . . . . .Eastw	Netherfield: NG4 . . . . .Neth
Awsworth: NG16 . . . . .Aws	Edwalton: NG12 . . . . .Edwal	Newthorpe: NG16 . . . . .Newth
Babbington: NG16 . . . . .Babb	Epperstone: NG14 . . . . .Epp	Newton: NG13 . . . . .Newt
Barton in Fabis: NG11 . . . . .Bart F	Gamston: NG2 . . . . .Gam	Normanton-on-the-Wolds: NG12 . . . .Norm W
Basford: NG5-8 . . . . .Bas	Gedling: NG3-4 . . . . .Ged	Nottingham: NG1-3,NG7,NG9 . . . . . . .Nott
Beeston: NG9 .Bee	Giltbrook: NG16 . . . . .Gilt	Nuthall: NG16 . . . . .Nuth
Bestwood: NG5-6 . . . . .Bestw	Gonalston: NG14 . . . . .Gon	Ockbrook: DE72 . . . . .Ock
Bestwood Village: NG6,NG15 . . . . . . .Bestw V	Gotham: NG11 . . . . .Goth	Owthorpe: NG12 . . . . .Owt
Bilborough: NG8 . . . . .Bilb	Greasley: NG16 . . . . .Grea	Oxton: NG25 . . . . .Oxton
Bingham: NG13 . . . . .Bing	Heanor: DE7,DE75 . . . . .Hea	Papplewick: NG15 . . . . .Pap
Borrowash: DE72 . . . . .Bor	Holme Pierrepont: NG12 . . . . .Hol P	Plumtree: NG12 . . . . .Plum
Bramcote: NG9 . . . . .Bram	Hoveringham: NG14 . . . . .Hove	Radcliffe on Trent: NG12 . . . . .Rad T
Breaston: DE72 . . . . .Brea	Hucknall: NG15 . . . . .Huck	Radford: NG7-8 . . . . .Radf
Brinsley: NG16 . . . . .Brins	Hyson Green: NG7-8 . . . . .Hys G	Ratcliffe on Soar: NG11 . . . . .Rat
Broxtowe: NG8 . . . . .Brox	Ilkeston: DE7 .Ilk	Ravenshead: NG15 . . . . .Rave
Bulcote: NG14 . . . . .Bulc	Keyworth: NG12 . . . . .Key	Redhill: NG5 .Redh
Bulwell: NG6 . . . . .Bulw	Kimberley: NG16 . . . . .Kimb	Risley: DE72 . . . . .Ris
Bunny: NG11 . . . . .Bunny	Kingston on Soar: NG11 . . . . .King	Ruddington: NG11 . . . . .Rudd
Burton Joyce: NG14 . . . . .Bur J	Kirk Hallam: DE7 . . . . .Kirk H	Sandiacre: NG10 . . . . .Sand
Calverton: NG5,NG14 . . . . .Calv	Kneeton: NG13 . . . . .Knee	Saxondale: NG13 . . . . .Saxon
Car Colston: NG13 . . . . .Car C	Lambley: NG4 . . . . .Lamb	Screveton: NG13 . . . . .Scre
Carlton: NG4 .Car	Langar: NG13 . . . . .Lang	Shardlow: DE72 . . . . .Shar
Chilwell: NG9 . . . . .Chil	Langley Mill: NG16 . . . . .Lang M	Shelford: NG12 . . . . .S'frd
Cinderhill: NG6,NG8,NG16 . . . . .Cin	Lenton: NG7-9 . . . . .Lent	Sherwood: NG5,NG7 . . . . .Sher
Clifton: NG11 . . . . .Clftn	Lenton Abbey: NG9 . . . . .Lent A	Shipley: DE75 . . . . .Ship
Clipston: NG12 . . . . .C'ton	Linby: NG15 . . . . .Lin	Smalley: DE7 . . . . .Smal
Colwick: NG2,NG4 . . . . .Colw	Lockington: DE74 . . . . .Lock	Southwell: NG25 . . . . .S'well
Cossall: NG16 . . . . .Coss	Long Eaton: NG10 . . . . .Long E	Stanley: DE7 .Stly
Cotgrave: NG12 . . . . .Cotg		

Stanley Common: DE7 ...Stan C	Tithby: NG13 ...Tith	West Hallam: DE7 ...West H
Stanton-by-Dale: DE7 ...Stant D	Tollerton: NG12 ...Toll	Whatton: NG13 ...What
Stanton-on-the-Wolds: NG12 ...Stant W	Top Valley: NG5 ...Top V	Widmerpool: NG12 ...Widm
Stapleford: NG9 ...Stfrd	Toton: NG9 ...Toton	Wilford: NG11 ...Wilf
Stoke Bardolph: NG4,NG14 ...Stoke B	Trowell: NG9 ...Trow	Wollaton: NG8 ...Woll
Strelley: NG8 ...Stre	Watnall: NG16 ...Want	Woodborough: NG5,NG14 ...Woodbo
Thrumpton: NG11 ...Thru	West Bridgford: NG2,NG11 ...West Br	Woodthorpe: NG5 ...Woodt

A

Aaron Cl. NG11: Wilf ...4F 57
Abba Cl. NG16: Kimb ...6H 17
Abbey Bri. NG7: Lent ...1C 56
Abbey Cir. NG2: West Br ...4C 58
Abbey Cl. NG15: Huck ...4E 7
Abbey Ct. NG9: Bee ...3F 55
Abbey Dr. NG9: Bee ...4F 55
Abbeyfield Rd. NG7: Lent ...3D 56
Abbey Gro. NG3: Nott ...2B 46
Abbey Rd. NG2: West Br ...4C 58
  NG9: Bee ...3F 55
  NG13: Bing ...4G 51
  NG16: Eastw ...3D 16
Abbey St. DE7: Ilk ...5B 28
  NG7: Lent ...1C 56
Abbot Cl. NG12: Key ...3G 79
Abbot Rd. DE7: Kirk H ...3G 39
Abbotsbury Cl. NG5: Top V ...4B 20
Abbots Cl. NG5: Arn ...1H 33
Abbots Dr. NG15: Huck ...5E 7
Abbotsford Dr. NG3: Nott ...1F 5 (3H 45)
Abbotsford M. DE7: Ilk ...4H 27
Abbots Rd. NG15: Huck ...5E 7
Abbot St. NG16: Aws ...3E 29
Abbots Wlk. NG15: Huck ...5E 7
Abbots Way NG8: Woll ...5H 43
Abbott St. DE75: Hea ...4C 14
  NG10: Long E ...1F 73
Abercarn Cl. NG6: Bulw ...6H 19
Abercarn M. NG6: Bulw ...6H 19
Aberdeen St. NG3: Nott ...3H 5 (4A 46)
Aberford Av. NG8: Bas ...1B 44
Abingdon Dr. NG11: Rudd ...5H 67
Abingdon Gdns. NG5: Woodt ...2C 34
  NG9: Chil ...1D 64
Abingdon Rd. NG2: West Br ...4C 58
Abingdon Sq. NG8: Aspl ...6H 31
Ablard Gdns. NG9: Chil ...3C 64
Acacia Cl. NG15: Huck ...6H 7
Acacia Cres. NG4: Car ...1H 47
Acacia Gdns. NG16: Want ...5H 17
Acacia Wlk. NG9: Bee ...5F 55
Acacia Way NG12: Edwal ...4C 68
Academy Cl. NG6: Bas ...4C 32
Acaster Cl. NG9: Bee ...1H 65
Access 26 Bus. Pk. NG16: Lang M ...2G 15
Acle Gdns. NG6: Bulw ...4H 19
Acorn Av. NG16: Gilt ...5D 16
Acorn Bank NG2: West Br ...1F 67
Acorn Cen. ...2G 15
Acorn Dr. NG4: Ged ...4A 36
Acorn Pk. NG7: Lent ...3C 56
A'court St. NG7: Hys G ...3D 44
Acre Cl. NG2: West Br ...2E 59
Acton Av. NG6: Bas ...3B 32
  NG10: Long E ...1G 73
Acton Cl. NG10: Long E ...1G 73
Acton Gro. NG10: Long E ...1G 73
Acton Rd. NG5: Arn ...5H 21
  NG10: Long E ...6G 63
Acton Rd. Ind. Est. NG10: Long E ...1G 73
  (not continuous)
Acton St. NG10: Long E ...1G 73
Adale Rd. DE7: Smal ...5A 14
Adams Cl. DE75: Hea ...6B 14
Adams Ct. DE7: Ilk ...4A 28
Adams Hill NG7: Nott ...1H 55
  NG12: Key ...4H 79
Adam St. DE7: Ilk ...4F 5
Adams Wlk. NG1: Nott ...3G 7
Ada Pl. NG15: Huck ...6G 35
Adbolton Av. NG4: Ged ...1D 58
Adbolton Gro. NG2: West Br ...2D 58
Adbolton La. NG2: West Br ...2E 59
  NG12: Hol P ...3G 47
Adbolton Lodge NG4: Car ...1E 33
Adderley Cl. NG5: Bestw ...5G 49
Addington Ct. NG12: Rad T ...3D 44
Addington Rd. NG7: Radf ...3E 7
Addison Dr. NG15: Huck ...1D 46
Addison Rd. NG4: Car ...1C 4 (2F 45)
Addison St. NG1: Nott ...4A 16
Addison Vs. NG16: Eastw ...4A 16
  (not continuous)
Adelaide Cl. NG9: Stfrd ...2H 53
Adelaide Gro. NG5: Top V ...5C 20
Adel Dr. NG4: Ged ...5G 35

Adenburgh Dr. NG9: Atten ...4D 64
Admiral Cl. DE75: Hea ...3C 14
Admiral Ct. DE7: Ilk ...3B 28
Adrian Cl. NG9: Toton ...4H 63
Aeneas Ct. NG5: Sher ...6F 7
Aerial Way NG15: Huck ...2E 19
The Aerodrome NG15: Huck ...5A 34
Agnes Vs. NG3: Mapp ...3E 21
Aidan Gdns. NG5: Top V ...4G 31
Ainsdale Cres. NG8: Cin ...3B 44
Ainsley Rd. NG8: Aspl ...6G 17
Ainsworth Dr. NG2: Nott ...2F 57
Aintree Cl. NG16: Kimb ...5F 59
Aira Cl. NG2: Gam ...1C 72
Airedale Cl. NG10: Long E ...1A 64
Airedale Ct. NG9: Chil ...6C 42
Airedale Wlk. NG8: Woll ...4F 7
Aitchison Av. NG15: Huck ...6A 18
Alandene Av. NG16: Want ...6A 22
Albany Cl. NG5: Arn ...6C 6
  NG15: Huck ...6C 6
Albany Ct. NG9: Stfrd ...2G 53
Albany Rd. NG7: Bas ...1E 45
Albany St. DE7: Ilk ...3C 40
Albemarle Rd. NG5: Woodt ...3H 33
Alberta Ter. NG7: Hys G ...1E 45
Albert Av. NG4: Car ...2D 46
  NG8: Aspl ...1B 44
  NG9: Stfrd ...4F 53
  NG16: Nuth ...1C 30
Albert Ball Cl. NG5: Top V ...5D 20
Albert Ball Ho. NG5: Top V ...5E 21
Albert Cl. NG15: Huck ...6A 8
Albert Einstein Cen. NG7: Nott ...2B 56
Albert Gro. NG7: Lent, Radf ...4D 44
Albert Hall
  Nottingham ...4C 4 (5F 45)
Albert Mill NG7: Radf ...1A 4 (3E 45)
Albert Rd. NG2: West Br ...3B 58
  NG3: Nott ...6H 33
  NG7: Lent ...6D 44
  NG9: Bee ...3G 55
  NG10: Long E ...5F 63
  NG10: Sand ...5D 52
  NG11: Bunny ...6A 78
Albert Sq. NG7: Lent ...6C 44
Albert St. DE7: Ilk ...1A 40
  NG1: Nott ...5E 5 (5G 45)
  NG4: Ged ...6H 35
  NG9: Stfrd ...4F 53
  NG12: Rad T ...6F 49
  NG15: Huck ...4H 7
  (not continuous)
  NG16: Eastw ...2B 16
Albion Cen. ...1B 40
Albion Ri. NG5: Arn ...4B 22
Albion Rd. NG10: Long E ...5H 63
Albion St. DE7: Ilk ...6B 28
  NG1: Nott ...6D 4 (6G 45)
  NG9: Bee ...4F 55
Albion Ter. DE7: Ilk ...6B 28
  (off Northgate St.)
Albury Dr. NG8: Aspl ...6H 31
Albury Sq. NG7: Nott ...4A 4 (5E 45)
Alcester St. NG7: Lent ...3C 56
Aldene Ct. NG9: Chil ...6D 54
Aldene Way NG14: Woodbo ...1C 24
ALDERCAR ...1F 15
Aldercar La. NG16: Lang M ...1F 15
Alder Gdns. NG6: Bulw ...6G 19
Alderman Cl. NG9: Bee ...3F 55
Aldermens Cl. NG2: Nott ...1G 57
Alderney St. NG7: Lent ...6D 44
Alderton Rd. NG5: Bestw ...1G 33
Alder Way NG12: Key ...5A 80
Aldgate Cl. NG6: Bulw ...5G 19
Aldred's La. NG16: Lang M ...4E 15
Aldreds La. DE75: Hea ...4E 15
Aldridge Cl. NG9: Toton ...3G 63
Aldrin Cl. NG6: Bulw ...2F 31
Aldworth Cl. NG5: Bestw ...1F 33
Aldwych Cl. NG5: Arn ...4E 21
  NG16: Nuth ...5D 30
Alexander Cl. NG15: Huck ...2H 7
Alexander Fleming Bldg. NG7: Nott ...3B 56
Alexander Rd. NG7: Nott ...5A 4 (5E 45)
Alexandra Cres. NG9: Bee ...5G 55
Alexandra Gdns. NG5: Sher ...6F 33
Alexandra M. NG5: Sher ...1F 45
ALEXANDRA PARK ...1H 45
Alexandra Rd. NG10: Long E ...5F 63

Alexandra St. NG5: Sher ...1F 45
  NG9: Stfrd ...5F 53
  NG16: Eastw ...3B 16
Alford Cl. NG9: Bee ...6G 55
Alford Rd. NG2: West Br ...5D 58
  NG12: Edwal ...5D 58
Alfred Av. NG3: Mapp ...5C 34
Alfred Cl. NG3: Nott ...3G 45
Alfred St. Central NG3: Nott ...1F 5 (3G 45)
Alfred St. Nth. NG3: Nott ...3G 45
Alfred St. Sth. NG3: Nott ...2H 5 (4A 46)
Alfreton Rd. NG7: Hys G, Radf, Nott ...2A 4 (2C 44)
Alison Av. NG15: Huck ...2A 8
Alison Wlk. NG3: Nott ...1F 5 (3H 45)
Allen Av. NG3: Mapp ...6C 34
Allendale DE7: Ilk ...2A 40
Allendale Av. NG8: Aspl ...6F 31
  NG9: Atten ...3D 64
Allendale Rd. DE75: Hea ...3B 14
Allen Fld. Ct. NG7: Lent ...6D 44
Allen St. NG15: Huck ...3G 7
Allen's Wlk. NG5: Arn ...4B 22
All Hallows Dr. NG4: Ged ...5H 35
Allington Av. NG7: Lent ...6D 44
Allison Gdns. DE7: Ilk ...6C 28
  NG9: Chil ...1D 64
All Saints St. NG7: Radf ...1A 4 (3E 45)
All Saints Ter. NG7: Radf ...1A 4 (3E 45)
Allwood Dr. NG4: Car ...1G 47
Allwood Gdns. NG15: Huck ...5H 7
Alma Cl. DE7: Ilk ...2A 28
  NG1: Nott ...1D 4 (3G 45)
  NG4: Ged ...5A 36
Alma Hill NG16: Kimb ...5G 17
Alma Rd. NG3: Nott ...3B 46
Alma St. NG7: Bas ...1E 45
Almond Cl. NG15: Huck ...6H 7
  NG16: Kimb ...6G 17
Almond Ct. NG2: Nott ...1G 57
Almond Wlk. NG4: Ged ...5A 36
Almond Way NG8: Bilb ...2D 42
Alnwick Cl. NG6: Bulw ...1B 32
Alpha Ter. NG1: Nott ...3F 45
Alpine Cres. NG4: Car ...1G 47
Alpine St. NG6: Bas ...5C 32
Althea Ct. NG7: Bas ...6E 33
  (off Poyser La.)
Althorpe St. NG7: Radf ...4E 45
Alton Av. NG11: Wilf ...1F 67
Alton Cl. NG2: West Br ...2G 67
Alton Dr. NG16: Gilt ...5D 16
Alum Ct. NG5: Top V ...5D 20
Alvenor St. DE7: Ilk ...6B 28
Alverstone Rd. NG3: Mapp P ...6G 33
Alvey Ter. NG7: Radf ...4C 44
Alvina Gdns. NG8: Stre ...6C 30
Alwood Gro. NG16: Clftn ...2B 66
Alwyn Ct. NG9: Bee ...6F 55
Alwyn Rd. NG8: Brox ...5F 31
Alyth Ct. NG6: Bas ...4D 32
Amber Cl. NG15: Huck ...6F 21
Amber Ct. NG16: Lang M ...3F 15
Ambergate Rd. NG8: Bilb ...2G 43
  (not continuous)
Amber Hill NG5: Bestw ...6F 21
Amberley Cl. DE7: Ilk ...3B 40
Amber Rd. NG9: Bee ...2G 65
Amber Trad. Cen. NG16: Kimb ...6F 17
Ambleside NG2: Gam ...4E 59
Ambleside Dr. NG16: Eastw ...2H 15
Ambleside Rd. NG8: Aspl ...6G 31
Ambleside Way NG4: Ged ...1B 48
Amelia Cl. DE72: Brea ...5A 62
Amersham Ri. NG8: Aspl ...6H 31
Amesbury Cir. NG8: Cin ...4G 31
Amilda Av. DE7: Ilk ...1B 40
Ampthill Ri. NG5: Sher ...3F 33
Ancaster Gdns. NG8: Woll ...4G 43
The Anchorage NG14: Bur J ...3F 37
Anchor Cl. NG8: Aspl ...5H 31
Anchor Ct. NG5: Bestw ...6F 21
Anchor Rd. NG16: Eastw ...2G 15
Anders Dr. NG6: Bulw ...2F 31
Anderson Cl. NG5: Top V ...5E 21
Anderson Cres. NG9: Bee ...3E 55
Andover Cl. NG8: Bilb ...3H 43
Andover Rd. NG5: Bestw ...1C 32
Andrew Av. DE7: Ilk ...2D 40
  NG3: Mapp ...5C 34

Andrews Ct.—Awsworth & Cossall By-Pass

Andrews Ct. NG9: Chil 5C 54
Andrews Dr. NG16: Lang M 1E 15
Anfield Cl. NG9: Toton 3A 64
Anford Cl. NG6: Bulw 2H 31
Angela Cl. NG5: Arn 3A 22
Angela Ct. NG9: Toton 3A 64
Angel All. NG1: Nott 4F 5 (5H 45)
Angelica Ct. NG13: Bing 5C 50
Angell Grn. NG11: Clftn 5A 66
Angel Row NG1: Nott 4D 4 (5G 45)
Angletarn Cl. NG2: West Br 5E 59
Angrave Cl. NG3: Nott 2A 46
Angus Cl. NG5: Arn 4D 22
NG16: Kimb 2A 30
Anmer Cl. NG2: Nott 2F 57
Annan Ct. NG8: Aspl 1H 43
Anne's Cl. NG3: Mapp 5C 34
Annesley Gro. NG1: Nott 1C 4 (3F 45)
Annesley Rd. NG2: West Br 4B 58
NG15: Ann, Huck 1D 6
Annies Cl. NG15: Huck 6F 7
Anslow Av. NG9: Lent A 3G 55
Anson Rd. NG13: Newt 2B 50
Anson Wlk. DE7: Ilk 4B 28
Anstee Rd. NG10: Long E 2E 73
Anstey Ri. NG3: Nott 4B 46
Anthony Wharton Ct. NG11: Clftn 2C 66
Antill St. NG9: Stfrd 5F 53
Antonia Dr. NG15: Huck 3B 8
Apollo Dr. NG6: Bulw 2F 31
Appleby Cl. DE7: Ilk 3B 40
Appledore Av. NG8: Woll 1D 54
Appledorne Way NG5: Arn 4A 22
Appleton Cl. NG11: Clftn 4A 66
Appleton Ct. NG9: Bee 1H 65
Appleton Gdns. NG3: Mapp 2D 34
Appleton Rd. NG9: Bee 1H 65
Apple Tree Cl. NG12: Edwal 1C 68
Appletree La. NG4: Ged 5H 35
Apple Wlk. NG3: Nott 1C 46
Applewood Gro. NG5: Sher 4H 33
The Approach NG11: Rudd 5G 67
Arboretum St. NG1: Nott 1B 4 (3F 45)
Arbour Hill DE7: D Ab 6C 38
Arbrook Dr. NG8: Aspl 3B 44
Arbutus Cl. NG11: Clftn 4A 66
Archdale Rd. NG5: Bestw 1G 33
Archer Cres. NG8: Woll 4F 43
Archer Rd. NG9: Stfrd 6G 53
Archer St. DE7: Ilk 4A 28
Arches Cl. NG16: Aws 2E 29
Arch Hill NG5: Redh 2A 22
Archway Ct. *NG7: Radf 3D 44*
(off Limpenny St.)
Arden Cl. NG9: Lent A 3G 55
NG15: Huck 6A 8
Arden Gro. NG13: Bing 4C 50
Ardleigh Cl. NG5: Top V 4B 20
Ardmore Cl. NG2: Nott 6B 46
Ardsley Cl. DE75: Hea 3E 15
The Arena NG1: Nott 5C 4 (5F 45)
Argyle Ct. NG7: Radf 4D 44
Argyle M. NG16: Eastw 3B 16
Argyle St. NG7: Radf 4D 44
NG16: Lang M 1F 15
Aria Ct. NG9: Stfrd 5F 53
Ariel Cl. NG6: Bas 2D 32
Arkers Cl. NG6: Bas 4B 32
Arklow Cl. NG8: Aspl 5G 31
Arkwright St. NG2: Nott 6G 45
(Queens Rd.)
NG2: Nott 2H 57
(Radcliffe St.)
Arkwright St. Sth. NG2: Nott 2H 57
Arkwright Wlk. NG2: Nott 1H 57
(not continuous)
Arleston Dr. NG8: Woll 6D 42
Arlington Cl. NG15: Huck 1G 19
Arlington Dr. NG3: Mapp P 6G 33
Armadale Cl. NG5: Arn 5E 23
Armes Cl. DE7: Ilk 4B 28
Armfield Rd. NG5: Arn 1E 35
Armitage Dr. NG10: Long E 6A 64
Armstrong Rd. NG6: Bulw 2F 31
Armstrong Way NG7: Bas 6C 32
Arncliff Cl. NG8: Woll 5C 42
Arndale Rd. NG5: Sher 2G 33
Arne Ct. NG2: Nott 2G 57
Arnesby Rd. NG7: Lent 6B 44
Arno Av. NG7: Hys G 1F 45
ARNOLD 6B 22
Arnold Av. NG10: Long E 3C 72
Arnold Cres. NG10: Long E 3C 72
Arnold La. NG3: Ged, Mapp 2D 34
NG4: Ged 4G 35
Arnold Leisure Cen. 5B 22
Arnold Rd. NG5: Bestw 3C 32
NG6: Bas, Bestw 3C 32
Arnos Gro. NG16: Nuth 4D 30
Arnot Hill Pk. 1A 34
Arnot Hill Pk. NG5: Arn 1A 34
Arnot Hill Rd. NG5: Arn 6A 22
Arnot Ho. *NG4: Car 1G 47*
(off Foxhill Rd. E.)
Arno Va. Gdns. NG5: Woodt 2B 34
Arno Va. Rd. NG5: Woodt 2A 34
Arnside NG9: Stfrd 6G 53
Arnside Cl. NG5: Bestw 2F 33
Arnside Rd. NG5: Bestw 2E 33
A Rd. NG7: Nott 5A 56
Arran Cl. NG9: Stfrd 1G 53
Arrow Cen. NG15: Huck 2E 7
Arthur Av. NG7: Lent 5D 44
NG9: Stfrd 3H 53
Arthur Cres. NG4: Car 2E 47
Arthur Mee Rd. NG9: Stfrd 6G 53
Arthur St. NG4: Neth 3A 48
NG7: Radf 1A 4 (3E 45)
Artic Way NG16: Kimb 6F 17
Arundel Cl. NG10: Sand 1D 62
Arundel Dr. NG9: Bram 1B 54
Arundel St. NG7: Lent 4E 45
Ascot Av. NG16: Kimb 6G 17
Ascot Cl. DE7: West H 2B 38
Ascot Dr. NG5: Redh 5H 21
NG15: Huck 6D 6
Ascot Pk. Est. NG10: Sand 4E 53
Ascot Pl. DE7: Kirk H 4G 39
Ascot Rd. NG8: Aspl 2B 44
Ascott Gdns. NG2: West Br 6F 57
Ashbourne Cl. NG9: Bram 2A 54
Ashbourne Ct. DE7: Ilk 6H 27
NG6: Bulw 1F 31
Ashbourne St. NG7: Lent 4E 45
Ashburnham Av. NG7: Lent 5D 44
Ashchurch Dr. NG8: Woll 1D 54
Ash Cl. NG13: Bing 5G 51
NG14: Bur J 3E 37
NG14: Woodbo 1C 24
NG15: Huck 6C 6
Ash Ct. NG4: Car 2F 47
NG16: Newth 1D 16
Ash Cres. NG16: Nuth 1B 30
Ashdale Av. NG15: Huck 6G 7
Ashdale Rd. DE7: Ilk 3C 40
NG3: Nott 3D 46
NG5: Arn 5C 22
Ashdown Cl. NG11: Wilf 5F 57
Ashdown Gro. NG13: Bing 5D 50
Ashe Cl. NG5: Arn 6D 22
Asher La. NG11: Rudd 1G 77
Ashfield Av. NG9: Bee 6H 55
Ashfield Rd. NG2: Nott 5B 46
Ashford Ct. DE7: West H 1B 38
Ashford Pl. DE7: Ilk 2A 28
Ashford Ri. NG8: Woll 1D 54
Ashforth Av. DE75: Hea 4E 15
Ashforth Bus. Cen. *NG3: Nott 3H 45*
(off Ashforth St.)
Ashforth St. NG3: Nott 3H 45
Ashgate Retail Pk. 4A 8
Ashgate Rd. NG15: Huck 4H 7
Ash Gro. NG9: Stfrd 6F 53
NG10: Long E 1E 73
NG10: Sand 4C 52
NG12: Key 5H 79
NG14: Woodbo 6C 12
Ashiana NG2: Nott 4H 5 (5A 46)
Ashington Dr. NG5: Arn 3B 22
Ash La. NG15: Pap 1H 9
Ash Lea Cl. NG12: Cotg 3F 71
Ashley Cl. NG9: Chil 5D 54
Ashley Ct. NG9: Bee 5E 55
Ashley Cres. NG12: Key 4H 79
Ashley Gro. NG15: Huck 4E 7
Ashley Rd. NG12: Key 4G 79
Ashley St. NG3: Nott 3H 5 (4A 46)
Ashling Ct. NG2: Nott 1A 58
Ashling St. NG2: Nott 1A 58
Ashmore Cl. NG4: Ged 4G 35
Ash Mt. Rd. NG16: Lang M 2F 15
Ashness Cl. NG2: Gam 5E 59
Ashover Cl. NG3: Nott 1A 46
Ashridge Way NG12: Edwal 1E 69
Ash St. DE7: Ilk 3A 28
Ashton Av. NG5: Arn 3B 22
Ashton Ct. NG8: Bilb 2D 42
Ash Tree Ct. NG8: Stre 4C 30
Ash Tree Sq. NG9: Bram 3B 54
Ashurst Gro. NG15: Huck 1E 19
Ash Vw. NG7: Radf 3D 44
Ashview Cl. NG10: Long E 5D 62
Ash Vs. NG5: Sher 6F 33
Ashville Cl. NG2: Nott 2E 57
Ashwater Dr. NG3: Mapp 1F 35
Ashwell Ct. NG5: Woodt 3A 34
Ashwell Gdns. NG7: Hys G 1C 44
Ashwell St. NG4: Neth 3H 47
Ashwick Cl. NG11: Wilf 6E 57
Ashworth Av. NG11: Rudd 5G 67
Ashworth Cl. NG3: Nott 4E 47
Ashworth Cres. NG3: Mapp 5D 34
Askeby Dr. NG8: Stre 6D 30
Askew Rd. NG15: Huck 2B 8
Askham Ct. *NG2: Gam 4E 59*
(off Radcliffe Rd.)
Aslockton Dr. NG8: Aspl 5B 32
Aspect Bus. Pk. NG6: Bulw 5F 19
Aspen Cl. NG13: Bing 5G 51
Aspen Rd. NG6: Bulw 1F 31
Asper St. NG4: Neth 2A 48
Aspinall Ct. NG8: Woll 4A 44
ASPLEY 1H 43
Aspley La. NG8: Aspl, Bilb 6F 31
Aspley Pk. Dr. NG8: Bilb 1G 43
Aspley Pl. NG7: Radf 3D 44
Assarts Rd. NG16: Nuth 3E 31
Astcote Cl. DE75: Hea 4E 15
Aster Rd. NG3: Nott 2H 45
Astill Pine Cl. DE72: Brea 6A 62
Astle Ct. NG5: Arn 1E 35
Astley Dr. NG3: Nott 6B 34
Aston Av. NG9: Lent A 3G 55
Aston Ct. DE7: Ilk 6B 28
NG7: Lent 2C 56
Aston Dr. NG6: Bulw 3A 20
Aston Grn. NG9: Toton 2G 63
Astral Dr. NG15: Huck 1E 19
Astral Gro. NG15: Huck 1D 18
Astrid Gdns. NG5: Bestw 1D 32
Astron Ct. NG15: Huck 1E 19
Astwood Cl. NG8: Bilb 2E 43
Atherfield Gdns. NG16: Eastw 2B 16
Atherton Ri. NG8: Cin 4H 31
Atherton Rd. DE7: Ilk 4G 27
Athorpe Gro. NG6: Bas 4C 32
Atkinson Gdns. NG16: Nuth 2B 30
Atlas St. NG2: Nott 3H 57
The Atrium NG2: Nott 6G 5 (6H 45)
ATTENBOROUGH 3D 64
Attenborough Cl. NG10: Long E 2B 72
Attenborough La. NG9: Atten, Chil 2C 64
(not continuous)
Attenborough Nature Cen. 5C 64
Attenborough Nature Reserve 3E 65
Attenborough Sailing Club 5C 64
Attenborough Station (Rail) 3D 64
Attercliffe Ter. NG2: Nott 2G 57
Attewell Rd. NG16: Aws 2D 28
Aubrey Av. NG2: Nott 5H 5 (5A 46)
Aubrey Rd. NG5: Sher 5F 33
Auburn Cl. DE7: Stan C 1A 38
Auckland Cl. NG7: Radf 4C 44
Auckland Rd. NG15: Huck 6D 6
Audley Cl. DE7: Ilk 4H 27
Audley Dr. NG9: Lent A 2F 55
Audon Av. NG9: Chil 6E 55
Augustine Gdns. NG5: Top V 4E 21
Austen Av. NG7: Hys G 2E 45
NG10: Long E 2E 73
Austin's Dr. DE72: Ris 1A 62
Austins Dr. NG10: Sand 1D 62
Austin St. NG6: Bulw 6A 20
Austrey Av. NG9: Lent A 3G 55
Autumn Cl. NG2: West Br 6H 57
Autumn Ct. NG15: Huck 5G 7
Autumn Rd. NG12: Cotg 6G 61
Autumn Way NG9: Bee 4H 55
Avalon Cl. NG6: Bulw 1C 32
Avebury Cl. NG11: Clftn 5B 66
Aveline Cl. NG5: Top V 5D 20
The Avenue NG11: Rudd 2H 77
NG12: Rad T 5F 49
NG14: Calv 4H 11
Avenue A NG1: Nott 4G 5 (5H 45)
Avenue B NG1: Nott 4G 5 (5H 45)
Avenue C NG1: Nott 4H 5 (5A 46)
Avenue D NG1: Nott 4H 5 (5A 46)
Avenue E NG1: Nott 3H 5 (4A 46)
Averton Sq. NG8: Woll 6B 44
Aviemore Cl. NG5: Arn 4D 22
Avis Av. DE75: Hea 6D 14
Avocet Cl. DE75: Hea 4F 15
NG13: Bing 6G 51
NG15: Huck 2H 7
Avocet Wharf NG7: Lent 1E 57
Avon Av. NG15: Huck 2E 19
Avonbridge Cl. NG5: Arn 4E 23
Avondale NG12: Cotg 2G 71
Avondale Cl. NG10: Long E 1C 72
Avondale Rd. DE7: Kirk H 4G 39
NG4: Car 3F 47
Avon Gdns. NG2: West Br 4B 58
Avonlea Cl. DE7: Ilk 3D 40
Avon Pl. NG9: Bee 4G 55
Avon Rd. NG3: Nott 4D 46
NG4: Ged 5H 35
AWSWORTH 2E 29
Awsworth & Cossall By-Pass
NG16: Aws 3D 28

Awsworth La. NG16: Coss 5E **29**
 NG16: Kimb 2F **29**
Awsworth Rd. DE7: Ilk 5B **28**
Axford Cl. NG4: Ged 5H **35**
Axmouth Dr. NG3: Mapp 2F **35**
Aylesham Av. NG5: Arn 1B **34**
Aylestone Dr. NG8: Bilb 1H **43**
Ayr St. NG7: Radf 1A **4** (3E **45**)
Ayscough Av. NG16: Nuth 1C **30**
Ayton Cl. NG2: Nott 1F **57**
Ayton Gdns. NG9: Chil 3C **64**
Azalea Ct. NG16: Gilt 5E **17**

B

Babbacombe Dr. NG5: Bestw 1F **33**
Babbacombe Way NG15: Huck 5D **6**
BABBINGTON 3G **29**
Babbington Cl. DE7: Ilk 3D **40**
Babbington Cres. NG4: Ged 5G **35**
Babbington Dr. NG6: Cin 3H **31**
Babbington La. NG16: Kimb 3H **29**
Babington Ct. NG9: Chil 6C **54**
Back La.
 DE7: Ilk 5A **28**
 NG12: Norm W 1A **80**
 NG16: Nuth 1D **30**
Bacon Cl. NG16: Gilt 5C **16**
Bacton Av. NG6: Bulw 5H **19**
Bacton Gdns. NG6: Bulw 5C **46**
Baden Powell Rd. NG2: Nott 4F **57**
Bader Rd. NG4: Car 1G **47**
 NG15: Huck 5C **6**
Bagnall Av. NG5: Arn 1G **33**
Bagnall Cotts. NG6: Bulw 2H **31**
Bagnall Rd. NG6: Bas, Cin 3H **31**
Bagot St. DE7: West H 1A **38**
Bagthorpe Cl. NG5: Sher 4E **33**
Baildon Cl. NG8: Woll 6A **44**
Bailey Brook Cres. NG16: Lang M 2E **15**
Bailey Brook Dr. NG16: Lang M 2D **14**
Bailey Brook Ind. Est. NG16: Lang M 3F **15**
Bailey Brook Wlk. NG16: Lang M 2E **15**
Bailey Cl. DE75: Los 1A **14**
 NG5: Arn 6H **21**
Bailey Ct. NG4: Neth 2A **48**
 NG12: Rad T 1E **61**
Bailey Dr. NG3: Mapp 2D **34**
BAILEY GROVE 3H **15**
Bailey Gro. Rd. NG16: Eastw 3H **15**
Bailey La. NG12: Rad T 1E **61**
Bailey St.
 NG4: Neth 2A **48**
 NG6: Bas 5C **32**
 NG9: Stfrd 5E **53**
The Bainbridge NG14: Calv 4A **12**
Bainton Gro. NG11: Clftn 4D **66**
Baird-Parker Dr. NG4: Car 2F **47**
Baker Av. DE75: Hea 6D **14**
 NG5: Arn 4C **22**
Baker Brook Cl. NG15: Huck 5B **8**
Baker Cl. NG10: Long E 4E **63**
Bakerdale Rd. NG3: Nott 3D **46**
Baker Rd. NG16: Gilt, Newth 5E **17**
Bakers Brothers Mobile Home Cvn. Site ..6C **28**
Bakers Cl. NG7: Radf 3C **44**
 NG12: Cotg 2E **71**
BAKERS FIELDS 3D **46**
Baker St.
 DE7: Ilk 6B **28**
 NG1: Nott 2F **45**
 NG15: Huck 4G **7**
Bakewell Av. NG4: Car 6G **35**
Bakewell Dr. NG5: Top V 6C **20**
Bakewell La. NG15: Huck 1H **19**
Bakewell Rd. NG10: Long E 2G **73**
Bala Dr. NG5: Bestw 6E **21**
Baldwin Ct. NG7: Radf 4D **44**
Baldwin St. NG7: Radf 4E **45**
 NG16: Newth 4E **17**
Bale Cl. NG10: Long E 1A **74**
Balfour Rd. NG7: Lent, Radf 4D **44**
 NG9: Stfrd 5F **53**
Balfron Gdns. NG2: Nott 1F **57**
Balisier Ct. NG3: Nott 3D **45**
Ballantrae Cl. NG5: Arn 5D **22**
Ballerat Cres. NG5: Top V 5C **20**
Balloon Wood Ind. Est. NG9: Bram 5A **42**
Ball St. NG3: Nott 3A **58**
Balmoral Av. NG2: West Br 4A **14**
Balmoral Cl. DE75: Hea 4A **14**
 NG10: Sand 2D **62**
Balmoral Cres. NG8: Woll 4C **42**
Balmoral Dr. NG9: Bram 1B **54**
Balmoral Gro. NG4: Colw 3H **47**
 NG15: Huck 3H **7**
Balmoral Ho. NG5: Woodt 3H **33**

Balmoral Rd. DE7: Kirk H 4H **39**
 NG1: Nott 3F **45**
 NG4: Colw 3H **47**
 NG13: Bing 5C **50**
Balshaw Way NG9: Chil 3B **64**
Bamkin Cl. NG15: Huck 5H **7**
Bampton Ct. NG2: Gam 4E **59**
Banbury Av. NG9: Toton 2H **63**
Bancroft St. NG6: Bulw 6A **20**
Bandstand Yard 5C **4**
Banes Rd. NG13: Bing 5H **51**
Bangor Wlk. NG3: Nott 2G **45**
Bankfield Dr. DE7: Kirk H 3F **39**
 NG9: Bram 2C **54**
Bank Hill NG14: Woodbo 2H **23**
Bank Pl. NG1: Nott 4E **5** (5G **45**)
The Banks NG13: Bing 5E **51**
Banksburn Cl. DE75: Hea 4A **14**
Banks Cl. NG5: Arn 1D **34**
Banks Cres. NG13: Bing 5E **51**
Banksman Cl. NG3: Nott 2B **46**
Banks Paddock NG13: Bing 5F **51**
Banks Rd. NG6: Toton 2G **63**
Bank St. NG10: Long E 6G **63**
 NG16: Lang M 1G **15**
Banks Yd. NG6: Bulw 6H **19**
 (off Main St.)
Bankwood Cl. NG8: Aspl 6G **31**
Bannerman Rd. NG6: Bulw 1A **32**
Barbara Sq. NG15: Huck 2F **7**
Barber Cl. DE7: Ilk 4A **28**
Barber St. NG16: Eastw 3C **16**
Barbrook Cl. NG8: Woll 4H **43**
Barbury Dr. NG11: Clftn 6B **66**
Barclay Ct. DE7: Ilk 4H **27**
Barden Rd. NG3: Mapp 2C **34**
Bardfield Gdns. NG5: Top V 3B **20**
Bardney Dr. NG6: Bulw 5G **19**
Bardsey Gdns. NG5: Bestw 6E **21**
Barent Cl. NG5: Bestw 1D **32**
Barent Wlk. NG5: Bestw 1D **32**
Barker Av. E. NG10: Sand 5D **52**
Barker Av. Nth. NG10: Sand 5C **52**
Barker Ga. DE7: Ilk 5B **28**
 NG1: Nott 4F **5** (5H **45**)
 NG15: Huck 4F **7**
Barkers La. NG9: Chil 1F **65**
Barkla Cl. NG11: Clftn 5A **66**
Bar La. NG6: Bas 5A **32**
 NG8: Aspl 5A **32**
Bar La. Ind. Pk. NG6: Bas 5B **32**
Barlborough Rd. DE7: Ilk 2B **28**
Barley Cft. NG2: West Br 1G **67**
Barleydale Dr. NG9: Trow 1F **53**
Barleylands NG11: Rudd 1G **77**
Barling Dr. DE7: Ilk 5G **27**
Barlock Rd. NG6: Bas 3C **32**
Barlow Dr. Nth. NG16: Aws 3D **28**
Barlow Dr. Sth. NG16: Aws 3D **28**
Barlows Cotts. NG16: Aws 2E **29**
Barlows Cotts. La. NG16: Aws 2E **29**
Barnby Wlk. NG5: Sher 2G **33**
Barn Cl. NG6: Bulw 2F **31**
 NG10: Long E 2E **73**
 NG12: Cotg 3E **71**
Barn Cft. NG9: Chil 5B **54**
Barndale Cl. NG2: West Br 2G **67**
Barnes Cl. NG11: Wilf 1F **67**
Barnes Cft. DE75: Hea 5A **14**
Barnes Rd. NG5: Top V 5D **20**
Barnet Rd. NG3: Nott 2D **46**
Barnett Ct. NG12: Key 4G **79**
Barnfield NG11: Wilf 1F **67**
Barnsley Cl. NG6: Bestw V 5F **9**
Barnsley Ter. NG2: Nott 2G **57**
Barnston Rd. NG2: Nott 4B **46**
Barnum Cl. NG8: Woll 4E **43**
Barons Cl. NG4: Ged 6G **35**
Barrack La. NG7: Nott 5D **44**
Barra M. NG2: Nott 1F **57**
Barratt Cl. NG9: Atten 4D **64**
Barratt Cres. NG9: Atten 3D **64**
Barratt La. NG9: Atten 3C **64**
Barrhead Cl. NG5: Top V 4C **20**
Barrington Cl. NG12: Rad T 1E **61**
Barrique Rd. NG7: Lent 2C **56**
Barrow Slade NG12: Key 5G **79**
Barrydale Av. NG9: Bee 6F **55**
Barry St. NG6: Bulw 6H **19**
Bartley Gdns. NG14: Calv 3E **11**
Bartlow Rd. NG8: Bilb 2D **42**
Barton Cl. NG11: Rudd 1F **77**
BARTON IN FABIS 1E **75**
Barton La. NG9: Atten, Chil 4B **64**
 NG11: Bart F 1G **75**
 NG11: Clftn 5A **66**
 NG11: Rat, Thru 6C **74**
Barton Rd. NG10: Long E 1A **74**

Bartons Cl. NG16: Newth 3E **17**
Barton St. NG9: Bee 6G **55**
Barton Way NG9: Chil 6E **55**
Barwell Dr. NG8: Stre 6D **30**
Basa Cres. NG5: Top V 5D **20**
Basford Rd. NG6: Bas 6B **32**
Basford Stop (NET) 4C **32**
Baskin La. NG9: Chil 1C **64**
Baslow Av. NG4: Car 6F **35**
Baslow Cl. NG10: Long E 2C **72**
Baslow Dr. NG9: Lent A 2G **55**
Bass Cl. NG15: Huck 2A **8**
Bassett Cl. DE7: Ilk 4G **27**
 NG16: Kimb 6G **17**
Bassford Av. DE75: Hea 3D **14**
BASSINGFIELD 4H **59**
Bassingfield La. NG2: Gam 4F **59**
 (not continuous)
 NG12: Rad T 3H **59**
Bastion St. NG7: Radf 4C **44**
Bateman Gdns. NG7: Hys G 2D **44**
Bathley St. NG2: Nott 2G **57**
Baths La. NG15: Huck 4H **7**
Bath St. DE7: Ilk 6A **28**
 NG1: Nott 2F **5** (4H **45**)
Bathurst Dr. NG8: Bilb 3G **43**
Battle Cl. NG13: Newt 2B **50**
Baulk La. NG9: Stfrd 3H **53**
Bawtry Wlk. NG3: Nott 3B **46**
Baxter Cl. NG15: Huck 1A **8**
Bayard Ct. NG8: Woll 4A **44**
Bayliss Rd. NG4: Ged 4F **35**
Bayswater Rd. NG16: Kimb 6H **17**
Baythorn Rd. NG8: Bilb 3D **42**
Beacon Flatts NG9: Bee 5H **55**
Beacon Hill Dr. NG15: Huck 6C **6**
Beacon Hill Ri. NG3: Nott 2H **5** (4A **46**)
Beacon Rd. NG9: Bee 5H **55**
Beaconsfield St. NG7: Hys G 1D **44**
 NG10: Long E 6G **63**
Beaconsfield Street Stop (NET) 1D **44**
Bean Cl. NG6: Bulw 2F **31**
Beanford La. NG14: Oxton 1H **11**
Beardall St. NG15: Huck 4H **7**
Beardsall Ho. NG7: Lent 5C **44**
 (off Faraday Rd.)
Beardsall M. NG8: Stre 5C **30**
Beardsley Gdns. NG2: Nott 1F **57**
Beardsmore Gro. NG15: Huck 2F **7**
Beastmarket Hill NG1: Nott 4D **4** (5G **45**)
Beatty Wlk. DE7: Ilk 4B **28**
Beauclerk Dr. NG5: Top V 5C **20**
Beaufort Cl. NG2: West Br 2G **67**
Beaufort Dr. NG9: Chil 6C **54**
Beaulieu Gdns. NG2: West Br 6G **57**
Beaumaris Dr. NG4: Ged 6B **36**
 NG9: Chil 1B **64**
Beaumont Cl. NG9: Stfrd 2G **53**
 NG12: Key 3G **79**
Beaumont Gdns. NG2: West Br 1H **67**
Beaumont Sq. NG8: Woll 4B **42**
Beaumont St. NG2: Nott 5H **5** (5A **46**)
BEAUVALE
 NG15 ....5E **7**
 NG16 ....2D **16**
Beauvale NG16: Newth 3D **16**
Beauvale Ct. NG15: Huck 5E **7**
Beauvale Cres. NG15: Huck 5D **6**
Beauvale Dr. DE7: Ilk 2H **27**
Beauvale Ri. NG16: Eastw 2D **16**
Beauvale Rd. NG2: Nott 2G **57**
 NG15: Huck 5D **6**
Beaver Grn. NG2: West Br 4H **57**
Beck Av. NG14: Calv 3H **11**
Beckenham Rd. NG7: Radf 3D **44**
Becket Gro. NG11: Wilf 6E **57**
Beckett Ct. NG4: Ged 4F **35**
The Becket Way NG2: West Br 5F **57**
Beckford Rd. NG2: Nott 6B **46**
Beckhampton Rd. NG5: Bestw 5F **21**
Beckinsale Ct. NG4: Car 1A **48**
Beckley Rd. NG8: Brox 5F **31**
Beckside NG2: West Br 1E **69**
Beck St. NG1: Nott 3F **5** (4H **45**)
 NG4: Car 1F **47**
Bedale Ct. NG9: Chil 1A **64**
Bedale Rd. NG5: Sher 2G **33**
Bedarra Gro. NG7: Lent 5C **44**
Bede Ling NG2: West Br 5G **57**
Bedford Cl. NG7: Hys G 1D **44**
 NG9: Stfrd 2G **53**
Bedford Gro. NG6: Bulw 2B **32**
Bedford Row NG1: Nott 3G **5** (4H **45**)
Bedlington Gdns. NG3: Mapp 5A **34**
Beecham Av. NG3: Nott 3B **46**
Beech Av. DE72: Brea 5B **62**
 NG3: Mapp 3B **34**
 NG4: Neth 3H **47**
 NG7: Bas 1E **45**
 NG9: Bee 6H **55**

Beech Av.—Blenheim Pk. Rd.

Beech Av. NG10: Long E .4G **63**
NG10: Sand .4D **52**
NG12: Key .5H **79**
NG13: Bing .5G **51**
NG15: Huck .4G **7**
NG16: Nuth .1B **30**
Beech Cl. NG2: West Br .2F **59**
NG6: Cin .3A **32**
NG12: Edwal .1D **68**
NG12: Rad T .1F **61**
Beech Ct. NG3: Mapp .3C **34**
Beechcroft DE7: West H .2C **38**
BEECHDALE .3G 43
Beechdale Rd. NG8: Aspl, Bilb .6F **31**
The Beeches DE7: Smal .5A **14**
NG3: Nott .1C **46**
NG10: Long E .5G **63**
Beech La. DE7: West H .2B **38**
Beech Lodge NG13: Bing .5G **51**
Beechwood Rd. NG5: Arn .5C **22**
BEESTON .4G 55
Beeston Bus & Tram Interchange .5F 55
Beeston Bus. Pk. NG9: Bee .1G **65**
Beeston Centre Stop (NET) .5F 55
Beeston Cl. NG6: Bestw V .1C **20**
Beeston Ct. NG6: Bulw .6B **20**
Beeston Flds. Dr. NG9: Bee, Bram .3C **54**
Beeston Fields Golf Course .3D 54
Beeston La. NG7: Nott .2H **55**
Beeston Marina Mobile Home Pk. .2G **65**
Beeston Rd. NG7: Nott .2B **56**
Beeston Sailing Club .3G 65
Beeston Station (Rail) .6G 55
Beetham Cl. NG13: Bing .5F **51**
Beggarlee Pk. NG16: Newth .1D **16**
Bel-Air Res. Homes .4F **59**
Belconnen Rd. NG5: Bestw .2D **32**
Beldover Dr. NG8: Stre .5C **30**
Beldover Ho. *NG7: Lent .5C 44*
(off Faraday Rd.)
Belfield Ct. DE75: Los .1A **14**
Belfield Gdns. NG10: Long E .6G **63**
Belfield St. DE7: Ilk .5B **28**
Belford Cl. NG6: Bulw .5F **19**
Belfry Way NG12: Edwal .1E **69**
Belgrave M. NG2: West Br .2G **67**
Belgrave Rd. NG6: Bulw .6G **19**
Belgrave Sq. NG1: Nott .3C **4** (4F **45**)
Bella Cl. NG16: Lang M .1F **15**
Bellar Ga. NG1: Nott .4G **5** (5H **45**)
Belle Isle Rd. NG15: Huck .5G **7**
Belleville Dr. NG5: Bestw .6F **21**
Bellevue Ct. NG3: Nott .3A **46**
Bell Ho. NG7: Nott .3C **56**
Bell La. DE7: Smal .2A **26**
DE75: Ship .2A **26**
NG11: Wilf .4F **57**
Bells La. NG8: Cin .5G **31**
Bell St. NG4: Car .1F **47**
Belmont Av. DE72: Brea .5A **62**
NG6: Bulw .6A **20**
Belmont Cl. NG9: Chil .1B **64**
NG15: Huck .1G **19**
Belmore Gdns. NG8: Bilb .4D **42**
Belper Av. NG4: Car .6F **35**
Belper Cres. NG4: Car .6F **35**
Belper Rd. DE7: Stan C, West H .6A **26**
NG7: Hys G .2D **44**
Belper St. DE7: Ilk .2B **40**
Belsay Rd. NG5: Bestw .6E **21**
Belsford Ct. NG16: Want .5A **18**
Belton Cl. NG10: Sand .1D **62**
Belton Dr. NG2: West Br .1F **67**
Belton St. NG7: Hys G .1D **44**
Belvedere Av. NG7: Hys G .1D **44**
Belvedere Cl. NG12: Key .3G **79**
Belvoir Cl. DE7: Kirk H .3H **39**
NG10: Long E .2G **73**
Belvoir Hill NG2: Nott .5B **46**
Belvoir Lodge NG4: Car .3G **47**
Belvoir Rd. NG2: West Br .2C **58**
NG4: Neth .2A **48**
Belvoir St. NG3: Mapp .5B **34**
NG15: Huck .3F **7**
Belvoir Ter. NG2: Nott .5B **46**
Belvoir Va. Gro. NG13: Bing .5F **51**
Belward St. NG1: Nott .4G **5** (5H **45**)
Belwood Cl. NG11: Clftn .3D **66**
Bembridge Ct. NG9: Bram .3A **54**
Bembridge Dr. NG5: Bestw .1F **33**
(not continuous)
Bencaunt Gro. NG15: Huck .3G **7**
Bendigo La. NG2: Nott .6C **46**
Benedict Ct. NG5: Top V .4E **21**
Benington Dr. NG8: Woll .6C **42**
Ben Mayo Ct. NG7: Radf .3D **44**
Benner Av. DE7: Ilk .4C **40**
Bennerley Av. DE7: Ilk .3B **28**
Bennerley Ct. NG6: Bulw .5F **19**
Bennerley Rd. NG6: Bulw .5F **19**
Bennett Rd. NG3: Mapp .4C **34**
Bennett St. NG3: Mapp .5B **34**
NG10: Long E .2E **63**
NG10: Sand .6D **52**
Benneworth Cl. NG15: Huck .6F **7**
Ben St. NG7: Radf .3D **44**
Bentinck Av. NG12: Toll .4F **69**
Bentinck Ct. NG2: Nott .4H **5**
Bentinck Rd. NG4: Car .5E **35**
NG7: Hys G, Radf .3D **44**
Bentinck St. NG15: Huck .3F **7**
Bentley Av. NG3: Nott .3C **46**
Bentwell Av. NG5: Arn .6C **22**
Beresford Dr. DE7: Ilk .2A **28**
Beresford Rd. NG10: Long E .2C **72**
Beresford St. NG7: Radf .4C **44**
Berkeley Av. NG3: Mapp P .1G **45**
NG10: Long E .1E **73**
Berkeley Ct. NG5: Sher .6G **33**
Berle Av. DE75: Hea .2C **14**
Ber Mar Anda Res. Mobile Home Pk. .1F **15**
Bernard Av. NG15: Huck .2H **7**
Bernard St. NG5: Sher .6F **33**
Bernard Ter. NG5: Sher .6F **33**
Bernisdale Cl. NG5: Top V .4D **20**
Berridge Rd. NG7: Hys G .1E **45**
Berridge Rd. Central NG7: Hys G .1D **44**
Berridge Rd. W. NG7: Hys G .2C **44**
Berriedale Cl. NG5: Arn .4D **22**
Berrydown Cl. NG8: Aspl .6A **32**
Berry Hill Gro. NG4: Ged .5G **35**
Berwick Cl. NG5: Bestw .1G **33**
Berwin Cl. NG10: Long E .4C **62**
Beryldene Av. NG16: Want .6A **18**
Besecar Av. NG4: Ged .5G **35**
Besecar Cl. NG4: Ged .5G **35**
Bessell La. NG9: Stfrd .6E **53**
Bestwick Av. DE75: Hea .4F **15**
Bestwick Cl. DE7: Ilk .5C **40**
BESTWOOD .6F 21
Bestwood Av. NG5: Arn .5A **22**
Bestwood Bus. Pk. NG6: Bestw V .2C **20**
Bestwood Cl. NG5: Arn .5A **22**
Bestwood Country Pk. .2C 20
Mill Lakes .6B 8
Mill Lakes .1B 20
Bestwood Footpath NG15: Bestw V, Huck .6B **8**
Bestwood Lodge Dr. NG5: Arn .4G **21**
Bestwood Lodge Stables NG5: Arn .3F **21**
Bestwood Pk. NG5: Arn .3F **21**
Bestwood Pk. Dr. NG5: Top V .4F **21**
Bestwood Pk. Dr. W. NG5: Top V .4B **20**
Bestwood Pk. Vw. NG5: Arn .4A **22**
Bestwood Rd. NG6: Bulw .5A **20**
NG15: Huck .6A **8**
Bestwood Ter. NG6: Bulw .5B **20**
BESTWOOD VILLAGE .1C 20
Bethel Gdns. NG15: Huck .6C **6**
Bethnal Wlk. NG6: Bulw .6H **19**
Betony Cl. NG13: Bing .5C **50**
Bettison Ct. NG3: Mapp .3C **34**
Betts Av. NG15: Huck .1G **19**
Betula Cl. NG11: Clftn .4A **66**
Bevel St. NG7: Hys G .2D **44**
Beverley Cl. NG8: Woll .5B **42**
Beverley Dr. NG16: Kimb .6G **17**
Beverley Gdns. NG4: Ged .6H **35**
Beverley Sq. NG3: Nott .2A **46**
Bewcastle Rd. NG5: Arn, Top V .4E **21**
Bewick Dr. NG3: Nott .4E **47**
Bexhill Ct. NG9: Bee .2E **55**
Bexleigh Gdns. NG8: Bilb .1G **43**
Bexon Ct. NG4: Car .2G **47**
Bexwell Cl. NG11: Clftn .5C **66**
Biant Cl. NG8: Cin .4H **31**
Bideford Cl. NG3: Mapp .2F **35**
Bidford Rd. NG8: Brox .6F **31**
Bidwell Cres. NG11: Goth .5H **75**
Biggart Cl. NG9: Chil .3C **64**
Biko Sq. NG7: Hys G .1D **44**
Bilberry Wlk. NG3: Nott .3A **46**
Bilbie Wlk. NG1: Nott .2C **4** (4F **45**)
BILBOROUGH .2E 43
Bilborough Rd. NG8: Bilb, Stre .4B **42**
Bilborough Sports Cen. .2C 42
Bilby Gdns. NG3: Nott .4B **46**
Billesdon Dr. NG5: Sher .3D **32**
Binch Fld. Cl. NG14: Calv .3E **11**
Binding Cl. NG5: Sher .6F **33**
Binding Ho. NG5: Sher .6F **33**
BINGHAM .5E 51
Bingham By-Pass NG13: Bing .5B **50**
Bingham Ind. Pk. NG13: Bing .4E **51**
Bingham Leisure Cen. .5F 51
Bingham Rd.
NG5: Sher .5G **33**
NG12: Cotg .2F **71**
NG12: Rad T .6F **49**
Bingham Station (Rail) .4F 51
Bingley Cl. NG8: Bilb .3H **43**
Birch Av. DE7: Ilk .2C **40**
NG4: Car .2F **47**
NG9: Bee .1H **65**
NG16: Nuth .1B **30**
Birch Cl. NG16: Nuth .1B **30**
Birchdale Av. NG15: Huck .6G **7**
Birchfield Pk. DE75: Hea .6D **14**
Birchfield Rd. NG5: Arn .4C **22**
Birch Lea NG5: Redh .5H **21**
Birchover Pl. DE7: Ilk .2A **28**
Birchover Rd. NG8: Bilb .4C **42**
Birch Pk. NG16: Gilt .6C **16**
NG16: Newth .1D **16**
Birch Pas. NG7: Radf .2A **4** (4E **45**)
Birch Ri. NG14: Woodbo .6C **12**
Birch Wlk. NG5: Sher .4H **33**
Birchwood DE75: Los .1A **14**
Birchwood Av. DE72: Brea .6B **62**
NG10: Long E .1E **73**
Birchwood Rd. NG8: Woll .5C **42**
Bircumshaw Rd. DE75: Hea .3C **14**
Birdcroft La. DE7: Ilk .4B **40**
Birdsall Av. NG8: Woll .5E **43**
Birkdale Cl. DE7: Ilk .6H **27**
NG12: Edwal .2C **68**
Birkdale Way NG5: Top V .5D **20**
Birkin Av. NG7: Hys G .2D **44**
NG9: Toton .3A **64**
NG11: Rudd .5G **67**
NG12: Rad T .5G **49**
Birkland Av. NG1: Nott .1D **4** (3G **45**)
NG3: Mapp .3C **34**
Birley St. NG9: Stfrd .6F **53**
Birling Cl. NG6: Bulw .6F **19**
Birrell Rd. NG7: Hys G .1E **45**
Bisham Dr. NG2: West Br .4D **58**
Bishopdale Cl. NG10: Long E .1C **72**
Bishopdale Dr. NG16: Want .6B **18**
Bishops Cl. NG12: Key .3G **79**
Bishops Rd. NG13: Bing .4D **50**
Bishop St. NG16: Eastw .3B **16**
Bishops Way NG15: Huck .2H **7**
Bispham Dr. NG9: Toton .2H **63**
Blackacre NG14: Bur J .2E **37**
Blackburn Pl. DE7: Ilk .4A **28**
Blackburn Way NG5: Bestw .2E **33**
Blackcliffe Farm M. NG11: Rudd .4A **78**
Blackett's Wlk. NG11: Clftn .5A **66**
Blackfriars Cl. NG16: Nuth .5D **30**
Blackhill Dr. NG4: Car .1H **47**
Black Hills Dr. DE7: Ilk .3A **40**
Blackrod Cl. NG9: Toton .3A **64**
Blacksmith Ct. NG12: Cotg .1E **71**
Blacksmiths Ct. NG15: Pap .1B **8**
Blackstone Wlk. NG2: Nott .1G **57**
Black Swan Cl. NG5: Sher .3H **33**
Blackthorn Cl. NG4: Ged .5A **36**
NG13: Bing .5G **51**
Blackthorn Dr. NG16: Eastw .3A **16**
Blackthorne Dr. NG6: Cin .4H **31**
Blackwell Av. DE7: Ilk .2B **28**
Bladon Cl. NG3: Mapp .5A **34**
Bladon Rd. NG11: Rudd .6F **67**
Blair Ct. NG2: Nott .2G **57**
Blair Gro. NG10: Sand .1C **62**
Blaise Cl. NG11: Clftn .5C **66**
Blake Cl. NG3: Nott .4A **46**
NG5: Arn .6C **22**
Blake Ct. NG10: Long E .2D **72**
Blakeney Ho. *NG7: Hys G .2D 44*
(off St Paul's Av.)
Blakeney Rd. NG12: Rad T .6H **49**
Blakeney Wlk. NG5: Arn .2B **34**
Blake Rd. NG2: West Br .4B **58**
NG9: Stfrd .5G **53**
Blake St. DE7: Ilk .6B **28**
Blandford Av. NG10: Long E .1D **72**
Blandford Rd. NG9: Chil .6C **54**
Bland La. NG14: Epp .6G **13**
Blanford Gdns. NG2: West Br .6G **57**
Blankney St. NG6: Bas .3C **32**
Blants Cl. NG16: Kimb .1H **29**
Blantyre Av. NG5: Top V .4C **20**
Blatherwick Cl. NG15: Huck .3H **7**
Blatherwick's Yd. NG5: Arn .5B **22**
Bleaberry Cl. NG2: West Br .6E **59**
Bleachers Yd. NG7: Bas .6C **32**
Bleasby St. NG2: Nott .5B **46**
Bleasdale Cl. NG4: Ged .5A **36**
Blencathra Cl. NG2: West Br .6E **59**
BLENHEIM .4F 19
Blenheim NG3: Nott .2G **45**
Blenheim Av. NG3: Mapp .5E **35**
Blenheim Cl. NG11: Rudd .6F **67**
Blenheim Ct. NG6: Bulw .4E **19**
NG10: Sand .1D **62**
Blenheim Dr. NG9: Chil .6C **54**
Blenheim Ind. Est. NG6: Bulw .5F **19**
Blenheim La. NG6: Bulw .3D **18**
Blenheim Pk. Rd. NG6: Bulw .4E **19**

90 A-Z Nottingham

Blidworth Cl. NG8: Stre 5E 31
Blind La. DE72: Brea 5A 62
NG12: Key 5G 79
Bloomsbury Ct. NG1: Nott 3F 5
(off Beck St.)
Bloomsbury Dr. NG16: Nuth 4E 31
Bloomsgrove Ind. Est. NG7: Radf 4D 44
Bloomsgrove Rd. DE7: Ilk 5B 28
NG7: Radf 4D 44
Bloomsgrove St. NG7: Radf 4D 44
Bluebell Av. NG12: Cotg 6G 61
Bluebell Bank NG13: Bing 6D 50
Bluebell Cl. NG15: Huck 5C 6
Blue Bell Hill Rd. NG3: Nott 3A 46
Bluebell Way DE75: Hea 4F 15
Bluecoat Cl. NG1: Nott 1D 4 (3G 45)
Bluecoat Ho. NG1: Nott 1D 4 (3G 45)
Bluecoat St. NG1: Nott 1D 4 (3G 45)
Blundell Cl. NG3: Nott 1B 46
Blyth Gdns. NG3: Mapp 5A 34
Blyth St. NG3: Mapp 6A 34
Blyton Wlk. NG5: Bestw 6F 21
BMI THE PARK HOSPITAL 1H 9
Boatmans Cl. DE7: Ilk 5B 28
Boatswain Dr. NG15: Huck 3H 7
Bobbers Mill NG8: Hys G 2C 44
Bobbers Mill Bri. NG7: Hys G 2B 44
NG8: Hys G 2B 44
Bobbers Mill Rd. NG7: Hys G 2C 44
Boden Dr. NG16: Nuth 1C 30
Boden St. NG7: Radf 4D 44
Bodill Gdns. NG15: Huck 5A 8
Bodmin Av. NG15: Huck 6C 6
Bodmin Dr. NG8: Aspl 5A 32
Body Rd. NG9: Chil 2B 64
BOGEND 3G 17
Bohem Rd. NG10: Long E 2E 63
Bold Cl. NG6: Bulw 5H 19
Bolero Cl. NG8: Woll 4E 43
Bolero Sq. NG1: Nott 4G 5
Bolingey Way NG15: Huck 6C 6
Bolsover St. NG15: Huck 4H 7
Bolton Av. NG9: Chil 1C 64
Bolton Cl. NG2: West Br 5C 58
Bolton Ter. NG12: Rad T 6F 49
Bond Ho. NG5: Arn 5A 22
(off Bond St.)
Bonds Cl. DE7: Ilk 2B 28
Bond St. NG2: Nott 4H 5 (5A 46)
NG5: Arn 5A 22
Bonetti Cl. NG5: Arn 2D 34
Boniface Gdns. NG5: Top V 4E 21
Bonington Cl. NG6: Bulw 1G 31
Bonington Dr. NG5: Arn 6B 22
The Bonington Gallery 1C 4
Bonington Rd. NG3: Mapp 3B 34
Bonington Theatre 5B 22
Bonner Hill NG14: Calv 5H 11
Bonner La. NG14: Calv 4A 12
Bonner's Rd. NG16: Aws 3E 29
Bonnington Cres. NG5: Sher 3G 33
Bonnymead NG12: Cotg 3E 71
Bonsall Ct. NG10: Long E 5G 63
Bonsall St. NG10: Long E 5G 63
Bonser Cl. NG4: Car 2G 47
Bonser Hedge Ct. NG10: Long E 3D 72
Booth Cl. NG3: Nott 2F 5 (4H 45)
Booths Gdns. DE7: Ilk 3B 28
The Booth's Ind. Est. DE7: Ilk 5B 28
Boots Ct. NG10: Long E 6D 62
Borlace Cres. NG9: Stfrd 5G 53
Borman Cl. NG6: Bulw 2F 31
Borrowdale Cl. NG2: Gam 5F 59
Borrowdale Ct. NG9: Chil 1B 64
Borrowdale Dr. NG10: Long E 1C 72
Boscawen Ct. DE7: Ilk 4B 28
Bosden Cl. NG8: Bilb 3C 42
Bosley Sq. NG9: Lent A 3C 56
Bostock's La. DE72: Ris 1B 62
Bostocks La. NG10: Sand 2C 62
Boston M. NG5: Sher 4D 32
Boston St. NG1: Nott 3G 5 (4H 45)
Boswell Cl. NG7: Radf 4C 44
NG8: Stre 6C 30
Bosworth Cl. NG2: S'frd 1H 49
Bosworth Dr. NG16: Newth 2D 16
Bosworth Wlk. NG2: Nott 2F 57
Bosworth Way NG10: Long E 2F 73
Botany Av. NG3: Nott 2B 46
Botany Cl. NG2: West Br 2G 67
Botany Rd. NG3: Nott 2B 46
Bothe Cl. NG10: Long E 1E 73
Bottle La. NG1: Nott 4E 5 (5G 45)
Boulevard Ind. Pk. NG9: Bee 5H 55
Boundary Cres. NG9: Bee 2F 55
Boundary La. NG16: Lang M 2G 15
Boundary Rd. NG2: West Br 3D 58
NG9: Bee 2F 55
Bourne Cl. NG9: Bram 2D 54
Bourne Dr. NG16: Lang M 2F 15

Bourne M. NG4: Neth 3A 48
Bourne Sq. DE72: Brea 5A 62
Bourne St. NG4: Neth 3A 48
Bournmoor Av. NG11: Clftn 4C 66
Bovill St. NG7: Radf 3D 44
Bowden Av. NG6: Bestw V 1C 20
Bowden Cl. NG5: Arn 5H 21
NG5: Sher 4G 33
Bowden Dr. NG9: Bee 5H 55
Bowers Av. NG3: Mapp P 2H 45
Boweswell Rd. DE7: Ilk 5A 28
Bowland Cl. NG3: Nott 2C 46
Bowland Rd. NG13: Bing 5C 50
Bowling Cl. DE7: Stant D 3A 52
Bowlwell Av. NG5: Top V 5D 20
Bowness Av. NG6: Bas 5A 32
Bowness Cl. NG2: Gam 4E 59
Bowness Cl. NG2: West Br 6E 59
Bowscale Cl. NG2: West Br 1G 67
Boxley Dr. NG2: West Br 5F 7
Boxtree Av. NG15: Huck 6B 8
Boyce Gdns. NG3: Mapp 6B 34
Boycroft Av. NG3: Nott 1B 46
Boyd Cl. NG5: Arn .4D 22
Boynton Dr. NG3: Mapp 6B 34
Boythorpe Cl. DE7: Ilk 2B 28
Bracadale Rd. NG5: Top V 4D 20
Bracebridge Dr. NG8: Bilb 3D 42
Bracey Ri. NG2: West Br 2A 68
Bracken Cl. NG4: Car 5F 35
NG8: Bilb 6F 31
NG10: Long E 4D 62
Brackendale Av. NG5: Arn 5B 22
Brackendale Cl. NG13: Bing 6E 51
Brackenfield Dr. NG8: Gilt 5D 16
Bracken Ho. NG6: Bulw 6H 19
Bracken Rd. NG10: Long E 4D 62
Brackenwood Cl. NG8: Bas 6B 32
Bracton Dr. NG3: Nott 3B 46
Bradbourne Av. NG11: Wilf 6E 57
Bradbury Gdns. NG11: Rudd 6F 67
Bradbury/Midway Ind. Est. NG7: Lent 3C 56
Bradbury St. NG2: Nott 5C 46
Braddock Cl. NG7: Lent 5C 44
Braddon Av. NG9: Stfrd 2G 53
Bradfield Rd. NG8: Brox 6F 31
Bradford Cl. NG6: Bulw 1G 31
Bradford Way NG6: Bestw V 5F 9
Bradgate Cl. NG10: Sand 1D 62
Bradgate Rd. NG7: Hys G 1E 45
Bradley St. NG9: Bee 5G 55
Bradley St. NG10: Sand 6E 53
Bradleys Yd. NG12: Plum 6G 69
Bradley Wlk. NG11: Clftn 5D 66
Bradman Gdns. NG5: Arn 1D 34
BRADMORE 4B 78
Bradmore Av. NG11: Rudd 5G 67
Bradmore Bus. Pk. NG11: Bunny 5A 78
Bradmore La. NG12: Plum 3E 79
Bradmore Ri. NG5: Sher 3G 33
Bradshaw St. NG10: Long E 2D 72
Bradstone Dr. NG3: Ged, Mapp 1F 35
Bradwell Cl. NG16: Gilt 5E 17
Bradwell Dr. NG5: Top V 5D 20
Braefell Cl. NG2: West Br 6F 59
Braefield Cl. DE7: Kirk H 4G 39
Braemar Av. NG16: Eastw 5B 16
Braemar Dr. NG4: Ged 6B 36
Braemar Rd. NG6: Bulw 6A 20
Braidwood Ct. NG7: Hys G 2D 44
Brailsford Rd. NG7: Lent 2C 56
Brailsford Way NG9: Chil 4C 64
Bramber Gro. NG11: Clftn 6C 66
Bramble Cl.
NG6: Bas 4B 32
NG9: Atten 3D 64
NG10: Long E 4D 62
Bramble Ct.
NG4: Ged 6H 35
NG10: Sand 6E 53
Bramble Dr. NG3: Nott 2C 46
Bramble Gdns. NG8: Bilb 1G 43
Bramble Way NG12: Cotg 3G 71
Brambling Rd. NG4: Neth, Stoke B 3A 54
BRAMCOTE 5C 54
Bramcote Av. NG9: Chil 5C 54
Bramcote Crematorium 6A 42
Bramcote Dr. NG8: Woll 6D 42
NG9: Bee 4E 55
Bramcote Dr. W. NG9: Bee 5D 54
BRAMCOTE HILLS 2C 54
Bramcote La. NG8: Woll 1D 54
NG9: Chil 5C 54
Bramcote Lane Stop (NET) 6C 54
Bramcote Leisure Cen. 2B 54
Bramcote Rd. NG9: Bee 4D 54
Bramcote St. NG7: Radf 4C 44
Bramcote Wlk. NG7: Radf 4C 44
Bramerton Rd. NG8: Bilb 3C 42
Bramhall Rd. NG8: Bilb 3C 42
Bramley Ct. NG16: Kimb 1H 29

Bramley Grn. NG8: Brox 6E 31
Bramley Rd. NG8: Brox 6E 31
NG10: Long E 2D 72
Brampton Av. DE75: Hea 3E 15
Brampton Cl. DE7: Ilk 2B 28
Brampton Dr. NG9: Stfrd 6H 53
Bramwell Dr. NG9: Bram 5C 54
Brancaster Cl. NG6: Cin 3H 31
Brandish Cres. NG11: Clftn 4B 66
Brandreth Av. NG3: Nott 1B 46
Brandreth Rd. NG16: Gilt 5C 16
Brands Cl. DE7: Ilk 2B 28
Brand St. NG2: Nott 1B 58
Brangwen Ho. NG7: Lent 5C 44
(off Faraday Rd.)
Branklene Cl. NG16: Kimb 6G 17
Branksome Wlk. NG2: Nott 1G 57
Bransdale Cl. NG10: Long E 1D 72
Bransdale Rd. NG11: Clftn 4B 66
Branston Gdns. NG2: West Br 1H 67
Branston Wlk. NG5: Sher 3G 33
Brantford Av. NG11: Clftn 4D 66
Brassington Cl. DE7: West H 1C 38
NG16: Gilt 6D 16
Bratton Dr. NG5: Bestw 2E 33
Braunton Cl. NG15: Huck 5D 6
Braunton Cres. NG3: Mapp 1F 35
Brayton Cres. NG6: Bulw 2B 32
Breach Ho. NG7: Lent 5C 44
(off Faraday Rd.)
Breach Rd. DE75: Hea 5E 15
Breadsall Ct. DE7: Ilk 4B 28
BREASTON 5A 62
Breaston Cl. NG5: Top V 5E 21
(off Erewash Gdns.)
Breaston La. DE72: Ris 2A 62
Brechin Cl. NG5: Arn 4D 22
Breckhill Rd. NG3: Mapp 2A 34
NG5: Woodt 2A 34
Brecknock Dr. NG10: Long E 6C 62
Breckswood Dr. NG11: Clftn 6C 66
Brecon Cl. NG6: Cin 4G 31
NG10: Long E 5C 62
Breconshire Gdns. NG6: Bas 5C 62
Bredon Cl. NG10: Long E 5C 62
Breedon St. NG10: Long E 2D 62
Brendon Dr. NG9: Bram 3B 54
Brendon Dr. NG8: Woll 4G 43
NG16: Kimb 6H 17
Brendon Gdns. NG8: Woll 4G 43
Brendon Gro. NG13: Bing 4C 50
Brendon Lawrence Sports Hall 1H 45
Brendon Rd. NG8: Woll 4G 43
Brendon Way NG10: Long E 3C 62
Brentcliffe Av. NG3: Nott 2C 46
Brentnall Cl. NG10: Long E 6D 62
Brentnall Ct. NG9: Chil 2D 64
Bressingham Dr. NG2: West Br 2G 67
Brett Cl. NG15: Huck 6E 7
Brettsil Dr. NG11: Rudd 6F 67
Brewery St. NG16: Kimb 1H 29
Brewhouse Yd. NG1: Nott 6C 4 (6F 45)
Brewill Gro. NG11: Wilf 6F 57
Brewsters Cl. NG13: Bing 5E 51
Brewsters Rd. NG3: Nott 1A 46
Breydon Ind. Cen. NG10: Long E 6H 63
Brian Clough Way NG7: Nott, Lent 1H 55
(not continuous)
NG9: Stfrd, Bram .6F 53
Briar Av. NG10: Sand 2C 62
Briarbank Av. NG3: Nott 1C 46
Briarbank Wlk. NG3: Nott 2C 46
Briar Cl.
NG9: Bram 2E 55
NG12: Key 3H 79
NG15: Huck 6D 6
Briar Ct. NG2: Nott 2F 57
Briar Gdns. NG14: Calv 3E 11
Briar Ga. NG10: Long E 3C 62
Briargate NG12: Cotg 3G 71
Briar Rd. NG16: Newth 5D 16
Briarwood Av. NG3: Nott 2C 46
Briarwood Ct. NG5: Sher 4A 34
Brickenell Rd. NG14: Calv 5H 11
Brickyard NG15: Huck 5A 8
The Brickyard DE7: Stan C 6A 26
Brickyard Cotts. NG16: Newth 4C 16
Brickyard Dr. NG15: Huck 6A 8
Brickyard La. NG12: Rad T 6H 49
Brickyard Plantation Nature Reserve 1G 41
Bridge Av. NG9: Chil 6E 55
Bridge Cl. NG6: Bulw 4B 20
NG9: Bee 4H 55
NG15: Huck 5G 7
Bridge Farm La. NG11: Clftn 3C 66
Bridge Grn. NG8: Brox 6E 31
Bridge Grn. Wlk. NG8: Brox 6E 31
Bridge Gro. NG2: West Br 3A 58
Bridgend Cl. NG9: Stfrd 6F 53
Bridge Rd. NG8: Woll 4D 42

Bridge St.—Bush Cl.

Bridge St. DE7: Ilk 3B **28**
NG10: Long E 4F **63**
NG10: Sand 6E **53**
NG16: Lang M 2G **15**
Bridgewater Ct. NG5: Woodt 2H **33**
Bridgeway Cen. NG2: Nott 1G **57**
Bridgeway Ct. NG2: Nott 1H **57**
Bridgford Rd. NG2: West Br 2A **58**
Bridgnorth Dr. NG11: Clftn 3C **66**
Bridgnorth Way NG9: Toton 2G **63**
Bridle Rd. NG9: Bram 2B **54**
NG14: Bur J 1D **36**
Bridlesmith Ga. NG1: Nott 4E **5** (5G **45**)
Bridlesmith Wlk. NG1: Nott 4E **5**
Bridlington St. NG7: Hys G 2C **44**
Bridport Av. NG8: Radf 4B **44**
Brielen Ct. NG12: Rad T 6G **49**
Brielen Rd. NG12: Rad T 6G **49**
Brierfield Av. NG11: Wilf 1F **67**
Brierley Grn. NG4: Neth 2A **48**
Brightmoor Ct. NG1: Nott 4F **5**
Brightmoor Pl. NG1: Nott 4F **5**
Brightmoor St. NG1: Nott 4F **5** (5H **45**)
Bright St. DE7: Ilk 4A **28**
NG7: Lent 4C **44**
NG16: Kimb 1G **29**
Brimington Cl. DE7: Ilk 1B **28**
Brindley Ct. NG5: Woodt 3H **33**
Brindley Rd. NG8: Bilb 4C **42**
Brinkhill Cres. NG11: Clftn 2D **66**
Brinsley Cl. NG8: Aspl 6G **31**
Brisbane Dr. NG5: Top V 5C **20**
NG9: Stfrd 2H **53**
Bristol Rd. DE7: Ilk 6A **28**
Britannia Av. NG6: Bas 2C **32**
Britannia Cl. NG16: Want 6A **18**
Britannia Ct. NG4: Neth 3A **48**
Britannia Rd. NG10: Long E 4F **63**
British Geological Survey 3A **80**
Britten Gdns. NG3: Nott 3B **46**
Brixham Rd. NG15: Huck 6D **6**
Brixton Rd. NG7: Radf 4C **44**
B Rd. NG7: Nott 5B **56**
Broad Cl. NG14: Woodbo 1C **24**
Broad Eadow Rd. NG6: Bulw 6F **19**
Broadfields NG14: Calv 3H **11**
Broadgate NG9: Bee 4G **55**
Broadgate Av. NG9: Bee 4G **55**
Broadgate La. NG9: Bee 4G **55**
Broadgate Pk. NG9: Bee 3G **55**
Broadgate Pk. Student Village *NG9: Bee* *3G* ***55***
(off Salthouse La.)
Broadholme St. NG7: Lent 6D **44**
Broadhurst Av. NG6: Bas 5B **32**
Broadlands NG10: Sand 2D **62**
Broadleigh Cl. NG2: West Br 2G **67**
Broadmarsh Bus & Coach Station 6E **5** (6G **45**)
Broadmead NG14: Bur J 2F **37**
Broadmeer NG12: Cotg 2E **71**
Broadmere Ct. NG5: Arn 4D **22**
Broad Oak Cl. NG3: Nott 2A **46**
Broad Oak Dr. NG9: Stfrd 5F **53**
Broadstairs Rd. NG9: Toton 3H **63**
Broadstone Cl. NG2: West Br 6G **57**
Broad St. NG1: Nott 3F **5** (4H **45**)
NG10: Long E 6F **63**
Broad Valley Dr. NG6: Bestw V 1C **20**
Broad Wlk. NG6: Bas 4A **32**
Broadway DE7: Ilk 4A **28**
DE75: Hea 4C **14**
NG1: Nott 5F **5** (5H **45**)
Broadway Cinema 3F **5**
Broadway E. NG4: Car 3F **47**
Broadwood Ct. NG9: Bee 3G **55**
Broadwood Rd. NG5: Bestw 5F **21**
Brockdale Gdns. NG12: Key 3G **79**
Brockenhurst Gdns. NG3: Nott 3B **46**
Brockhall Ri. DE75: Hea 4E **15**
Brockhole Cl. NG2: West Br 6F **59**
Brockley Rd. NG2: West Br 4D **58**
Brockwood Cres. NG12: Key 3G **79**
Brodhurst Cl. NG14: Woodbo 1C **24**
Brodwell Gro. NG3: Nott 6B **34**
Bromfield Cl. NG3: Nott 2E **47**
Bromley Cl. NG6: Bulw 1H **31**
Bromley Ct. DE7: Ilk 2C **40**
Bromley Pl. NG1: Nott 4C **4** (5F **45**)
Bromley Rd. NG2: West Br 5A **58**
Brompton Cl. NG5: Arn 3E **21**
Brompton Way NG2: West Br 2G **67**
Bronte Cl. NG10: Long E 6C **62**
Bronte Ct. NG7: Radf 3E **45**
Brook Av. NG5: Arn 5D **22**
Brook Chase M. NG9: Chil 6C **54**
Brook Cl. NG6: Bulw 1H **31**
NG10: Long E 2G **73**
NG16: Newth 4D **16**
Brook Cotts. DE7: Ilk 4B **28**
Brook Ct. NG7: Radf 3D **44**
NG16: Lang M 3F **15**
Brookdale Ct. NG5: Sher 2H **33**
Brooke St. DE7: Ilk 3D **40**
NG10: Sand 6D **52**
Brookfield Av. NG15: Huck 6G **7**
Brookfield Cl. NG12: Rad T 6F **49**
Brookfield Ct. NG2: Nott 1G **57**
NG5: Arn 6C **22**
Brookfield Gdns. NG5: Arn 6C **22**
Brookfield M. NG10: Sand 5E **53**
Brookfield Rd. NG5: Arn 6B **22**
Brookfield Way DE75: Hea 4F **15**
Brook Gdns. NG5: Arn 5C **22**
BROOK HILL 5E **67**
Brookhill Cres. NG8: Woll 6E **43**
Brookhill Dr. NG8: Woll 6E **43**
Brookhill Leys Rd. NG16: Eastw 4A **16**
Brookhill St. NG9: Stfrd 6E **53**
Brookland Dr. NG9: Chil 6D **54**
Brooklands Av. DE75: Hea 3D **14**
Brooklands Bus. Cen. DE75: Los 1B **14**
Brooklands Ct. NG10: Long E 6F **63**
Brooklands Cres. NG4: Ged 6A **36**
Brooklands Dr. NG4: Ged 6A **36**
Brooklands Rd. NG3: Nott 2D **46**
Brook La. NG12: Stant W 4D **80**
Brooklyn Av. NG14: Bur J 2E **37**
Brooklyn Cl. NG6: Bulw 2B **32**
Brooklyn Rd. NG6: Bulw 1B **32**
Brook Rd. NG9: Bee 3F **55**
Brooksby La. NG11: Clftn 1D **66**
Brooks Cotts. NG4: Car 2E **47**
Brookside NG15: Huck 6H **7**
NG16: Eastw 1B **16**
Brookside Av. NG8: Woll 1D **54**
Brookside Cl. NG10: Long E 5D **62**
Brookside Cotts. NG14: Bur J 2E **37**
Brookside Gdns. NG11: Rudd 5F **67**
Brookside Ind. Units NG9: Stfrd 3F **53**
Brookside Rd. NG11: Rudd 5F **67**
Brook St. DE75: Los 1A **14**
NG1: Nott 3F **5** (4H **45**)
NG15: Huck 3G **7**
Brookthorpe Way NG11: Wilf 1E **67**
Brookvale Rd. NG16: Lang M 3G **15**
Brook Vw. Ct. NG12: Key 5G **79**
Brook Vw. Dr. NG12: Key 5G **79**
Brookwood Cres. NG4: Car 2E **47**
Broom Cl. NG14: Calv 3H **11**
Broomfield Cl. NG10: Sand 6C **52**
BROOMHILL 6A **8**
Broomhill Av. DE7: Ilk 3C **40**
(not continuous)
Broomhill Cotts. NG15: Huck 6A **8**
Broomhill Pk. Vw. NG15: Huck 6A **8**
Broomhill Rd. NG6: Bulw 1A **32**
NG15: Huck 6G **7**
NG16: Kimb 1A **30**
Broom Rd. NG14: Calv 4H **11**
Broom Wlk. NG3: Nott 1D **46**
Brora Rd. NG6: Bulw 6B **20**
Broughton Cl. DE7: Ilk 4A **28**
Broughton Dr. NG8: Woll 5A **44**
Broughton St. NG9: Bee 4E **55**
Brownes Rd. NG13: Bing 4G **51**
Browning Cl. NG5: Arn 6H **21**
Browning Ct. NG5: Sher 4F **33**
Brown La. NG11: Bart F 1E **75**
Brownlow Dr. NG5: Top V 4B **20**
Browns Cft. NG6: Bas 4B **32**
Brown's Flats NG16: Kimb 6H **17**
Browns La. NG12: Stant W 6B **80**
Browns La. Bus. Pk.
NG12: Stant W 6C **80**
Brown's Rd. NG10: Long E 5G **63**
Brown St. NG7: Hys G 2D **44**
BROXTOWE 5G **31**
Broxtowe Av. NG8: Aspl 5A **32**
NG16: Kimb 1F **29**
Broxtowe Country Pk. 5E **31**
Broxtowe Dr. NG15: Huck 2G **7**
Broxtowe Hall Cl. NG8: Brox 5G **31**
Broxtowe La. NG8: Aspl, Brox 6F **31**
Broxtowe Pk. Bus. Cen. NG8: Stre 5D **30**
Broxtowe Ri. NG8: Cin 4H **31**
Broxtowe St. NG5: Sher 5G **33**
Bruce Cl. NG2: Nott 1H **57**
Bruce Dr. NG2: West Br 4H **57**
Brunel Av. NG16: Newth 1D **16**
Brunel Ter. NG7: Nott 4E **45**
Brunswick Dr. NG9: Stfrd 6H **53**
Brushfield St. NG7: Hys G 2C **44**
Brussells Ter. DE7: Ilk 6A **28**
Brusty Pl. NG14: Bur J 2E **37**
Bryan Ct. NG8: Aspl 1A **44**
Buckfast Way NG2: West Br 4C **58**
Buckingham Av. NG15: Huck 3H **7**
Buckingham Ct. NG10: Sand 2C **62**
Buckingham Dr. DE75: Hea 3A **14**
Buckingham Rd. NG5: Woodt 2A **34**
NG10: Sand 1C **62**
Buckingham Way NG16: Want 6B **18**
Buckland Dr. NG14: Woodbo 1C **24**
Bucklee Dr. NG14: Calv 4G **11**
Bucklow Cl. NG8: Bas 6B **32**
Buckminster Rd. DE7: Kirk H 5G **39**
Budby Ri. NG15: Huck 4H **7**
The Buildings NG11: Thru 4C **74**
BULCOTE 1H **37**
Bulcote Dr. NG14: Bur J 4D **36**
Bulcote Ho. *NG4: Car* *1G* ***47***
(off Garden City)
Bulcote Rd. NG11: Clftn 2D **66**
Bullace Rd. NG3: Nott 2B **46**
Bull Cl. Rd. NG7: Lent 3C **56**
Buller St. DE7: Ilk 3C **40**
Buller Ter. NG5: Sher 4H **33**
Bullfinch Rd. NG6: Bas 3B **32**
Bullins Cl. NG5: Arn 4G **21**
Bullivant St. NG3: Nott 1F **5** (3H **45**)
Bull Mdw. NG14: Calv 3F **11**
BULWELL 6A **20**
Bulwell Bus. Cen. NG6: Bulw 6G **19**
Bulwell Bus Station 6H **19**
BULWELL FOREST 5A **20**
Bulwell Forest Golf Course 6C **20**
Bulwell Forest Stop (NET) 5A **20**
Bulwell Hall Pk. 3H **19**
Bulwell High Rd. NG6: Bulw 1H **31**
Bulwell La. NG6: Bas 3B **32**
Bulwell Station (Rail) 1A **32**
Bulwell Stop (NET) 1A **32**
Bulwer Rd. NG7: Radf 4D **44**
Bunbury St. NG2: Nott 2H **57**
Bunny La. NG11: Bunny 5D **78**
NG12: Key 5D **78**
Bunting Cl. DE7: Kirk H 3G **39**
Buntings La. NG4: Car 2E **47**
Bunting St. NG7: Lent 2C **56**
Burberry Av. NG15: Huck 1A **20**
Burcot Cl. DE7: West H 1C **38**
Burford Rd. NG7: Hys G 1D **44**
Burford St. NG5: Arn 5A **22**
Burgass Rd. NG3: Nott 2C **46**
Burge Cl. NG2: Nott 1G **57**
Burgh Hall Cl. NG9: Chil 3C **64**
Burhill NG12: Cotg 3G **71**
Burke St. NG7: Radf 2A **4** (4E **45**)
Burleigh Cl. NG4: Car 2H **47**
Burleigh Rd. NG2: West Br 5B **58**
Burleigh Sq. NG9: Chil 1C **64**
Burleigh St. DE7: Ilk 6B **28**
Burlington Av. NG5: Sher 4F **33**
Burlington Ct. NG5: Sher 4G **33**
Burlington Rd. NG4: Car 1G **47**
NG5: Sher 4G **33**
Burnaby St. NG6: Bas 3B **32**
Burnbank Cl. NG2: West Br 6F **59**
Burnbreck Gdns. NG8: Woll 5E **43**
Burncroft DE7: West H 2C **38**
Burndale Wlk. NG5: Top V 5C **20**
Burnham Av. NG9: Chil 1F **65**
Burnham Cl. DE7: West H 1B **38**
Burnham Lodge NG5: Top V 4C **20**
Burnham St. NG5: Sher 5G **33**
Burnham Way NG2: Nott 6G **45**
Burnor Pool NG14: Calv 4H **11**
Burns Av. NG7: Radf 1A **4** (3E **45**)
Burns Ct. NG5: Sher 4F **33**
Burnside Dr. NG9: Bram 1C **54**
Burnside Grn. NG8: Bilb 3D **42**
Burnside Gro. NG12: Toll 4E **69**
Burnside Rd. NG2: West Br 6A **58**
NG8: Bilb 3D **42**
Burns St. DE7: Ilk 1A **40**
DE75: Hea 3B **14**
NG7: Radf 1A **4** (3E **45**)
Burnthouse Rd. DE75: Hea 4B **14**
Burnt Oak Cl. NG16: Nuth 4D **30**
Burntstump Country Pk. 1H **9**
Burntstump Hill NG5: Arn 1G **9**
Burnwood Dr. NG8: Woll 4D **42**
Burr La. DE7: Ilk 6B **28**
Burrows Av. NG9: Bee 2F **55**
Burrows Ct. NG3: Nott 4B **46**
Burrows Cres. NG9: Bee 2F **55**
Bursar Way NG10: Long E 2E **63**
Burtness Rd. NG11: Clftn 4C **66**
Burton Av. NG4: Car 1D **46**
Burton Cl. NG4: Car 6A **36**
Burton Dr. NG9: Chil 1C **64**
BURTON JOYCE 3F **37**
Burton Joyce Station (Rail) 4E **37**
Burton Manderfield Ct. NG2: Nott 1G **57**
Burton Rd. NG4: Car, Ged 2G **47**
NG14: Bur J 5C **36**
(not continuous)
Burton St. DE75: Hea 3C **14**
NG1: Nott 3D **4** (4G **45**)
Burwell St. NG7: Hys G 3D **44**
Bush Cl. NG5: Top V 5D **20**

92 A-Z Nottingham

Bushy Cl. NG10: Long E 1C 72
Bute Av. NG7: Lent .5D 44
Butler Av. NG12: Rad T 5G 49
Butlers Cl. NG15: Huck 6A 8
BUTLER'S HILL 5A 8
Butlers Hill Stop (NET) 6B 8
Butterfield Ct. NG16: Want 6A 18
Butterley Cl. DE7: Ilk 2B 28
Buttermead Cl. NG9: Trow 1F 53
Buttermere Cl. NG2: Gam 4F 59
    NG10: Long E 3C 62
Buttermere Ct. NG5: Sher 5G 33
Buttermere Dr. NG9: Bram 3D 54
Butterton Cl. DE7: Ilk 2C 40
Buttery Gdns. NG11: Rudd 1G 77
Butt Ho's. NG7: Lent 5C 44
Butt Rd. NG13: Bing 5G 51
Butts Cl. DE7: Ilk 5C 40
Butt St. NG10: Sand 6D 52
Buxton Av. DE75: Hea 5D 14
    NG4: Car 6F 35
Buxton Cl. NG5: Top V 5D 20
Buxton Ct. DE7: Ilk 5H 27
Buxton Grn. DE75: Hea 6D 14
Byard La. NG1: Nott 5E 5 (5G 45)
Bye Pass Rd. NG9: Chil 3D 64
Byfield Cl. NG7: Radf 3D 44
Byford Cl. NG3: Mapp 5A 34
Byley Rd. NG8: Bilb .4B 42
Byrne Ct. NG5: Arn .2D 34
Byron Av. NG10: Long E 2D 62
Byron Bingo
    Hucknall 4H 7
The Byron Cen. NG15: Huck 4G 7
Byron Ct. NG2: Nott 4H 5 (5A 46)
    NG9: Stfrd 2G 53
Byron Cres. NG16: Aws 3E 29
Byron Gro. NG5: Sher 4G 33
Byron Ind. Est. NG5: Arn 6C 22
Byron Pl. NG7: Lent 4C 44
                                         (off Wragby Rd.)
Byron Rd. NG2: West Br 4B 58
Byron Sq. NG15: Huck 4G 7
                                          (off Baker St.)
Byron St. DE7: Ilk .6B 28
    NG5: Arn 6H 21
    NG15: Huck 5G 7

C

Caddaw Av. NG15: Huck 5G 7
Cadlan Cl. NG5: Bestw 6E 21
Cadlan Ct. NG5: Bestw 6E 21
Caernarvon Pl. NG9: Chil 1B 64
Caincross Rd. NG8: Bilb 2D 42
Cairngorm Dr. NG5: Arn 3F 21
Cairns Cl. NG5: Bestw 2E 33
Cairnsmore Cl. NG10: Long E 4C 62
Cairns St. NG1: Nott 2E 5 (4G 45)
Cairo St. NG7: Bas .6D 32
Caister Rd. NG11: Clftn 5C 66
Caithness Ct. NG5: Sher 6F 33
Calcroft Cl. NG8: Aspl 5A 32
Caldbeck Cl. NG2: Gam 4E 59
Caldbeck Ct. NG9: Chil 1B 64
Caldbeck Wlk. NG5: Bestw 6F 21
Calderdale NG8: Woll 6B 42
Calder Gdns. NG13: Bing 6D 50
Calderdale Dr. NG10: Long E 1C 72
Calderhall Gdns. NG5: Bestw 5G 21
Calder Wlk. NG6: Bulw 6H 19
Caldon Grn. NG6: Bulw 3A 20
Caledon Rd. NG5: Sher 4F 33
Calladine Cl. DE75: Hea 3B 14
Calladine Ct. NG6: Bulw 1G 31
Callaway Cl. NG8: Woll 4E 43
Calley Av. DE7: Ilk .1B 28
Calstock Rd. NG5: Woodt 2A 34
Calveley Rd. NG8: Bilb 1E 43
Calver Cl. NG8: Woll 5A 44
Calvert Cl. NG9: Chil 1D 64
    NG16: Lang M 2F 15
CALVERTON
Calverton Av. NG4: Car 6D 34
Calverton Bus. NG14: Calv 1H 11
Calverton Cl. NG9: Toton 3A 64
Calverton Dr. NG8: Stre 5D 30
Calverton Folk Mus. 4G 11
Calverton Leisure Cen.
Calverton Rd. NG5: Arn 4B 22
Camberley Ct. NG6: Bulw 5G 19
Camberley Rd. NG6: Bulw 5G 19
Camborne Dr. NG8: Aspl 2G 45
Cambria M. NG3: Nott 3A 58
Cambridge Ct. NG2: West Br 1F 53
Cambridge Cres. NG9: Stfrd 1F 53
Cambridge Gdns. NG5: Woodt 2D 34
Cambridge Rd. NG2: West Br 4C 58
    NG8: Woll 5G 43

Cambridge St. NG4: Car 6G 35
Camdale Cl. NG9: Chil 5B 54
Camden Cl. NG2: Nott 4H 5 (5A 46)
Camelia Av. NG11: Clftn 4A 66
Camelot Av. NG5: Sher 5E 33
Camelot Cres. NG11: Rudd 5F 67
Camelot St. NG11: Rudd 5F 67
Cameo Cl. NG4: Colw 3H 47
Camer Ct. NG9: Bee 5G 55
                                      (off Waverley Av.)
Cameron St. NG5: Sher 5G 33
Camish Ho. NG10: Sand 6D 52
                                       (off Bennett St.)
Camomile Cl. NG5: Top V 6C 20
Camomile Gdns. NG7: Hys G 2C 44
Campbell Cl. NG8: Brox 6G 31
Campbell Dr. NG4: Car 1E 47
Campbell Gdns. NG5: Arn 4E 23
Campbell Gro. NG3: Nott 2G 5 (4H 45)
Campbell St. NG3: Nott 2H 5 (4A 46)
    NG16: Lang M 1G 15
Campden Grn. NG11: Clftn 3C 66
Campion Cl. NG5: Arn 5A 22
Campion Way NG13: Bing 5D 50
Camrose Cl. NG8: Bilb 1F 43
Canal Side DE7: Ilk 4B 28
    NG9: Bee 2H 65
Canalside NG1: Nott 6E 5 (6G 45)
Canalside Wlk. NG1: Nott 6B 4 (6G 45)
Canal St. DE7: Ilk .6C 28
    NG1: Nott 6D 4 (6G 45)
    NG10: Long E 4D 62
    NG10: Sand 6D 52
Canberra Cl. NG9: Stfrd 2G 53
Canberra Cres. NG2: West Br 1H 67
    NG15: Huck 3D 18
Canberra Gdns. NG2: West Br 2H 67
Candleby Cl. NG12: Cotg 2F 71
Candleby Ct. NG12: Cotg 2F 71
Candleby La. NG12: Cotg 2F 71
Candle Mdw. NG2: Colw 1A 58
Canning Cir. NG7: Nott 3A 4 (4E 45)
Canning Ter. NG7: Nott 3A 4 (4E 45)
Cannock Way NG10: Long E 6H 63
Cannon St. NG5: Sher 4G 33
Canonbie Cl. NG5: Arn 4D 22
Cantelupe Gdns. NG16: Gilt 1D 44
Cantelupe Rd. DE7: Ilk 1B 40
Canterbury Cl. NG16: Nuth 3D 30
Canterbury Ct. NG1: Nott 1C 4 (3F 45)
Canterbury Rd. NG8: Radf 4B 44
Cantley Av. NG4: Ged 5G 35
Cantrell Rd. NG6: Bulw 1A 32
Canver Cl. NG8: Bilb 3C 42
Canwick Cl. NG8: Bilb 4C 42
Capenwray Gdns. NG5: Bestw 5G 21
Capital FM Arena 4G 5 (5H 45)
Capitol Cl. NG8: Woll 4G 43
Caporn Cl. NG6: Bulw 2A 32
Cardale Rd. NG3: Nott 3C 46
Cardiff St. NG3: Nott 4B 46
Cardigan Cl. NG3: Nott 2G 45
Cardinal Cl. NG3: Nott 3A 46
Cardington Cl. NG5: Top V 4C 20
Cardwell St. NG7: Hys G 1D 44
Carew Rd. NG11: Clftn 3C 66
Carey Rd. NG6: Bulw 5A 20
Carisbrooke Av. NG3: Mapp 6G 33
    NG4: Ged 6B 36
    NG9: Bee 3G 55
Carisbrooke Dr. NG3: Mapp P 6G 33
Carlight Gdns. Pk. Homes 2D 58
Carlile Rd. NG4: Car 1G 47
Carlin St. DE72: Brea 5A 62
Carlingford Rd. NG15: Huck 3G 7
Carlin St. NG6: Bulw 6H 19
Carlisle Av. NG6: Bulw 6A 20
Carlswark Gdns. NG5: Top V 4D 20
CARLTON 2H 47
Carlton Bus. Cen. NG4: Car 2H 47
Carlton Cl. DE75: Hea 2E 15
Carlton Fold NG2: Nott 6B 46
Carlton Forum Leisure Cen. 6E 35
Carlton Grange NG4: Car 2E 47
Carlton Hgts. NG4: Car 2E 47
Carlton Hill NG4: Car 2D 46
Carlton M. NG4: Car 2E 47
Carlton Rd. NG3: Nott 4H 5 (4A 46)
    NG10: Long E 2D 72
Carlton Sq. NG4: Car 2G 47
Carlton Station (Rail) 1H 47
Carlton St. NG1: Nott 4F 5 (5H 45)
Carlton Va. Cl. NG4: Car 6F 35
Carlyle Gdns. DE75: Hea 2B 14
Carlyle Pl. DE75: Hea 2B 14
Carlyle Rd. NG2: West Br 4A 58
Carlyle St. DE75: Hea 2B 14
Carman Cl. NG16: Want 5A 18
Carmel Gdns. NG5: Arn 1B 34

Carnarvon Cl. NG13: Bing 4E 51
Carnarvon Dr. NG14: Bur J 2F 37
Carnarvon Gro. NG4: Car 1F 47
    NG4: Ged 6H 35
Carnarvon Pl. NG13: Bing 5D 50
Carnarvon Rd. NG2: West Br 5B 58
Carnarvon St. NG4: Neth 3A 48
Carnforth Cl. NG9: Stfrd 6F 53
Carnforth Ct. NG5: Bestw 5G 21
Carnwood Rd. NG5: Bestw 1E 33
Caroline Ct. DE7: Ilk 3C 40
Caroline Wlk. NG3: Nott 3H 45
Carradale Cl. NG5: Arn 5E 23
Carrfield Av. NG9: Toton 4H 63
    NG10: Long E 5H 63
Carriage Cl. NG3: Nott 6H 33
CARRINGTON 5F 33
Carrington Cl. DE7: Ilk 4C 40
Carrington Ct. NG5: Sher 6G 33
Carrington La. NG14: Calv 2H 11
Carrington St. NG1: Nott 6E 5 (6G 45)
    NG2: Nott 6G 45
Carrock Av. DE75: Hea 4F 15
Carroll Gdns. NG2: Nott 2G 57
Carr Rd. NG13: Bing 4H 51
Cartbridge NG12: Cotg 3F 71
Carter Av. NG11: Rudd 1G 77
    NG12: Rad T 6H 49
Carter Cl. NG10: Long E 1D 72
Carter Ga. NG1: Nott 5G 5 (5H 45)
Carter Rd. NG9: Chil 3A 64
                                      (not continuous)
Carterswood Dr. NG16: Nuth 4F 31
Cartledge Dr. NG3: Arn 1E 35
Cartwright Way NG9: Bee 6F 55
Carver St. NG7: Hys G 1D 44
Carwood Rd. NG9: Bram 2D 54
Casper Ct. NG5: Top V 5E 21
                                     (off Birkdale Way)
Castellan Ri. NG5: Bestw 5G 21
Casterton Rd. NG5: Bestw 5F 21
Castle Blvd. NG7: Lent, Nott 6A 4 (6D 44)
Castlebridge Office Village NG7: Lent 1E 57
Castle Bri. Rd. NG7: Lent 6E 45
Castle Cl. NG14: Calv 4G 11
Castle Ct. DE75: Hea 4E 15
    NG2: Nott 6C 4 (6F 45)
Castle Exchange NG1: Nott 3F 5
Castlefields NG2: Nott 1G 57
Castle Gdns. NG7: Lent 6D 44
Castle Ga. NG1: Nott 5D 4 (5G 45)
Castle Gro. NG7: Nott 5C 4 (5F 45)
Castle Ind. Pk. NG15: Huck 6F 7
Castle Marina Pk. NG7: Lent 6E 45
Castle Marina Retail Pk. 6F 45
Castle Marina Rd. NG7: Lent 1E 57
Castle Mdw. NG2: Nott 6F 45
Castle M. NG7: Nott 6E 45
Castle Mus. & Art Gallery 5C 4 (6F 45)
Castle Pk. NG7: Nott 1F 57
Castle Pk. Ind. Est. NG2: Nott 2F 57
Castle Pl. NG1: Nott 5C 4 (5F 45)
Castle Quay NG7: Nott 6B 4 (6F 45)
Castle Quay Cl. NG7: Lent 6E 45
Castle Retail Pk. 3C 44
Castlerigg Cl. NG2: West Br 6E 59
Castle Rd. NG1: Nott 5C 4 (5F 45)
Castle Rock NG7: Nott 6C 4 (6F 45)
Castle St. NG2: Nott 5B 46
    NG4: Eastw 4C 16
    NG4: Car 6G 35
    NG5: Arn 6B 22
Castleton Av. DE7: Ilk 2A 28
    NG4: Car 6G 35
Castleton Cl. NG2: Nott 1F 57
    NG15: Huck 5D 6
Castleton Ct. NG6: Bulw 1F 31
Castle Vw. NG2: West Br 5H 57
    NG16: Lang M 1E 15
Castle Vw. Cotts. NG9: Bee 5A 56
Castle Vs. NG7: Nott 5B 46
                                        (off Castle St.)
Castle Wlk. NG7: Hys G 2D 44
Castle Wharf NG1: Nott 6D 4 (6G 45)
Cat & Fiddle La. DE7: West H 3B 38
Cat & Fiddle Windmill 5D 38
Caterham Cl. NG8: Bilb 2D 42
Catfoot La. NG4: Lamb 5F 23
Catherine Av. DE7: Ilk 3B 40
Catherine Cl. NG6: Bulw 6G 19
Catherine St. NG6: Bulw 6G 19
Catkin Dr. NG16: Gilt 5E 17
Catlow Wlk. NG5: Bestw 5G 21
Cator Cl. NG4: Ged .4F 35
Cator La. NG9: Chil .5D 54
Cator La. Nth. NG9: Chil 5D 54
Cator Lane Stop (NET) 6D 54
Catriona Cres. NG5: Arn 3C 22
Catt Cl. NG9: Chil 4B 64
Catterley Hill Rd. NG3: Nott 2C 46
Cattle Mkt. Rd. NG2: Nott 1H 57

Catton Rd. NG5: Arn 5C 22
Caudale Ct. NG2: Gam 4E 59
Caulton St. NG7: Hys G 3D 44
             (not continuous)
Caunton Av. NG3: Nott 6A 34
Causeway M. NG2: Nott 1F 57
Cavan Ct. NG2: Nott 2G 57
Cavell Cl. NG11: Clftn 3B 66
Cavendish Av. NG4: Ged 5F 35
  NG5: Sher 4H 33
Cavendish Cl. NG15: Huck 5A 8
Cavendish Ct. NG3: Mapp 4B 34
  NG7: Nott 4A 4 (5E 45)
Cavendish Cres. NG4: Car 5E 35
  NG9: Stfrd 1F 53
Cavendish Cres. Nth. NG7: Nott 4A 4 (5E 45)
Cavendish Cres. Sth. NG7: Nott 6A 4 (6E 45)
Cavendish Dr. NG4: Car 1G 47
Cavendish Ho. NG4: Car 1G 47
             (off Garden City)
Cavendish M. NG7: Nott 4A 4 (5E 45)
  NG12: Cotg 3F 71
              (off Daleside)
Cavendish Pl. NG7: Nott 6A 4 (6E 45)
  NG9: Bee 5F 55
Cavendish Rd. DE7: Ilk 3B 40
  NG4: Car 5E 35
  NG10: Long E 3E 63
Cavendish Rd. E. NG7: Nott 4A 4 (5E 45)
Cavendish Rd. W. NG7: Nott 5E 45
Cavendish St. NG5: Arn 5A 22
  NG7: Lent 2C 56
             (not continuous)
Cavendish Va. NG5: Sher 4H 33
Caversham Way DE7: West H 1B 38
Cawdron Wlk. NG11: Clftn 3C 66
Cawston Gdns. NG6: Bulw 5H 19
Caxmere Dr. NG8: Woll 4F 43
Caxton Cl. NG4: Neth 2A 48
Caxton Rd. NG5: Sher 6F 33
Caythorpe Cres. NG5: Sher 3G 33
Caythorpe Ri. NG5: Sher 3G 33
Cecil St. NG7: Lent 6D 44
Cedar Av. NG9: Bee 4G 55
  NG10: Long E 2E 73
  NG16: Nuth 3F 31
Cedar Cl. NG10: Sand 4D 52
  NG13: Bing 5G 51
Cedar Ct. NG9: Bee 4G 55
Cedar Dr. NG12: Key 5G 79
Cedar Gro. NG5: Arn 5D 22
  NG8: Woll 5F 43
  NG15: Huck 6H 7
Cedarland Cres. NG16: Nuth 3F 31
Cedar Lodge NG7: Nott 4A 4 (5E 45)
Cedar Lodge Cvn. Pk. 1C 60
Cedar Pk. DE7: Ilk 1A 40
Cedar Rd. NG7: Hys G 1E 45
  NG9: Chil 6E 55
The Cedars NG5: Sher 3H 33
Cedar Tree Rd. NG5: Arn 4F 21
Celandine Cl. NG5: Top V 6C 20
Celandine Gdns. NG13: Bing 5C 50
Celia Dr. NG4: Car 2F 47
Cemetery Rd. NG9: Stfrd 4G 53
Cemetery Wlk. NG16: Eastw 4A 16
Central Av. NG2: West Br 3B 58
  NG3: Mapp 3D 34
  NG5: Arn 6B 22
  NG7: Bas 6E 33
  NG9: Bee 2E 55
  NG9: Chil 5D 54
  NG9: Stfrd 3G 53
  NG10: Sand 5D 52
  NG15: Huck 5G 7
Central Av. Sth. NG5: Arn 6B 22
Central Ct. NG7: Lent 2D 56
Central St. NG3: Nott 3A 46
Central Wlk. NG15: Huck 4G 7
Centre Way NG12: Rad T 5E 49
Centurion Bus. Pk. NG6: Bulw 4E 19
Centurion Cl. NG15: Huck 3B 8
Centurion Way NG2: Nott 3E 57
Century Ct. NG1: Nott 1G 4
          (off Nth. Sherwood St.)
Cernan Ct. NG6: Bulw 2F 31
Cerne Cl. NG11: Clftn 5D 66
Chaceley Way NG11: Wilf 2E 67
Chadborn Av. NG11: Goth 6H 75
Chadburn Rd. NG15: Huck 1A 8
The Chaddesden NG3: Mapp P 2G 45
Chad Gdns. NG5: Top V 3E 21
Chadwick Rd. NG7: Hys G 2C 44
Chain La. NG7: Lent 2C 56
Chalfield Cl. NG11: Clftn 4B 66
Chalfont Dr. NG8: Aspl 2H 43
Challond Ct. NG5: Bestw 6G 21
Chalons Cl. DE7: Ilk 6B 28
Chalons Way DE7: Ilk 6B 28
Chamberlain Cl. NG11: Clftn 4A 66

Chambers Av. DE7: Ilk 2D 40
Chambers Ct. NG5: Bestw 2D 32
Champion Av. DE7: Ilk 4G 27
The Chancery NG9: Bram 4C 54
Chancery Ct. NG11: Wilf 5E 57
Chandos Av. NG4: Neth 1A 48
Chandos St. NG3: Nott 2A 46
  NG4: Neth 2A 48
Chantrey Rd. NG2: West Br 4A 58
Chantry Cl. NG9: Chil 1D 64
  NG10: Long E 3C 72
  NG16: Kimb 2A 30
Chapel Bar NG1: Nott 4C 4 (5F 45)
Chapel Cl. NG11: Goth 6H 75
Chapel Ct. DE7: Ilk 3B 28
Chapelfield Gro. NG13: Bing 6E 51
Chapel La. NG4: Lamb 6B 24
  NG5: Arn 5A 22
  NG12: Cotg 2F 71
  NG13: Bing 2D 50
  NG14: Epp 5G 13
Chapel M. Ct. NG9: Bram 3B 54
Chapel Pl. NG16: Kimb 1H 29
Chapel Quarter NG1: Nott 4C 4 (5F 45)
Chapel St. DE7: Ilk 6B 28
             (not continuous)
  DE75: Hea 5E 15
  NG7: Radf 4E 45
  NG9: Bram 3B 54
  NG10: Long E 6G 63
  NG11: Rudd 1G 77
  NG15: Huck 4G 7
  NG16: Eastw 4B 16
  NG16: Kimb 1H 29
Chapel Yd. NG12: Norm W 6A 70
Chapman Ct. NG8: Bilb 2H 43
Chapmans Wlk. NG6: Bestw V 5F 9
Chapter Dr. NG16: Kimb 2A 30
Chardlace Wlk. NG1: Nott 5G 5
Chard St. NG7: Bas 5D 32
Chard Ter. NG7: Bas 5D 32
Charlbury Ct. NG9: Bram 5B 42
Charlbury Rd. NG8: Woll 3G 43
Charlecote Dr. NG8: Woll 6D 42
Charlecote Pk. Dr. NG2: West Br 1G 67
Charles Av. NG9: Chil 2C 64
  NG9: Lent A 2G 55
  NG9: Stfrd 3H 53
  NG10: Sand 5D 52
  NG16: Eastw 3D 16
Charles Cl. DE7: Ilk 3D 40
  NG4: Ged 5H 35
Charles Ct. NG15: Huck 4G 7
Charles Ho. NG1: Nott 5C 4
Charles St. NG5: Arn 6A 22
  NG10: Long E 1F 73
  NG11: Rudd 6G 67
  NG15: Huck 4G 7
Charleston Ho. NG1: Nott 1C 4 (3F 45)
Charles Way NG6: Bulw 2H 31
Charles Way Bus. Pk. NG6: Bulw 2A 32
Charlesworth Av. NG7: Bas 1C 44
Charlock Cl. NG5: Top V 6C 20
Charlock Gdns. NG13: Bing 6D 50
Charlotte Cl. NG5: Arn 3A 22
Charlotte Gro. NG9: Bram 2D 54
Charlotte St. DE7: Ilk 4A 28
Charlton Av. NG10: Long E 4H 63
Charlton Gro. NG9: Bee 1F 65
Charnock Av. NG8: Woll 6B 44
Charnos St. DE7: Ilk 5C 40
Charnwood Av. NG9: Bee 5D 54
  NG10: Long E 3D 72
  NG10: Sand 1C 62
  NG12: Key 5G 79
Charnwood Gdns. NG5: Sher 6F 33
Charnwood Gro. NG2: West Br 4A 58
  NG13: Bing 5D 50
  NG15: Huck 4E 7
Charnwood La. NG5: Arn 1C 34
Charnwood Way NG14: Woodbo 1D 24
Charter Pk. DE7: Ilk 2A 40
Chartwell Av. NG11: Rudd 6F 67
Chartwell Gro. NG3: Mapp 2E 35
Chase Farm NG4: Ged 3G 35
Chase Pk. NG2: Nott 6C 46
Chatham St. NG1: Nott 3G 45
Chatsworth Av. NG4: Car 1G 47
  NG7: Bas 5D 32
  NG9: Chil 3C 64
  NG10: Long E 1A 74
  NG12: Rad T 5G 49
Chatsworth Cl. NG10: Sand 1D 62
Chatsworth Ct. DE7: West H 1C 38
  NG15: Huck 5G 7
Chatsworth Pl. DE7: Kirk H 4F 39
Chatsworth Rd. NG2: West Br 3D 58

Chatsworth Way DE75: Hea 3A 14
Chatterley Ct. NG7: Lent 4C 44
             (off Wragby Rd.)
Chatterley Parkway NG8: Stre 5C 30
Chaucer St. DE7: Ilk 6B 28
  NG1: Nott 2C 4 (4F 45)
Chaworth Av. NG15: Want 4H 17
Chaworth Cl. NG15: Huck 1F 7
Chaworth Rd. NG2: West Br 5A 58
  NG4: Colw 3H 47
  NG13: Bing 5D 50
Cheadle Cl. NG3: Mapp 5D 34
  NG8: Bilb 1D 42
Cheapside NG1: Nott 4E 5 (5G 45)
Cheddar Rd. NG11: Clftn 5C 66
Chedington Av. NG3: Mapp 1F 35
Chediston Va. NG5: Bestw 5F 21
Chedworth Cl. NG3: Nott 4B 46
Chelmsford Rd. NG7: Bas 5D 32
Chelmsford Ter. NG7: Bas 5D 32
             (off Zulu Rd.)
Chelsbury Ct. NG5: Arn 6A 22
Chelsea Cl. NG16: Nuth 4E 31
Chelsea St. NG7: Bas 6D 32
Cheltenham Cl. NG9: Toton 3H 63
Cheltenham St. NG6: Bas 3C 32
Chelwood Dr. NG3: Mapp 4E 35
Chennel Nook NG12: Cotg 3G 71
Chepstow Rd. NG11: Clftn 5C 66
Cherhill Cl. NG11: Clftn 6B 66
Cheriton Dr. DE7: Ilk 4G 27
The Cherries NG11: Wilf 5F 57
Cherry Av. NG15: Huck 6H 7
Cherry Blossom Rd. NG14: Stoke B 2C 48
Cherry Cl. DE72: Brea 5A 62
  NG2: West Br 2E 59
  NG5: Arn 5A 22
  NG5: Bestw 1F 33
Cherry Hill NG12: Key 4H 79
Cherry Orchard NG12: Cotg 2F 71
Cherry Orchard Mt. NG5: Bestw 1F 33
Cherry St. NG13: Bing 5F 51
Cherry Tree Cl. DE7: Kirk H 3H 39
  DE72: Ris 1B 62
  NG14: Calv 3G 11
Cherrytree Cl. NG12: Rad T 1F 61
Cherry Tree La. NG12: Edwal 2D 68
Cherry Tree Way NG16: Lang M 1G 15
Cherry Vw. NG8: Aspl 2H 43
Cherry Wood Dr. NG8: Aspl 2H 43
Cherrywood Gdns. NG3: Nott 1C 46
Chertsey Cl. NG3: Nott 6B 34
Chertsey Ct. DE7: West H 1B 38
Cherwell Cl. NG6: Bulw 1F 31
Cherwell Gdns. NG13: Bing 6C 50
Chesham Dr. NG5: Sher 5F 33
  NG9: Bram 6B 42
Cheshire Cl. NG2: West Br 6H 57
Chesil Av. NG8: Radf 4B 44
Chesil Cotts. NG8: Radf 4B 44
             (off Chesil Av.)
Cheslyn Dr. NG8: Aspl 1A 44
The Chesnuts NG4: Ged 6B 36
Chesterfield Av. NG4: Ged 4F 35
  NG10: Long E 6H 63
  NG13: Bing 5E 51
Chesterfield Cl. NG4: Ged 4F 35
Chesterfield Dr. NG4: Bur J 2G 37
Chesterfield St. NG4: Car 2F 47
Chester Grn. NG9: Toton 3G 63
Chester Ho. NG3: Mapp P 1G 45
Chesterman Cl. NG16: Aws 3D 28
Chester Rd. NG3: Nott 4E 47
Chestnut Av. NG3: Mapp 5D 34
  NG9: Bee 5F 55
  NG13: Bing 5E 51
Chestnut Bank DE75: Hea 4B 14
Chestnut Cl. NG12: Key 4G 79
Chestnut Dr. NG12: Cotg 6G 61
  NG16: Nuth 6B 18
Chestnut Gro.
  NG2: West Br 4H 57
  NG3: Mapp P 2G 45
  NG4: Ged 6H 35
  NG5: Arn 4C 22
  NG10: Sand 4C 52
  NG12: Rad T 5F 49
  NG14: Bur J 3F 37
  NG15: Huck 1H 19
Chestnut La. NG11: Bart F 1E 75
Chestnut M. NG12: Toll 2H 69
Chestnut Rd. NG16: Lang M 2E 15
The Chestnuts NG3: Nott 6B 34
  NG10: Long E 5C 62
  NG12: Rad T 6E 49
Chestnut Wlk. NG5: Sher 4A 34
Chettles Ind. Est. NG7: Radf 4B 44
Chettles Trade Pk. NG7: Radf 4B 44
Chetwin Rd. NG8: Bilb 4D 42
Chetwynd Bus. Pk. NG9: Chil 3B 64

Chetwynd Rd. NG9: Chil 2A 64
  NG9: Toton 3A 64
Chevin Gdns. NG5: Top V 4E 21
Cheviot Cl. NG5: Arn 3F 21
Cheviot Ct. NG9: Chil 2C 64
Cheviot Dr. NG6: Bulw 5F 19
Cheviot Rd. NG10: Long E 4C 62
Chewton Av. NG16: Eastw 4C 16
Chewton St. NG16: Eastw 4B 16
Cheyne Wlk. NG15: Huck 3H 7
Cheyny Cl. NG2: Nott 2G 57
Chichester Cl. DE7: Ilk 1C 40
  NG5: Top V 6C 20
Chichester Dr. NG12: Cotg 1E 71
Chidlow Rd. NG8: Bilb 2D 42
Chigwell Cl. NG16: Nuth 4E 31
Chilton Way NG15: Huck 5D 6
Chiltern Cl. NG5: Arn 3F 21
Chiltern Dr. DE7: West H 1C 38
Chiltern Gdns. NG10: Long E 1F 33
Chiltern Way NG5: Bestw 6A 18
Chilton Dr. NG16: Want 6E 21
Chilvers Cl. NG5: Bestw 5C 54
CHILWELL 5B 20
Chilwell Ct. NG6: Bulw 6H 19
Chilwell La. NG9: Bram 4B 54
Chilwell Manor Golf Course 1E 65
Chilwell Meadow Nature Reserve 1D 64
Chilwell Olympia Leisure Cen. 4B 64
Chilwell Retail Pk. .6F 55
Chilwell Rd. NG9: Bee 6F 55
Chilwell Road Stop (NET) 6D 44
Chilwell St. NG7: Lent 6G 57
Chine Gdns. NG2: West Br 1E 43
Chingford Rd. NG8: Bilb 2B 50
Chipmunk Way NG13: Newt 6D 44
Chippendale St. NG7: Lent 1F 33
Chippenham Rd. NG5: Bestw 6B 66
Chisbury Grn. NG11: Cliftn 1E 33
Chisholm Way NG5: Bestw 4G 33
Chiswick Ct. NG5: Sher 1D 18
Christchurch Rd. NG15: Huck 3A 32
Christina Av. NG6: Cin 3A 32
Christina Cres. NG6: Cin 2A 8
Christine Cl. NG15: Huck 2C 46
Christine Ct. NG3: Nott 3F 43
Christopher Cl. NG8: Woll 1F 19
Christopher Cl. NG15: Huck 2G 15
Chrysalis Way NG16: Eastw 2G 15
Chrysalis Way Ind. Pk. NG16: Eastw 6A 22
Church Av. NG5: Arn 6D 44
  NG7: Lent 3C 72
  NG10: Long E 6A 22
Church Cl. NG5: Arn 6E 49
  NG9: Trow 5E 41
  NG12: Rad T 4F 51
  NG13: Bing 2E 71
Church Ct. NG12: Cotg 6H 21
Church Cres. NG5: Arn 1A 64
  NG9: Chil 3B 58
Church Cft. NG2: West Br 2G 53
Churchdale Av. NG9: Stfrd 2H 27
Church Dr. DE7: Ilk 4B 58
  NG2: West Br 6H 21
  NG5: Arn 6F 33
  NG5: Sher 4D 52
  NG10: Sand 4G 79
  NG12: Key 4G 7
  NG15: Huck 6A 22
Church Dr. E. NG5: Arn 4E 21
Churchfield Ct. NG5: Top V 2C 44
Churchfield La. NG7: Radf 5C 32
Churchfield Ter. NG6: Bas 4E 21
Churchfield Way NG5: Top V 5C 70
Church Gro. NG7: Lent 6C 44
Church Hill NG12: Plum 1G 79
  NG16: Kimb 1H 29
Churchill Cl. NG5: Arn 1B 34
Churchill Dr. NG9: Stfrd 3G 53
  NG11: Rudd 6F 67
Churchill Pk. NG4: Colw 4H 47
Church La. DE7: Mapp 5C 26
  DE7: Stant D 2B 52
  NG5: Arn 4B 22
  NG6: Bulw 6A 20
  NG9: Atten 4D 64
  NG9: Stfrd 4F 53
  NG11: Bart F 1E 75
  NG11: Thru 2E 71
  NG12: Cotg 6G 69
  NG12: Plum 5F 51
  NG13: Bing 5G 13
  NG14: Epp 1G 7
  NG15: Lin 1G 7
  NG16: Coss 5E 29
Church Mdw. NG14: Calv 5H 11
Church M. NG2: Nott 2H 57
Churchmoor Ct. NG5: Arn 4A 22
Churchmoor La. NG5: Arn 4A 22

Church Rd. NG3: Nott 2H 45
  NG6: Bestw V 1C 20
  NG14: Bur J 3F 37
  NG16: Grea. Want 2F 17
Churchside Gdns. NG7: Hys G 1C 44
Church Sq. DE75: Hea 4D 14
Church St. DE7: Ilk 3H 27
  DE75: Hea 4D 14
  NG4: Car 2G 47
  NG4: Lamb 5C 24
  NG5: Arn 5B 22
  NG6: Bas 5C 32
  NG7: Lent 6C 44
  NG9: Bee 5F 55
  NG9: Bram 3B 54
  NG9: Stfrd 4F 53
  NG10: Sand 4D 52
  NG11: Goth 6H 75
  NG11: Rudd 6G 67
  NG12: S'frd 6H 37
  NG13: Bing 5F 51
  NG16: Eastw 3A 16
Church Vw. DE7: Ilk 2A 40
  DE72: Brea 6A 62
  DE75: Los 1A 14
  NG4: Ged 6H 35
Church Vw. Cl. NG5: Arn 4F 21
Church Wlk. NG4: Car 2G 47
  NG9: Stfrd 4G 53
  NG14: Woodbo .1C 24
  NG16: Eastw 3B 16
Churnet Cl. NG11: Cliftn 1C 66
Churston Ct. NG9: Bee 5G 55
Cider Orchard Pl. NG16: Kimb 1H 29
The Cigar Factory NG7: Nott 3A 4
                                      (off Derby Rd.)
CINDERHILL 3H 31
Cinderhill Footway NG6: Bulw 3B 32
Cinderhill Gro. NG4: Ged 5G 35
Cinderhill Gym 4H 31
Cinderhill Rd. NG6: Bulw, Cin 3H 31
Cinderhill Stop (NET) 3H 31
Cinderhill Wlk. NG6: Bulw 3H 31
Cineworld Cinema 3D 4 (4G 45)
CIRCLE NOTTINGHAM HOSPITAL 1C 56
Circuit Dr. NG10: Long E 5H 63
Cirrus Dr. NG16: Want 6A 18
Citadel St. NG7: Radf 4C 44
The City NG9: Bee .5G 55
                                    (not continuous)
City Bus. Pk. NG4: Colw 3H 47
City Ground 2A 58
CITY HOSPITAL (NOTTINGHAM UNIVERSITY) . .2F 33
City Link NG2: Nott 6G 5 (6H 45)
City of Caves 5E 5
City Point NG1: Nott 5C 4 (5F 45)
City Rd. NG7: Nott .2B 56
  NG9: Bee 4G 55
City Vw. NG3: Mapp 5B 34
Clandon Dr. NG5: Sher 5F 33
Clanfield Rd. NG8: Bilb 2E 43
Clapham St. NG7: Radf 4C 44
Claramount Rd. DE75: Hea 4E 15
Clarborough Dr. NG5: Arn 1C 34
Clare Cl. NG6: Bas .3C 32
Clarehaven NG9: Stfrd 6G 53
Claremont Av. NG9: Bram 3C 54
  NG15: Huck 6G 7
Claremont Dr. NG2: West Br 2G 67
Claremont Gdns. NG5: Sher 6F 33
Claremont Rd. NG5: Sher 6F 33
Clarence Cl. NG5: Top V 3H 5 (4A 46)
Clarence Rd. NG9: Chil 3D 64
  NG10: Long E 1E 73
Clarence St. NG3: Nott 2H 5 (4A 46)
Clarendon Chambers NG1: Nott 2B 4 (4F 45)
Clarendon Ct. NG5: Sher 1F 45
Clarendon Ho. NG1: Nott 3B 4 (4F 45)
Clarendon Pk. NG5: Sher 1F 45
Clarendon St. NG1: Nott 2B 4 (4F 45)
Clare St. NG1: Nott 3E 5 (4G 45)
Clare Valley NG7: Nott 5B 4 (5F 45)
Clarewood Gro. NG11: Cliftn 6C 66
Clarges St. NG6: Bulw 1A 32
Clarke Av. DE75: Los 3A 14
  NG5: Arn 5B 22
Clarke Dr. NG10: Long E 3C 72
Clarke Rd. NG2: Nott 1A 58
Clarke's La. NG9: Chil 1D 64
Clarkson Dr. NG9: Bee 5H 55
Claude St. NG7: Lent 2C 56
Claxton St. DE75: Hea 3B 14
Claxton Ter. DE75: Hea 3B 14
Clay Av. NG3: Mapp 4C 34
Claye St. NG10: Long E 6G 63
Clayfield Cl. NG6: Bulw 1G 31
Claypit Wlk. NG11: Wilf 5E 57
Claypole Rd. NG7: Hys G 2D 44

Clayton Ct. NG7: Radf 4D 44
  NG9: Bee 6G 55
Clayton Gro. DE75: Los 1A 14
Claytons Dr. NG7: Lent 1C 56
Claytons Wharf NG7: Lent 1C 56
Clementine Dr. NG3: Mapp 2E 35
Clether Rd. NG8: Bilb 3D 42
Cleve Av. NG9: Toton 2G 63
Clevedon Dr. NG5: Arn 4E 23
Cleveland Av. NG10: Long E 4H 63
Cleveland Cl. NG7: Radf 4C 44
Cleveley's Rd. NG9: Toton 2G 63
Clevely Way NG11: Cliftn 2C 66
The Cliff NG6: Bulw 3H 31
Cliff Blvd. NG16: Kimb 6H 17
Cliff Cres. NG12: Rad T 5F 49
Cliff Dr. NG12: Rad T 5F 49
Cliffe Hill Av. NG9: Stfrd 4F 53
Cliffgrove Av. NG9: Chil 5D 54
Cliffmere Wlk. NG11: Cliftn 4B 66
Clifford Av. NG9: Bee 5H 55
Clifford Cl. NG10: Long E 3C 72
  NG12: Key 6G 7
Clifford St. NG7: Radf 3D 44
  NG10: Long E 6G 63
Cliff Rd. NG1: Nott 5F 5 (5H 45)
  NG4: Car 3F 47
  NG12: Rad T 5E 49
The Cliffs NG12: Rad T 4G 49
Cliff Way NG12: Rad T 5F 49
CLIFTON 4D 66
Clifton Av. NG10: Long E 6A 64
  NG11: Rudd 5G 67
Clifton Blvd. NG7: Lent, Nott 1B 56
  NG11: Rudd, Wilf 1B 56
Clifton Centre Stop (NET) 4C 66
Clifton Cres. NG9: Atten 2E 65
Clifton Grn. NG11: Cliftn 3B 66
Clifton Gro. NG4: Ged 5G 35
Clifton Hall Dr. NG11: Cliftn 3H 65
Clifton La. NG11: Cliftn, Wilf 5B 66
  NG11: Rudd 5E 67
Clifton Leisure Cen. 4D 66
Clifton M. NG7: Nott 4A 4 (5E 45)
Clifton Pastures NG11: Goth 6A 66
Clifton Rd. NG11: Rudd 6F 67
Clifton South Park & Ride 6A 66
Clifton St. NG9: Bee 5G 55
Clifton Ter. NG7: Nott 6A 4 (6E 45)
Clinton Av. NG5: Sher 1F 45
Clinton Ct. NG1: Nott 2D 4 (4G 45)
Clinton St. NG5: Arn 6A 22
  NG9: Bee 4E 55
Clinton St. E. NG1: Nott 3E 5 (4G 45)
Clinton St. W. NG1: Nott 3E 5 (4G 45)
Clinton Ter. NG7: Nott 3A 4 (4E 45)
CLIPSTON 4D 70
Clipstone Av. NG1: Nott 1C 4 (3F 45)
  NG3: Mapp 3C 34
Clipstone Cl. NG8: Stre 5D 30
Clipston La. NG12: Norm W 6H 69
Clive Cres. NG16: Kimb 2A 30
Cliveden Grn. NG11: Cliftn 4B 66
Cloister Ho. NG7: Lent 1C 56
The Cloisters NG9: Bee 3G 55
Cloister St. NG7: Nott 1C 56
The Close NG5: Sher 4G 33
  NG9: Chil 1D 64
Close Quarters NG9: Bram 3C 54
Cloud Av. NG9: Stfrd 4H 53
Clouds Hill NG11: Cliftn 5C 66
Cloudside Ct. NG10: Sand 4D 52
Cloudside Rd. NG10: Sand 4D 52
Clough Ct. NG8: Bilb 2H 43
Clovelly Dr. NG3: Mapp 2E 35
Cloverdale NG12: Cotg 3G 71
Clover Flds. NG14: Calv 3A 12
Clover Grn. NG6: Bas 4B 32
Cloverlands NG2: West Br 2G 67
Cloverlands Ct. NG16: Want 6A 18
Cloverlands Dr. NG16: Want 6A 18
Clover Ri. NG6: Newth 4D 16
Clumber Av. NG3: Mapp 3C 34
  NG4: Neth 2A 48
  NG5: Sher 1F 45
  NG9: Chil 6D 54
Clumber Cres. Nth. NG7: Nott 4A 4 (5E 45)
Clumber Cres. Sth. NG7: Nott 6A 4 (6E 45)
Clumber Dr. NG12: Rad T 4G 49
Clumber Rd. NG2: West Br 4B 58
Clumber Rd. E. NG7: Nott 5A 4 (5E 45)
Clumber Rd. W. NG7: Nott 5A 4 (5E 45)
Clumber St. NG1: Nott 3E 5 (4G 45)
  NG10: Long E 6F 63
  NG15: Huck 5A 8
Coach Dr. NG16: Eastw 1B 16
Coachmans Cft. NG8: Woll 4G 43
Coachways DE7: Mapp 4D 26
Coates Av. NG15: Huck 2F 7

Coatsby Rd. NG16: Kimb 6H 17
Cobden Chambers NG1: Nott 4E 5
Cobden Cl. NG7: Lent 4C 44
NG10: Long E 6F 63
Cockayne Cl. NG10: Sand 2D 62
Cocker Beck NG4: Lamb 6C 24
Cockerhouse Rd. NG16: Eastw 1A 16
Cockington Rd. NG8: Bilb 4C 42
Cockleys NG10: Long E 1E 73
Codrington Gdns. NG5: Bestw 5G 21
Cogenhoe Wlk. NG5: Arn 3B 22
Coggan Wlk. NG14: Calv 3E 11
Cogley La. NG13: Bing .5G 51
Cohen Cl. NG5: Arn 1D 34
NG9: Chil 3B 64
Cokefield Av. NG16: Nuth 4F 31
Colborn St. NG3: Nott .2B 46
Colbrook Pl. NG4: Car .2H 47
Colchester Rd. NG8: Brox 6E 31
Coleby Av. NG7: Lent .1C 56
Coleby Rd. NG8: Brox .5F 31
Coledale NG2: West Br 5E 59
Coleridge Cres. NG5: Arn 6H 21
Coleridge St. NG7: Radf 3C 44
Colesbourne Pl. NG11: Clftn 3D 66
Colesbourne Rd. NG11: Clftn 3D 66
Colin Broughton Ct. NG6: Bulw 6B 20
Colindale Gdns. NG16: Nuth 4E 31
Colinwood Av. NG5: Top V 4C 20
College Dr. NG11: Clftn 3B 66
(not continuous)
College Rd. NG3: Mapp 4E 35
NG9: Chil 6E 55
College St. NG1: Nott 3B 4 (4F 45)
NG10: Long E 2D 62
College Way NG8: Bilb .2C 42
Colleymoor Leys La. NG11: Clftn 3D 66
Colliers Bus. Pk. NG12: Cotg 6G 61
Colliers Way NG8: Cin .3G 31
NG12: Cotg 6G 61
Colliery Cl. NG2: Nott .2F 57
Collin Av. NG10: Sand .1D 62
Collin Grn. NG5: Sher .3H 33
Collington St. NG9: Bee 5E 55
Collington Way NG2: West Br 6H 57
Collingwood Cl. NG11: Clftn 1C 66
Collingwood Rd. NG10: Long E 1F 73
Collins Cl. NG6: Bulw .2F 31
Collins Homes NG7: Bee 2E 55
Collin St. NG1: Nott 6E 5 (6G 45)
NG9: Bee 5F 55
Collison St. NG7: Hys G 3D 44
Collyer Rd. NG14: Calv 3E 11
Colly Ga. NG16: Kimb .2A 30
Collygate Rd. NG2: Nott 2H 57
Colmon Cl. NG5: Bestw 6E 21
Colmon Wlk. NG5: Bestw 6E 21
Colonsay Cl. NG9: Trow 6F 41
Colston Cres. NG2: West Br 1H 67
Colston Ga. NG12: Cotg, Crop Bi 2F 71
Colston Rd. NG6: Bulw 5A 20
Coltsfoot Cl. NG13: Bing 6C 50
Colville St. NG1: Nott .2F 45
Colville St. NG1: Nott .2F 45
Colville Ter. NG1: Nott 3F 45
Colville Vs. NG1: Nott .2F 45
COLWICK 4G 47
Colwick Bus. Pk. NG4: Colw 4H 47
Colwick Country Pk. 6F 47
Colwick Crossing NG2: Nott 5C 46
Colwick Ind. Est. NG4: Colw 4H 47
(Private Rd. No. 2)
NG4: Colw 4B 48
(Private Rd. No. 5)
NG4: Colw 4G 47
(Private Rd. No. 8)
Colwick Lodge NG4: Car 3H 47
Colwick Loop Rd. NG4: Car, Colw, Neth 1A 48
Colwick Mnr. Farm NG4: Colw 4G 47
Colwick Pk. Cl. NG4: Colw 4G 47
Colwick Quays Bus. Pk. NG4: Colw 4A 48
Colwick Rd. NG2: Nott 6B 46
NG2: West Br 2A 58
COLWICK VALE 3G 47
Colwick Woods Ct. NG2: Nott 5C 46
Comery Av. NG3: Nott .3C 46
Comet Dr. NG16: Eastw 3C 16
Comfrey Cl. NG5: Top V 6C 20
Commerce Sq. NG1: Nott 5F 5 (5H 45)
Commercial Av. NG9: Bee 5F 55
Commercial Rd. NG6: Bulw 6H 19
NG12: Key 5G 79
Commodore Ct. NG8: Aspl 5A 32
Commodore Gdns. NG8: Aspl 5A 32
The Common NG15: Huck 5C 6
Common La.
DE7: Stly, Stan C 4A 38
NG9: Bram 5A 54
NG15: Huck 5D 6
NG16: Want 6B 18

Commons Cl. NG16: Newth 5C 16
COMMON SIDE 4B 14
Compton Acres NG2: West Br 5F 57
Compton Acres Shop. Cen. 6G 57
Compton Rd. NG5: Sher 4F 33
Comyn Gdns. NG3: Nott 1F 5 (3H 45)
Condor Rd. DE7: Ilk 5B 40
Conduit Cl. NG2: Nott .1G 57
Coney Wlk. NG5: Top V 5D 20
Conifer Cres. NG11: Clftn 6C 66
Conifer Wlk. NG3: Nott 2C 46
Coningsby Gdns. E. NG5: Woodt 3B 34
Coningsby Rd. NG5: Woodt 2B 34
Coningswath Rd. NG4: Car 5E 35
Conisborough Ter. NG2: Nott 2G 57
Conisbrough Av. NG4: Ged 6B 36
Coniston Av. NG6: Bas .5A 32
Coniston Cl. NG2: Gam 4E 59
Coniston Dr. DE7: Kirk H 4H 39
Coniston Rd. NG9: Bram 2D 54
NG10: Long E 3C 62
NG15: Huck 3F 7
Connelly Cl. NG5: Arn .1E 35
Connelly Cl. NG6: Bulw 1A 32
The Connery NG15: Huck 3H 7
Connery M. NG9: Toton 4B 64
Conrad Ct. NG6: Bulw .2F 31
Constance St. NG7: Bas 6E 33
The Convent NG1: Nott 3B 4
Convent St. NG1: Nott 3F 5 (4H 45)
Conway Av. NG4: Car .2A 48
Conway Cl. NG3: Nott .2G 45
Conway Cres. NG4: Car 1A 48
Conway Gdns. NG5: Arn 1A 34
Conway Rd. NG4: Car .2H 47
NG15: Huck 2D 18
Conway St. NG10: Long E 5G 63
Conway Wlk. NG3: Nott 2G 45
Cook Dr. DE7: Ilk 3C 40
Cooke Cl. NG10: Long E 1D 72
Cookson Av. NG4: Ged .5F 35
Coombe Cl. NG8: Woll .6A 44
Coombe Rd. NG16: Newth 1D 16
Co-operative Av. NG15: Huck 3H 7
Co-operative St. NG10: Long E 6G 63
NG6: Bulw 1F 31
Cooper Cl. NG5: Arn 1E 35
Cooper Gdns. NG11: Rudd 6F 67
Coopers Grn. NG8: Woll 1E 55
Cooper St. NG4: Neth .3A 48
Copeland Av. NG9: Stfrd 3G 53
Copeland Gro. NG13: Bing 4C 50
Copeland Rd. NG15: Huck 3A 8
Copenhagen Ct. NG3: Nott 6H 33
Copestake Cl. NG10: Long E 6C 62
Cope St. NG7: Hys G 3D 44
Coppice Av. DE7: Ilk 2H 27
Coppice Cl. NG15: Huck 6E 7
Coppice Ct. DE75: Hea 6D 14
Coppice Dr. DE75: Hea 6D 14
NG16: Eastw 2H 15
Coppice Ga. NG5: Arn .5B 22
Coppice Gro. NG3: Mapp 5B 34
Coppice Lodge NG5: Arn 5C 22
Coppice M. DE75: Hea .6D 14
Coppice Rd. NG5: Arn .5B 22
Copplestone Dr. NG3: Mapp 1E 35
The Copse DE7: Ilk 2H 27
NG9: Chil 5C 54
NG15: Huck 5A 8
Copse Cl. NG14: Bur J .2F 37
Copseside Cl. NG10: Long E 5C 62
Copsey Cft. Ct. NG10: Long E 6H 63
Corben Gdns. NG6: Bulw 6F 19
Corbett Chase NG4: Ged 4G 35
Corbiere Av. NG16: Want 6A 18
Corby Rd. NG3: Nott 6A 34
Corfield Av. DE75: Hea .6D 14
Coriander Dr. NG6: Bas 4B 32
Corinthian Cl. NG15: Huck 2A 8
Corinth Rd. NG11: Clftn 3C 66
Corke Ho. NG7: Lent 5C 44
(off Faraday Rd.)
Corn Cl. NG12: Cotg 3E 71
Corncrake Av. NG6: Bas 4B 32
Corncrake Dr. NG5: Arn 6E 23
Corn Cft. NG11: Clftn 4D 66
Cornfield Rd. NG16: Kimb 6G 17
The Cornfields NG5: Bestw 5F 21
Cornhill Rd. NG4: Car .1D 46
Cornwall Av. NG9: Bee .1A 66
Cornwall Dr. NG10: Long E 3A 64
Cornwallis Cl. NG10: Long E 1F 73
Cornwall Rd. NG5: Arn .6G 21
Cornwall's Hill NG4: Lamb 6D 24
Coronation Av. NG10: Sand 4C 52
NG11: Wilf 3F 57
Coronation Pk.
Eastwood 3C 16

Coronation Rd. DE7: Ilk 5C 28
DE7: Mapp 4C 26
(not continuous)
DE7: Stly 3A 38
NG3: Mapp 4B 34
NG6: Bestw V 6C 8
NG15: Huck 3F 7
NG16: Coss 5C 28
Coronation St. DE7: Ilk .1B 40
Coronation Wlk. NG4: Ged 6A 36
Corporation Cotts. NG14: Bulc 2H 37
Corporation Oaks NG3: Nott 2G 45
Corporation Rd. DE7: Ilk 4C 40
Corsham Gdns. NG3: Nott 2C 46
Corve Dale Wlk. NG2: West Br 6B 58
Cosby Rd. NG2: Nott 6B 46
COSSALL 6E 29
Cossall Ind. Est. DE7: Ilk 5D 28
COSSALL MARSH 5E 29
Cossall Rd. NG9: Trow .2E 41
NG16: Coss 2E 41
Cossethay Dr. NG8: Stre 6C 30
Costock Av. NG5: Sher .3F 33
COTGRAVE 2F 71
Cotgrave Av. NG4: Ged .5H 35
Cotgrave Cl. NG8: Stre .5E 31
Cotgrave Country Pk. 5F 61
Cotgrave La. NG12: Toll 2H 69
Cotgrave Leisure Cen. 2G 71
Cotgrave Park & Ride 2F 71
Cotgrave Rd. NG12: C'ton, Plum 6H 69
NG12: Crop Bi, Owt 5H 71
Cotgrave Shop. Cen. 2F 71
COTMANHAY 3A 28
Cotmanhay Rd. DE7: Ilk 4A 28
Coton Cl. NG11: Wilf 2E 67
Cotswold Cl. NG10: Long E 5D 62
Cotswold Rd. NG9: Bram 2D 54
Cotswold Rd. NG8: Stre 6E 31
Cottage Cl. DE7: Ilk 4H 27
Cottage Gdn. La. DE75: Hea 3B 14
Cottage Gdns. NG2: West Br 2E 59
Cottage Mdw. NG4: Colw 5H 47
Cottage Ter. NG1: Nott 3A 4 (4E 45)
Cottage Wlk. NG8: Woll 4E 43
Cottam Dr. NG5: Top V .5D 20
Cottam Gdns. NG5: Top V 5E 21
Cottesmore Rd. NG7: Lent 5D 44
Cotton Ho. NG7: Radf .3C 44
(off Radford Blvd.)
County Archives 6D 4 (6G 45)
County Bus. Pk. NG2: Nott 1A 58
County Court NG1: Nott 6G 55
County Court
Nottingham 6E 5 (6G 45)
County Rd. NG2: Nott 1A 58
NG4: Ged 4E 35
Coupe Gdns. NG15: Huck 5A 8
The Court NG9: Toton 3A 64
Court Cres. NG8: Woll 5F 43
Courtenay Gdns. NG3: Nott 2H 45
Court Gdns. NG2: West Br 1F 67
Courtleet Way NG6: Bulw 2H 31
Courtney Cl. NG8: Woll .4E 43
Court Rd. NG7: Hys G 2D 44
Court Vw. NG7: Nott 4A 4 (5E 45)
Court Yd. NG9: Bram 3B 54
The Courtyard NG16: Kimb 5G 17
Covedale Rd. NG5: Sher 2G 33
Coventry Ct. NG6: Bulw 2H 31
Coventry La. NG9: Bram 2H 53
Coventry Rd. NG6: Bulw 6H 19
(Gilead St.)
NG6: Bulw 1H 31
(Main St.)
NG9: Bee 4G 55
The Covers NG2: West Br 2B 58
Covert Cl. NG12: Key 3H 79
NG14: Bur J 3F 37
NG15: Huck 5A 8
Covert Cres. NG12: Rad T 6H 49
Covert Rd. NG2: West Br 5D 58
Cowan St. NG1: Nott 3F 5 (4H 45)
Cowdrey Gdns. NG5: Arn 1D 34
Cowlairs NG5: Top V 6C 20
Cow La. NG9: Bram 3B 54
Cowley Cl. DE7: Ilk 2B 28
Cowley St. NG6: Bas 4B 32
Cowper Rd. NG5: Woodt 3A 34
NG16: Newth 5C 16
Cowslip Cl. NG13: Bing .5D 50
Coxmoor Cl. NG12: Edwal 1E 69
Coxmoor Ct. NG5: Top V 4E 21
Crabapple Dr. NG16: Lang M 1G 15
Crab Apple Gro. NG15: Huck 1A 20
Crabtree Fld. NG2: Colw 5F 47
Crabtree Rd. NG6: Bulw 1G 31
Cragdale Rd. NG5: Sher 2G 33
Cragmoor Rd. NG14: Bur J 4E 37

Craig Moray NG12: Rad T 5G 49
Craig St. NG10: Long E 6G 63
Crammond Cl. NG2: Nott 1F 57
Crampton Ct. NG5: Top V 5E 21
Cramworth Gro. NG5: Sher 4H 33
Cranberry Cl. NG2: West Br 5F 57
Cranborne Cl. NG9: Trow 1F 53
Cranbourne Gro. NG15: Huck 4E 7
Cranbrook Ho. NG1: Nott 4G 5
Cranbrook St. NG1: Nott 3F 5 (4H 45)
Cranfield Wlk. NG11: Clftn 3D 66
(off Southchurch Dr.)
Cranfleet Way NG10: Long E 6C 62
Cranford Gdns. NG2: West Br 1G 67
Cranmer Gro. NG3: Nott 2G 45
Cranmer St. DE7: Ilk 6B 28
  NG3: Nott 2G 45
  NG10: Long E 5F 63
Cranmer Wlk. NG3: Nott 2G 45
Cranmore Cl. NG5: Arn 3C 22
Cransley Av. NG8: Woll 1D 54
Cranston Av. NG5: Arn 4B 22
Cranston Rd. NG9: Bram 2C 54
Cranswick Cl. NG15: Huck 1B 8
Cranthorne Dr. NG5: Nott 3E 47
Crantock Gdns. NG12: Key 4H 79
Cranwell Ct. NG6: Bulw 1F 31
Cranwell Rd. NG8: Stre 6D 30
Craster Dr. NG5: Arn 3C 22
  NG6: Bulw 5F 19
Craven Rd. NG7: Hys G 2C 44
Crawford Av. NG9: Stfrd 3F 53
Crawford Cl. NG8: Woll 4E 43
Crawford Ri. NG5: Arn 5E 23
Crawford Wlk. NG11: Clftn 3D 66
Creamery Cl. NG8: Bilb 2H 43
Creeton Grn. NG11: Clftn 5D 66
Cremorne Dr. NG2: Nott 2F 57
The Crescent
  DE7: Stan C 1A 38
  DE72: Ris 2A 62
  NG3: Nott 1H 45
  NG5: Woodt 3A 34
  NG9: Chil 2C 64
  NG9: Stfrd 2G 53
  NG9: Toton 3A 64
  NG12: Rad T 6G 49
  NG16: Eastw 2C 16
Crescent Av. NG4: Car 6G 35
Cresswell Rd. NG9: Chil 6B 54
Cressy Rd. NG11: Clftn 3D 66
Cresta Gdns. NG3: Mapp 5H 33
Crest Vw. NG5: Sher 4F 33
Crewe Cl. NG7: Radf 3D 44
Cribb Cl. NG11: Wilf 4F 57
Crich Vw. NG5: Sher 5G 33
Cricketers Ct. NG2: West Br 3D 12
Criftin Ent. Cen. NG14: Epp 3D 12
Criftin Rd. NG14: Bur J 4G 37
Cripps Hill NG7: Nott 1A 56
Crispin Way NG8: Aspl 2A 44
Critchley St. DE7: Ilk 6B 28
Critch's Flats NG16: Kimb 1H 29
Crocus St. NG2: Nott 1G 57
Croft Av. NG15: Huck 6G 7
Croft Cres. NG16: Aws 2E 29
Crofton Cl. NG8: Bilb 3H 43
  NG9: Chil 3D 64
Crofton Rd. NG9: Chil 3D 64
Croft Rd. NG5: Arn 5B 22
  NG12: Edwal 2D 74
  NG12: Key 4F 79
The Crofts NG13: Bing 5E 51
Cromdale Cl. NG5: Arn 4E 23
Cromer Rd. NG3: Nott 2A 46
Cromford Av. NG4: Car 1F 47
Cromford Cl. NG10: Long E 2C 72
  NG16: Lang M 1F 15
Cromford Rd. NG2: West Br 5B 58
  NG16: Lang M 1D 14
Cromford Rd. Ind. Est. NG16: Lang M 1F 15
Crompton Rd. DE7: Ilk, Stant D 1D 52
Crompton Rd. Ind. Est. DE7: Ilk 6C 40
Cromwell Av. DE7: Ilk 4C 40
Cromwell Cres. NG4: Lamb 6B 24
Cromwell Rd. NG9: Bee 4E 55
Cromwell St. NG4: Car 2G 47
  NG7: Radf 2A 4 (4E 45)
  NG16: Gilt 5D 16
Cromwell Ter. DE7: Ilk 4B 28
Crookdole La. NG14: Calv 4H 11
Cropston Cl. NG2: West Br 1A 68
Cropton Cres. NG8: Bilb 3H 43
Cropton Gro. NG13: Bing 5C 50
Cropwell Gdns. NG12: Rad T 1G 61
Cropwell Grn. NG3: Nott 3B 46
Cropwell Rd. NG12: Rad T 6F 49
Crosby Rd. NG2: West Br 2B 58
The Cross NG12: Cotg 2E 71
Crossdale Dr. NG12: Key 3G 79

Crossdale Wlk. NG5: Top V 5C 20
Crossfield Ct. NG5: Top V 5E 21
Crossfield Dr. NG5: Top V 5E 21
Crossgate Dr. NG2: Nott 3E 57
Crosshill NG12: Cotg 2G 71
Crosshill Dr. DE7: Kirk H 4F 39
Crossland Rd. NG5: Bestw 2E 33
Crosslands Mdw. NG4: Colw 5H 47
Crossley St. NG5: Sher 5F 33
Cross St.
  NG4: Car 1F 47
  NG4: Neth 2A 48
  NG5: Arn 5H 21
  NG9: Bee 4F 55
  NG10: Long E 5G 63
  NG10: Sand 5E 53
  NG16: Eastw 3C 16
Crowborough Av. NG8: Woll 1E 55
Crow Ct. NG13: Bing 5G 51
Crowcroft Way NG10: Long E 3D 62
Crow Hill Rd. NG4: Car 2H 47
Crowley Cl. NG8: Bilb 3C 42
Crown Cl. NG10: Long E 6C 62
Crown Court
  Nottingham 6E 5 (6G 45)
Crown Hill Way DE7: Stan C 1A 38
Crown St. NG15: Huck 1A 20
Crown Way NG16: Lang M 1F 15
Crow Pk. Dr. NG14: Bur J 4E 37
Crowthorne Cl. NG5: Top V 4C 20
Crowthorne Gdns. NG5: Top V 4C 20
Croxall Cl. NG11: Clftn 1C 66
Croxley Gdns. NG16: Nuth 4D 30
Croyde Gdns. NG2: Gam 4D 58
Croydon Rd. NG7: Radf 4C 44
Crummock Cl. NG9: Bram 3C 54
Crusader Ct. NG11: Clftn 4A 66
Crusader Ho. NG1: Nott 3E 5 (5D 45)
Cudworth Dr. NG3: Mapp 5B 34
Cuillin Cl. NG5: Top V 3D 20
  NG10: Long E 4C 62
Culbert Lodge NG7: Bas 6D 32
Culbert Pl. NG7: Bas 6D 32
Cullens Ct. NG5: Sher 5G 33
Cultivation Rd. NG16: Eastw 4C 16
Cumberland Av. NG9: Bee 5D 54
Cumberland Cl. NG11: Rudd 6G 67
Cumberland Pl. NG1: Nott 4C 4 (5F 45)
Cumbria Grange NG2: Gam 4E 59
Curie Ct. NG7: Nott 1C 56
Curlew Cl. NG3: Nott 4E 47
Curlew Wharf NG7: Lent 1E 57
Cursley Way NG9: Chil 3C 64
Curtis St. NG15: Huck 5G 7
Curzon Av. NG4: Car 2D 46
Curzon Ct. NG3: Nott 1G 5 (3H 45)
Curzon Gdns. NG3: Nott 1G 5 (3H 45)
Curzon Pl. NG3: Nott 2F 5 (4H 45)
Curzon St. NG3: Nott 2F 5 (4H 45)
  NG4: Neth 2A 48
  NG10: Long E 3D 62
  NG11: Goth 6H 75
Cuthrough La. NG7: Nott 3H 55
Cutlers Ct. NG12: Rad T 6E 49
Cuxton Cl. NG8: Stre 6D 30
Cycle Rd. NG7: Lent 5C 44
CYGNET HOSPITAL 3B 66
Cypress Ct. NG15: Huck 6C 6
Cyprus Av. NG9: Bee 4F 55
Cyprus Dr. NG9: Bee 4F 55
Cyprus Rd. NG3: Mapp P 1G 45
Cyril Av. NG8: Aspl 1B 44
  NG9: Bee 4E 55
  NG9: Stfrd 4F 53
Cyril Cotts. NG8: Aspl 1B 44
Cyril Rd. NG2: West Br 3C 58
Cyril's Nut Hut Indoor Play Cen. 1G 73

D

Dabell Av. NG6: Bulw 5E 19
Daffodil Gdns. NG12: Edwal 3C 68
Dagmar Gro. NG3: Nott 6H 33
  NG9: Bee 5G 55
Dairy Sq. NG8: Bilb 2H 43
Daisy Cl. NG12: Cotg 3E 71
Daisy Farm Rd. NG16: Newth 4D 16
Daisy Rd. NG3: Nott 6C 34
Dakeyne St. NG3: Nott 3H 5 (4A 46)
Dakota Rd. NG13: Newt 2B 50
Dalbeattie Cl. NG5: Arn 5D 22
Dalby Sq. NG8: Woll 6A 44
DALE ABBEY 6D 38
Dale Av. NG3: Mapp 5C 34
  NG4: Car 2E 47
  NG10: Long E 4F 63
Dalebrook Cres. NG15: Huck 5C 6

Dale Cl. DE72: Brea 5A 62
  NG2: West Br 4D 58
  NG15: Huck 5C 6
Dale Farm Av. NG3: Nott 4C 46
Dale Gro. NG2: Nott 5B 46
Dalehead Rd. NG11: Clftn 3B 66
Dale La. DE7: D Ab 6D 38
  NG9: Chil 5E 55
Dalemoor Gdns. NG8: Bilb 1H 43
Dale Rd. DE7: D Ab, Stant D 2A 52
  DE7: Stly 4A 38
  NG4: Car 2E 47
  NG12: Key 4G 79
  NG16: Kimb 2H 29
The Dales DE7: West H 2C 38
Daleside NG12: Cotg 3E 71
Daleside Rd. NG2: Nott 6B 46
Daleside Rd. E. NG2: Nott 5D 46
Dale St. DE7: Ilk 2B 40
  NG2: Nott 5A 46
Dale Ter. NG2: Nott 5B 46
Dale Vw. DE7: Ilk 3A 40
Dale Vw. Rd. NG3: Nott 2D 46
Dalkeith Ter. NG7: Hys G 2D 44
Dallaglio M. NG9: Chil 3B 64
Dallas York Rd. NG9: Bee 5H 55
Dalley Cl. NG9: Stfrd 4G 53
Dallimore Rd. DE7: Kirk H 5H 39
Dallman Cl. NG15: Huck 6G 7
Dalton Cl. NG9: Stfrd 6G 53
Daltons Cl. NG16: Lang M 1E 15
Damson Wlk. NG3: Nott 5H 33
Danbury M. NG5: Sher 5H 33
Dance4 .... 4B 4 (5F 45)
Dane Cl. NG3: Nott 1F 5
Dane Cl. NG3: Nott 1F 5 (3H 45)
Danehurst Dr. NG4: Ged 6A 36
Danes Cl. NG5: Arn 5H 21
Danethorpe Va. NG5: Sher 3G 33
Daniel M. NG10: Sand 6C 52
Daniels Way NG15: Huck 1E 19
Dann Pl. NG11: Wilf 3F 57
Darfield Dr. DE75: Hea 3E 15
Darkey La. NG9: Stfrd 6G 53
(not continuous)
Dark La. NG13: Bing 5G 51
  NG14: Calv 5G 11
Darley Av. NG4: Car 6G 35
  NG7: Hys G 2C 44
  NG9: Toton 2G 63
Darley Dr. DE7: West H 1C 38
  NG10: Long E 2C 72
Darley Rd. NG7: Hys G 2C 44
Darley Sq. DE7: Ilk 2A 28
Darlison St. NG15: Huck 3G 7
(off Ogle St.)
Darlton Dr. NG5: Arn 6C 22
Darnal Cl. NG5: Top V 6C 20
Darnhall Cres. NG8: Bilb 2D 42
Daron Gdns. NG5: Bestw 6E 21
Dart Cl. NG13: Bing 6D 50
Dartmeet Ct. NG7: Radf 2B 44
Dartmoor Cl. NG11: Clftn 5B 66
Darvel Cl. NG8: Bilb 3H 43
Darwin Cl. NG5: Top V 5C 20
Darwin Av. DE7: Ilk 2A 40
Darwin Rd. NG10: Long E 2D 72
David Gro. NG9: Bram 2D 54
David La. NG6: Bas 4B 32
David Lane Stop (NET) 4B 32
David Lloyd Leisure
  Nottingham 2B 44
  West Bridgford 5H 57
Davidson Cl. NG5: Arn 6E 23
Davidson Gdns. NG11: Rudd 6E 67
Davidson St. NG2: Nott 6B 46
Davies Rd. NG2: West Br 4B 58
Davies Way NG5: Bestw 2E 33
Davis Rd. NG9: Chil 2B 64
Davy Cl. NG15: Lin 1H 7
Dawes Way NG7: Lent 4C 44
Dawlish Cl. NG3: Mapp 2E 35
  NG15: Huck 5D 6
Dawlish Ct. NG3: Mapp 1F 35
  NG16: Eastw 2H 15
Dawlish Dr. NG5: Bestw 2F 33
Dawn Cl. NG15: Huck 2A 8
Dawn Vw. NG9: Trow 1F 53
Dawson Cl. NG16: Newth 4C 16
Dawver Rd. NG16: Kimb 1H 29
DAYBROOK 1A 34
Daybrook Av. NG5: Sher 4G 33
Daybrook Bus. Cen. NG5: Arn 1H 33
DAYBROOK SQUARE 1A 34
Daybrook St. NG5: Sher 4G 33
Deabill Cl. NG4: Neth 3A 48
Deabill St. NG4: Neth 3A 48
Dead La. NG16: Coss 6F 29
Deakins Pl. NG7: Radf 4C 44

Deal Gdns. NG6: Bulw 6F 19
Dean Av. NG3: Mapp 4D 34
Dean Cl. NG8: Woll 4D 42
Deane Ct. NG11: Wilf 5E 57
Deane Rd. NG11: Wilf 5E 57
Dean Rd. NG5: Woodt 2A 34
Deans Ct. NG12: Cotg 2G 71
Deans Cft. NG9: Bram 2B 54
Dean St. NG1: Nott 5G 5 (5H 45)
  NG16: Lang M 2G 15
Debdale La. NG12: Key 4F 79
De Buseli Cl. NG4: Ged 6A 36
Deddington La. NG9: Bram 1B 54
Deeley Cl. NG16: Want 5A 18
Deepdale Av. NG9: Stfrd 5F 53
Deepdale Cl. NG2: Gam 4E 59
Deepdale Ct. DE75: Hea 4C 14
Deepdale Rd. NG8: Woll 5D 42
  NG10: Long E 1C 72
Deepdene Cl. NG8: Brox 5G 31
Deepdene Way NG8: Brox, Cin 5G 31
Deep Furrow Av. NG4: Car 1F 47
Deering Ct. NG2: Nott 1F 57
Deerleap Dr. NG5: Arn 6G 21
Deer Pk. NG8: Woll 5E 43
Deer Pk. Dr. NG5: Arn 5F 21
Defiant Cl. NG15: Huck 2E 19
Delia Av. NG15: Huck 2A 8
Dell Way NG11: Clftn 3D 66
Dellwood Cl. NG4: Car 5D 34
Delta Ct. NG1: Nott 3G 45
Delta St. NG7: Bas 6D 32
Deltic Cl. NG16: Want 6A 18
Delves Ct. DE75: Hea 5C 14
Delves Rd. DE75: Hea 5B 14
Delville Av. NG12: Key 3G 79
Denacre Av. NG10: Long E 4H 63
Denbury Ct. NG3: Mapp 2F 35
Denby Ct. NG4: Neth 2A 48
Denby Hall Rd. DE7: Ilk 1A 28
Denehurst Av. NG8: Aspl 6A 32
Denewood Av. NG9: Bram 1C 54
Denewood Cres. NG8: Bilb 1E 43
Denholme Rd. NG8: Bilb 4D 42
Denison Ct. NG7: Radf 3D 44
Denison St. NG7: Radf 3D 44
  NG9: Bee 4E 55
Denman St. Central NG7: Radf 4C 44
Denman St. E. NG7: Radf 4D 44
Denman St. W. NG7: Radf 4C 44
Denmark Gro. NG3: Nott 6H 33
Dennett Cl. NG3: Nott 1H 5 (3A 46)
Dennis Av. NG9: Bee 3E 55
Dennis St. NG4: Neth 2A 48
Denstone Rd. NG3: Nott 4A 46
Dentdale Dr. NG8: Woll 5B 42
Denton Av. NG10: Sand 5C 52
Denton Dr. NG2: West Br 1H 67
Denton Grn. NG8: Brox 5F 31
Denver Ct. NG9: Stfrd 2G 53
Denz Childrens Play Cen. 5H 55
Depedale Av. DE7: Kirk H 4H 39
Deptford Cres. NG6: Bulw 1A 32
Derby Gro. NG7: Lent, Radf 4D 44
Derby Rd. DE7: Ilk 2G 39
  DE7: Stly 4A 38
  DE72: Ris 1A 62
  DE75: Hea 4B 14
  (not continuous)
  NG1: Nott 3A 4 (4E 45)
  NG7: Lent, Nott 1B 56
  NG9: Bee, Bram, Nott 3A 54
  NG9: Lent, Nott 2F 55
  NG9: Stfrd 6E 53
  NG10: Long E 5C 62
  NG10: Sand 1A 62
  NG16: Eastw 3H 15
  NG16: Lang M 2G 15
Derby Rd. Ind. Est. DE75: Hea 4B 14
  NG10: Sand 6D 52
Derbyshire Av. DE7: West H 1C 38
  NG9: Trow 5F 41
Derbyshire Cl. DE7: West H 1C 38
Derbyshire Cres. NG8: Woll 4G 43
Derbyshire Dr. DE7: Ilk 3A 40
Derbyshire La. NG15: Huck 4G 7
Derby St. DE7: Ilk 1B 40
  NG1: Nott 3B 4 (4F 45)
  NG5: Arn 6B 22
  NG9: Bee 4F 55
Derby Ter. NG7: Nott 3A 4 (4E 45)
Dereham Dr. NG5: Arn 1B 34
Derry Dr. NG5: Arn 3B 22
Derry Hill Rd. NG5: Arn 4A 22
Derry La. NG13: Bing 5H 51
Derwent Av. DE7: Ilk 5H 27
  DE7: West H 1C 38
Derwent Cl. NG2: Gam 4E 59
  NG9: Atten 2E 55
Derwent Ct. NG7: Radf 3E 45

Derwent Cres. NG5: Arn 1C 34
Derwent Dr. NG15: Huck 5H 7
Derwent St. NG10: Long E 1E 73
Derwent St. Ind. Est. NG10: Long E 1E 73
Derwent Ter. NG5: Sher 5G 33
Derwent Way NG7: Lent 3A 44
Desford Cl. NG5: Sher 3E 33
De Vere Gdns. NG5: Woodt 2B 34
Devitt Dr. NG15: Huck 2A 8
Devon Cir. NG5: Redh 4H 21
Devon Cl. NG10: Sand 6D 52
  NG16: Newth 3D 16
Devon Dr. NG5: Sher 5F 33
  NG11: Rudd 5H 67
Devonshire Av. NG9: Bee 5F 55
  NG10: Long E 5A 64
Devonshire Cl. DE7: Ilk 2A 28
Devonshire Cres. NG5: Sher 5F 33
Devonshire Dr. NG9: Stfrd 1F 53
  NG16: Eastw 3B 16
Devonshire Prom. NG7: Lent 6C 44
Devonshire Rd. NG2: West Br 5A 58
  NG5: Sher 5F 33
Devon St. DE7: Ilk 4B 40
  NG3: Nott 4B 46
Dewberry La. NG12: Rad T 1H 61
Dexters Gro. NG15: Huck 4F 7
DH Lawrence Birthplace Mus. 2B 16
DH Lawrence Craft Cen. 2B 16
  (off Scargill Wlk.)
DH Lawrence Pavilion 2B 56
DH Lawrence 'Sons & Lovers' Cottage 2C 16
The Dial NG12: Cotg 4E 71
Diamond Cl. NG10: Long E 2C 72
Dickens Ct. NG16: Newth 2D 16
Dickinson St. NG3: Nott 3A 46
Dicks La. NG16: Newth 2E 17
Dickson Dr. NG11: Rudd 1H 77
Didcot Dr. NG8: Bas 6B 32
Digby Av. NG3: Mapp 4D 34
  NG8: Woll 5G 43
Digby Hall Dr. NG4: Ged 4E 35
Digby Ind. Est. NG16: Kimb 6F 17
Digby St. DE7: Ilk 6C 28
  NG16: Kimb 1F 29
Dirac Cl. NG11: Clftn 5A 66
Discovery Dr. NG8: Aspl 2A 44
Diseworth Gro. NG2: Nott 2H 57
Disraeli Cres. DE7: Ilk 1B 40
Distillery St. NG11: Rudd 1G 77
Dizzy Rascalz 5F 67
Djanogly Art Gallery 2B 56
Djanogly Community Leisure Cen. 2E 45
DOBPARK 3F 7
Dob Pk. Cl. NG6: Bas 3B 32
Dockholm Rd. NG10: Long E 3E 63
Dodford Ct. DE75: Hea 4E 15
Dogwood Av. NG6: Bulw 6F 19
Dolphin Ct. NG5: Top V 5E 21
Donbas Cl. NG6: Bulw 3H 31
Doncaster Av. NG10: Sand 5D 52
Doncaster Gro. NG10: Long E 4H 63
Doncaster Ter. NG2: Nott 2G 57
Donington Rd. NG11: Clftn 4C 66
Donkey La. NG11: Rudd 4A 78
Donner Cres. DE7: Ilk 2A 28
Dooland Dr. NG3: Nott 6B 34
Dorchester Gdns. NG2: West Br 2A 68
Dorchester Rd. NG16: Kimb 6H 17
Doris Ct. NG9: Toton 3H 64
Doris Rd. DE7: Ilk 2C 40
Dorket Cl. NG5: Arn 4C 22
Dorket Dr. NG8: Woll 6B 44
DORKET HEAD 2C 22
Dorket Ho. NG4: Car 1G 47
  (off Garden City)
Dorking Rd. NG7: Radf 3C 44
Dormy Cl. NG9: Bram 4C 54
  NG12: Rad T 6H 49
Dormy Ct. NG6: Bulw 6B 20
Dornoch Av. NG5: Sher 5H 33
Dorothy Av. NG10: Sand 6D 52
  NG15: Huck 2H 7
  NG16: Newth 2C 16
The Dorothy Boot Homes 3F 57
Dorothy Gro. NG8: Aspl 3A 44
Dorset Gdns. NG2: West Br 6G 57
Dorset St. NG8: Radf 4B 44
Dorterry Cres. DE7: Ilk 4C 40
Douglas Av. DE75: Hea, Los 3A 14
  NG4: Car 3F 47
  NG16: Aws 2E 29
Douglas Cl. NG12: Rad T 1F 61
Douglas Cres. NG4: Car 3G 47
Douglas Rd. NG7: Lent, Radf 4D 44
  NG10: Long E 3D 62
  NG13: Bing 5H 51
Douro Dr. NG5: Arn 4D 22
Dove Cl. NG13: Bing 6F 51

Dovecote Dr. NG8: Woll 5E 43
Dovecote La. NG9: Bee 5F 55
Dovecote Rd. NG16: Eastw, Newth 3D 16
The Dovecotes NG9: Bee 6F 55
Dovedale Av. NG10: Long E 1D 72
Dovedale Circ. DE7: Ilk 2A 28
Dovedale Cl. NG10: Long E 1D 72
Dovedale Rd. NG2: West Br 6C 58
  NG3: Nott 3E 47
Dove La. NG10: Long E 5E 63
Dovenby Rd. NG11: Clftn 2D 66
Dover Beck Cl. NG4: Calv 4A 12
Doverbeck Dr. NG14: Woodbo 1C 24
Doveridge Av. NG4: Car 1A 48
Doveridge Rd. NG4: Car 1H 47
Dove St. NG6: Bulw 6H 19
Doveys Orchard NG14: Calv 4F 11
Downes Cl. NG6: Bulw 6G 19
Downham Cl. NG5: Arn 1C 34
Downing Gdns. NG6: Bulw 5H 19
Downing St. NG6: Bulw 5H 19
The Downs NG11: Wilf 1E 67
Dowson Cl. NG12: Rad T 5H 49
Dowson St. NG3: Nott 3B 46
Doyne Ct. NG2: Nott 2G 57
Drakemyre Cl. NG5: Arn 4D 22
Drake Rd. NG4: Neth 3B 48
Draycott Cl. DE75: Los 1A 14
Draycott Ct. DE7: Ilk 4B 28
Draycott Rd. DE72: Brea 5A 62
  NG10: Long E 2B 72
Draymans Ct. NG7: Bas 6D 32
Drayton St. NG5: Sher 5G 33
DREWRY ISLAND 6F 31
The Drift NG11: Clftn 2C 66
  NG15: Huck 2H 7
The Drive NG7: Atten 2E 65
Dronfield Pl. DE7: Ilk 2A 28
Drummond Av. NG4: Neth 2B 48
Drummond Dr. NG16: Nuth 3E 31
Drummond Rd. DE7: Ilk 6A 28
Drury Cl. NG15: Huck 4H 7
Drury Wlk. NG1: Nott 5E 5 (5G 45)
Dryden Ct. NG9: Stfrd 2G 53
Dryden St. NG1: Nott 1C 4 (3F 45)
Drysdale Cl. NG6: Bulw 2H 31
Duchess Gdns. NG6: Bulw 5H 19
Duchess St. NG6: Bulw 5H 19
Duckworth Cl. NG4: Ged 4G 35
Dudley Cl. NG9: Bram 3A 54
Duffield Cl. NG10: Long E 2C 72
Duffield Cres. NG5: Top V 5D 20
Duke Cl. NG6: Bulw 2F 31
Duke Cres. NG16: Gilt 4E 17
Dukes Cl. NG15: Huck 4H 7
Dukes Pl. DE7: Ilk 3A 28
  NG1: Nott 4G 5 (5H 45)
Duke St. DE7: Ilk 4B 28
  NG5: Arn 6H 21
  NG6: Bulw 6H 19
  NG7: Bas 1D 44
  NG15: Huck 4H 7
Duke St. E. NG15: Huck 4H 7
Dukes Wharf NG7: Nott 6C 4 (6F 45)
Duke William Mt. NG7: Nott 5A 4 (5H 45)
Dulverton Va. NG8: Cin 4G 31
Dulwich Rd. NG7: Radf 4C 44
The Dumbles NG4: Lamb 5B 24
Dumbles Cl. DE7: Kirk H 3G 39
Dunbar Cl. NG10: Long E 3G 73
Dunblane Rd. NG11: Rudd 1G 77
Duncombe Cl. NG3: Nott 2A 46
Duncroft Av. NG4: Ged 6H 35
Dundas Cl. NG1: Nott 1D 4 (3G 45)
Dunelm Dr. NG14: Calv 4A 12
Dungannon Rd. NG11: Clftn 5C 66
Dunholme Cl. NG6: Bulw 5H 19
Dunkery Rd. NG11: Clftn 5D 66
DUNKIRK 1C 56
Dunkirk Rd. NG7: Lent 2C 56
  (not continuous)
Dunlin Wharf NG7: Lent 1E 57
Dunlop Av. NG7: Lent 5C 44
Dunn Dr. NG10: Long E 6D 62
Dunoon Cl. NG5: Top V 3C 20
Dunsby Cl. NG11: Clftn 4C 66
Dunsford Dr. NG3: Mapp 1F 35
Dunsil Dr. NG2: Nott 3E 57
Dunsil Rd. NG16: Newth 1D 16
Dunsmore Cl. NG9: Bee 1H 65
Dunstan St. NG4: Neth 2A 48
  (not continuous)
Dunster Rd. NG2: West Br 5C 58
  NG16: Newth 3D 16
Dunston Cl. NG10: Long E 6H 63
Dunvegan Cl. NG5: Top V 3D 20
Durham Av. NG2: Nott 5B 46
Durham Chambers NG1: Nott 4E 5
Durham Cl. NG2: Nott 5B 46
Durham Cres. NG6: Bulw 1A 32

Durham Ho. NG3: Mapp P 1G 45
Durham St. DE7: Ilk 6B 28
Durlston Cl. NG2: West Br 6F 57
Durnford St. NG7: Bas 5D 32
Dursley Cl. NG6: Bulw 2H 31
Dusk till Dawn Casino 3C 56
DW Fitness
    Nottingham 3B 48
Dyce Cl. NG6: Bulw 6F 19
Dylan M. NG8: Bilb 1E 43
Dylan Thomas Rd. NG5: Bestw 5F 21

E

Eagle Cl. NG5: Arn 6C 22
    NG9: Bee 3D 54
Eagle Ct. NG6: Bulw 6B 20
Eagle Rd. DE7: Ilk 5B 40
Ealing Av. NG6: Bas 3B 32
Eardley Rd. NG5: Bestw 4B 14
Eames Cl. DE75: Hea 4B 14
Eardley Rd. NG5: Bestw 4B 14
Earl Cres. NG4: Ged 4H 35
Earl Dr. NG16: Gilt 4E 17
Earlham Cl. DE7: Kirk H 3G 39
Earls Cl. NG8: Bilb 4C 42
Earlsfield Dr. NG5: Top V 4B 20
Earlswood Dr. NG12: Edwal 1D 68
Easedale Cl. NG2: Gam 4E 59
Easegill Cl. NG5: Top V 5D 20
    (off Aveline Cl.)
East Acres NG12: Cotg 2F 71
E. Bridgeford Rd. NG13: Newt 1B 50
E. Circus St. NG1: Nott 4C 4 (5F 45)
Eastcliffe Av. NG4: Ged 4F 35
East Cl. NG12: Key 5G 79
Eastcote Av. NG9: Bram 1B 54
East Cres. NG9: Bee 6H 55
Eastdale Rd. NG3: Nott 3E 47
East Dr. NG7: Nott 2A 56
Easter Pk. NG7: Lent 1D 56
Eastglade Rd. NG5: Bestw 1D 32
East Gro. NG7: Bas 1E 45
    NG13: Bing 5F 51
Eastham Cl. NG3: Nott 2H 5 (3A 46)
Eastham Rd. NG5: Arn 1D 34
Eastholme Cft. NG2: Colw 4F 47
Easthorpe Cotts. NG11: Rudd 6H 67
Easthorpe St. NG11: Rudd 6G 67
East Midlands Conference Cen. 2H 55
East Moor NG12: Cotg 4G 71
Eastmoor Dr. NG4: Car 1H 47
E. Nelson St. DE75: Hea 3C 14
East Rd. NG7: Nott 1B 56
East St.
    DE7: Ilk 1B 40
    DE75: Hea 5E 15
    NG1: Nott 3F 5 (4H 45)
    NG10: Long E 5H 63
    NG11: Goth 6H 75
    NG13: Bing 5F 51
East Vw. NG2: West Br 5H 57
Eastview Ter. NG16: Lang M 2F 15
Eastwell Ct. NG15: Huck 3G 7
    (off Annesley Rd.)
Eastwell St. NG15: Huck 3G 7
Eastwold NG12: Cotg 3G 71
EASTWOOD 3B 16
Eastwood Cl. NG15: Huck 1E 19
Eastwood Rd. NG12: Rad T 6G 49
    NG16: Kimb 6F 17
Eastwood St. NG6: Bulw 2A 32
Eastwood Town FC 3C 16
Eaton Av. DE7: Kirk H 3H 39
    NG5: Arn 6C 22
Eaton Cl. NG9: Bee 5H 55
Eaton Grange Dr. NG10: Long E 5C 62
Eaton Pl. NG13: Bing 5E 51
Eatons Rd. NG9: Stfrd 5F 53
Eaton St. NG3: Mapp 4B 34
Eaton Ter. NG3: Mapp 4B 34
Ebenezer St. DE7: Ilk 4B 28
    NG16: Lang M 1F 15
Ebers Gro. NG3: Mapp P 1G 45
Ebers Rd. NG3: Mapp P 6G 33
Ebony Wlk. NG3: Nott 1D 46
Ebury Rd. NG5: Sher 6F 33
Eccles Way NG3: Nott 2B 46
Eckington Cl. DE7: West H 1C 38
Eckington Ter. NG2: Nott 2G 57
Ecton Cl. NG5: Top V 4D 20
Ecton M. NG5: Top V 5D 20
    (off Ecton Cl.)
Edale Cl. NG10: Long E 1D 72
    NG15: Huck 5C 6
Edale Ri. NG9: Toton 2G 63
Edale Rd. NG2: Nott 4C 46
Edale Sq. DE7: Ilk 2A 28
Eddleston Dr. NG11: Clftn 4D 66
Edenbridge Ct. NG8: Woll 1D 54

Eden Cl. NG5: Arn 1C 34
    NG15: Huck 5C 6
Edenhall Gdns. NG11: Clftn 3D 66
Eden Wlk. NG13: Bing 6D 50
Edern Cl. NG5: Bestw 6E 21
Edern Gdns. NG5: Bestw 6E 21
Edgbaston Gdns. NG8: Aspl 1B 44
Edgcote Way NG5: Bestw 1E 33
Edge Hill Ct. NG10: Long E 3F 73
Edgeway NG8: Stre 6D 30
Edgewood Dr. NG15: Huck 6D 6
Edgewood Leisure Cen. 1D 18
Edgington Cl. NG12: Cotg 3G 71
Edgington St. NG3: Nott 2B 46
Edgware Rd. NG6: Bulw 6B 20
Edgwood Rd. NG16: Kimb 1H 29
Edinbane Cl. NG5: Top V 3D 20
Edinboro Row NG16: Kimb 6G 17
Edinburgh Dr. NG13: Bing 4D 50
Edingale Ct. NG9: Bram 5B 42
Edingley Av. NG5: Sher 3G 33
Edingley Sq. NG5: Sher 3F 33
Edison Village NG7: Nott 2C 56
Edison Way NG5: Arn 6E 23
Edith Ter. NG7: Radf 3C 44
    (off Hartley Rd.)
Edlington Dr. NG8: Woll 6C 42
Edmond Gro. NG15: Huck 3A 8
Edmonds Cl. NG5: Top V 3E 21
Edmonstone Cres. NG5: Bestw 2D 32
Edmonton Ct. NG2: West Br 5H 57
Ednaston Rd. NG7: Nott 2B 56
Edwald Rd. NG12: Edwal 2D 68
EDWALTON 2D 68
Edwalton Av. NG2: West Br 4B 58
Edwalton Cl. NG12: Edwal 2D 68
Edwalton Ct. NG6: Bulw 1C 32
Edwalton Golf Course 2E 69
Edwalton Hall NG12: Edwal 2C 68
Edwalton Lodge Cl. NG12: Edwal 2C 68
Edward Av. NG8: Aspl 1B 44
Edward Cl. NG15: Huck 1D 18
Edward Rd. NG2: West Br 2B 58
    NG10: Long E 5F 63
    NG16: Eastw 3C 16
    NG16: Nuth 2C 30
Edwards Ct. NG5: Sher 2F 33
Edwards La. NG5: Bestw, Sher 1F 33
Edward St. NG9: Stfrd 4F 53
    NG16: Lang M 1F 15
Edwinstowe Av. NG2: West Br 4B 58
Edwinstowe Dr. NG5: Sher 3G 33
Edwin St. NG5: Arn 1H 33
Eelwood Rd. NG15: Huck 1D 18
Egerton Dr. NG9: Stfrd 1F 53
Egerton Rd. NG5: Woodt 3H 33
Egerton St. NG3: Nott 2G 45
Egerton Wlk. NG3: Nott 2G 45
Egling Cft. NG4: Colw 5H 47
Egmont Ct. NG2: Nott 1G 57
Egreaves Av. DE75: Los 1A 14
Egypt Rd. NG7: Bas 6D 32
    (not continuous)
Eileen Rd. NG9: Bee 2G 65
Eisele Cl. NG6: Bulw 1F 31
Ekowe St. NG7: Bas 5D 32
Eland St. NG7: Bas 6D 32
Elder Cl. NG5: Arn 4C 22
Elder Gdns. NG5: Top V 5E 21
Elder Gro. NG15: Huck 1H 19
Elder Rd. NG14: Stoke B 2C 48
Eldon Bus. Pk. NG9: Atten 4C 64
Eldon Chambers NG1: Nott 5D 4 (5G 45)
Eldon Rd. NG9: Atten 4C 64
Eldon Rd. Ind. Est. NG9: Atten 4C 64
Eldon Rd. Trad. Est. NG9: Chil 4C 64
Eleanor Av. DE7: Ilk 4C 40
Eleanor Cres. NG9: Stfrd 4H 53
Electric Av. NG2: Nott 4E 57
Eley Cl. DE7: Ilk 5G 27
Elgar Dr. NG10: Long E 2D 72
Elgar Gdns. NG3: Nott 3B 46
Eliot Cl. NG10: Long E 2D 72
Eliot Dr. DE7: Kirk H 4H 39
Eliot Wlk. NG11: Clftn 5A 66
Elizabeth Cl. DE7: Ilk 6H 27
    NG15: Huck 6E 7
Elizabeth Gro. NG4: Ged 5G 35
Elizabeth Rd. NG5: Woodt 2H 33
Elka Rd. DE7: Ilk 5B 40
Ella Bank Rd. DE75: Hea 4E 15
Ella Rd. NG2: West Br 2B 58
Ellastone Av. NG5: Bestw 4D 20
Ellerby Av. NG11: Clftn 3C 66
Ellerslie Gro. NG10: Sand 6C 52
Ellesmere Bus. Pk. NG5: Sher 5F 33

Ellesmere Cl. NG5: Arn 6D 22
Ellesmere Ct. DE7: Ilk 6H 27
Ellesmere Cres. NG5: Sher 5F 33
Ellesmere Dr. NG9: Trow 4E 41
Ellesmere Rd. NG2: West Br 1B 68
Ellington Rd. NG5: Arn 3B 22
Elliot St. NG7: Nott 3A 4 (4E 45)
Ellis Av. NG15: Huck 5H 7
Ellis Cl. NG10: Long E 1E 73
Ellis Ct. NG3: Nott 3H 45
Ellis Gro. NG9: Bee 6F 55
Ellsworth Ri. NG5: Bestw 1D 32
Ellwood Cres. NG8: Woll 4G 43
Elm Av.
    NG3: Nott 2G 45
    NG4: Car 2H 47
    NG9: Atten 3D 64
    NG9: Bee 5E 55
    NG10: Long E 4E 63
    NG10: Sand 4D 52
    NG12: Key 5H 79
    NG13: Bing 5G 51
    NG15: Huck 6E 7
    NG16: Nuth 1B 30
Elm Bank NG3: Mapp P 1G 45
Elm Bank Dr. NG3: Mapp P 1G 45
Elmbridge NG5: Bestw 6F 21
Elm Cl. NG3: Mapp P 2G 45
    NG12: Key 5H 79
Elmdale Gdns. NG8: Bilb 1H 43
Elm Dr. NG4: Car 2H 47
Elm Gro. NG5: Arn 4C 22
Elmhurst Av. NG3: Mapp 5E 35
Elmhurst Cl. NG7: Radf 3E 45
The Elms NG4: Colw 3H 47
    NG16: Want 6H 17
Elms Cl. NG11: Rudd 1H 77
Elmsdale Gdns. NG4: Bur J 3F 37
Elmsfield Av. DE75: Hea 3E 15
Elms Gdns. NG11: Rudd 1G 77
Elmsham Av. NG5: Top V 4C 20
Elms Pk. NG11: Rudd 1H 77
Elmsthorpe Av. NG7: Lent 5C 44
Elmswood Gdns. NG5: Sher 4H 33
Elm Tree Av. NG2: West Br 4H 57
Elmtree Rd. NG14: Calv 4F 11
Elm Vw. NG7: Radf 3D 44
Elnor St. NG16: Lang M 3G 15
Elson St. NG7: Bas 1D 44
Elston Gdns. NG11: Clftn 1C 66
Elston M. NG3: Nott 2D 46
Elstree Dr. NG8: Bilb 3G 43
Elswick Cl. NG5: Bestw 5F 21
Elswick Dr. NG9: Bee 1H 65
Elterwater Dr. NG2: Gam 4E 59
Eltham Cl. NG3: Nott 4F 31
Eltham Dr. NG8: Cin 4F 31
Eltham Rd. NG2: West Br 4B 58
Elton Cl. NG9: Stfrd 3G 53
Elton M. NG5: Sher 6F 33
Elton Rd. Nth. NG5: Sher 6F 33
Elton Ter. NG7: Hys G 2D 44
Elvaston Ct. NG5: Bestw 2D 32
Elvaston Dr. NG10: Long E 3B 72
Elvaston Rd. NG8: Woll 4G 43
Elveden Dr. DE7: Ilk 3G 27
Elwes Lodge NG4: Car 3H 47
Elwin Dr. NG9: Bram 2C 54
Embley Rd. NG5: Sher 2E 33
Emerys Rd. NG4: Ged, Neth 1B 48
Emmanuel Av. NG3: Mapp 6C 34
    NG5: Arn 4E 21
Emneth Cl. NG3: Nott 1B 46
Emperor Cl. NG5: Sher 6F 33
Emperors Way NG15: Huck 3A 8
Empingham Cl. NG9: Toton 3B 64
Empire Ct. DE75: Hea 3C 14
    (off Fletcher St.)
Empire Gallery 4D 4
Emsworth Cl. DE7: Ilk 4H 27
Ena Av. NG2: Nott 4B 46
Enderby Gdns. NG5: Redh 4A 22
Enderby Sq. NG9: Lent A 3F 55
Endsleigh Gdns. NG9: Bee 4F 55
    NG12: Edwal 1C 68
Enfield Chambers NG1: Nott 5E 5 (5G 45)
Enfield St. NG9: Bee 5E 55
England Cres. DE75: Hea 3E 15
Ennerdale Cl. NG2: Gam 4E 59
Ennerdale Ct. NG10: Long E 3D 62
Ennerdale Rd. NG5: Sher 2H 33
    NG10: Long E 3D 62
Enthorpe St. NG8: Bilb 3H 43
EPPERSTONE 5G 13

Epperstone By-Pass NG14: Woodbo 5E 13
Epperstone Ct. NG2: West Br 3A 58
Epperstone Mnr. NG14: Epp 5F 13
Epperstone Rd. NG2: West Br 3A 58
  NG25: Oxton 1B 12
Epsom Rd. NG9: Toton .2G 63
Erdington Way NG9: Toton 2G 63
Erewash Ct. DE7: Ilk 6H 27
  NG10: Long E 4F 63
Erewash Dr. DE7: Ilk 3C 40
Erewash Gdns. NG5: Top V 5E 21
Erewash Gro. NG9: Toton 3H 63
                    (not continuous)
Erewash Indoor Bowling Club 5A 64
Erewash Mus. 1B 40
Erewash Sq. DE7: Ilk 3D 40
Erewash Valley Golf Course 2D 52
Eric Av. NG15: Huck 2F 7
Erith Cl. NG8: Stre 6D 30
Ernest Rd. NG4: Car 1D 46
Erskine Rd. NG5: Sher .6F 33
Escape Family Entertainment Cen. 6E 17
Esher Gro. NG3: Mapp P 6G 33
Eskdale Cl. NG10: Long E 2D 72
Eskdale Ct. NG2: Gam .4E 59
Eskdale Dr. NG8: Aspl .1H 43
  NG9: Chil 6A 54
Eskdale Drive Stop (NET) 6B 54
Esk Hause Cl. NG2: West Br 1E 69
Essex St. DE7: Ilk 6B 28
  NG16: Eastw 3B 16
Estwic Av. NG16: Eastw 2B 16
Ethel Av. NG3: Mapp 6C 34
  NG15: Huck 2H 7
Ethel Rd. NG2: West Br 4B 58
Eton Cl. NG8: Aspl 2B 44
Eton Ct. DE7: West H 1B 38
Eton Gro. NG8: Woll 5H 43
Eton Pl. NG2: West Br .6A 58
Eton Rd. NG2: West Br .5A 58
NG5: Sher 6F 33
                  (off Claremont Rd.)
Eucalyptus Av. NG11: Clftn 4A 66
Eugene Gdns. NG2: Nott 1H 57
Eugene St. NG2: Nott 6H 45
Europa Way NG2: West Br 2G 67
Evans Rd. NG6: Bas 4B 32
Evedon Wlk. NG5: Top V 4F 21
Evelyn St. NG2: Nott 5H 5 (5A 46)
  NG9: Bee 4H 55
Eversley Wlk. NG5: Bestw 5F 21
Evesham Ct. NG9: Toton 4A 64
Ewart Rd. NG7: Hys G .1D 44
Ewe Lamb Cl. NG9: Bram 2H 53
Ewe Lamb La. NG9: Bram 2H 53
Ewell Rd. NG8: Woll 4E 43
Exbourne Rd. NG8: Aspl 6F 31
Exbury Gdns. NG2: West Br 1F 67
Exchange Arc. NG1: Nott 4E 5
Exchange Rd. NG2: West Br 4B 58
Exchange Wlk. NG1: Nott 4E 5 (5G 45)
Excise Chambers NG1: Nott 4F 5
Exeter Cl. NG4: Ged 5H 35
Exeter Rd. NG2: West Br 5B 58
  NG7: Hys G 1E 45
Experian Way NG2: Nott 1E 57
Exton Rd. NG5: Sher 4E 33
Eyam Cl. NG9: Bram 1C 54
Eyre's Gdns. DE7: Ilk 5B 28
Eyre St. NG2: Nott 4H 5 (5A 46)

F

Fabis Dr. NG11: Clftn 1C 66
Factory La. DE7: Ilk 5A 28
  NG9: Chil 6E 55
Failsworth Cl. NG11: Clftn 2C 66
Fairbank Cres. NG5: Sher 5H 33
Fairburn Cl. NG8: Woll .3H 43
Fairburn Way NG16: Want 6A 18
Faircroft Av. NG10: Sand 6D 52
Fairdale Dr. NG16: Newth 3D 16
Fairfax Cl. NG5: Bas 5D 32
Fairfield Cl. NG11: Wilf .6F 57
Fairfield Cres. NG10: Long E 3C 72
Fairfield St. NG13: Bing .5E 51
Fairham Av. NG11: Goth 6H 75
Fairham Brook Nature Reserve 5D 66
Fairham Cl. NG11: Rudd 6H 67
Fairham Ct. NG11: Wilf .2E 67
Fairham Dr. NG8: Woll .5B 44
Fairham Rd. NG12: Key .4F 79
Fairholm Cl. NG3: Nott 1H 5 (3A 46)
Fairisle Cl. NG11: Clftn .4E 67
Fairland Cres. NG2: West Br 1H 67
Fairlawn Pl. NG5: Sher .5H 33
Fair Lea Cl. NG10: Long E 1F 73
Fairlight Way NG5: Bestw 6F 21
Fairmaid Gro. NG11: Clftn 3C 66

Fairmead Cl. NG3: Nott .1C 46
Fairnley Rd. NG8: Bilb 1D 42
Fairview Ct. NG2: West Br 3H 67
Fairview Rd. NG5: Woodt 3A 34
Fairway NG12: Key 4H 79
The Fairway NG4: Ged 4G 35
Fairway Cres. NG13: Newt 1B 50
Fairway Dr. NG4: Car 1E 47
  NG6: Bulw 6B 20
  NG9: Chil 5D 54
Falcon Cl. NG7: Lent 5C 44
Falcon Ct. DE7: Ilk 6H 27
Falcon Gro. NG7: Bas 6E 33
Falcon St. NG7: Bas 6E 33
Falcon Way NG15: Huck .2B 8
Falconwood Gdns. NG11: Clftn 4A 66
Fallow Cl. NG11: Clftn 3C 66
Fall Rd. DE75: Hea 1A 14
Falstaff M. NG7: Bas 6E 33
Falston Rd. NG8: Bilb 3G 43
Faraday Bldg. NG7: Nott 2B 56
Faraday Ct. NG9: Stfrd 2G 53
Faraday Rd. NG7: Lent .4C 44
Far Dales Rd. DE7: Ilk 5A 28
Farfield Av. NG9: Bee 3E 55
Farfield Gro. NG9: Bee .3E 55
Farfield Rd. DE7: Ilk 6C 28
FARLEYS 2H 19
Farleys Gro. NG15: Huck 6G 7
Farleys La. NG15: Huck .5G 7
                  (not continuous)
Farley St. NG6: Bulw 6H 19
Farm Av. NG15: Huck 1D 18
Farm Ct. DE7: Ilk 1C 40
  NG10: Long E 2G 73
  NG11: Clftn 3C 66
Farmer St. NG11: Rudd .4A 78
Farm M. NG7: Bas 6E 33
Farm Rd. NG5: Arn 6D 22
  NG9: Chil 6C 54
Farnborough Rd. NG11: Clftn 1D 66
Farndale Cl. NG10: Long E 2C 72
Farndale Dr. NG8: Woll .5B 42
Farndon Dr. NG9: Toton .3F 63
Farndon Grn. NG8: Woll .5A 44
Farndon M. NG3: Nott 1C 46
Far New Cl. NG10: Sand 6D 52
Farnham Wlk. DE7: West H 1B 38
Farnsfield Av. NG14: Bur J 2G 37
Farnsworth Cl. NG16: Want 4A 18
Far Pastures Cl. NG12: Key 5G 79
Farriers Cft. DE7: Ilk 4G 27
Farriers Grn. NG11: Clftn 3A 66
Farringdon Cl. NG16: Nuth 4D 30
Farrington Way NG16: Eastw 3A 16
Far Row NG5: Bestw 2E 33
Far Rye NG8: Woll 3F 43
Far St. NG11: Rudd 4A 78
Farthing Ct. NG10: Long E 6D 62
The Farthings NG7: Lent 5C 44
Farwells Cl. NG6: Bas 4A 32
Faulconbridge Cl. NG6: Bulw 1H 31
Fearn Chase NG4: Car 2G 47
Fearn Cl. DE72: Brea 6C 62
Fearnleigh Dr. NG6: Bas 5B 32
Featherstone Cl. NG4: Ged 4F 35
Feignies Ct. NG12: Key .4G 79
Felen Cl. NG5: Bestw 6E 21
Fellbarrow Cl. NG2: West Br 6E 59
Felley Cl. NG15: Huck 6E 7
Fellows Rd. NG9: Bee 4E 55
Fellows Yd. NG12: Plum 6G 69
Fell Side NG5: Woodt 2C 34
Fellside Cl. NG2: Gam 5E 59
Felstead Ct. NG9: Bram .2C 54
Felstead Rd. NG8: Bilb .3G 43
Felton Cl. NG9: Chil 6B 54
Felton Rd. NG2: Nott 2H 57
Felton Way NG5: Arn 3B 22
Fenchurch Cl. NG5: Arn .4E 21
Fenimore Ct. NG12: Rad T 5H 49
Feniton Ct. NG3: Ged 2G 35
Fenman Cl. DE7: Ilk 2B 28
Fenroth Cl. NG6: Bulw 5F 19
Fenton Ct. NG5: Sher 3D 32
Fenton Dr. NG6: Bulw 3A 20
Fenton Rd. NG5: Sher 3D 32
Fenwick Cl. NG8: Brox 5F 31
Fenwick Ct. NG4: Neth .2A 48
Fenwick Rd. NG8: Brox .5F 31
Fergus Cl. NG11: Clftn 5D 66
Ferguson Cl. NG9: Chil .3C 64
Fern Av. NG5: Sher 6F 33
Fern Cl. NG9: Bram 4B 54
Fern Cres. NG16: Eastw .2A 16
Ferndale Cl. NG9: Atten .3D 64
Ferndale Gro. NG3: Nott 3D 46
Ferndale Rd. NG3: Nott .3D 46
Ferndene Dr. NG10: Long E 6C 62
Ferngill Cl. NG2: Nott 2F 57

Fernilee Cl. DE7: West H 1C 38
Fern Lea Av. NG12: Cotg 3E 71
Fernleigh Av. NG3: Mapp 5D 34
Fernwood Commercial Workshops
  NG16: Want 5A 18
Fernwood Cres. NG8: Woll 5C 42
Fernwood Dr. NG12: Rad T 5F 49
  NG16: Want 5A 18
Ferny Hollow Cl. NG5: Top V 5C 20
Ferrers Wlk. NG3: Nott 2H 5 (4A 46)
Ferriby Ter. NG2: Nott 2G 57
Ferry Lodge NG4: Car 3G 47
Ferryman Rd. NG11: Wilf 5E 57
Festival Cres. NG9: Trow 5E 41
Festival Rd. DE7: Kirk H .4G 39
Festus Cl. NG3: Nott 3H 45
Festus St. NG4: Neth 2A 48
The Field DE75: Ship 6E 15
Field Av. NG15: Huck 1D 18
Field Cl. DE72: Brea 6B 62
  NG2: West Br 2E 59
  NG4: Ged 5H 35
  NG9: Chil 1A 64
Field Dr. DE7: Smal 5A 14
Fieldfare Cl. NG9: Bram .5C 54
Fieldfare Rd. NG12: Cotg 6G 61
Field Ho. Cl. NG8: Woll .4D 42
Field La. NG9: Chil 1A 64
  NG14: Woodbo .1C 24
Field Maple Dr. NG7: Hys G 1C 44
Field Rd. DE7: Ilk 3B 40
Fields Av. NG11: Rudd 2G 77
Flds. Farm Rd. NG10: Long E 2E 73
Fields Vw. NG12: Cotg 1E 71
Field Vw. NG12: Rad T 5H 49
Fieldway NG11: Wilf 1F 67
Fiennes Cres. NG7: Nott 6A 4 (6E 45)
Fifth Av. NG7: Nott 5A 56
Filey St. NG6: Bulw 5A 20
Finch Cl. NG7: Lent 3D 56
Finchley Cl. NG11: Clftn .4A 66
Findern Grn. NG3: Nott .3C 46
Fingal Cl. NG11: Clftn 4D 66
Finsbury Av. NG2: Nott .5B 46
Finsbury Pk. Cl. NG2: West Br 6G 57
Finsbury Rd. NG5: Arn 3E 21
  NG9: Bram 6C 42
Firbank Ct. NG9: Chil 6B 54
Firbeck Rd. NG5: Arn 5C 22
  NG8: Woll 5B 42
Fir Cl. NG6: Bulw 6F 19
  NG15: Huck 1H 19
Fircroft Av. NG8: Bilb 1E 43
Fircroft Dr. NG15: Huck 6C 6
Firdale NG12: Cotg 2G 71
Firecrest Way NG6: Bas .3B 32
Firefly Cl. NG13: Newt 2B 50
The Fire Ho. NG5: Arn 1A 34
Firfield Av. DE72: Brea 5A 62
The Firs NG5: Sher 4H 33
Firs Av. NG9: Bee 4F 55
Firsby Rd. NG8: Brox 5F 31
Firs Ho. NG5: Sher 4H 33
Firs Rd. NG12: Edwal 6D 58
Firs St. NG10: Long E 3C 72
First Av.
  DE7: Ilk 2B 40
  DE72: Ris 6B 52
  NG4: Car 2E 47
  NG4: Colw 4G 47
  NG4: Ged 6H 35
  NG6: Bulw 6H 19
  NG7: Hys G 1F 45
  NG7: Nott 5A 56
Firth Cl. NG5: Arn 4E 23
Firth Dr. NG9: Chil 3C 64
Firth Way NG6: Bulw 5G 19
Fir Wlk. NG3: Nott 2D 46
Fisher Av. NG5: Woodt 2B 34
Fisher Ct. DE7: Ilk 4B 28
Fisher Ga. NG1: Nott 5G 5 (5H 45)
Fisher La. NG13: Bing 5E 51
Fisher St. NG7: Bas 1D 44
                  (not continuous)
Fishpond Dr. NG7: Nott 6A 4 (6E 45)
Fitzgerald Ct. NG15: Huck 5G 7
Five Acres NG11: Wilf 1E 67
Flagholme NG12: Cotg 3F 71
Flake La. DE7: Stant D 2A 52
Flamingo Ct. NG7: Lent .1E 57
Flamstead Av. DE75: Los 1A 14
  NG4: Lamb 6B 24
Flamstead Rd. DE7: Ilk .6B 28
Flamsteed Rd. NG8: Stre 6D 30
The Flatts NG9: Chil 6B 54
Flatts La. NG14: Calv 1G 11
Flawborough Ri. NG2: West Br 2G 67
Flawforth Av. NG11: Rudd 6H 67
Flawforth La. NG11: Rudd 6H 67
Flaxendale NG12: Cotg .3G 71

Flaxton Way. NG5: Top V 6D **20**
Fleam Rd. NG11: Clftn 1C **66**
Fleeman Gro. NG2: West Br 2C **58**
Fleet Cl. NG7: Radf 3B **44**
Fleetway Cl. NG16: Newth 4D **16**
Fleetwith Cl. NG2: West Br 6E **59**
Fleming Cl. NG16: Want 5A **18**
Fleming Dr. NG4: Car 2E **47**
Fleming Gdns. NG11: Clftn 4A **66**
Fleming Ho. NG3: Mapp 5B **34**
Fletcher Ga. NG1: Nott 4E **5** (5G **45**)
Fletcher Rd. NG9: Bee 4G **55**
Fletcher St. DE75: Hea 3C **14**
    NG10: Long E .5F **63**
Fletcher Ter. NG3: Mapp 5A **34**
Fletton Ct. NG3: Nott 2C **46**
Flewitt Gdns. NG3: Nott 1H **5** (3A **46**)
Flinders Orchard NG12: Key 5G **79**
Flintham Dr. NG5: Sher 3F **33**
Flixton Rd. NG16: Kimb 6H **17**
Florence Av. NG10: Long E 4H **63**
Florence Boot Cl. NG7: Nott 3H **55**
Florence Ct. DE7: Ilk 6B **28**
Florence Cres. NG4: Ged 1B **48**
Florence Gro. NG3: Nott 2C **46**
Florence Rd.
    NG2: West Br .3C **58**
    NG3: Nott 6C **34**
    NG4: Ged 6B **36**
Florence St. NG15: Huck 6G **7**
Florey Wlk. NG11: Clftn 5A **66**
Florimel Ct. NG5: Arn 6G **21**
Florin Gdns. NG10: Long E 6C **62**
Flowers Cl. NG5: Arn 1D **34**
Flying Horse Wlk. NG1: Nott 4E **5** (5G **45**)
Foljambe Ter. NG3: Nott 2G **5** (4H **45**)
Folkton Gdns. NG3: Mapp 6B **34**
Forbes Cl. NG10: Long E 2G **73**
Forbes Hole Local Nature Reserve 2G **73**
Ford Av. DE75: Los 1A **14**
Fordham Grn. NG11: Clftn 5C **66**
Ford St. NG7: Bas 6E **33**
Ford St. Nth. NG7: Bas 6E **33**
Foredrift Cl. NG11: Goth 6G **75**
Forest Cl. NG12: Cotg 2E **71**
Forest Cotts. NG6: Bulw 4B **20**
Forest Ct. NG7: Radf 3E **45**
Forester Cl. NG9: Chil 1C **64**
Forester Gro. NG4: Car 2F **47**
Forester Rd. NG3: Nott 1C **46**
Forester St. NG4: Neth 2A **48**
FOREST FIELDS 1E **45**
Forest Gro. NG1: Nott 2F **45**
    NG7: Radf 3E **45**
Forest La. NG15: Pap 1C **8**
The Forest Park & Ride 2E **45**
Forest Rd. NG13: Bing 5C **50**
    NG14: Calv 3F **11**
Forest Rd. E. NG1: Nott 3E **45**
Forest Rd. W. NG7: Radf 1A **4** (3E **45**)
The Forest Stop (NET) 2E **45**
Forest Vw. Dr. NG15: Huck 4E **7**
The Forge NG9: Trow 4D **40**
Forge Av. NG14: Calv 3H **11**
Forge Hill NG9: Chil 1D **64**
Forge Mill Gro. NG15: Huck 6B **8**
Forman Ho. NG5: Sher 6F **33**
Forman St. NG1: Nott 3D **4** (4G **45**)
Forster St. NG7: Radf 3C **44**
    (not continuous)
Forsythia Gdns. NG7: Lent 1C **56**
Forum Rd. NG5: Bestw 1C **32**
Fosbrooke Dr. NG10: Long E 2F **73**
The Fosse NG12: Cotg, Crop Bi, Owt 6H **71**
    (not continuous)
Fosse Rd. NG13: Bing, Newt, Saxon 5B **50**
    NG13: Car C, East B 1E **51**
Fosse Wlk. NG12: Cotg 3G **71**
Fosse Way NG13: Bing 6A **50**
Foster Av. NG9: Bee 5F **55**
Foster Dr. NG5: Sher 3H **33**
Fosters La. NG13: Bing 5F **51**
Fothergill Ct. NG3: Mapp P 2G **45**
Fountain Dale Ct. NG3: Nott 2H **45**
Fountains Cl. NG2: West Br 5D **58**
Fountains Ct. NG9: Bee 5G **55**
Fountayne Cl. NG15: Huck 1F **7**
Fourth Av. NG4: Car 1D **46**
    NG7: Hys G 1F **45**
    NG7: Nott 5A **56**
Fowler M. NG16: Want 6A **18**
Fowler St. NG3: Mapp P 1H **45**
Fox Cl. NG10: Long E 2F **73**
Fox Covert NG4: Colw 5H **47**
Fox Covert La. NG11: Clftn 5H **65**
Fox Covert Local Nature Reserve 6F **63**
Foxearth Av. NG11: Clftn 3E **67**
Fox End NG5: Sher 5H **33**
Foxes Cl. NG7: Nott 6A **4**
Foxglove Cl. NG15: Huck 1A **20**

Foxglove Rd. NG16: Newth 5D **16**
The Foxgloves NG13: Bing 6D **50**
Foxglove Way NG12: Cotg 6G **61**
Fox Gro. NG5: Bas 4C **32**
Fox Gro. Ct. NG5: Bas 4C **32**
Foxhall Rd. NG7: Hys G 1E **45**
Foxhill NG12: Cotg 3E **71**
Foxhill Cl. NG4: Car 1G **47**
Foxhill Rd. NG4: Car 1E **47**
    NG14: Bur J 2E **37**
Foxhill Rd. Central NG4: Car 1D **46**
Foxhill Rd. E. NG4: Car 1F **47**
Foxhill Rd. W. NG4: Car 1C **46**
Foxhollies Gro. NG5: Sher 4F **33**
Foxley Rd. DE7: Ilk 2B **28**
Fox Mdw. NG15: Huck 5F **7**
Fox Rd. NG2: West Br 2B **58**
Foxton Cl. DE7: Ilk 4G **27**
    NG6: Bulw 5F **19**
Foxwood Gdns. NG8: Bilb 2G **43**
Foxwood Gro. NG14: Calv 4H **11**
Foxwood La. NG14: Woodbo 5H **11**
Fradley Cl. NG6: Bulw 3A **20**
Frampton Rd. NG8: Bilb 2G **43**
Frances Gro. NG15: Huck 2H **7**
Francis Gro. NG6: Bas 4C **32**
Francis Mill NG9: Bee 4F **55**
Francis St. NG7: Radf 1H **47**
Francis St. NG7: Radf 1A **4** (3E **45**)
    (not continuous)
Franklin Cl. NG5: Arn 5G **21**
Franklin Dr. NG12: Toll 4F **69**
Franklin Ho. NG3: Mapp 5B **34**
    (off Ockbrook Dr.)
Franklyn Gdns. NG8: Aspl 3A **44**
    NG12: Key 3G **79**
Fraser Cres. NG4: Car 6D **34**
Fraser Rd. NG2: Nott 3H **57**
    NG4: Car 5D **34**
Fraser Sq. NG4: Car 6D **34**
Frearson Farm Ct. NG16: Eastw 4B **16**
Freckingham St. NG1: Nott 3H **5** (4H **45**)
Freda Av. NG4: Ged 5F **35**
Freda Cl. NG4: Ged 4F **35**
Frederic Av. DE75: Hea 6D **14**
Frederick Av. DE7: Ilk 4C **40**
    NG4: Car 2D **46**
Frederick Gro. NG7: Lent 6D **44**
Frederick Rd. NG9: Stfrd 4F **53**
Frederick St. NG10: Long E 6H **63**
Freeland Cl. NG9: Toton 2H **63**
Freemans Rd. NG4: Car 1A **48**
Freemans Ter. NG4: Car 1H **47**
Freemantle Wlk. NG5: Top V 5C **20**
Freeston Dr. NG6: Bulw 5F **19**
Freeth Ct. NG2: Nott 1B **58**
Freeth St. NG2: Nott 1A **58**
Freiston St. NG7: Hys G 2C **44**
Fremount Dr. NG8: Bilb 3F **43**
French St. DE7: Ilk 3C **40**
Fretwell St. NG7: Hys G 2C **44**
Friar La. NG1: Nott 5C **4** (5F **45**)
Friars Ct. DE7: Kirk H 3G **39**
    NG7: Nott 6A **4** (6E **45**)
Friar St. NG7: Lent 1C **56**
    NG10: Long E .6F **63**
Friar Wlk. NG13: Newt 1C **50**
The Friary NG7: Lent 1C **56**
Friary Cl. NG7: Lent 1C **56**
Friday La. NG4: Ged 5H **35**
Friesland Dr. NG10: Sand 6B **52**
Frinton Rd. NG8: Brox 6E **31**
Frisby Av. NG10: Long E 1G **73**
Frobisher Gdns. NG5: Arn 1H **33**
Frogmore St. NG1: Nott 1D **4** (3G **45**)
Frome Gdns. NG13: Bing 6D **50**
Front St. NG5: Arn 5H **21**
Frost Av. NG16: Lang M 1E **15**
Fryar Rd. NG16: Eastw 1B **16**
Fulforth St. NG1: Nott 1D **4** (3G **45**)
Fullwood Av. DE7: Ilk 6A **28**
Fullwood St. DE7: Ilk 6A **28**
Fulwood Cl. NG9: Chil 1C **64**
Fulwood Cres. NG8: Aspl 1H **43**
Fulwood Dr. NG10: Long E 6C **62**
Funky Pots
    West Bridgford 5A **58**
Furleys Cotts. NG16: Lowd 2H **25**
Furlong Av. NG5: Arn 5A **22**
Furlong Cl. NG9: Stfrd 3F **53**
Furlong Ct. NG5: Arn 5A **22**
Furlong Pl. NG2: Nott 5C **46**
Furlong St. NG5: Arn 6A **22**
Furnace La. DE75: Los 1A **14**
Furnace Rd. DE7: Ilk 2D **40**
Furness Cl. NG2: West Br 4D **58**
Furness Rd. NG6: Bas 4A **32**
Furzebrook Rd. NG4: Colw 3G **47**
Furze Gdns. NG3: Nott 2H **45**

Fylde Cl. NG9: Toton 3G **63**
Fylingdale Way NG8: Woll 6B **42**

G

The Gables NG3: Mapp 3C **34**
    NG7: Bas 6E **33**
Gabor Cl. NG11: Clftn 5A **66**
Gabor Ct. NG11: Clftn 4A **66**
Gabrielle Cl. NG6: Bulw 3B **32**
Gadd St. NG7: Radf 3D **44**
Gadsby Cl. DE7: Ilk 5C **40**
Gadwall Cres. NG7: Lent 1E **57**
Gainsborough Cl. NG9: Stfrd 5G **53**
    NG10: Long E .2G **73**
Gainsborough Ct. NG9: Bee 4G **55**
Gainsford Cl. NG5: Bestw 2D **32**
Gainsford Cres. NG5: Bestw 2D **32**
Gala Bingo
    Nottingham St Anns 2F **5** (4H **45**)
    Nottingham Top Valley 1C **32**
Gala Way NG5: Bestw 1C **32**
The Galeb NG7: Lent 1C **56**
    (off Leen Ct.)
Gale Cl. NG9: Bee .5H **55**
Galena Dr. NG3: Nott 2C **46**
The Gallery NG7: Nott 6C **4** (6F **45**)
GALLOWS INN 3C **40**
Gallows Inn Cl. DE7: Ilk 3C **40**
Gallows Inn Ind. Est. DE7: Ilk 3D **40**
Galway Rd. NG5: Arn 5H **21**
    NG7: Lent 6D **44**
Gamble St. NG7: Radf 2A **4** (3E **45**)
GAMSTON 4E **59**
Gamston Cres. NG5: Sher 4G **33**
Gamston District Cen. 5E **59**
Gamston Lings Bar Rd.
    NG2: Gam 4F **59**
    NG12: Toll, Edwal 4C **68**
Gamston Lodge NG4: Car 3G **47**
Ganton Cl. NG3: Mapp 6B **34**
Garden Av. DE7: Ilk 4B **40**
    NG4: Car 2F **47**
Garden City NG4: Car 1G **47**
Gardendale Av. NG11: Clftn 4B **66**
Gardeners Cl. NG4: Car 6F **35**
    NG4: Car 4D **50**
    NG15: Huck 4F **7**
Gardeners Wlk. NG5: Sher 3D **32**
Gardenia Cl. NG9: Toton 3A **64**
Gardenia Cres. NG3: Mapp 5D **34**
Gardenia Gro. NG3: Mapp 5D **34**
Garden Rd. NG13: Bing 5D **50**
    NG15: Huck 4F **7**
    NG16: Eastw 2B **16**
The Gardens DE75: Los 1A **14**
Gardens Ct. NG2: West Br 4C **58**
Garden St. NG7: Radf 4D **44**
Garfield Cl. NG9: Stfrd 2G **53**
Garfield Ct. NG7: Radf 4D **44**
Garfield Rd. NG7: Radf 3C **44**
    (not continuous)
Garforth Cl. NG8: Bas 1C **44**
The Garland NG7: Lent 1C **56**
    (off Leen Ct.)
Garner Rd. NG16: Gilt 6D **16**
Garners Hill NG1: Nott 5E **5** (5H **45**)
Garnet Ct. NG3: Nott 2H **5** (4A **46**)
Garnet St. NG4: Neth 2H **47**
Garnett Av. DE75: Hea 3D **14**
Garrett Gro. NG11: Clftn 3A **66**
Garsdale Cl. NG2: Gam 5E **59**
Garsdale Dr. NG11: Wilf 2E **67**
Garton Cl. NG6: Bulw 2H **31**
    NG9: Chil 6B **54**
Gas St. NG10: Sand 5E **53**
Gatcombe Cl. NG12: Rad T 6G **49**
Gatcombe Gro. NG10: Sand 2C **62**
Gateford Cl. NG9: Bram 1C **54**
Gatehouse Ct. NG9: Chil 6D **54**
Gateside Rd. NG2: Nott 2E **57**
Gatling St. NG7: Radf 4C **44**
Gaul St. NG6: Bulw 6H **19**
Gauntley Ct. NG7: Bas 1C **44**
Gauntley St. NG7: Bas 1C **44**
Gautries Cl. NG5: Top V 5E **21**
Gavin M. NG7: Hys G 1D **44**
Gawthorne St. NG7: Bas 6D **32**
Gayhurst Grn. NG6: Bulw 2C **32**
Gayhurst Rd. NG6: Bulw 2C **32**
Gaynor Ct. NG8: Bilb 3H **43**
Gayrigg Ct. NG9: Chil 6B **54**
Gayton Cl. NG8: Bilb 1D **42**
Gayton Rd. DE7: Ilk 1H **39**
Gaywood Cl. NG11: Clftn 5D **66**
GEDLING 5H **35**
Gedling Country Pk. 2H **35**
Gedling Country Pk. Visitor Cen. 2G **35**
Gedling Crematorium 4F **23**

Gedling Gro. NG5: Arn 6B 22
   NG7: Radf 1A 4 (3E 45)
Gedling Rd. NG4: Car 1H 47
   NG5: Arn 6B 22
Gedling St. NG1: Nott 4G 5 (5H 45)
Gedney Av. NG3: Nott 1B 46
Gell Rd. NG9: Chil 1A 64
Genesis Pk. NG7: Radf 4B 44
George Av. NG9: Bee 6F 55
   NG10: Long E 4H 63
George Grn. Ct. NG2: Nott 5B 46
   (off Sneinton Blvd.)
George Grn. Way NG7: Nott 3B 56
George Rd. NG2: West Br 4A 58
   NG4: Car 2G 47
George's La. NG5: Calv, Woodbo 6D 10
   NG14: Calv 6D 10
George St. NG1: Nott 3F 5 (4H 45)
   NG5: Arn 1A 34
   NG15: Huck 3G 7
   NG16: Lang M 2F 15
George St. Trad. Ho. NG1: Nott 3F 5 (4H 45)
Georgia Dr. NG5: Arn 3A 22
Georgina Rd. NG9: Bee 6F 55
Geraldine Cl. NG5: Bestw 5F 21
Gerrard Cl. NG5: Arn 3E 21
Gertrude Rd. NG2: West Br 3C 58
Gervase Gdns. NG11: Clftn 3A 66
Ghost Ho. La. NG9: Chil 6B 54
   (not continuous)
Gibbons Av. NG9: Stfrd 4F 53
Gibbons St. NG7: Lent 3C 56
Gibb St. NG10: Long E 6G 63
Gibson Rd. NG7: Hys G 1E 45
Gifford Gdns. NG2: Nott 1G 57
Gilbert Av. NG11: Goth 6H 75
Gilbert Blvd. NG5: Arn 6E 23
Gilbert Cl. NG5: Bestw 2E 33
Gilbert Gdns. NG3: Nott 3C 46
Gilbert St. NG15: Huck 4G 7
   (not continuous)
Gilead St. NG6: Bulw 6H 19
Giles Av. NG2: West Br 5H 57
Giles Ct. NG2: West Br 4A 58
Gillercomb Cl. NG2: West Br 6F 59
Gilliver La. NG12: C'ton 3D 75
Gillotts Cl. NG13: Bing 4E 51
Gillott St. DE75: Hea 5A 14
Gill St. NG1: Nott 1C 4 (3E 45)
Gilpet Av. NG16: Nuth 1B 46
GILTBROOK 5E 17
Giltbrook Cres. NG16: Gilt 5E 17
Giltbrook Ind. Pk. NG16: Gilt 6E 17
Giltbrook Retail Pk. 6E 17
Gilt Hill NG16: Kimb 6F 17
Giltway NG16: Gilt 6E 17
Gimson Cl. DE7: Ilk 4G 27
Gin Cl. Way NG16: Aws, Gilt 1E 29
Gipsy La. NG11: Clftn 3A 66
   NG15: Huck 1D 6
Girton Rd. NG5: Sher 4E 33
Gisburn Cl. NG11: Wilf 1E 67
The Glade NG11: Clftn 6C 66
Glade Av. NG8: Woll 4A 44
The Glade Bus. Cen. NG5: Bestw 1C 32
Gladehill Rd. NG5: Arn, Bestw 6G 21
The Glades NG5: Top V 5D 20
Gladstone Av. DE75: Hea 3C 14
   NG11: Goth 6H 75
Gladstone Dr. DE7: Ilk 2B 40
   DE75: Hea 3C 14
   NG4: Car 2F 47
   NG7: Bas, Hys G 1D 44
   (not continuous)
   NG9: Bee 6E 55
   NG10: Long E 1F 73
   NG16: Lang M 2G 15
Gladys St. NG7: Bas 6E 33
Glaisdale Dr. E. NG8: Bilb 3D 42
Glaisdale Dr. W. NG8: Bilb 4D 42
Glaisdale Pk. Ind. Est. NG8: Bilb 4D 42
Glaisdale Parkway NG8: Bilb 4D 42
Glamis Rd. NG5: Sher 5E 33
Glanton Way NG5: Arn 3C 22
Glapton La. NG11: Clftn 3B 66
Glapton Rd. NG2: Nott 2G 57
Glaramara Cl. NG2: Nott 2F 57
The Glasshouse NG3: Nott 2F 5 (4G 45)
Glasshouse St. NG1: Nott 2E 5 (4G 45)
The Glebe NG16: Coss 3D 28
Glebe Cotts. NG11: Wilf 3F 57
Glebe Cres. DE7: Ilk 2C 40
   DE7: Stly 3A 38
Glebe Dr. NG14: Bur J 4D 36
Glebe Farm Cl. NG2: West Br 1G 67
Glebe Farm Vw. NG4: Ged 4H 35
Glebe La. NG12: Rad T 6F 49
Glebe Rd. NG2: West Br 4B 58
   NG4: Car 5E 35
   NG16: Nuth 1C 30

Glebe St. NG9: Bee 5E 55
   NG15: Huck 3G 7
The Glen NG11: Clftn 4C 66
Glen Av. NG16: Eastw 4D 16
Glenbrook NG12: Cotg 2G 71
Glenbrook Cres. NG8: Bilb 2G 43
Glencairn Dr. NG8: Bilb 1G 43
Glencairn M. NG8: Bilb 1G 43
Glencoe Rd. NG11: Clftn 4E 67
Glencoyne Rd. NG11: Clftn 5C 66
Glencross Cl. NG2: West Br 2E 59
Glendale Cl. NG4: Car 5F 35
Glendale Ct. NG9: Chil 2E 65
Glendale Gdns. NG5: Arn 6B 22
Glendoe Gro. NG13: Bing 5C 50
Glendon Dr. NG5: Sher 4E 33
   NG15: Huck 6G 7
Glendon Rd. DE7: Kirk H 5G 39
Gleneagles Ct. NG12: Edwal 2D 68
Gleneagles Dr. NG5: Arn 4D 22
Glenfield Av. NG16: Kimb 6F 17
Glenfield Rd. NG10: Long E 2F 73
Glen Helen NG4: Colw 3H 47
Glenlivet Gdns. NG11: Clftn 4D 66
Glenloch Dr. NG11: Clftn 5D 66
Glenmore Rd. NG2: West Br 5D 58
Glenorchy Cres. NG5: Top V 5C 20
Glen Parva Av. NG5: Redh 4A 22
Glenridding Cl. NG2: West Br 6F 59
Glen Rd. NG14: Bur J 2E 37
Glensford Gdns. NG5: Top V 3C 20
Glenside NG5: Woodt 2D 34
Glenside Rd. NG9: Bram 2C 54
Glenstone Ct. NG7: Hys G 1D 44
Glentworth Rd. NG7: Radf 3C 44
Glenwood Av. NG8: Woll 5D 42
Glins Rd. NG5: Top V 5D 20
Gloucester Av. NG7: Lent 5C 44
   NG9: Bee 6F 55
   NG10: Sand 1C 62
   NG16: Nuth 4F 31
Glover Av. NG8: Woll 5D 42
Glover Ho. NG5: Arn 1C 34
   (off Derwent Cres.)
Glue La. DE75: Los 3A 14
Goatchurch Ct. NG5: Top V 5E 21
Goathland Cl. NG5: Bestw 5F 21
Godber Cl. NG16: Gilt 5C 16
Godber Rd. NG15: Huck 6E 7
Goddard Ct. NG3: Arn 1E 35
Godfrey Dr. DE7: Kirk H 4G 39
Godfrey La. NG7: Lent 5D 44
Godfrey St. DE75: Hea 4C 14
   (not continuous)
   NG4: Neth 3A 48
Godkin Dr. NG16: Lang M 1E 15
Goldcrest Cl. NG13: Bing 6G 51
Goldcrest Rd. NG6: Cin 4H 31
Goldenbrook Cl. DE72: Brea 6A 62
Goldham Rd. NG8: Stre 1D 42
Goldrill Cl. NG2: Gam 4D 58
Goldsmith Ct. NG1: Nott 2C 4
Goldsmith St. NG1: Nott 2C 4 (4F 45)
Goldswong Ter. NG3: Nott 2G 45
Golf Cl. NG6: Bulw 3A 20
Golf Club Rd. DE7: Stant D 2C 52
Golf Course Rd. NG12: Stant W 5B 80
Golf Rd. NG12: Rad T 6G 49
Gonalston La. NG14: Epp 6H 13
Goodall Cres. NG15: Huck 5A 8
Goodall St. NG7: Hys G 2D 44
Goodhill Ct. DE7: Ilk 5D 40
Goodliffe St. NG7: Hys G 1D 44
Goodman Cl. NG16: Gilt 5E 17
Goodwin Cl. NG10: Sand 5C 52
Goodwin Dr. NG16: Kimb 1G 29
Goodwin St. NG7: Radf 1A 4 (3E 45)
Goodwood Av. NG5: Arn 5A 22
Goodwood Cres. DE7: Kirk H 5H 39
Goodwood Dr. NG9: Toton 3H 63
Goodwood Rd. NG8: Woll 5D 42
Goole Rd. DE7: Kirk H 4H 39
Goosedale La. NG6: Bestw V 5A 6
Goose Ga. NG1: Nott 4F 5 (5H 45)
   NG12: Cotg 2E 71
Gordon Cl. NG9: Atten 3D 64
Gordon Gro. NG7: Bas 6D 32
Gordon Ri. NG3: Mapp 5A 34
Gordon Rd. NG2: West Br 4B 58
   NG3: Nott 3A 46
   NG14: Bur J 2G 37
Gordon Sq. NG2: West Br 4B 58
Gordon St. DE7: Ilk 6B 28
   NG6: Bas 3B 32
Gorman Ct. NG5: Arn 6D 22
Gorse Cl. NG10: Long E 3D 62
   NG14: Calv 4F 11
   NG16: Newth 4D 16
Gorse Ct. NG6: Bulw 2C 32
Gorse Rd. NG12: Key 4F 79

Gorse Wlk. NG3: Nott 2D 46
Gorsey Rd. NG3: Mapp P 2H 45
Gosforth Av. DE7: Ilk 1A 28
Gosforth Ct. NG2: Nott 2H 57
Goshawk Rd. DE7: Ilk 6C 40
GOTHAM 6H 75
Gotheridge Dr. NG4: Ged 3F 35
Gothic Cl. NG6: Bas 3C 32
Gough Rd. NG10: Long E 1E 73
Goverton Sq. NG6: Bulw 2B 32
Gowan Cl. NG9: Chil 3C 64
Goyden Cl. NG5: Top V 5E 21
Grace Av. NG9: Bee 5H 55
Grace Cres. DE75: Hea 3D 14
Grace Dr. NG8: Aspl 1B 44
Grafton Av. NG5: Woodt 2A 34
Grafton Cl. NG7: Radf 3A 4 (4E 45)
Graham St. DE7: Ilk 2B 40
   NG7: Radf 4D 44
Grainger Av. NG2: West Br 2A 68
Graingers Ter. NG15: Huck 5H 7
Grainger St. NG2: Nott 1A 58
Grampian Dr. NG5: Arn 3F 21
Grampian Way NG10: Long E 5C 62
Granby Cl. NG13: Bing 5D 50
Granby St. DE7: Ilk 5A 28
Granby Vs. NG2: Nott 5B 46
Grandfield Av. NG12: Rad T 5F 49
Grandfield Cres. NG12: Rad T 5F 49
Grandfield St. DE75: Los 1A 14
The Grange DE7: Smal 5A 14
Grange Av. DE72: Brea 5A 62
   NG9: Bee 5F 55
   NG11: Rudd 5F 67
Grange Cl. NG4: Lamb 6C 24
   NG11: Wilf 3F 57
Grange Ct. NG11: Rudd 3G 67
Grange Cres. NG4: Ged 4H 35
Grange Dr. NG10: Long E 5H 63
Grange Est. NG16: Coss 6F 29
Grange Farm NG2: Gam 4E 59
Grange Farm Cl. NG9: Toton 4A 64
Grange Farm Cotts. NG14: Lowd 2F 25
Grange Gdns. DE75: Los 2A 14
   NG15: Pap 2B 8
Grangelea Gdns. NG9: Bram 3B 54
Grange La. NG11: Rudd 3G 67
Grangemoor NG15: Pap 2B 8
GRANGE PARK 5A 64
Grange Pk. NG2: West Br 6D 58
   NG10: Long E 5H 63
Grange Rd. NG5: Woodt 3A 34
   NG6: Bas 4B 32
   NG10: Long E 5H 63
   NG12: Edwal 1C 68
   NG13: Bing 5F 51
Grange Vw. NG16: Eastw 2B 16
Grange Vw. Rd. NG4: Ged 5H 35
Grangewood Av. DE7: Ilk 2B 40
Grangewood Ct. NG8: Woll 6C 42
Grangewood Rd. NG8: Woll 6C 42
Grannis Dr. NG8: Bilb 1G 43
Grantham Cl. NG16: Gilt 6E 17
Grantham Rd. NG12: Rad T 1D 60
   NG13: Bing 5F 51
Grantleigh Cl. NG8: Woll 4F 43
Granton Av. NG11: Clftn 5D 66
Grant St. NG7: Radf 4D 44
Granville Av. NG10: Long E 4F 63
Granville Ct. NG3: Nott 4B 46
Granville Cres. NG12: Rad T 1E 61
Granville Gro. NG3: Nott 4B 46
Grasby Wlk. NG11: Clftn 3B 66
Grasmere Av. NG8: Aspl 5A 32
Grasmere Ct. NG15: Huck 3F 7
Grasmere Gdns. NG11: Goth 5H 75
Grasmere Rd. NG9: Bram 3D 54
   NG10: Long E 3D 62
Grasmere St. NG10: Sand 6D 52
Grassmoor Cl. NG3: Nott 1B 46
Grassingdale Cl. NG4: Car 5F 35
Grassington Rd. NG8: Aspl 3B 44
Grassmere NG12: Cotg 2G 71
Grass St. DE7: Ilk 4A 28
Grassy La. NG9: Bee 6G 55
Gravelly Hollow NG14: Calv 1B 10
Graveney Gdns. NG5: Arn 1D 34
Graylands Rd. NG8: Bilb 2D 42
Grayson M. NG9: Chil 3B 64
Graystones Cl. NG2: West Br 6E 59
Grazingfield NG11: Wilf 1E 67
GREASLEY 2G 17
Greasley Av. NG16: Newth 3E 17
Greasley Sports & Comm. Cen. 3D 16
Greasley St. NG6: Bulw 6H 19
Great Central Railway
   Ruddington Station 2G 77
Great Central Railway (Nottingham) Mus. 2G 77
Gt. Freeman St. NG3: Nott 1E 5 (3G 45)
Gt. Hoggett Dr. NG9: Chil 5A 54

Gt. Northern Cl. DE7: Ilk 5B 28
The Gt. Northern Cl. NG2: Nott 6G 5 (6H 45)
Gt. Northern Cotts. NG15: Huck 2H 7
Gt. Northern Rd. NG16: Eastw 3H 15
Gt. Northern Way NG4: Neth 3B 48
Greaves Cl. NG5: Arn 2D 34
NG8: Stre 6D 30
Grebe Cl. NG14: Stoke B 2C 48
Greek St. NG7: Radf 4E 45
The Green DE72: Brea 5A 62
NG4: Car 1E 47
NG9: Chil 1E 65
NG11: Rudd 1G 77
NG12: Rad T 6E 49
NG14: Lowd 3F 25
Green Acre NG8: Woll 4B 42
Greenacre NG12: Edwal 1D 68
NG14: Bur J 2E 37
Greenacre Av. NG4: Car 1E 47
Greenacres Cl. NG16: Newth 3E 17
Greenacres Pk. NG2: West Br 2F 59
Green App. NG4: Car 1E 47
Green Av. NG4: Neth 2A 48
Greenbank NG4: Car 3F 47
Greenbank Ct. NG5: Sher 5G 33
Greenbanks NG5: Woodt 3A 34
Greenburn Cl. NG2: Gam 5F 59
Green Cl. NG7: Nott 1A 56
NG12: Key 3H 79
NG15: Huck 6A 8
Green Ct. NG13: Bing 4E 51
Greencroft NG11: Clftn 2D 66
Greendale Gdns. NG8: Bilb 1H 43
Greendale Rd. NG3: Nott 3E 47
NG5: Arn 1B 34
Greenfield Gro. NG4: Car 1D 46
Greenfields NG16: Lang M 1E 15
Greenfields Dr. NG12: Cotg 3F 71
Greenfield St. NG7: Nott 2B 56
Greenford Cl. NG16: Nuth 4E 31
Greengage Rd. NG12: Cotg 6G 61
Greengates Av. NG3: Mapp 4B 34
The Grove DE72: Brea 5B 62
NG5: Sher 5F 33
NG7: Radf 3D 44
NG14: Calv 4A 12
Greenhalgh Cres. DE7: Ilk 5A 28
Greenhill Cres. NG4: Car 3G 47
Greenhill Ri. NG4: Car 2G 47
Greenhill Rd. NG4: Car 3G 47
Greenhills Av. NG16: Eastw 2C 16
Greenhills Rd. NG16: Eastw 2B 16
Greenland Cres. NG9: Chil 1C 64
Green La. DE7: Ilk 2C 40
NG4: Lamb 4B 24
NG11: Clftn 3B 66
Green Leys NG2: West Br 1G 67
The Green M. NG5: Bestw 2E 33
Green Platt NG12: Cotg 2E 71
Greens Ct. DE7: Ilk 5H 27
Greens Farm La. NG4: Ged 5A 36
Greenside Cl. NG10: Long E 6G 63
Greenside Wlk. NG3: Nott 3E 47
Greens La. NG16: Kimb 1H 29
Green St. NG2: Nott 2H 57
NG11: Bart F, Thru 3E 75
Green's Windmill & Science Cen. 5B 46
The Greenway NG10: Sand 5D 52
Greenway Cl. NG12: Rad T 6E 49
Greenwich Av. NG6: Bas 3A 32
Greenwich Pk. Cl. NG2: West Br 6G 57
Greenwood Av. DE7: Ilk 2C 40
NG3: Nott 4F 47
NG15: Huck 3F 7
Greenwood Bonsai Studio 4A 10
Greenwood Ct. NG9: Chil 6D 54
Greenwood Cres. NG4: Car 3G 47
Greenwood Gdns. NG8: Bilb 2C 42
NG11: Rudd 1H 77
Greenwood Rd. NG3: Nott 4C 46
NG4: Car 4E 47
Greenwood Va. NG15: Huck 3E 7
Greet Ct. NG7: Radf 2B 44
Greetwell Cl. NG8: Bilb 3G 43
Gregg Av. DE75: Hea 3D 14
The Gregory NG7: Lent 1C 56
(off Leen Ct.)
Gregory Av. NG3: Mapp 5C 34
NG7: Lent 6D 44
NG16: Lang M 2E 15
Gregory Blvd. NG7: Hys G 2C 44
Gregory Cl. NG9: Stfrd 3H 53
Gregory Ct. NG7: Hys G 1D 44
NG7: Lent 6C 44
NG9: Chil 1B 64
Gregory St. DE7: Ilk 1A 40
NG7: Lent 6C 44
Gregory Street Stop (NET) 1C 56
Gregson Gdns. NG9: Bram 4B 64
Gregson Rd. NG9: Chil 2A 64
Grenay Ct. NG11: Rudd 5F 67
Grenfell Ter. NG6: Bas 3C 32
Grenville Dr. DE7: Ilk 4B 28
NG2: West Br 4H 57

Grenville Dr. NG9: Stfrd 3G 53
Grenville Ri. NG5: Arn 4B 22
Grenville Rd. NG9: Bee 1H 65
Gresham Cl. NG2: West Br 4G 57
Gresham Gdns. NG2: West Br 4H 57
NG5: Woodt 2C 34
Gresham Pk. Rd. NG2: West Br 4G 57
Gresley Dr. NG2: Nott 6B 46
Gresley Rd. DE7: Ilk 6B 28
Gretton Rd. NG3: Mapp 2C 34
Greyfriar Ga. NG1: Nott 6D 4 (6G 45)
Greyfriars Cl. DE75: Hea 4D 14
Greyhound St. NG1: Nott 4E 5 (5G 45)
Grey Mdw. Rd. DE7: Ilk 5A 28
Greymede Av. NG8: Stre 5C 30
Greys Rd. NG5: Woodt 5C 34
Greystoke Dr. NG8: Bilb 2C 42
Greythorn Dr. NG2: West Br 1H 67
Grierson Av. NG5: Bestw 5F 21
Griffiths Way NG15: Huck 5H 7
Griffon Cl. DE7: Ilk 5B 40
Griffon Rd. DE7: Ilk 5B 40
Griffs Hollow NG4: Car 2G 47
Grimesmoor Rd. NG14: Calv 3A 12
Grimsby Ter. NG3: Nott 1E 5 (3G 45)
Grimston Rd. NG7: Radf 3C 44
Grindon Cres. NG6: Bulw 3A 20
Grindslow Av. DE7: West H 1C 38
Grinsbrook NG7: Lent 5C 44
Gripps Comn. NG12: Cotg 3F 71
Grisedale Ct. NG9: Chil 1A 64
Grizedale Gro. NG13: Bing 5B 50
Gritley M. NG2: Nott 1F 57
Groome Av. DE75: Los 1A 14
Grosvenor Av. DE72: Brea 5B 62
NG3: Mapp P 6G 33
NG10: Long E 3C 72
Grosvenor Ct. NG3: Mapp P 1G 45
Grosvenor Rd. NG16: Eastw 2B 16
Grouville Dr. NG5: Woodt 2C 34
Grove Av. NG7: Radf 4E 45
NG9: Chil 5E 55
Grove Cl. NG14: Bur J 2F 37
Grove Ct. NG9: Chil 5D 54
Grove M. NG16: Eastw 4A 16
Grover Av. NG3: Mapp 4C 34
Grove Rd. NG7: Lent 6D 44
NG13: Bing 4F 51
Groveside Cres. NG11: Clftn 2A 66
Grove St. NG9: Bee 6G 55
Grundy St. NG7: Hys G 2C 44
Guardian Ct. NG8: Aspl 1A 44
Guinea Cl. NG10: Long E 6C 62
Gumtree Cl. NG12: Edwal 6C 68
Gunnersbury Way NG16: Nuth 4D 30
Gunthorpe Cl. NG5: Sher 4F 33
Gunthorpe Dr. NG5: Sher 4F 33
Gunthorpe Rd. NG4: Ged 4E 35
Gutersloh Ct. NG9: Stfrd 3H 53
Guy Cl. NG9: Stfrd 5G 53
Gwenbrook Av. NG9: Chil 6E 55
Gwenbrook Rd. NG9: Chil 6E 55
Gwndy Gdns. NG5: Bestw 6E 21
Gypsum Way NG11: Goth 6G 75

H

H2 Fitness
Nottingham 2E 5 (4G 45)
The Habitat NG1: Nott 4F 5
Hackworth Cl. NG16: Newth 2D 16
Hadbury Rd. NG5: Sher 4D 32
Hadden Ct. NG8: Bilb 4D 42
Haddon Cl. DE7: West H 1C 38
DE75: Hea 3A 14
NG4: Car 5F 35
NG15: Huck 5G 7
Haddon Cres. NG9: Chil 2C 64
Haddon Nurseries DE7: Ilk 4A 28
Haddon Rd. NG2: West Br 5B 58
Haddon St. DE7: Ilk 4A 28
NG5: Sher 5F 33
Haddon Way NG10: Long E 3B 72
NG12: Rad T 5G 49
Hadleigh Cl. NG9: Toton 3G 63
Hadley Cl. NG15: Huck 1A 8
Hadley St. DE7: Ilk 4C 40
Hadrian Gdns. NG5: Top V 3E 21
Hadstock Cl. NG10: Sand 1D 62
Hadston Dr. NG5: Arn 3B 22
Hagg La. DE7: D Ab, West H 4B 38
NG14: Epp 6H 13

Hagley Cl. NG3: Nott 3C 46
Haileybury Cres. NG2: West Br 6B 58
Haileybury Rd. NG2: West Br 6B 58
Haise Ct. NG6: Bulw 2F 31
Halberton Dr. NG2: West Br 1H 67
Hales Cl. NG12: Cotg 2E 71
Halfacre Gdns. DE7: Ilk 5B 28
Halfpenny Wlk. NG11: Wilf 5E 57
Halifax Ct. NG8: Stre 5D 30
Halifax Pl. NG1: Nott 5F 5 (5H 45)
Halina Ct. NG9: Bee 4F 55
Hallam Ct. DE7: Ilk 4B 28
HALLAM FIELDS 5C 40
Hallam Flds. Rd. DE7: Ilk 5C 40
Hallam Rd. NG3: Mapp 5C 34
NG9: Bee 5F 55
Hallam's La. NG5: Arn 6B 22
Hallams La. NG9: Chil 1C 64
Hallam Way DE7: West H 1B 38
NG16: Lang M 2G 15
Hall Cl. NG12: Rad T 6E 49
Hall Ct. DE7: West H 2C 38
Hall Cft. NG9: Bee 6F 55
Hallcroft Rd. DE7: Ilk 1B 40
Hall Dr. NG5: Arn 5C 22
NG8: Woll 6E 43
NG9: Chil 6C 54
NG10: Sand 5D 52
NG11: Goth 6G 75
Hall Farm Cl. NG12: Toll 4F 69
Hall Farm Ct. DE7: Stant D 3B 52
NG2: Gam 4A 60
Hallfields NG12: Edwal 2D 68
Hall Gdns. NG9: Bram 3B 54
Hallington Dr. DE75: Hea 4B 14
Hallowell Dr. NG8: Woll 3F 43
Hall Pk. Dr. NG16: Eastw 2A 16
Hall Rd. NG16: Lang M 1G 15
Halls La. NG16: Newth 5C 16
Halls Rd. NG9: Stfrd 5F 53
Hall St. NG5: Sher 4H 33
Hall Vw. Dr. NG8: Bilb 3D 42
Halstead Cl. NG8: Cin 4H 31
NG9: Chil 1C 64
Haltham Wlk. NG11: Clftn 5B 66
Hambledon Dr. NG8: Woll 4H 43
Hambleton Cl. NG10: Long E 4C 62
Hambling Cl. NG6: Bulw 6G 19
The Hamilton NG7: Lent 1C 56
(off Leen Ct.)
Hamilton Cl. NG5: Arn 4E 23
NG9: Toton 3H 63
Hamilton Ct. NG7: Nott 6B 4 (6F 45)
NG11: Clftn 2D 66
Hamilton Dr. NG7: Nott 6B 4 (6F 45)
NG12: Rad T 5F 49
Hamilton Gdns. NG5: Sher 6F 33
(off Alexandra St.)
Hamilton Pl. NG2: Nott 5B 46
Hamilton Rd. NG5: Sher 1F 45
NG10: Long E 4F 63
The Hamlet DE75: Hea 2C 14
Hammersmith Cl. NG16: Nuth 3E 31
Hampden Gro. NG1: Nott 1C 4 (3F 45)
Hampden Gro. NG9: Bee 5E 55
Hampden Rd. NG13: Newt 2B 50
Hampden St. NG1: Nott 1C 4 (3F 45)
NG16: Gilt 5D 16
NG16: Lang M 2F 15
Hampshire Dr. NG10: Sand 6D 52
Hampstead Ct. NG5: Sher 4G 33
(off St Albans St.)
Hampstead Rd. NG3: Nott 6A 34
Hampton Cl. DE7: West H 1B 38
NG9: Toton 2G 63
Hampton Dr. DE75: Hea 3B 14
Hampton Rd. NG2: West Br 5A 58
Handel St. NG3: Nott 3H 5 (4A 46)
Hand's Rd. DE75: Hea 4D 14
Hankin St. NG15: Huck 5A 8
Hanley Av. NG9: Bram 3B 54
Hanley St. NG1: Nott 3C 4 (4F 45)
Hannah Cres. NG11: Wilf 4F 57
Hanover Ct. NG8: Bilb 3D 42
Hanselin Cl. NG4: Ged 6A 36
Hanslope Cres. NG8: Bilb 3D 42
Hanson Cl. NG16: Kimb 6H 17
Hanson Cres. NG15: Huck 4G 7
Hanworth Gdns. NG5: Arn 5H 21
Harberton Cl. NG5: Redh 4A 22
Harby Dr. NG8: Woll 5A 44
Harcourt Cl. DE7: Ilk 6H 27
Harcourt Cres. NG16: Nuth 4F 31
Harcourt Rd. NG7: Hys G 1E 45
Harcourt St. NG9: Bee 5E 55
Harcourt Ter. NG3: Nott 2G 5 (4H 45)
Harden Ct. NG11: Clftn 5A 66
Hardstaff Almshouses NG4: Ged 5G 35
The Hardstaff Homes 5E 17
Hardstaff Rd. NG2: Nott 4C 46

Hardwick Av. DE7: West H 1C 38
Hardwick Ct. NG10: Long E 3B 72
Hardwicke Rd. NG9: Chil 2C 64
Hardwick Gro. NG2: West Br 2B 58
   NG7: Nott 5E 45
   NG13: Bing 5D 50
Hardwick Pl. DE7: Kirk H 4G 39
Hardwick Rd. NG5: Sher 4G 33
   NG7: Nott 6A 4 (6E 45)
Hardwood Cl. NG6: Bulw 5E 15
Hardy Barn DE75: Ship 5E 15
Hardy Cl. NG10: Long E 1F 73
   NG16: Kimb 6H 17
Hardy's Dr. NG4: Ged 6H 35
Hardy St. NG7: Radf 3E 45
   NG16: Kimb 6H 17
Harebell Gdns. NG13: Bing 5C 50
Harewood Av. NG6: Bulw 2B 32
Harewood Cl. NG10: Sand 1C 62
   NG12: Rad T 6G 49
Hargreaves Ct. DE7: Ilk 3C 40
Harkstead Rd. NG5: Top V 4F 21
Harlaxton Dr. NG7: Lent 5D 44
                (not continuous)
   NG10: Long E 4A 64
Harlaxton Wlk. NG3: Nott 1E 5 (3G 45)
Harlech Cl. DE7: Ilk .4G 27
Harlech Ri. NG9: Chil 1B 64
HARLEQUIN 6H 49
Harlequin Cl. NG12: Rad T 6H 49
Harlequin Ct. NG16: Eastw 2H 15
Harlequin M. NG12: Rad T 6H 49
Harley St. NG7: Lent 6D 44
Harlow Ct. DE7: West H 2B 38
Harlow Gro. NG4: Ged 5G 35
Harmston Ri. NG5: Sher 3D 32
                (not continuous)
Harnett Cl. NG1: Nott 5F 5 (5H 45)
Harold Av. NG16: Lang M 1F 15
Harold Ct. NG2: Nott 5A 46
Harold St. NG2: Nott 4H 5 (5A 46)
Harpenden Sq. NG8: Cin 4G 31
Harpole Wlk. NG5: Arn 3B 22
Harrier Gro. NG15: Huck 1E 19
Harriett St. NG9: Stfrd 4F 53
Harrimans Ct. NG7: Lent 3C 56
Harrimans Dr. DE72: Brea 5B 62
Harrimans La. NG7: Lent 3B 56
Harrington Cl. NG4: Ged 6B 36
Harrington Dr. NG7: Lent 5D 44
                (not continuous)
Harrington St. NG10: Long E 2D 72
Harris Cl. NG8: Woll .4F 43
Harrison Ct. NG13: Bing 5C 50
Harrison Rd. NG9: Stfrd 3F 53
Harrison's Plantation Nature Reserve 4G 43
Harris Rd. NG9: Chil .5D 54
Harrogate Rd. NG3: Nott 4E 47
Harrogate St. NG4: Neth 2H 47
Harrowby M. NG7: Lent 5D 44
Harrowby Rd. NG7: Lent 5D 44
Harrow Dr. DE7: Ilk .5C 40
Harrow Gdns. NG8: Woll 5A 44
Harrow Rd. NG2: West Br 6A 58
   NG8: Woll 5G 43
   NG15: Huck 6D 6
Harry Peel Ct. NG9: Bee 5G 55
Harry's Ct. NG16: Newth 1D 16
Harston Gdns. NG2: West Br 2F 67
Hart Av. NG10: Sand 5C 52
Hartcroft Rd. NG5: Bestw 1E 33
Hartford Cl. NG2: Nott 1H 57
Hartill Cl. NG9: Chil .3C 64
Hartington Av. NG4: Car 6F 35
   NG15: Huck 5C 6
Hartington Cl. DE7: West H 1C 38
Hartington Pl. DE7: Ilk 2A 28
Hartington Rd. NG5: Sher 4G 33
Hartland Dr. NG3: Ged 2G 35
Hart Lea NG10: Sand 5D 52
                (Charles Av.)
   NG10: Sand 5D 52
                (Hall Dr.)
Hartley Ct. NG7: Radf 3D 44
Hartley Dr. NG9: Bee 5H 55
Hartley Rd. NG7: Radf 3D 44
Hartness Rd. NG11: Clftn 4A 66
Hartshay Cl. DE7: Ilk 2B 28
Hartside Cl. NG2: Gam 4E 59
Hartside Gdns. NG10: Long E 5C 62
Hartside Way DE75: Hea 4F 15
Hart St. NG7: Lent 6D 44
Hartwell St. NG3: Nott 3H 45
Hartwood Dr. NG9: Stfrd 2F 53
Harvest Cl. NG5: Top V 5D 20
   NG9: Bee 4H 55
   NG13: Bing 5D 50
Harvest Dr. NG12: Cotg 6G 61
Harvest Rd. NG16: Eastw 4C 16
Harvey Cl. NG11: Rudd 2H 77

Harvey Ct. NG7: Nott 1C 56
Harvey Cft. NG9: Trow 5E 41
Harvey Hadden Sports Village 2F 43
Harvey Hadden Stadium 2F 43
Harvey Rd. NG7: Nott 1B 56
   NG8: Bilb 2F 43
Harviston Av. NG4: Ged 3F 35
Harwich Cl. NG6: Bulw 5G 19
Harwill Cres. NG8: Aspl 5H 31
Harwood Cl. NG5: Arn 5D 22
Haslam St. NG7: Nott 6C 4 (6F 45)
Haslemere Rd. NG8: Aspl 1B 44
   NG10: Long E 5D 62
Hassall Ct. NG13: Bing 5F 51
Hassock La. Nth. DE75: Ship 6F 15
Hassock La. Sth. DE75: Ship 1G 27
Hassocks Cl. NG9: Bee 4H 55
Hassocks La. NG9: Bee 4H 55
Hastings St. NG4: Car 2E 47
Haswell Rd. NG6: Bulw 2H 31
Hatfield Av. NG10: Sand 1D 62
Hatfield Dr. NG2: West Br 1G 67
Hatfield Rd. NG3: Mapp P 6G 33
Hatherleigh Cl. NG3: Mapp 1E 35
Hathern Cl. NG10: Long E 2F 73
Hathern Grn. NG9: Lent A 3G 55
Hathersage Av. NG10: Long E 2B 72
Hathersage Cl. NG5: Top V 5D 20
Hatley Cl. NG2: Nott .2F 57
Hatton Cl. NG5: Arn .3E 21
Hatton Crofts NG10: Long E 1E 73
Hatton Gdns. NG16: Nuth 4E 31
Havelock Gdns. NG3: Nott 1G 5 (3H 45)
Havelock St. DE7: Ilk 2B 40
Haven Cl. NG2: West Br 6H 57
Havenwood Ri. NG11: Clftn 5B 66
Haverhill Cres. NG5: Top V 3B 20
Haversham Cl. NG6: Bas 5B 32
Hawarden Ter. NG7: Hys G 2D 44
Hawker Cl. NG9: Chil 6B 54
Hawkhurst Dr. NG8: Woll 1D 54
Hawkins Ct. DE7: Ilk .3B 28
Hawkridge Gdns. NG3: Nott 2G 5 (4A 46)
                (not continuous)
Hawkshead Cl. NG2: West Br 6F 59
Hawksley Gdns. NG11: Clftn 3A 66
Hawksley Rd. NG7: Hys G 2D 44
Hawkswood Cl. NG9: Chil 1B 64
Hawksworth Av. NG5: Sher 3H 33
Hawksworth Rd. NG2: West Br 2B 58
Hawksworth St. NG3: Nott 3H 5 (4A 46)
Hawley Mt. NG5: Sher 4B 34
Haworth Ct. NG11: Clftn 4A 66
Hawthorn Av. DE72: Brea 5B 62
Hawthorn Cl. NG2: Nott 2F 57
   NG12: Edwal 1D 68
   NG12: Key 5G 79
   NG14: Woodbo 1C 24
Hawthorn Cres. NG5: Arn 4C 22
Hawthorne Av. NG9: Stfrd 5F 53
   NG10: Long E 1E 73
   NG12: Cotg 3F 71
   NG15: Huck 4F 7
Hawthorne Gro. NG9: Bee 5H 55
Hawthorne Lodge NG2: West Br 2D 58
Hawthorne Ri. NG16: Aws 3D 28
Hawthorn Vw. NG2: Nott 1F 57
Hawthorn Wlk. NG3: Nott 2D 46
Hawton Cres. NG8: Woll 5A 44
Hawton Spinney NG8: Woll 5A 44
Hayden La. NG15: Lin 1H 7
Haydn Av. NG5: Sher .5F 33
Haydn Rd. NG5: Sher 5E 33
Haydock Cl. NG16: Kimb 6G 17
Hayes Cl. DE7: West H 1C 38
Hayes Rd. NG12: Key 4F 79
Hayles Cl. NG5: Bestw 1F 33
Hayley Cl. NG16: Kimb 1F 29
Hayling Cl. DE7: Ilk 4G 27
Hayling Dr. NG8: Bas 6B 32
Haynes Av. NG9: Trow 4E 41
Haynes Cl. NG11: Clftn 2D 66
Hay's Cl. DE7: Ilk 5H 27
Haywood Cl. NG2: Nott 4H 5
HAYWOOD HOUSE HOSPICE 3F 33
Haywood Rd. NG3: Mapp 5B 34
Haywood St. NG2: Nott 4H 5 (5A 46)
Hayworth Rd. NG10: Sand 6D 52
Hazelbank Av. NG3: Nott 6B 34
Hazel Cl. DE75: Hea .4B 14
   NG2: West Br 2E 59
   NG13: Bing 5G 51
Hazel Dr. NG16: Nuth 1B 30
HAZELGROVE 1H 19
Hazel Gro. NG3: Mapp 3C 34
   NG15: Huck 6G 7
Hazel Hill Cres. NG5: Bestw 5F 21
Hazel Hill Pl. NG5: Bestw 5F 21
Hazelhurst Gdns. NG6: Bulw 6H 19
Hazel Mdws. NG15: Huck 6G 7

Hazelmere Gro. NG7: Lent 5C 44
Hazel St. NG6: Bulw .5H 19
                (not continuous)
Hazel Way NG15: Lin .1H 7
Hazelwood NG12: Cotg 2G 71
Hazelwood Cl. NG16: Newth 3D 16
Hazelwood Dr. NG15: Huck 5C 6
Hazelwood Rd. NG7: Hys G 2C 44
Headingley Gdns. NG8: Aspl 1B 44
Healey Cl. NG2: Nott .1G 57
HEANOR 4C 14
Heanor & District Heritage Cen. 5D 14
HEANOR GATE 5A 14
Heanor Ga. DE75: Hea 4B 14
Heanor Ga. Ind. Est. DE75: Hea 4B 14
                (not continuous)
Heanor Ga. Rd. DE75: Hea 4A 14
HEANOR MEMORIAL HOSPITAL 4D 14
Heanor Retail Pk. 3C 14
Heanor Rd.
   DE7: Ilk 2H 27
   DE7: Smal 5A 14
   DE75: Hea 5A 14
   DE75: Los 1A 14
Heanor Small Bus. Cen. DE75: Hea 5A 14
Heard Cres. NG9: Bee 3F 55
The Heath NG16: Gilt 5C 16
Heath Cl. NG7: Lent .5D 44
Heathcoat Bldg. NG7: Nott 2B 56
Heathcoat Ho. NG1: Nott 5F 5 (5H 45)
Heathcoat St. NG1: Nott 4F 5 (5H 45)
Heather Cl. NG3: Nott 2H 45
   NG16: Newth 4D 16
Heather Ct. DE75: Hea 4F 15
Heather Cres. DE72: Brea 5B 62
Heather Cft. NG2: West Br 1G 67
Heatherington Gdns. NG5: Top V 4E 21
Heatherley Dr. NG6: Bas 3D 32
Heather Ri. NG9: Bram 2E 55
Heather Rd. NG4: Car 6F 35
Heathervale NG2: West Br 5F 57
Heathfield Av. DE7: Ilk 1C 40
Heathfield Gro. NG9: Chil 2C 64
Heathfield Rd. NG5: Huck 3D 32
Heath Gdns. DE72: Brea 5C 62
Heaton Cl. NG3: Nott .6B 34
Heckington Dr. NG8: Woll 4H 43
Hedderley Wlk. NG3: Nott 1F 5 (3H 45)
Heddington Gdns. NG5: Arn 5H 21
Hedges Dr. DE7: Ilk 5B 40
Hedingham Cl. DE7: Ilk 1H 39
Hedley St. NG7: Bas .1E 45
Hedley Vs. NG7: Bas .6E 33
Hellebore Cl. NG5: Top V 5D 54
Helm Cl. NG6: Bulw 6C 20
Helmsdale Cl. NG5: Arn 6F 19
Helmsdale Gdns. NG5: Top V 4D 22
Helmsley Dr. NG16: Eastw 4D 20
Helston Dr. NG8: Stre 2H 15
Helvellyn Cl. NG2: Nott 5D 30
Helvellyn Way NG10: Long E 1G 57
Hemingway Cl. NG4: Car 3D 62
   NG16: Newth 2E 47
Hemlock Av. NG9: Stfrd 4E 17
   NG10: Long E 3G 53
Hemlock Gdns. NG6: Bulw 4F 63
Hemlock La. DE7: Kirk H 1F 31
Hemlock Rd. NG12: Edwal 4H 39
Hempshill Barns NG6: Bulw 4C 68
Hempshill La. NG6: Bulw 2E 31
                (Lillington Rd.)
   NG6: Bulw 1F 31
                (Rochester Ct.)
HEMPSHILL VALE 2F 31
Hemsby Cl. NG5: Arn .1B 34
Hemsby Gdns. NG6: Bulw 5H 19
                (not continuous)
Hemscott Cl. NG6: Bulw 5F 19
Hemswell Cl. NG3: Nott 4C 46
Hendon Ct. NG3: Nott 1B 46
Hendon Ri. NG3: Nott 1B 46
Hendre Gdns. NG5: Top V 6E 21
Henley Cl. NG4: Neth .3A 48
Henley Gdns. NG9: Stfrd 2G 53
Henley Ri. NG5: Sher .4E 33
Henley Way DE7: West H 1B 38
Hennessey Cl. NG9: Chil 3C 64
Henning Gdns. NG5: Top V 5E 21
Henrietta St. NG6: Bulw 1A 32
Henry Ct. NG2: Nott 1G 57
Henry Rd. NG2: West Br 3A 58
   NG7: Lent 6D 44
   NG9: Bee 5G 55
Henry St. NG2: Nott 4H 5 (5A 46)
   NG5: Redh 3A 22
   NG15: Huck 5H 7
Henshaw Av. DE7: Kirk H 4H 39
Henshaw Pl. DE7: Ilk .3A 28
Hensons Row NG6: Bas 5B 32

Hensons Sq. NG9: Bram 3B 54
    (not continuous)
Hepple Dr. NG6: Bulw 6F 19
Hepworth Dr. NG16: Gilt 6D 16
Herald Cl. NG9: Bee 4H 55
Herbert Buzzard Ct. NG15: Huck 5A 8
    (off Hankin St.)
Herbert Rd. NG5: Sher 6E 33
Hereford Rd. NG3: Nott 4D 46
  NG4: Ged 4H 35
  NG5: Woodt 2A 34
Hermitage Sq. NG2: Nott 5B 46
Hermitage Wlk. DE7: Ilk 4B 40
  NG7: Nott 6A 4 (6E 45)
Hermon St. NG7: Nott 3A 4 (4E 45)
Heron Ct. DE7: Ilk .5B 40
Heron Cres. NG12: Cotg 6G 61
Heron Dr. NG7: Lent 5C 44
Herons Ct. NG2: West Br 1E 69
Heron Wharf NG7: Lent 1D 56
Herrywell La. NG12: Owt 6H 71
Hertford M. NG4: Car 1E 47
Hervey Grn. NG11: Clftn 3C 66
Heskey Cl. NG3: Nott 3G 45
Heskey Wlk. NG3: Nott 3G 45
Heslington Av. NG8: Bas 1C 44
Hethbeth Ct. NG1: Nott 1G 57
Hethersett Gdns. NG6: Bulw 5H 19
Hetley Rd. NG9: Bee 3F 55
Hexham Av. DE7: Ilk 5C 40
Hexham Cl. NG2: West Br 5C 58
Hexham Gdns. NG5: Top V 3E 21
Heyford Ct. DE75: Hea 4E 15
Hey St. NG10: Long E 3D 72
The Hicking Bldg. NG2: Nott 6H 45
Hickings La. NG9: Stfrd 3G 53
Hickling Cl. NG10: Long E 2E 73
Hickling Rd. NG3: Mapp 5C 34
Hickling Way NG12: Cotg 4G 71
Hickton Dr. NG9: Chil 4B 64
Highbank Dr. NG11: Clftn 5C 66
Highbury Av. NG6: Bulw 2A 32
Highbury Cl. NG16: Nuth 4D 30
HIGHBURY HOSPITAL 2A 32
Highbury Rd. NG6: Bulw 6A 20
  NG12: Key 3G 79
HIGHBURY VALE 2B 32
Highbury Vale Stop (NET) 3B 32
Highbury Wlk. NG6: Bulw 1A 32
High Chu. St. NG7: Stfrd 6D 32
    (not continuous)
Highclere Dr. NG4: Car 1H 47
Highcliffe Rd. NG3: Nott 4C 46
High Ct. Dr. NG12: Key 5F 79
Highcroft NG3: Mapp 3B 34
High Cft. Cl. NG10: Long E 2G 73
Highcroft Dr. NG8: Woll 4B 42
High Cross Leys NG3: Nott 1E 5 (3G 45)
High Cross St. NG1: Nott 3F 5 (4H 45)
Highfield Ct. NG9: Bee 5F 55
Highfield Dr. DE7: Kirk H 4F 39
  NG4: Car 2D 46
  NG16: Nuth 3F 31
Highfield Gro. NG2: West Br 4B 58
Highfield Rd. NG2: West Br 4B 58
  NG7: Nott 2B 56
  NG9: Chil 1A 64
  NG12: Key 3G 79
  NG16: Nuth 3E 31
Highfields Ct. NG15: Huck 5G 7
Highfield St. NG10: Long E 3E 63
Highgate Cl. NG4: Car 5E 35
Highgate Dr. DE7: Ilk 4G 27
Highgrove Av. NG9: Chil 5D 54
Highgrove Cl. DE75: Hea 4A 14
Highgrove Gdns. NG12: Edwal 1C 68
High Hazels Ct. NG16: Newth 1D 16
High Hazles Cl. NG4: Ged 4G 35
High Hazles Rd. NG12: Cotg 1G 71
High Holborn DE7: Ilk 4A 28
High Hurst NG14: Calv 4G 11
Highland Ct. NG5: Bas 5D 32
Highgrove Av. NG9: Chil 5D 54
High La. Central DE7: West H 6D 26
High La. E. DE7: West H 6E 27
High La. W. DE7: West H 1A 38
High Leys Rd. NG15: Huck 5F 7
High Main Dr. NG6: Bestw V 1C 20
High Mdw. NG12: Toll 4F 69
High Pavement NG1: Nott 5F 5 (5H 45)
High Rd. NG9: Bee .5F 55
  NG9: Chil 2C 64
  NG9: Toton 3A 64
High Road / Central College Stop (NET) . . .6E 55
High School Stop (NET) 3E 45
High Spannia NG16: Kimb 6H 17
High St. DE7: Ilk 1B 40
  DE75: Hea 3C 14
  DE75: Los 1A 14
  NG1: Nott 4E 5 (5G 45)
  NG5: Arn 6A 22

High St. NG9: Stfrd 4G 53
  NG10: Long E .5G 63
  NG11: Rudd 6G 67
  NG15: Huck 4G 7
  NG16: Kimb 1H 29
High St. Av. NG5: Arn 6A 22
High St. Pl. NG1: Nott 4E 5 (5G 45)
Highurst Ct. NG7: Radf 4E 45
Highurst St. NG7: Radf 4E 45
High Vw. Av. NG12: Key 4H 79
High Vw. Ct. NG3: Mapp P 1H 45
Highwood Av. NG8: Bilb 1F 43
Highwray Gro. NG11: Clftn 4B 66
Hilary Cl. NG8: Woll 6D 42
Hilcot Dr. NG8: Aspl 6H 31
Hillary Pl. DE7: Kirk H 4F 39
Hillbeck Cres. NG8: Woll 5C 42
Hill Cl. NG2: West Br 5D 58
  NG16: Newth 4E 17
Hillcrest NG16: Want 6A 18
Hillcrest Dr. NG15: Huck 5D 6
Hillcrest Gdns. NG14: Bur J 2E 37
Hillcrest Gro. NG5: Sher 4F 33
Hill Crest Pk. NG14: Calv 2H 11
Hillcrest Rd. NG12: Key 3G 79
Hillcrest Vw. NG4: Car 6D 34
Hill Dr. NG13: Bing .4D 50
Hill Farm Ct. NG12: Edwal 3C 68
Hillfield Gdns. NG5: Top V 3C 20
Hillfield Rd. NG9: Stfrd 3H 53
Hillgrove Gdns. NG5: Top V 5E 21
    (off Whitchurch Cl.)
Hilliers Ct. NG5: Top V 5D 20
Hillingdon Av. NG16: Nuth 4D 30
Hillingdon Dr. DE7: Ilk 2C 40
Hillington Ri. NG5: Bestw 6G 21
Hill Ri. NG9: Trow 5E 41
Hill Rd. DE75: Hea .4B 14
  NG6: Bestw V .1C 20
  NG9: Chil 2B 64
Hillsford Cl. NG8: Woll 4G 43
Hill Side NG7: Nott .6B 44
Hillside NG16: Lang M 2E 15
Hillside Av. NG3: Mapp 3C 34
Hillside Cres. NG9: Bram 3E 55
Hillside Dr. NG10: Long E 5D 62
  NG14: Bur J 2F 37
Hillside Gro. NG10: Sand 5C 52
Hillside Rd. NG9: Bram 2C 54
  NG9: Chil 2A 64
  NG12: Rad T 6G 49
Hills Rd. NG5: Woodt 3A 34
Hill Syke NG14: Lowd 3G 25
Hilltop NG16: Eastw 3D 16
Hilltop Rd. NG16: Eastw 3D 16
Hillview Av. NG3: Mapp 5H 33
Hillview Rd. NG4: Car 6C 34
  NG9: Toton 3A 64
Hilton Cl. NG10: Long E 3B 72
Hilton Ct. NG2: West Br 6D 58
Hilton Cres. NG2: West Br 6D 58
Hilton Rd. NG3: Mapp 5B 34
Hine Hall NG3: Nott 5C 44
Hinchin Brook NG7: Lent 6B 34
Hinshelwood Ct. NG11: Clftn 5D 22
Hinsley Cl. NG5: Arn 4C 42
Hinsley Ct. NG8: Bilb 3B 22
Hirst Cl. NG5: Arn 3B 22
Hirst Ct. NG7: Radf 2A 4 (4E 45)
Hirst Cres. NG8: Woll 5F 43
Hitchen Rd. NG10: Long E 6D 62
HMP Lowdham Grange 3E 25
HMP Nottingham 4F 33
Hobart Cl. NG2: Nott 2G 57
Hobart Dr. NG9: Stfrd 2H 53
Hobben Cres. NG15: Huck 2B 8
Hobson Dr. DE7: Ilk 3A 40
Hockerton Rd. NG11: Clftn 1C 66
Hockley NG1: Nott 4G 5 (5H 45)
Hockley Ho. NG1: Nott 4G 5
Hodgkin Cl. NG11: Clftn 4A 66
Hodgkinson St. NG4: Neth 3A 48
Hodson Ho. NG5: Sher 5G 33
Hoefield Cres. NG6: Bulw 1G 31
Hoe Hill Vw. NG12: Toll 4F 69
Hoewood Rd. NG6: Bulw 6G 19
Hogan Gdns. NG5: Top V 4E 21
Hogarth Cl. NG9: Stfrd 5G 53
Hogarth St. NG3: Nott 3B 46
Hoggbarn La. DE75: Los 1B 14
Hoggetts Cl. NG9: Chil 5B 54
Hogg La. NG12: Rad T 6E 49
Hoggs Fld. NG16: Eastw 3B 16
Holbeck Rd. NG8: Aspl 3A 44
  NG15: Huck 2H 7
Holborn Av. NG2: Nott 4B 46
Holborn Cl. NG16: Nuth 4D 30
Holborn Pl. NG6: Bulw 6A 20
Holbrook Cl. NG11: Clftn 5C 66
Holbrook St. DE75: Hea 3E 15

Holby Cl. NG5: Top V 5D 20
Holcombe Cl. NG8: Aspl 5H 31
Holdale Rd. NG3: Nott 3D 46
Holden Ct. NG7: Radf 2A 4 (4E 45)
Holden Cres. NG16: Nuth 1C 30
Holden Gdns. NG9: Stfrd 5G 53
Holden Rd. NG9: Bee 4E 55
Holden St. NG7: Radf 2A 4 (4E 45)
Holgate NG11: Clftn 3A 66
Holgate Rd. NG2: Nott 2G 57
Holgate Wlk. NG15: Huck 5E 7
Holkham Av. NG9: Chil 6C 54
Holkham Cl. DE7: Ilk 4G 27
  NG5: Arn 1C 34
Holland Cl. NG11: Goth 6H 75
Holland Mdw. NG10: Long E 2F 73
Holland St. NG7: Hys G 2D 44
Holles Cres. NG7: Nott 6A 4 (6E 45)
The Hollies NG5: Sand 6C 52
  NG16: Eastw 3B 16
Hollies Dr. NG12: Edwal 1C 68
Hollington Rd. NG8: Bilb 3G 43
Hollingworth Av. NG10: Sand 6D 52
The Hollins NG14: Calv 3A 12
Hollins Ct. NG7: Radf 4E 45
Hollinwell Av. NG8: Woll 4H 43
Hollinwell Cl. NG12: Edwal 2D 68
Hollinwood La. NG14: Calv 4D 10
Hollis St. NG7: Bas .6E 33
The Hollows NG10: Long E 5A 64
  NG11: Wilf 1E 67
Hollowstone NG1: Nott 5G 5 (5H 45)
Holly Av. DE72: Brea 4B 62
  NG3: Nott 2C 46
  NG4: Car 2F 47
  NG11: Wilf 3F 57
Hollybrook Gro. NG16: Want 6B 18
Holly Cl. NG13: Bing 5G 51
  NG15: Huck 6H 7
Holly Copse Nature Reserve 5H 29
Holly Ct. NG3: Nott .2B 46
  NG9: Bram 3C 54
Hollycroft NG2: West Br 1C 68
Hollydale Rd. NG3: Nott 3D 46
Hollydene Cl. NG15: Huck 6C 6
Hollydene Cres. NG6: Cin 3H 31
Holly Farm Cotts. NG12: Key 1G 71
Holly Farm Ct. NG16: Newth 4E 17
Holly Gdns. NG3: Nott 2B 46
Hollygate Ind. Pk. NG12: Cotg 1G 71
Hollygate La. NG12: Cotg 2F 71
Holly La. NG9: Chil .6E 55
Holly Leaf Rd. NG15: Huck 1A 20
Holly Lodge NG2: West Br 2D 58
Holly Rd. NG16: Want 6H 17
Hollythorpe Pl. NG15: Huck 6C 6
Holme Cl. DE7: Ilk .5H 27
  NG14: Woodbo 1D 24
Holme Cft. DE7: West H 2C 38
Holmefield Cres. DE7: Ilk 1C 40
Holme Gro. NG2: West Br 1D 58
Holme La. NG12: Hol P, Rad T 6B 48
  NG3: Rad T 3H 59
Holme Lea NG10: Sand 5D 52
Holme Lodge NG4: Car 3G 47
HOLME PIERREPONT 6A 48
Holme Pierrepont Country Pk. 6A 48
Holme Pierrepont Hall 6B 48
Holme Rd. NG2: West Br 2B 58
  NG13: Bing 5F 51
Holmes Cl. NG16: Lang M 2E 15
Holmefield Dr. DE75: Hea 5D 14
Holmes Rd. DE72: Brea 5A 62
Holmes St. DE75: Hea 3B 14
Holme St. NG2: Nott 1A 58
Holmewood Av. DE7: Ilk 2B 28
Holmewood Cres. NG5: Bestw 1E 33
Holmewood Dr. NG16: Gilt 5D 16
Holmfield Rd. NG9: Chil 2C 64
Holmsfield NG12: Key 5G 79
Holroyd Av. NG2: Nott 5B 46
Holt Gro. NG14: Calv 3H 11
Holwood Ct. NG6: Bulw 1G 31
Holyoake Dr. NG10: Long E 6H 63
Holyoake Rd. NG3: Mapp 4E 35
Holyoake Vs. NG4: Colw 3H 47
Holyrood Ct. NG9: Bram 2C 54
Holy Trinity Stop (NET) 5C 66
Holywell Rd. DE7: Ilk 4G 27
Home Cl. NG5: Arn .5H 21
The Home Cft. NG9: Bram 4B 54
Home Farm Cl. NG11: Goth 6G 75
Homefield Av. NG5: Arn 3C 22
Homefield Rd. NG8: Aspl 2B 44
Homestead NG16: Lang M 1E 15
Homewell Wlk. NG11: Clftn 2D 66
Honeysuckle Cl. NG8: Brox 6E 31
Honeysuckle Gro. NG6: Cin 3H 31
  NG13: Bing 6D 50
Honeywood Ct. NG3: Nott 2C 46

Honeywood Dr. NG3: Nott ...2C 46
Honingham Cl. NG5: Arn ...2B 34
Honingham Rd. DE7: Ilk ...4G 27
Honister Cl. NG2: Gam ...4E 59
 NG11: Clftn ...6B 66
Honiton Cl. NG9: Toton ...3A 64
Honiton Rd. NG8: Brox ...6E 31
Hood Cotts. NG5: Sher ...5H 33
Hood St. NG5: Sher ...5H 33
Hook Cl. NG9: Chil ...3C 64
Hooley Cl. NG10: Long E ...1D 72
Hooley Pl. NG5: Sher ...4H 33
Hoopers Wlk. NG2: Nott ...1G 57
Hooton Rd. NG4: Car ...2E 47
Hooton St. NG3: Nott ...4B 46
Hope Cl. NG2: Nott ...1F 57
Hopedale Cl. NG7: Radf ...4C 44
Hope Dr. NG7: Nott ...6B 4 (6F 45)
Hope St. DE7: Ilk ...2B 40
 NG9: Bee ...4E 55
Hopewell Cl. NG12: Rad T ...4G 49
HOPEWOOD ...3H 33
Hopkin Ct. NG3: Mapp ...1E 35
Hopkins Ct. NG16: Eastw ...2B 16
Hopkinson Ct. NG6: Bestw V ...2C 20
Hopwood Dr. NG4: Ged ...3F 35
Hopwood Rd. NG4: Ged ...4G 35
Horace Av. NG9: Stfrd ...4E 53
Horizon Pl. NG8: Stre ...5C 30
Hornbeam Cl. DE7: Ilk ...2D 40
Hornbeam Gdns. NG6: Bulw ...6F 19
Hornbuckle Ct. NG7: Radf ...4D 44
Hornchurch Rd. NG8: Bilb ...1D 42
Hornsby Wlk. NG5: Top V ...5C 20
Horridge St. DE7: Ilk ...3B 28
Horsecroft Cl. DE7: Ilk ...5G 27
Horsendale Av. NG16: Nuth ...3E 31
Horsham Dr. NG5: Top V ...5D 20
Horsley Cres. NG16: Lang M ...2E 15
Horsley La. NG4: Ged ...4G 35
Horwood Dr. NG11: Wilf ...6E 57
Hoselett Fld. Rd. NG10: Long E ...2G 73
Hoten Rd. NG2: Nott ...6B 46
Hotspur Cl. NG6: Bas ...2C 32
Hotspur Dr. NG4: Colw ...3G 47
Houghton Av. DE7: Ilk ...4G 27
Houghton Cl. NG16: Nuth ...3E 31
Houghton Dr. NG8: Stre ...6C 30
Houldsworth Ri. NG5: Arn ...3A 22
Hound Rd. NG2: West Br ...3A 58
Hounds Ga. NG1: Nott ...5C 4 (5G 45)
 (not continuous)
Houseman Gdns. NG2: Nott ...1G 57
Houston Cl. NG5: Top V ...4C 20
Hovenden Gdns. NG7: Hys G ...2C 44
Hove Rd. NG5: Bestw ...2C 32
Howard Cl. NG10: Long E ...4G 63
Howard St. NG1: Nott ...2F 5 (4G 45)
Howarth Cl. NG10: Long E ...6C 62
Howbeck Rd. NG5: Arn ...4D 22
Howden Rd. NG6: Bulw ...3A 20
Howell Jones Rd. NG9: Chil ...2B 64
Howells Cl. NG5: Arn ...5G 21
Howick Dr. NG6: Bulw ...6F 19
Howieson Ct. NG3: Mapp ...2D 34
Howitt St. DE75: Hea ...3D 14
 NG10: Long E ...6G 63
Hoylake Cres. NG8: Bilb ...2D 42
Hoyland Av. NG7: Lent ...1C 56
Hoyle Rd. NG14: Calv ...2H 11
Hubert Cl. NG7: Hys G ...3D 44
Hubert St. NG7: Hys G ...3D 44
Huckerby Rd. DE7: Ilk ...5G 27
Huckerbys Fld. NG4: Car ...6E 35
HUCKNALL ...4G 7
Hucknall Aerodrome ...3E 19
Hucknall By-Pass NG15: Huck ...4E 7
Hucknall Cl. NG8: Stre ...5D 30
Hucknall Cres. NG4: Ged ...5G 35
Hucknall Ind. Pk. NG15: Huck ...1F 19
Hucknall La. NG6: Bulw ...5A 20
Hucknall Leisure Cen. ...3H 7
Hucknall Park & Ride ...4A 8
Hucknall Rd. NG5: Bestw, Sher, Top V ...4B 20
 NG6: Bulw ...4B 20
Hucknall Station (Rail & NET) ...4A 8
Hudson St. NG3: Nott ...3B 46
Hudson Way NG12: Rad T ...5H 49
Hufton's Ct. DE75: Hea ...6E 15
Hufton's Dr. DE75: Hea ...6D 14
Hugessen Av. NG15: Huck ...3A 8
Huggett Gdns. NG5: Top V ...5E 21
Hughes La. NG4: Ged ...3G 35
Humber Cl. NG2: Nott ...1G 57
Humber Lodge NG9: Bee ...4G 55
Humber Rd. NG9: Bee ...4G 55
 (not continuous)
Humber Rd. Sth. NG9: Bee ...5H 55
Humberston Rd. NG8: Woll ...6C 42

HUNGERHILL GARDENS ...2H 45
Hungerhill La. NG14: Woodbo ...3H 23
Hungerhill Rd. NG3: Nott ...2H 45
Hungerton St. NG7: Lent ...6D 44
Hunston Cl. NG8: Bilb ...2G 43
Hunt Av. DE75: Hea ...3C 14
Hunt Cl. NG12: Rad T ...6F 49
Hunter Rd. NG5: Arn ...1E 35
Hunters Cl. NG11: Wilf ...5E 57
Hunter St. NG2: Nott ...2H 57
Huntingdon Dr. NG7: Nott ...5B 4 (5F 45)
Huntingdon St. NG1: Nott ...1D 4 (3G 45)
Huntingdon Wlk. NG10: Sand ...6D 52
Huntingdon Way NG9: Toton ...3H 63
Huntly Cl. NG11: Clftn ...4E 67
Hurcomb St. NG3: Nott ...2B 46
Hurley Ct. DE7: West H ...1C 38
Hurricane Rd. NG15: Huck ...2E 19
Hurst Dr. DE7: Stly ...3A 38
Hurts Cft. NG9: Chil ...1D 64
Hurt's Yd. NG1: Nott ...3D 4 (4G 45)
Hussar Ter. NG2: West Br ...2H 67
Huss's La. NG10: Long E ...6H 63
Hutchinson Grn. NG3: Nott ...1F 5 (3H 45)
Hutton Cl. NG9: Bram ...2D 54
Hutton St. NG2: Nott ...6B 46
Huxley Cl. NG8: Bilb ...2D 42
Hyde Cl. NG11: Clftn ...1D 66
Hyde Pk. Cl. NG2: West Br ...6G 57
HYSON GREEN ...2D 44
Hyson Green Market Stop (NET) ...2D 44
Hyson St. NG7: Hys G ...2D 44

Ian Gro. NG4: Car ...1G 47
Ibbinson Cl. NG4: Ged ...3F 35
The Ice Ho. NG1: Nott ...4G 5
Ikea Way NG16: Gilt ...6E 17
Ilam Sq. DE7: Ilk ...2A 28
Ilford Cl. DE7: Ilk ...4H 27
ILKESTON ...6A 28
ILKESTON COMMUNITY HOSPITAL ...3H 27
ILKESTON JUNCTION ...6C 28
Ilkeston Rd. DE7: Stant D ...2E 53
 (Stanton Ga.)
 DE7: Stant D ...6B 40
 (Twelve Ho's.)
 DE75: Hea ...4D 14
 NG7: Lent, Nott, Radf ...3A 4 (4B 44)
 NG9: Stfrd, Bram ...1G 53
 NG9: Trow ...4D 40
 NG10: Sand ...2E 53
Ilkeston Station (Rail) ...5C 28
Ilkeston Town FC ...4C 28
Imex Ent. Pk. NG15: Huck ...5B 8
Imperial Av. NG4: Ged ...6G 35
 NG9: Bee ...5E 55
Imperial Rd. NG6: Bulw ...1B 32
 NG9: Bee ...5E 55
Incher M. NG4: Car ...6E 35
Inchwood Cl. NG9: Toton ...3H 63
Incinerator Rd. NG2: Nott ...1A 58
Independent St. NG7: Radf ...3D 44
Ingham Gro. NG7: Lent ...6C 44
Ingham Rd. NG10: Long E ...3E 63
Ingleborough Gdns. NG10: Long E ...5C 62
Ingleby Cl. NG8: Woll ...5B 42
 NG12: Cotg ...3E 71
Ingleby Rd. NG10: Long E ...3B 72
Inglefield Rd. DE7: Ilk ...3B 40
Inglewood Rd. NG11: Clftn ...4C 66
Ingram Rd. NG6: Bulw ...1A 32
Ingram Ter. NG6: Bulw ...1B 32
Inham Cir. NG9: Chil ...5C 54
Inham Cl. NG9: Chil ...6A 54
Inham Rd. NG9: Chil ...6A 54
Inham Road Stop (NET) ...6A 54
Inkerman Cl. DE7: Ilk ...2A 28
Innes Cl. NG4: Car ...2E 47
Innovation Pk. NG7: Lent ...5B 44
Instow Cl. NG3: Ged ...2F 35
Instow Ri. NG3: Nott ...1G 5 (3H 45)
Intake Rd. NG12: Key ...4F 79
Interchange 25 Bus. Pk. NG10: Sand ...1C 62
intu Broadmarsh Shop. Cen. ...5E 5 (5G 45)
intu Victoria Cen. ...2E 5 (4G 45)
Invaders Cl. NG10: Long E ...5H 63
Iona Dr. NG9: Trow ...6F 41
Iona Gdns. NG5: Top V ...4E 21
Ipswich Cir. NG3: Nott ...4C 46
Ireland Av. NG9: Bee ...6G 55
Ireland Cl. NG9: Bee ...6G 55
Iremonger Rd. NG2: Nott ...1H 57
Irene Ter. NG7: Bas ...5D 32
Ireton Gro. NG9: Atten ...3D 64
Ireton St. NG7: Radf ...2A 4 (4E 45)
 NG9: Bee ...5E 55

Ironwood Cl. NG12: Edwal ...3C 68
Irwin Dr. NG6: Bulw ...2F 31
Isaac Newton Cen. NG7: Nott ...2B 56
Isaacs La. NG9: Stfrd ...4F 53
Isabella Cl. NG1: Nott ...6D 4 (6G 45)
Isandula Rd. NG7: Bas ...5D 32
The Island NG16: Eastw ...4B 16
Island La. NG12: Rad T ...5D 48
Islay Cl. NG5: Arn ...4B 22
 NG9: Trow ...6F 41
Ivatt Dr. NG2: Nott ...6B 46
Ives Cl. NG2: West Br ...1G 67
Ivy Cl. NG16: Want ...4H 17
Ivy Gro. NG4: Car ...2F 47
 NG7: Bas ...1E 45
Ivy La. NG16: Eastw ...3A 16

Jacklin Gdns. NG5: Top V ...4E 21
Jackson Av. DE7: Ilk ...6A 28
 NG10: Sand ...5C 52
Jackson Dr. NG5: Bestw ...2E 33
Jackson Rd. NG15: Huck ...1A 20
Jacobite Cl. DE75: Hea ...5A 14
Jacoby Cl. NG5: Arn ...6G 21
Jake Rd. NG9: Bee ...2G 65
James Dr. NG14: Calv ...2G 11
James St. NG5: Arn ...5A 22
 NG16: Kimb ...1H 29
Japonica Dr. NG6: Cin ...3H 31
The Jardines NG9: Bram ...2C 54
Jarrow Gdns. NG5: Top V ...3D 20
Jarvis Av. NG3: Nott ...3D 46
Jasmine Cl. NG8: Brox ...6E 31
 NG9: Bram ...2D 54
 NG11: Clftn ...4A 66
Jasmine Dr. DE75: Hea ...4G 15
Jasmine Rd. NG5: Bas ...4C 32
Jasper Cl. NG12: Rad T ...1E 61
Jayne Cl. NG4: Ged ...5A 36
 NG8: Woll ...3E 43
Jebb's La. NG13: Bing ...5F 51
Jedburgh Cl. NG3: Nott ...1G 5 (3H 45)
 NG16: Kimb ...6G 17
Jedburgh Wlk. NG3: Nott ...1G 5 (3H 45)
Jeffries Cl. DE7: Ilk ...3H 27
Jenned Rd. NG5: Arn ...3C 22
Jenner Rd. NG5: Mapp ...5B 34
Jenner St. NG5: Sher ...6F 33
Jenness Av. NG5: Top V ...4C 20
Jennison St. NG6: Bulw ...6A 20
Jenny Burton Way NG15: Huck ...6A 8
Jensen Way NG5: Sher ...6F 33
Jermyn Dr. NG5: Arn ...4E 21
Jersey Gdns. NG3: Nott ...3A 46
Jervis Ct. DE7: Ilk ...4B 28
Jesmond Rd. NG6: Bulw ...1B 32
Jessamine Cl. NG9: Bee ...5G 55
Jesse Boot Av. NG7: Nott ...2B 56
Jessops La. NG4: Ged ...4H 35
Jewitt Way NG11: Rudd ...6F 67
Jill-Iain Ct. NG9: Stfrd ...5G 53
Joan Av. DE75: Hea ...3C 14
John & Eliza Jelley Homes ...6B 44
John Carroll Ct. NG3: Nott ...3B 46
John Carroll Leisure Cen. ...5F 9
John Quinn Ct. NG7: Bas ...6D 32
Johnson Av. NG15: Huck ...6H 7
Johnson Cl. NG16: Want ...6A 18
Johnson Dr. DE75: Hea ...3D 14
Johnson Rd. NG7: Lent ...5C 44
Johnson Way NG9: Chil ...3B 64
John's Pl. DE75: Hea ...4B 14
Johns Rd. NG9: Bee ...2G 65
 NG12: Rad T ...6G 49
Johnstone Way NG6: Bestw V ...5F 9
John St. DE7: Ilk ...6B 28
 DE75: Hea ...3B 14
 NG7: Bas ...6D 32
John Wright Cl. NG6: Bulw ...4B 20
Joseph Cl. DE7: Ilk ...4A 28
Joshua Bus. Pk. NG16: Lang M ...2G 15
Joyce Av. NG5: Sher ...3H 33
 NG9: Toton ...2H 63
Joyce Cl. NG5: Sher ...3H 33
Jubilee Ct.
 DE7: West H ...1A 38
 NG8: Stre ...6D 30
 NG15: Huck ...6E 7
Jubilee Rd. NG5: Arn ...1A 34
Jubilee St. NG2: Nott ...5B 46
 NG16: Kimb ...6G 17
Judes Cl. NG3: Mapp ...5A 34
Judson Av. NG9: Stfrd ...5H 53
Julian Cl. DE7: Ilk ...3D 40
Julian Rd. NG2: West Br ...3D 58
Julie Av. DE75: Hea ...4E 15
Julius Cl. NG16: Lang M ...1F 15

Jumelles Dr. NG14: Calv ...4F 11
The Junction NG15: Huck ...4H 7
Junction Rd. NG10: Long E ...1A 74
Jungletastic Play Cen. ...3F 31
Juniper Cl. NG11: Clftn ...4A 66
Juniper Ct. NG7: Radf ...3E 45
   (off Waterloo Prom.)
  NG16: Gilt ...5E 17
Juniper Gdns. NG13: Bing ...5G 51
Justice Cen.
  Nottingham ...6E 5 (6G 45)
Justnian Cl. NG15: Huck ...3A 8

K

Kappler Cl. NG4: Neth ...2A 48
Kapwood Cl. NG7: Radf ...4D 44
Karen Gdns. NG9: Chil ...1D 64
Karen Ri. NG5: Arn ...4C 22
Katherine Dr. NG9: Toton ...1H 63
Kayes Ct. NG9: Stfrd ...4F 53
Kayes Wlk. NG1: Nott ...5F 5 (5H 45)
Kay's Mdw. NG9: Bee ...4G 55
Keats Cl. NG5: Arn ...6H 21
  NG10: Long E ...2D 72
  NG16: Nuth ...1B 30
Keats Dr. NG15: Huck ...5D 6
Keble Cl. DE75: Hea ...5C 14
Kedleston Cl. NG9: Chil ...6C 54
  NG10: Long E ...2C 72
Kedleston Dr. DE7: Ilk ...4H 27
  DE75: Hea ...3A 14
Kedleston Dr. Sth. DE7: Ilk ...4A 28
Keeling Cl. NG16: Newth ...4D 16
Keepers Cl. NG6: Bestw V ...1C 20
Kegworth Rd. NG11: Goth ...6F 75
Keighton Dr. NG7: Nott ...2A 56
Kelfield Cl. NG6: Bulw ...2C 32
Kelham Dr. NG5: Sher ...5E 33
Kelham Grn. NG3: Nott ...3B 46
Kelham M. NG3: Nott ...1D 46
Kelham Way NG16: Eastw ...1E 33
Kelling Cl. NG5: Bestw ...4F 57
Kelly Wlk. NG11: Wilf ...2E 65
Kelsey Cl. NG9: Atten ...1F 57
Kelso Gdns. NG2: Nott ...4H 31
Kelstern Cl. NG8: Cin ...1H 5 (3A 46)
Kelvin Cl. NG9: Stfrd ...6E 53
Kelvin Ct. NG2: Nott ...2C 46
Kelvin Rd. NG3: Nott ...2B 32
Kemmel Rd. NG6: Bulw ...5C 20
Kempsey Cl. NG5: Top V ...5C 20
Kempson St. NG11: Rudd ...6G 67
Kempton Cl. NG16: Kimb ...6G 17
Kempton Dr. NG5: Arn ...4C 22
Kenbrook Rd. NG15: Huck, Pap ...2A 8
Kendal Cl. NG15: Huck ...3F 7
Kendal Ct. NG2: West Br ...3D 58
Kendal Dr. NG9: Bram ...3D 54
Kendale Gro. NG3: Nott ...6B 34
Kendrew Ct. NG11: Clftn ...4A 66
Kenia Cl. NG4: Car ...1F 47
Kenilworth Ct. NG7: Nott ...6B 4 (6F 45)
  NG9: Bee ...3G 55
Kenilworth Dr. DE7: Kirk H ...4G 39
Kenilworth Rd. NG7: Nott ...6B 4 (6F 45)
  NG9: Bee ...4G 55
Ken Martin Leisure Cen. ...4A 20
Kenmore Gdns. NG3: Nott ...1G 5 (3H 45)
Kennedy Av. NG10: Long E ...2E 73
Kennedy Cl. NG5: Arn ...6H 21
Kennedy Dr. NG9: Stfrd ...2G 53
Kennel La. NG15: Ann ...2A 6
Kenneth Rd. NG5: Arn ...3B 22
Kennington Rd. NG8: Radf ...4B 44
Kenny Av. NG11: Wilf ...6E 57
Ken Reid Gdns. ...5A 20
   (off Ragdale Rd.)
Kenrick Rd. NG3: Mapp ...6C 34
Kenrick St. NG4: Neth ...2A 48
Kensal Ct. NG2: West Br ...3A 58
Kensington Av. DE75: Hea ...4A 14
Kensington Cl. NG9: Toton ...4A 64
Kensington Ct. NG5: Sher ...4G 33
   (off St Albans St.)
Kensington Gdns. DE7: Ilk ...2C 40
  NG4: Car ...2G 47
Kensington Pk. Cl. NG2: West Br ...6G 57
Kensington Rd. NG10: Sand ...1C 62
Kensington St. DE7: Ilk ...3B 40
Kenslow Av. NG7: Hys G ...2A 44
Kent Av. NG9: Bee ...1F 65
Kentmere Cl. NG2: Gam ...4E 59
Kenton Av. NG16: Nuth ...4D 30
Kenton Cl. NG2: Gam ...5A 48
Kent Rd. NG3: Mapp ...5B 34
  NG16: Gilt ...4E 17
Kent St. NG1: Nott ...3F 5 (4H 45)
Kentwood Rd. NG2: Nott ...5B 46

Kenyon Rd. NG7: Lent ...6B 44
Keppel Ct. DE7: Ilk ...4B 28
Kersall Ct. NG6: Bulw ...2B 32
Kersall Dr. NG6: Bulw ...2B 32
Kersall Gdns. NG15: Huck ...4H 7
Kestrel Cl. DE7: Ilk ...5B 40
  NG4: Car ...6D 34
Kestrel Dr. NG13: Bing ...6F 51
Kestrel Gro. NG15: Huck ...5F 7
Keswick Cl. DE7: Kirk H ...4H 39
  NG2: Gam ...4E 59
  NG9: Bram ...3D 54
Keswick Ct. NG2: Nott ...4H 5 (5A 46)
  NG10: Long E ...3D 62
Keswick St. NG2: Nott ...4H 5 (5A 46)
Ketton Cl. NG5: Bestw ...5F 21
Kett St. NG6: Bulw ...6H 19
Keverne Cl. NG8: Aspl ...5A 32
   (not continuous)
Kevin Rd. NG8: Woll ...1D 54
Kew Cl. NG2: West Br ...2G 67
Kew Cres. DE75: Hea ...4F 15
Kew Gdns. NG16: Nuth ...4E 31
Key VI Fitness ...5G 79
Keys Cl. NG6: Bulw ...6G 19
Key St. NG3: Nott ...4B 46
KEYWORTH ...5G 79
Keyworth La. NG11: Bunny ...6B 78
Keyworth Leisure Cen. ...4H 79
Keyworth Rd. NG4: Ged ...4F 35
Kibworth Cl. NG5: Sher ...3D 32
Kiddier Av. NG5: Arn ...6D 22
Kidney Cl. DE7: Smal, Hea ...5A 14
Kielder Dr. NG13: Bing ...5C 50
Kilbourne Rd. NG5: Arn ...4D 22
Kilbourn St. NG3: Nott ...3G 45
Kilburn Cl. NG9: Bram ...1B 54
Kilburn Dr. DE7: Ilk ...4H 27
Kilby Av. NG3: Nott ...3C 46
Kilby Ho. NG10: Long E ...6F 63
Kildare Rd. NG3: Nott ...1B 46
Kildonan Cl. NG8: Stre ...5D 30
Killarney Pk. NG6: Bestw V ...5F 9
Killerton Grn. NG11: Clftn ...6D 66
Killerton Pk. Dr. NG2: West Br ...1F 67
Killisick La. NG5: Arn ...3D 22
Killisick Rd. NG5: Arn ...5D 22
Kilnbrook Av. NG5: Arn ...4D 22
Kiln Cl. DE7: West H ...6C 26
Kiln Pl. NG6: Bulw ...1G 31
Kilnwood Cl. NG3: Nott ...2C 46
Kilsby Rd. NG11: Clftn ...3D 66
Kilverston Rd. NG10: Sand ...5C 52
Kilverton Cl. NG8: Woll ...5A 44
Kilvington Rd. NG5: Arn ...6D 22
Kimber Cl. NG8: Bilb ...1H 29
KIMBERLEY ...1H 29
Kimberley Cl. NG16: Kimb ...2H 29
Kimberley Eastwood By-Pass
  NG16: Eastw ...1A 30
Kimberley Leisure Cen. ...2B 30
Kimberley Rd. NG16: Nuth ...5C 46
Kimberley St. NG2: Nott ...4D 44
Kimbolton Av. NG7: Lent, Radf ...3B 64
Kindlewood Dr. NG9: Toton ...3B 64
King Charles St. NG1: Nott ...5C 4 (5F 45)
King Edward Ct. NG1: Nott ...3F 5 (4H 45)
King Edward Gdns. NG10: Sand ...5D 52
King Edward St. NG1: Nott ...3F 5 (4H 45)
  NG10: Sand ...5D 52
  NG15: Huck ...5G 7
Kingfisher Cl. NG6: Bas ...3B 32
  NG9: Bee ...6H 55
Kingfisher Dr. NG12: Cotg ...1G 71
Kingfisher Rd. NG4: Neth, Stoke B ...2C 48
Kingfishers Ct. NG2: West Br ...1E 69
Kingfisher Wharf NG7: Lent ...1E 57
King George Av. DE7: Ilk ...1A 40
King John's Arc. NG1: Nott ...4E 5
King John's Chambers
  NG1: Nott ...4E 5
Kinglake Pl. NG2: Nott ...1G 57
Kingrove Av. NG9: Chil ...5D 54
Kings Av. NG4: Ged ...5G 35
Kingsbridge Av. NG3: Mapp ...1E 35
Kingsbridge Way NG9: Bram ...5C 54
Kingsbury Dr. NG8: Bilb ...1G 43
Kings Cl. DE75: Hea ...4A 14
Kingsdale Cl. NG10: Long E ...2C 72
Kingsdown Mt. NG8: Woll ...1E 55
Kingsford Av. NG7: Radf ...3C 44
Kingsley Cres. NG10: Long E ...3D 72
Kingsley Dr. NG4: Neth ...3A 48
Kingsley Rd. NG2: Nott ...5C 46
Kingsmead Av. NG9: Trow ...1F 53
Kingsmoor Cl. NG5: Top V ...6C 20
King's Pl. NG1: Nott ...4F 5 (5H 45)
Kings Rd. NG10: Sand ...5D 52
Kingsthorpe Cl. NG3: Nott ...6B 34
Kingston Av. DE7: Ilk ...5C 40

Kingston Ct. DE7: West H ...1B 38
  NG2: Nott ...4H 5 (5A 46)
  NG12: Rad T ...6F 49
   (off Bingham Rd.)
Kingston Dr. NG12: Cotg ...4F 71
Kingston Rd. NG2: West Br ...5A 58
King St. DE7: Ilk ...6B 28
  NG1: Nott ...3D 4 (5G 45)
  NG9: Bee ...5G 55
  NG10: Long E ...5F 63
  NG16: Eastw ...3B 16
Kings Wlk. NG1: Nott ...3D 4 (4G 45)
Kingsway DE7: Ilk ...4B 40
  DE75: Hea ...3B 14
  NG12: Rad T ...1E 61
Kingsway Gdns. NG15: Huck ...1E 19
Kingsway Rd. NG15: Huck ...1E 19
Kingswell Rd. NG5: Arn ...6B 22
Kingswell Rd. NG5: Arn ...6B 22
Kingswood Cl. NG2: West Br ...6H 57
Kingswood Rd. NG2: West Br ...6H 57
  NG8: Woll ...4H 43
Kinlet Rd. NG5: Bestw ...1E 33
KINOULTON WOLDS ...6H 81
Kinross Cres. NG8: Bilb ...3G 43
Kinsale Wlk. NG11: Clftn ...3C 66
Kipling Cl. NG11: Clftn ...5A 66
Kipps St. NG1: Nott ...3F 5 (4H 45)
Kirby Cl. NG16: Newth ...2C 16
Kirby Rd. NG16: Newth ...2C 16
Kirkbride Cl. NG9: Chil ...1B 64
Kirkby Av. DE7: Ilk ...3B 40
Kirkby Gdns. NG2: Nott ...1H 57
Kirk Cl. NG9: Chil ...1D 64
Kirkdale Cl. NG8: Woll ...5B 42
Kirkdale Gdns. NG10: Long E ...1D 72
Kirkdale Rd. NG3: Nott ...3D 46
  NG10: Long E ...2D 72
Kirkewhite Ct. NG4: Nott ...1H 57
Kirkewhite St. W. NG2: Nott ...1G 57
Kirkewhite Wlk. NG2: Nott ...1G 57
Kirkfell Cl. NG2: West Br ...6E 59
Kirkfield Dr. DE72: Brea ...5A 62
KIRK HALLAM ...4H 39
Kirkham Cl. DE75: Hea ...4B 14
Kirkham Dr. NG9: Toton ...3H 63
Kirkhill NG13: Bing ...5G 51
Kirkland Dr. NG9: Chil ...3C 64
Kirk La. NG11: Rudd ...6G 67
Kirkley Dr. DE75: Hea ...4A 14
Kirkley Gdns. NG5: Arn ...5C 22
Kirkman Rd. DE75: Los ...1A 14
Kirk Rd. NG3: Mapp ...5C 34
Kirk's Bldgs. NG4: Car ...2F 47
Kirkstead Gdns. NG7: Hys G ...2D 44
Kirkstead St. NG7: Hys G ...2D 44
Kirkstone Av. DE75: Hea ...4F 15
Kirkstone Ct. NG10: Long E ...3D 62
Kirkstone Dr. NG2: Gam ...4E 59
Kirkwhite Av. NG10: Long E ...6F 63
Kirkwhite Ho. NG10: Long E ...6F 63
   (off Kirkwhite Av.)
Kirtle Cl. NG8: Aspl ...1H 43
Kirtley Cl. NG8: Want ...5A 18
Kirtley Dr. NG7: Lent ...1E 57
Kirtling Cl. NG5: Bestw ...5G 21
Kirton Av. NG10: Long E ...6F 63
Kittiwake M. NG7: Lent ...5C 44
Kiwi Cl. NG15: Huck ...6D 6
KK Sports & Leisure Cen. ...4B 16
Knapp Av. NG16: Eastw ...4H 7
Kneesall Gro. NG15: Huck ...5H 7
Kneeton Cl. NG4: Ged ...3F 35
  NG5: Sher ...3G 33
Kneeton Va. NG5: Sher ...3G 33
Knighton Av. NG7: Radf ...3H 43
Knighton Rd. NG5: Woodt ...2H 33
Knightsbridge Dr. NG3: Sher ...4G 33
   (off St Albans St.)
Knightsbridge Dr. NG2: West Br ...1G 67
  NG16: Nuth ...4E 31
Knightsbridge Gdns. NG15: Huck ...1F 7
Knightsbridge Way NG15: Huck ...2F 7
Knight's Cl. NG2: West Br ...2G 67
Knights Cl. NG5: Top V ...5D 20
  NG9: Toton ...3H 63
Knight St. NG4: Neth ...3H 47
Knightsyard Ct. NG10: Long E ...2E 73
Knightwood Dr. NG6: Bestw V ...6F 9
Kniveton Pk. DE7: Ilk ...2H 39
Knole Rd. NG8: Woll ...4E 43
Knoll Av. NG15: Huck ...6D 6
Knowle Hill NG16: Kimb ...2A 30
Knowle La. NG16: Kimb ...3A 30
Knowle Pk. NG16: Kimb ...2A 30
Knowles Wlk. NG5: Arn ...5H 21
Kozi Kots NG4: Neth ...2H 47
Krebs Cl. NG11: Clftn ...4A 66
Kyle Vw. NG5: Top V ...4E 21
Kyme St. NG7: Radf ...4D 44

Kynance Gdns. NG11: Wilf 6F 57
Kyte St. NG7: Lent 5D 44

L

Labray Rd. NG14: Calv 3G 11
Laburnum Av. NG12: Key 5A 80
Laburnum Cl. NG10: Sand 4D 52
Laburnum Gdns. NG6: Bulw 2C 32
Laburnum Gro. NG9: Bee 6H 55
 NG15: Huck 6H 7
Laburnum St. NG3: Nott 2H 45
Lace Ct. NG10: Long E 4E 63
LACE MARKET 5F 5 (5H 45)
Lace Mkt. Sq. NG1: Nott 4F 5
Lace Market Stop (NET) 4E 5 (5G 45)
Lace Market Theatre 5F 5 (5H 45)
Lace Mill Ct. NG6: Bas 4B 32
Lace Rd. NG9: Bee 4F 55
Lace St. NG7: Nott, Lent 2B 56
Lace Way NG1: Nott 5H 5 (5A 46)
Lacewood Cl. NG6: Bestw V 1B 20
Lacey Av. NG15: Huck .6F 7
Lacey Cl. DE7: Ilk 4G 27
Laceyfields Rd. DE75: Hea 4E 15
Ladbrooke Cres. NG6: Bas 4A 32
Ladybank Ri. NG5: Arn 5E 23
Lady Bay Av. NG2: West Br 2B 58
Lady Bay Bri. NG2: Nott, West Br 1A 58
Lady Bay Ct. NG2: West Br 2C 58
Lady Bay Rd. NG2: West Br 2C 58
Ladybay Workshops NG2: West Br 2B 58
 (off Lady Bay Av.)
Ladybridge Cl. NG9: Atten 2E 65
Ladycroft Av. NG15: Huck 4G 7
Ladylea Rd. NG10: Long E 3C 72
Ladysmith St. NG2: Nott 5C 46
Ladysmocks Gdns. NG2: Nott 1H 57
Ladywood Rd. DE7: D Ab, Kirk H 4F 39
Lake Av. DE75: Los 1A 14
Lake Gdns. DE75: Los 1A 14
Lakehead Ho. NG11: Clftn 4C 66
Lakeland Av. NG15: Huck 6A 8
Lakeland Rd. NG14: Calv 5C 12
Lakeside Av. NG10: Long E 3E 73
Lakeside Bus. Cen. DE75: Ship 1E 27
Lakeside Cres. NG10: Long E 2F 73
Lake St. NG7: Radf 3D 44
Lamartine St. NG3: Nott 2G 5 (4H 45)
Lamb Cl. Dr. NG16: Eastw, Newth 1C 16
Lambert Gdns. NG8: Aspl 1A 44
Lambert Hill NG15: Huck 4F 7
Lambert St. NG7: Hys G 2C 44
Lambeth Ct. NG9: Bee 4H 55
Lambeth Rd. NG5: Arn 3E 21
Lambie Cl. NG8: Woll 4A 44
LAMBLEY 6C 24
Lambley Almshouses NG3: Nott 1H 45
Lambley Av. NG3: Mapp 4D 34
Lambley Bridle Rd. NG14: Bur J 1D 36
Lambley Cl. NG3: Mapp 4B 34
Lambley La. NG4: Ged 4G 35
 NG14: Bur J 2D 36
Lambley Rd. NG14: Lowd 5G 25
Lambourne Cl. NG9: Bram 3C 54
Lambourne Dr. NG8: Woll 4F 43
Lambourne Gdns. NG5: Woodt 2C 34
Lambton Cl. DE7: Ilk .4A 28
Lamcote Gdns. NG12: Rad T 6E 49
Lamcote Gro. NG2: Nott 2H 57
Lamcote M. NG12: Rad T 6E 49
Lamcote St. NG2: Nott 2H 57
Laming Gap La. NG12: Cotg, Stant W 3C 80
Lamins La. NG6: Bestw V 6F 9
Lammas Gdns. NG2: Nott 1H 57
Lamorna Gro. NG11: Wilf 5F 57
Lamplands NG12: Cotg 2E 71
Lamp Wood Cl. NG14: Calv 4G 11
Lanark Cl. NG8: Woll .6A 44
Lancaster Av. NG9: Stfrd 5G 53
 NG10: Sand 1C 62
Lancaster Ct. NG3: Nott 2D 46
Lancaster Rd. NG3: Nott 2D 46
 NG6: Bestw V 1C 20
 NG15: Huck 1D 18
Lancaster Way NG8: Stre 5D 30
Lancelot Dr. NG16: Want 4H 17
Lancelyn Gdns. NG2: West Br 1A 68
Landcroft Cres. NG5: Bestw 1E 33
Landmere Cl. DE7: Ilk 4G 27
Landmere Gdns. NG3: Nott 6B 34
Landmere La. NG2: West Br 2F 67
 NG11: Rudd 3H 67
 NG12: Edwal 4B 68
Landsdown Gro. NG10: Long E 4H 63
Landseer Cl. NG7: Radf 3C 44
The Lane NG16: Aws .3E 29
Laneham Av. NG5: Arn 6C 22
Laneside Av. NG9: Toton 3G 63

Laneward Cl. DE7: Ilk 3H 27
Langar Cl. NG5: Sher 3G 33
Langar Rd. NG13: Bing 6E 51
Langbank Av. NG5: Top V 4C 20
Langdale Dr. NG10: Long E 1C 72
Langdale Gro. NG13: Bing 5B 50
Langdale Rd. NG3: Nott 4D 46
Langdon Cl. NG5: Sher 5E 33
 NG10: Long E 4C 62
Langdown Cl. NG6: Bulw 5G 19
Langen Ct. NG10: Long E 1G 73
Langford Rd. NG5: Arn 6D 22
Langham Av. NG3: Nott 3C 46
Langham Dr. NG14: Bur J 2F 37
Langham Pk. DE7: Stant D 2D 52
LANGLEY 4F 15
Langley Av. DE7: Ilk .2H 27
 NG5: Arn 1B 34
Langley Bri. Ind. Est. NG16: Lang M 2H 15
Langley Bus. Pk. NG16: Lang M 3F 15
Langley Cl. NG5: Bestw V 1C 20
Langley Farm Cl. DE75: Hea 4F 15
LANGLEY MILL 2G 15
Langley Mill By-Pass NG16: Lang M . . .1E 15, 1G 15
Langley Mill Station (Rail) 2F 15
Langley Pk. NG16: Lang M 2F 15
Langstrath Dr. NG2: West Br 1E 69
Langstrath Rd. NG11: Clftn 4C 66
Langton Cl. NG4: Colw 3G 47
Langtry Gdns. NG13: Bing 4F 51
Langtry Gro. NG7: Bas 6E 33
Langwith Cl. DE7: Ilk .2B 28
Lanky Bills Fun Shack 1F 15
Lansdown Cl. NG9: Chil 1B 64
Lansdowne Dr. NG2: West Br 1H 67
Lansdowne Rd. NG6: Bas 3C 32
Lansing Cl. NG11: Clftn 5D 66
Lanthwaite Cl. NG11: Clftn 4C 66
Lanthwaite Rd. NG11: Clftn 4D 66
Lapford Cl. NG3: Mapp 1F 35
Lapins Cl. NG8: Aspl .2H 43
Larch Cl.
 NG2: West Br 2E 59
 NG5: Arn 5G 21
 NG13: Bing 5G 51
 NG15: Huck 6H 7
Larch Cres. NG9: Bee 4E 55
 NG16: Eastw 3A 16
Larchdene Av. NG8: Woll 6D 42
Larch Dr. NG10: Sand 4D 52
Larch Gdns. NG6: Bulw 6G 19
Larch Ho. NG5: Sher .4H 33
Larch Way NG12: Key 5A 80
Largs Cl. NG5: Top V .3C 20
Lark Cl. NG9: Chil 6A 54
Larkdale St. NG7: Radf 1A 4 (3E 45)
Larkfield Rd. NG16: Nuth 2B 30
LARKFIELDS 2B 30
Lark Hill Village NG11: Clftn 5A 66
LARKLANDS 2C 40
Larkland's Av. DE7: Ilk 2C 40
Larkspur Av. NG5: Redh 3A 22
Larkwood Cl. NG8: Bilb 1G 43
Larwood Gro. NG5: Sher 3G 33
Lascelles Av. NG4: Ged 5F 35
Latham St. NG6: Bulw 6H 19
Lathkill Av. DE7: Ilk 2A 28
Lathkill Cl. DE7: West H 1C 38
 NG6: Bulw 6H 19
Lathkilldale Cres. NG10: Long E 2C 72
Latimer Cl. NG6: Bulw 1A 32
Latimer Dr. NG9: Bram 6B 42
Latin Gro. NG15: Huck .3A 8
Laughton Av. NG2: West Br 1G 67
Laughton Cres. NG15: Huck 1E 19
Launceston Cres. NG11: Wilf 1E 67
Launder St. NG2: Nott 1G 57
Laurel Av. NG12: Key 5H 79
Laurel Cres. NG10: Long E 1E 73
Laurel Rd. NG4: Car .1F 47
Lauren Gro. NG9: Toton 3H 63
Laurie Av. NG7: Hys G 1E 45
Laurie Cl. NG7: Hys G 1E 45
Lauriston Dr. NG6: Bulw 3B 32
Lavelle Ct. NG9: Chil .3C 64
Lavender Cl. NG8: Brox 6E 31
Lavender Cres. NG4: Car 6F 35
Lavender Gdns. DE75: Hea 4F 15
Lavender Gro. NG9: Bee 6H 55
 NG12: Cotg 6G 61
Lavender Wlk. NG3: Nott 2H 45
Laver Cl. NG5: Arn 6D 22
Laverock Cl. NG16: Kimb 1H 29
Lawdon Rd. NG5: Arn 4C 22
Lawley Av. NG9: Lent A 2G 55
Lawn Cl. DE75: Hea .3D 14
Lawn Gro. NG4: Car, Ged 6A 36
Lawn Mill Rd. NG16: Kimb 6G 17
Lawn Mills NG16: Kimb 6F 17

Lawrence Av. DE72: Brea 5A 62
 NG4: Colw 4G 47
 NG16: Aws 3E 29
 NG16: Eastw 3B 16
Lawrence Cl. NG12: Cotg 2F 71
Lawrence Dr. NG8: Stre 5C 30
Lawrence M. NG12: Cotg 2F 71
Lawrence St. NG9: Stfrd 5F 53
 NG10: Long E 5F 63
 NG10: Sand 4D 52
Lawrence Way NG7: Lent 1E 57
Lawson Av. NG10: Long E 6G 63
Lawson St. NG7: Radf 3E 45
Lawton Dr. NG6: Bulw 4A 20
Laxton Av. NG6: Bulw 2B 32
Laxton Cl. NG8: Aspl .2H 43
Laxton Dr. NG15: Huck 5E 7
Leabrook Cl. NG11: Clftn 2A 66
Leabrook Gdns. NG15: Huck 3A 8
Lea Ct. NG13: Bing 6D 50
Leacroft Rd. NG8: Aspl 2B 44
Leadale Av. NG15: Huck 3A 8
Leaf Cl. NG15: Huck 2H 7
Leafe Cl. NG9: Chil 3C 64
Leafield Gro. NG11: Clftn 3C 66
Leafy La. DE75: Hea .4D 14
Leahurst Gdns. NG2: West Br 6D 58
Leahurst Rd. NG2: West Br 6C 58
Leahy Gdns. NG5: Bestw 1D 32
Leake Rd. NG11: Goth 6H 75
Leamington Dr. NG9: Chil 1C 64
Leander Cl. NG11: Wilf 5F 57
The Leas NG14: Bulc .2H 37
Lechlade Cl. DE7: West H 1B 38
Lechlade Rd. NG5: Bestw 1E 33
Ledbury Va. NG8: Aspl 1H 43
Ledger Wlk. NG5: Sher 6F 33
 (off Jensen Way)
Leech Cl. NG16: Gilt 6D 16
Lee Cres. DE7: Ilk 1D 40
Lee La. DE75: Hea 2A 15
Leen Cl. NG6: Bestw V 1D 20
 NG15: Huck 3A 8
Leen Ct. NG7: Lent 1C 56
Leen Dr. NG6: Bulw 4A 20
 NG15: Huck 2H 7
Leen Ga. NG7: Lent, Nott 1B 56
Leen Mills La. NG15: Huck 2H 7
Leen Pl. NG7: Radf 4C 44
Leen Valley Golf Course 4A 8
Leen Valley Way NG15: Huck 6A 8
Lee Rd. NG14: Bur J .2G 37
 NG14: Calv 3F 11
Lees Barn Rd. NG12: Rad T 1D 60
Lees Hill Footpath NG2: Nott 6A 46
Lees Hill St. NG2: Nott 5A 46
Leeson St. NG4: Colw 4G 47
Lees Rd. NG3: Mapp .6C 34
Lee Westwood Sports Cen. 2B 66
Leicester Ho. NG9: Bram 3H 53
Leicester St. NG10: Long E 1G 73
Leigh Cl. NG2: West Br 5G 57
Leigh Rd. NG9: Toton 1H 63
Leighton St. NG3: Nott 3B 46
Leiston Gdns. NG5: Top V 5E 21
Leivers Av. NG5: Arn .5B 22
Leivers Ho. NG5: Arn .1C 34
 (off Derwent Cres.)
Lema Cl. NG6: Bulw 5B 20
Lendal Ct. NG7: Radf 2A 4 (4E 45)
Lendrum Ct. NG14: Bur J 3F 37
Leniscar Av. DE75: Los 1A 14
Len Maynard Ct. NG3: Nott 3C 46
Lennox St. NG1: Nott 3G 5 (4H 45)
LENTON ABBEY 2G 55
Lenton Av. NG7: Nott .5E 45
 NG12: Toll 4E 69
Lenton Blvd. NG7: Lent 4D 44
Lenton Bus. Pk. NG7: Lent 5C 44
The Lenton Cen. 6D 44
Lenton Cir. NG12: Toll 4E 69
Lenton Ct. NG7: Nott 6A 4 (6E 45)
Lenton Hall Dr. NG7: Nott 1A 56
Lenton Ind. Est. E. NG7: Lent 4D 56
Lenton Ind. Est. W. NG7: Lent 3D 56
Lenton La. NG7: Lent .1D 56
Lenton Mnr. NG7: Lent 6C 44
Lenton Rd. NG7: Nott 6A 4 (6E 45)
Lenton St. NG10: Sand 5E 53
Leonard Av. NG5: Sher 5G 33
Leonard Cheshire Cl. DE75: Hea 4F 15
Leonard M. NG9: Chil 3B 64
Leonard St. NG6: Bulw 2H 31
Leopold St. NG10: Long E 6F 63
Le Page Ct. NG8: Bilb 1G 43
Leroy Wallace Av. NG7: Radf 3D 44
Lerwick Cl. NG11: Clftn 4E 67
Leslie Av. NG7: Hys G 1E 45
 NG9: Bee 6F 55
 NG16: Kimb 2H 29

Leslie Gro. NG14: Calv 4H 11
Leslie Rd. NG7: Hys G 1E 45
(not continuous)
Letchworth Cres. NG9: Chil 1C 64
Letcombe Rd. NG11: Clftn 2C 66
Levens Cl. NG2: West Br 6E 59
Leverton Ct. NG2: West Br 6B 58
Leverton Grn. NG11: Clftn 3C 66
Levertons Pl. NG5: Huck 1H 19
Leverton Wlk. NG5: Arn 5C 22
Levick Ct. NG2: Nott 1G 57
Lewcote La. DE7: West H 6E 27
Lewindon Ct. NG5: Woodt 3A 34
Lewis Cl. NG3: Nott 1F 5 (3H 45)
Lewis Way NG6: Bestw V 6F 9
Lewsey Cl. NG9: Chil 3B 64
Lexington Gdns. NG5: Sher 3H 33
Lexington Pl. NG1: Nott 4G 5
Leybourne Dr. NG5: Bestw 1C 32
Leyland Cl. NG9: Toton 3H 63
The Leys NG11: Clftn 4A 66
NG12: Norm W 6H 69
Leys Ct. NG11: Rudd 1G 77
Leys Rd. NG11: Rudd 1G 77
Ley St. NG4: Neth 2A 48
Leyton Cres. NG9: Bee 6H 55
Library Rd. NG7: Nott 2A 56
Lichfield Cl. NG9: Toton 2G 63
NG10: Long E .6H 63
Lichfield Rd. NG2: Nott 5C 46
Liddell Gro. NG8: Woll 4F 43
Liddington St. NG7: Bas 6D 32
Lido Cl. NG6: Bulw 4A 20
Lievesley Gro. NG4: Ged 4G 35
Lightning Gro. NG15: Huck 2D 18
Lilac Av. NG4: Car 1E 47
Lilac Cl. NG8: Brox 6E 31
NG12: Key 5A 80
Lilac Ct. NG11: Clftn 4A 66
Lilac Cres. NG9: Bee 6H 55
Lilac Gro. DE75: Hea 4C 14
NG9: Bee 6H 55
Lilac M. DE7: Ilk 4H 27
Lilac Rd. NG15: Huck 6H 7
The Lilacs NG9: Bee 5F 55
Lilian Hind Ct. NG6: Bulw 5F 19
Lilleker Ri. NG5: Arn 4A 22
Lillie Ter. NG2: Nott 5B 46
Lillington Rd. NG6: Bulw 2A 48
Lily Av. NG4: Neth 2A 48
Lily Gro. NG9: Bee 6H 55
Lime Av. NG16: Lang M 3G 15
Lime Cl. NG12: Rad T 6F 49
NG16: Nuth 1A 30
Limefield Ct. NG2: West Br 2C 58
Lime Gro.
NG9: Stfrd 6F 53
NG10: Long E 5F 63
NG10: Sand 5D 52
Lime Gro. Av. NG9: Chil 6E 55
Limekiln Ct. NG6: Bulw 5G 19
Lime La. NG5: Arn 6A 10
The Limes DE7: Mapp 4C 26
NG11: Bart F 1E 75
Limes Cl. NG16: Lang M 1G 15
Lime St. DE7: Ilk .2B 40
NG6: Bulw 6H 19
Lime Ter. NG10: Long E 5F 63
Lime Tree Av. NG8: Cin 4H 31
NG8: Woll 6H 43
Limetree Cl. NG12: Key 5H 79
Lime Tree Ct. NG9: Nott 2G 55
Limetree Ct. DE7: Kirk H 3G 39
Lime Tree Ri. DE7: Kirk H 3G 39
Lime Tree Rd. NG15: Huck 1H 19
Limmen Gdns. NG3: Nott 1H 5 (3A 46)
Limpenny St. NG7: Radf 3D 44
LINBY 1H 7
Linby Av. NG15: Huck 4H 7
Linby Cl. NG4: Ged 5G 35
NG5: Sher 2H 33
Linby Dr. NG8: Stre 5D 30
Linby Gro. NG15: Huck 3H 7
Linby Ho. NG15: Huck 1H 7
Linby La. NG15: Lin, Pap 1A 8
Linby Rd. NG15: Huck 3H 7
Linby St. NG6: Bulw 5A 20
Linby Wlk. NG15: Huck 3G 7
Lincoln Av. NG10: Sand 1C 62
Lincoln Cir. NG7: Nott 5A 4 (5E 45)
Lincoln Cl. NG9: Stfrd 2G 53
Lincoln Ct. NG8: Bilb 2D 42
Lincoln Gro. NG12: Rad T 6F 49
Lincoln Ho. NG3: Mapp P 6H 21
Lincoln St. NG1: Nott 3E 5 (4G 45)
NG6: Bas 6A 32
Lindale Cl. NG2: Gam 5E 59
Lindbridge Rd. NG8: Brox 4A 66
Linden Av. NG11: Clftn 4A 66
Linden Ct. NG9: Bee 6G 55

Linden Gro. NG4: Ged 6B 36
NG9: Bee 6G 55
NG9: Stfrd 5G 53
NG10: Sand 4C 52
Linden Pl. NG3: Mapp 1E 35
Linden St. NG3: Nott 2H 45
Lindfield Cl. NG8: Brox 5G 31
Lindfield Rd. NG8: Brox 5F 31
Lindisfarne Gdns. NG5: Top V 4E 21
Lindley St. NG16: Newth 1D 16
Lindley Ter. NG7: Hys G 2C 44
Lindrick Cl. NG12: Edwal 1E 69
Lindsay St. NG7: Hys G 2D 44
Lindum Gro. NG2: Nott 6B 46
Lindum Rd. NG6: Bas 4B 32
Linen Ho. NG7: Radf 3C 44
(off Hartley Rd.)
Linette Cl. NG5: Sher 5E 33
Linford Ct. NG9: Bram 5B 42
Ling Cres. NG11: Rudd 5G 67
Lingdale Rd. NG8: Woll 6D 42
Lingford NG12: Cotg 2G 71
Lingford St. NG15: Huck 5H 7
Lingmell Cl. NG2: West Br 5E 59
LINGS BAR HOSPITAL 5F 59
Lings Bar Rd. NG2: Gam 5F 59
(off Ambleside)
Lings Cl. DE7: Ilk .2B 28
Lings La. NG12: Key 6G 79
Lingwood La. NG14: Woodbo 3B 24
Linkin Rd. NG9: Chil 5C 54
Linkmel Cl. NG2: Nott 2E 57
Linkmel Rd. NG16: Eastw 2G 15
Linksfield Ct. NG2: West Br 3G 67
Linley Ct. NG13: Bing 5E 51
(off Long Acre)
Linnell St. NG3: Nott 3B 46
Linnet Way NG15: Huck 4F 7
Linsdale Cl. NG8: Bilb 4B 42
Linsdale Gdns. NG4: Ged 3F 35
Linton Ri. NG3: Nott 3C 46
Linwood Cres. NG16: Eastw 4B 16
Lion Cl. NG8: Aspl 5A 32
Lismore Cl. NG7: Radf 4C 44
Lissett Av. DE7: Ilk 2A 40
Lister Ga. NG1: Nott 5E 5 (5G 45)
Listergate Sq. NG1: Nott 5E 5 (5G 45)
Lister Ho. NG3: Mapp 5B 34
Lister Rd. NG7: Nott 1C 56
Listowel Cres. NG11: Clftn 5C 66
Litchen Cl. DE7: Ilk 5B 28
Litchfield Ri. NG5: Arn 3A 22
The Litmus Bldg. NG1: Nott 2F 5
Lit. Bounds NG2: West Br 4H 57
Little Drivers Soft Play Cen. 5F 53
Littlegreen Rd. NG5: Woodt 3A 34
LITTLE HALLAM .3B 40
Lit. Hallam Hill DE7: Ilk 4A 40
Lit. Hallam La. DE7: Ilk 3B 40
Lit. Hayes NG2: West Br 1G 67
Lit. Holland Gdns. NG16: Nuth 1B 30
Lit. John Wlk. NG3: Nott 2H 45
Little La. NG12: Toll 2G 69
NG14: Calv 4F 11
NG16: Kimb 2H 29
Lit. Lime La. NG5: Arn 6A 10
Lit. Lunnon NG11: Bart F 1E 75
Lit. Meadow NG12: Cotg 3G 71
Little Mdw. Cl. DE7: Ilk 5A 28
Littlemoor La. NG11: Rudd 4A 78
Lit. Oakwood Dr. NG5: Top V 3B 20
Little Ox NG4: Colw 5H 47
Lit. Tennis St. NG2: Nott 6C 46
Lit. Tennis St. Sth. NG2: Nott 1C 58
Littlewell La. DE7: Stant D 1B 52
Lit. Wood Ct. NG15: Huck 6E 7
Littlewood Gdns. NG8: Bilb 4C 42
Litton Cl. DE7: Ilk .3A 28
NG5: Woodt 3A 34
Liverpool St. NG3: Nott 3H 5 (4A 46)
Livingstone Rd. NG3: Nott 3A 46
LivingWell Health Club
Nottingham 3E 5 (4G 45)
Llanberis Gro. NG8: Aspl 5A 32
Lloyd St. NG5: Sher 5G 33
Loach Ct. NG8: Woll 4A 44
Lobelia Cl. NG3: Nott 2H 45
Lock Cl. DE7: Kirk H 3G 39
NG9: Bee 2G 65
Lockerbie St. NG4: Colw 3H 47
Lock La. NG10: Long E 3D 72
NG10: Sand 6D 52
Locksley Ho. NG3: Nott 3H 45
Locksley La. NG11: Clftn 1C 66
Lockton Av. DE75: Hea 5C 14
Lockwood Cl. NG5: Top V 4E 21
NG9: Bee 1H 65
Lodge Cl. NG5: Redh 3A 22
NG8: Aspl 1B 44
Lodge Farm La. NG5: Arn 4A 22

Lodge Rd. DE7: Mapp 4D 26
NG10: Long E 2F 73
NG16: Newth 5C 16
Lodge Row DE7: Mapp 4C 26
Lodgewood Cl. NG6: Bulw 1G 31
Lodore Cl. NG2: West Br 5E 59
Logan Sq. NG6: Bas 2C 32
Logan St. NG6: Bulw 1A 32
Lois Av. NG7: Lent .6D 44
Lombard St. NG7: Lent 5D 44
Lombardy Lodge NG9: Toton 4A 64
London Rd. NG2: Nott 5G 5 (5H 45)
NG15: Huck 4D 6
Longacre NG5: Woodt 3B 34
Long Acre E. NG13: Bing 5E 51
NG15: Huck 4D 6
Longbeck Av. NG3: Nott 6C 34
Longbridge La. DE75: Los 2B 14
Longclose Ct. NG6: Bulw 1G 31
Longcroft Av. DE7: Ilk 2A 28
Longdale Rd. NG5: Arn 1H 33
Longden Cl. NG9: Bram 1H 53
Longden Mill NG3: Nott 3H 5
Longden St. NG3: Nott 3H 5 (4A 46)
LONG EATON 5G 63
Long Eaton Station (Rail) 2E 73
Longfellows Cl. NG5: Bestw 5F 21
Longfield Av. NG8: Bilb 2C 42
Longfield Cres. DE7: Ilk 4B 40
Longfield La. DE7: Ilk 4B 40
Longford Cres. NG6: Bulw 3A 20
Long Hill Ri. NG15: Huck 5F 7
Longhirst Dr. NG5: Arn 3B 22
Longlands Cl. NG9: Bee 1H 65
Longlands Dr. NG2: West Br 6F 59
Longlands Rd. NG9: Bee 1H 65
Long La. DE75: Ship 6H 15
NG9: Atten 3D 64
NG16: Want 4A 18
Longleat Cres. NG9: Chil 6C 54
Longmead Cl. NG5: Bestw 1G 33
Longmead Dr. NG5: Bestw 1G 33
Long Mdw. Hill NG14: Lowd 3F 25
Longmoor Gdns. NG10: Long E 3C 62
Longmoor La. DE72: Brea 4A 62
NG10: Sand 6D 52
Longmoor Rd. NG10: Long E, Sand 3C 62
Longore Sq. NG8: Woll 5B 44
Longridge Rd. NG5: Woodt 3B 34
Long Row NG1: Nott 4D 4 (5G 45)
(not continuous)
Long Row W. NG1: Nott 4D 4 (5G 45)
Long Stairs NG1: Nott 5G 5
Longthorpe Ct. NG5: Arn 6B 22
Longue Dr. NG14: Calv 4F 11
Longwall Av. NG2: Nott 2E 57
Long West Cft. NG14: Calv 4E 11
Longwood Ct. NG5: Top V 5D 20
Lonscale Ct. NG2: West Br 6E 59
Lonsdale Dr. NG9: Toton 3G 63
Lonsdale Rd. NG7: Radf 3C 44
Lord Haddon Rd. DE7: Ilk 6A 28
Lord Nelson St. NG2: Nott 5B 46
Lord St. NG2: Nott .5B 46
Lorimer Av. NG4: Ged 4H 35
Lorna Ct. NG3: Nott 6H 33
Lorne Gro. NG12: Rad T 6F 49
Lorne Wlk. NG3: Nott 2G 45
Lortas Rd. NG5: Sher 5D 32
LOSCOE 1A 14
Loscoe-Denby La. DE75: Los 1A 14
Loscoe Gdns. NG5: Sher 6F 33
Loscoe Grange DE75: Los 2A 14
Loscoe Mt. Rd. NG5: Sher 5G 33
Loscoe Rd. DE75: Hea 2B 14
NG5: Sher 6G 33
Lothian Rd. NG12: Toll 4E 69
Lothmore Ct. NG2: Nott 1F 57
Lotus Cl. NG3: Nott 2A 46
Loughborough Av. NG2: Nott 5B 46
Loughborough Rd. NG2: West Br 5A 58
NG11: Bunny, Rudd 3H 67
Loughrigg Cl. NG2: Nott 2F 57
Louisa Ct. NG5: Arn 5H 21
Louis Av. NG9: Bee 4E 55
Louise Av. NG4: Neth 1A 48
Lovelace Wlk. NG15: Huck 3H 7
Lovell Cl. NG6: Bulw 2F 31
Lovesey Av. NG15: Huck 3D 18
Lowater Pl. NG4: Car 2D 46
Lowater St. NG4: Car 2D 46
Lowcroft NG5: Woodt 3B 34
Lowdham La. NG14: Woodbo 1D 24
Lowdham Rd. NG4: Ged 4E 35
NG14: Epp 1G 25
Lowdham St. NG3: Nott 3H 5 (4A 46)
Lowe Av. DE7: Smal 5A 14
LOWER BEAUVALE 2C 16
Lwr. Beauvale NG16: Newth 2C 16
Lwr. Bloomsgrove Rd. DE7: Ilk 5B 28

Lwr. Brook St. NG10: Long E 6G **63**
Lwr. Canaan NG11: Rudd 5H **67**
Lwr. Chapel St. DE7: Ilk 6B **28**
Lwr. Claramount Rd. DE75: Hea 4E **15**
Lower Ct. NG9: Bee 4G **55**
Lwr. Dunstead Rd. NG16: Lang M 2E **15**
Lwr. Eldon St. NG2: Nott 5H **5** (5A **46**)
Lwr. Gladstone St. DE75: Hea 3C **14**
Lwr. Granby St. DE7: Ilk 5B **28**
Lwr. Maples DE75: Ship 5E **15**
Lwr. Middleton St. DE7: Ilk 6C **28**
Lwr. Orchard St. NG9: Stfrd 4G **53**
Lwr. Park St. NG9: Stfrd 4G **53**
Lwr. Parliament St. NG1: Nott 3E **5** (4G **45**)
Lwr. Regent St. NG9: Bee 5G **55**
Lower Rd. NG9: Bee 4H **55**
Lwr. Stanton Rd. DE7: Ilk 3B **40**
Lwr. Whitworth Rd. DE7: Ilk 3B **40**
Loweswater Ct. NG2: Gam 4E **59**
Lowlands Dr. NG12: Key 3H **79**
Lowlands Lea DE75: Hea 3H **79**
Low Pavement NG1: Nott 5E **5** (5G **45**)
Lows La. DE7: Stant D 1B **52**
Low Wood Rd. NG6: Bulw 2E **31**
Loxley Cl. NG15: Huck 6E **7**
Loxley Ho. 6H **45**
Loxley Mdw. NG14: Bur J 3E **37**
Lucerne Cl. NG11: Wilf 5F **57**
Lucillia Cl. NG15: Huck 3B **8**
Lucknow Av. NG3: Mapp P 1H **45**
Lucknow Ct. NG3: Mapp P 6H **33**
Lucknow Dr. NG3: Mapp P 1H **45**
Lucknow Rd. NG3: Mapp P 1H **45**
Ludford Cl. NG10: Long E 3G **73**
Ludford Rd. NG6: Bulw 5A **20**
Ludgate Cl. NG5: Arn 3E **21**
Ludham Av. NG6: Bulw 5H **19**
Ludlam Av. NG16: Gilt 6C **16**
Ludlow Av. NG2: West Br 4B **58**
Ludlow Cl. NG9: Bram 2D **54**
Ludlow Hill Rd. NG2: West Br 6B **58**
Lulworth Cl. NG2: West Br 6G **57**
Lulworth Ct. NG5: Kimb 6H **17**
Lune Cl. NG9: Atten 2E **65**
Lune Way NG13: Bing 6D **50**
Lupin Cl. NG3: Nott 2H **45**
Luther Cl. NG3: Nott 2A **46**
Luton Cl. NG8: Aspl 6B **32**
Lutterell Ct. NG2: West Br 6H **57**
Lutterell Way NG2: West Br 6D **58**
Lybster M. NG2: Nott 1F **57**
Lychgate Ct. NG16: Want 5H **17**
Lydia Gdns. NG16: Eastw 4A **16**
Lydney Pk. NG2: West Br 5F **57**
Lyle Cl. NG16: Kimb 6D **17**
Lyme Pk. NG2: West Br 6F **57**
Lymington Gdns. NG3: Nott 3C **46**
Lymn Av. NG4: Ged 5H **35**
Lynam Ct. NG6: Bulw 6H **19**
Lyncombe Gdns. NG12: Key 3H **79**
Lyndale Ct. DE7: Ilk 6H **27**
Lyndale Rd. NG9: Bram 3A **54**
Lynden Av. NG10: Long E 1F **73**
Lyndhurst Gdns. NG2: West Br 1H **67**
Lyndhurst Rd. NG2: Nott 5B **46**
Lynemouth Ct. NG5: Arn 3C **22**
Lyn Gilzean Ct. NG3: Nott 1G **5** (3H **45**)
Lynmoor Ct. NG15: Huck 2A **8**
Lynmouth Cres. NG7: Radf 2C **44**
Lynmouth Dr. DE7: Ilk 4H **27**
Lynncroft NG16: Eastw 2C **16**
Lynncroft St. NG8: Stre 5C **30**
Lynstead Dr. NG15: Huck 6C **6**
Lynton Ct. NG3: Nott 2B **46**
Lynton Gdns. NG5: Arn 5C **22**
Lynton Rd. NG9: Chil 5C **54**
Lyons Cl. NG11: Rudd 5F **67**
Lytham Dr. NG12: Edwal 2E **69**
Lytham Gdns. NG5: Top V 4E **21**
Lythe Cl. NG11: Wilf 6E **57**
Lytton Cl. NG3: Nott 2H **5** (4A **46**)

M

Mabel Gro. NG2: West Br 3C **58**
Mabel St. NG2: Nott 1H **57**
Macaulay Gro. NG16: Nuth 1B **30**
McClelland Av. NG6: Bestw V 6F **9**
McCracken Cl. NG5: Top V 4C **20**
Macdonald Sq. DE7: Kirk H 4G **39**
Machins La. NG12: Edwal 2C **68**
McIntosh Rd. NG4: Ged 4F **35**
Mackinley Av. NG9: Stfrd 2G **53**
Maclaren Gdns. NG11: Rudd 1H **77**
Maclean Rd. NG4: Car 2E **47**
Macmillan Cl. NG3: Mapp 5B **34**
Madden Cl. NG5: Bestw 2D **32**
Madford Bus. Pk. NG5: Arn 1H **33**
Madison Ct. NG7: Lent 5B **44**

Madryn Wlk. NG5: Bestw 6E **21**
Mafeking St. NG2: Nott 5C **46**
Magdala Rd. NG3: Mapp P 1G **45**
Magdalene Way NG15: Huck 3G **7**
Magenta Way
     NG4: Neth, Stoke B 2C **48**
Magnolia Cl. NG8: Brox 6E **31**
     NG12: Edwal 4C **68**
Magnolia Ct. NG9: Bram 2D **54**
Magnolia Gro. NG15: Huck 1H **19**
Magnus Ct. NG9: Bee 5G **55**
Magnus Rd. NG5: Sher 4G **33**
Magson Cl. NG3: Nott 4A **46**
Maiden La. NG1: Nott 4G **5** (5H **45**)
Maidens Dale NG5: Arn 5H **21**
Maid Marian Way NG1: Nott 4C **4** (5F **45**)
Maidstone Dr. NG8: Woll 1D **54**
Main Rd. NG4: Ged 6H **35**
     NG7: Nott 5A **56**
     NG11: Wilf 5F **57**
     NG12: Cotg, Rad T 4D **60**
     NG12: Plum 5G **69**
     NG12: Rad T 6E **49**
     NG12: S'frd 1H **49**
     NG14: Bulc, Lowd 2G **37**
     NG16: Want 4H **17**
Main St.
     DE7: Mapp 4C **26**
     DE7: Stant D 3B **52**
     DE72: Brea 5A **62**
     NG2: Gam 4E **59**
     NG4: Lamb 6B **24**
     NG6: Bulw 1H **31**
           (not continuous)
     NG8: Stre 6B **30**
     NG10: Long E 6G **63**
     NG11: Rudd 4A **78**
     NG12: Key 6G **79**
     NG13: Newt 1B **50**
     NG14: Bur J 3F **37**
     NG14: Calv 3D **10**
     NG14: Epp 5E **13**
     NG14: Woodbo 1B **24**
     NG15: Lin 1G **7**
     NG15: Pap 1B **8**
     NG16: Aws 2E **29**
     NG16: Eastw 4B **16**
     NG16: Kimb 1H **29**
     NG16: Newth 3E **17**
     NG25: Oxton 1B **12**
Maitland Av. NG5: Woodt 3B **34**
Maitland Rd. NG5: Woodt 3B **34**
Major St. NG1: Nott 2D **4** (4G **45**)
Malbon Cl. NG3: Nott 1B **46**
Malcolm Cl. NG3: Mapp P 2G **45**
Maldon Cl. NG9: Chil 1C **64**
     NG10: Long E 2G **73**
Malik Way DE75: Hea 5D **14**
Malin Cl. NG5: Arn 5D **22**
Malin Hill NG1: Nott 5F **5**
Malkin Av. NG12: Rad T 5G **49**
Mallard Cl. NG6: Bas 3D **32**
     NG13: Bing 6G **51**
Mallard Ct. NG9: Bee 6G **55**
Mallard Rd. NG4: Neth 3B **48**
Mallow Way NG13: Bing 5C **50**
Malmesbury Rd. NG3: Mapp 3C **34**
Maltby Cl. NG8: Aspl 5H **31**
Maltby Rd. NG3: Mapp 3C **34**
Malt Cotts. NG7: Bas 6D **32**
The Malt Cross Gallery 4D **4**
Malthouse Cl. NG16: Eastw 4B **16**
Malthouse Rd. DE7: Ilk 4B **40**
Malting Cl. NG11: Rudd 1G **77**
The Maltings NG3: Nott 2B **46**
     NG6: Bas 5C **32**
Malton Rd. NG5: Sher 5D **32**
Malt St. NG11: Goth 6H **75**
Malvern Cl. NG3: Nott 6A **34**
Malvern Ct. NG3: Mapp P 2G **45**
     NG9: Bee 5H **55**
Malvern Cres. NG2: West Br 6B **58**
Malvern Gdns. NG10: Long E 5C **62**
Malvern Rd. NG2: West Br 6A **58**
     NG3: Nott 6A **34**
Manchester St. NG10: Long E 1F **73**
Mandalay St. NG6: Bas 3B **32**
Mandeville Cl. NG15: Huck 4A **8**
Manesty Cres. NG11: Clftn 6C **66**
Manifold Gdns. NG2: Nott 1G **57**
Manly Cl. NG5: Top V 5C **20**
Manners Av. DE7: Ilk 6H **27**
Manners Ind. Est. DE7: Ilk 5H **27**
Manners Rd. DE7: Ilk 6A **28**
Manners St. DE7: Ilk 3C **40**
Manning St. NG3: Nott 2H **45**
Mannion Cres. NG10: Long E 2D **72**
Manns Leys NG12: Cotg 3E **71**
Mann St. NG7: Bas 1D **44**

Manor Av. NG2: Nott 5A **46**
     NG9: Atten 2E **65**
     NG9: Bee 5F **55**
     NG9: Stfrd 3F **53**
Manor Cl. NG12: Edwal 2D **68**
Manor Ct. DE72: Brea 5A **62**
     NG4: Car 2H **47**
     NG9: Bram 4C **54**
Manor Cres. NG4: Car 1H **47**
Manor Cft. NG6: Bas 4C **32**
Mnr. Farm Cvn. & Camping Site 4D **74**
Mnr. Farm Cl. NG11: Rudd 4A **78**
Mnr. Farm La. NG11: Clftn 3C **66**
Manor Flds. Dr. DE7: Ilk 2H **39**
Manor Grn. NG4: Car 1H **47**
Manor Grn. Wlk. NG4: Car 1H **47**
The Manor Health & Racquets Club 6A **28**
Manor Ho. Cl. NG11: Wilf 3F **57**
Manor Ho. Rd. NG10: Long E 1H **73**
Manorleigh DE72: Brea 5A **62**
Manor Pk. NG11: Rudd 6F **67**
Manor Pk. La. NG14: Epp 6G **13**
Manor Rd. DE7: Ilk 6A **28**
     NG4: Car 1H **47**
     NG11: Bart F 1E **75**
     NG12: Key 4G **79**
     NG13: Bing 5F **51**
     NG14: Calv 4G **11**
     NG16: Eastw 4B **16**
Manor St. NG2: Nott 5A **46**
Manor Wlk. NG14: Epp 6G **13**
Manorwood Rd. NG12: Cotg 3F **71**
Mansell Cl. NG16: Eastw 4D **16**
Mansfield Ct. NG5: Sher 1F **45**
Mansfield Gro. NG1: Nott 1C **4** (3F **45**)
Mansfield La. NG14: Calv 2H **11**
Mansfield Rd. DE75: Hea 3D **14**
     NG1: Nott 1D **4** (2F **45**)
     NG5: Arn, Redh, Sher 2G **9**
     NG5: Sher 1F **45**
     NG15: Pap 1F **9**
     NG16: Brins, Eastw 1A **16**
Mansfield St. NG5: Sher 5G **33**
Manston M. NG7: Radf 3D **44**
Manthorpe Cres. NG5: Sher 4B **34**
Manton Cres. NG9: Lent A 3F **55**
Manvers Bus. Pk. NG12: Cotg 1G **71**
Manvers Ct. NG2: Nott 4H **5** (5A **46**)
Manvers Gro. NG12: Rad T 6F **49**
Manvers Rd. NG2: West Br 5B **58**
Manvers St. NG2: Nott 4H **5** (5A **46**)
     NG4: Neth 3A **48**
Manville Cl. NG8: Aspl 3A **44**
     NG9: Bram 6B **42**
Maori Av. NG15: Huck 6D **6**
Maple Av. NG9: Bee 6H **55**
     NG10: Sand 4D **52**
Maplebeck Rd. NG5: Arn 6C **22**
Maple Cl. NG12: Key 5A **80**
     NG12: Rad T 1F **61**
     NG13: Bing 5G **51**
     NG14: Calv 4F **11**
Maple Ct. NG7: Lent 6D **44**
     NG16: Kimb 1H **29**
Mapledene Cres. NG8: Woll 6C **42**
Maple Dr. NG4: Ged 5B **36**
     NG15: Huck 6E **7**
     NG16: Nuth 1B **30**
Maple Gdns. DE75: Hea 4B **14**
     NG16: Lang M 2F **15**
Maple Gro. DE72: Brea 5B **62**
Maple Leaf Way NG15: Huck 1A **20**
The Maples DE75: Ship 5E **15**
Maples St. NG7: Hys G 2D **44**
Maplestead Av. NG11: Wilf 5F **57**
Mapletree Cl. NG5: Bestw 6F **21**
Maple Vw. NG11: Wilf 1F **67**
Maple Way NG2: West Br 1H **67**
MAPPERLEY
     DE7 ....5C **26**
     NG5 ....4B **34**
Mapperley Brook DE7: Mapp 5E **27**
Mapperley Cres. NG3: Mapp 3D **34**
Mapperley Golf Course 3D **34**
Mapperley Hall Dr. NG3: Mapp P 6G **33**
Mapperley Hall Gdns. NG3: Mapp P 6H **33**
Mapperley Hgts. NG5: Woodt 2D **34**
Mapperley La. DE7: Mapp 5C **26**
Mapperley Orchard NG5: Arn 6D **22**
MAPPERLEY PARK
     DE7 ....4B **26**
     NG3 ....4B **34**
Mapperley Pk. Dr. NG3: Mapp P 1G **45**
Mapperley Plains NG3: Mapp 2D **34**
Mapperley Ri. NG3: Mapp 5A **34**
Mapperley Rd. NG3: Mapp P 2G **45**
Mapperley Sports Village 6A **34**
Mapperley Wood Local Nature Reserve 4D **26**
March Cl. NG5: Top V 6C **20**

Marchesi Cl. NG15: Huck 1E **19**
Marchwood Cl. NG8: Radf 4B **44**
Marciana Gro. NG15: Huck 3A **8**
Marco Island NG1: Nott 3G **5**
Mardale Cl. NG2: West Br 6E **59**
Mardling Av. NG5: Bestw 1B **40**
Margaret Av. DE7: Ilk 4H **63**
  NG10: Long E 1D **62**
  NG10: Sand 5G **35**
Margaret Cres. NG4: Ged 4D **50**
Margaret Pl. NG13: Bing 3A **54**
Margarets Ct. NG9: Bram 6A **46**
Marham Cl. NG2: Nott 2H **47**
Marhill Rd. NG4: Car 6A 4 (6E **45**)
Maria Ct. NG7: Nott 6G **7**
Marie Gdns. NG15: Huck 6F **55**
Marina Av. NG9: Bee 5A **54**
Marina Rd. DE7: Smal 5G **14**
Mariner Cl. NG6: Bulw 1G **31**
Marion Av. NG15: Huck 3A **66**
Maris Cl. NG11: Clftn 3E **37**
Maris Dr. NG14: Bur J 1A **40**
Market Pl. DE7: Ilk 4C **14**
  DE75: Hea .4C **14**
    (off Market St.)
  NG5: Arn 6B **22**
  NG6: Bulw .6H **19**
  NG10: Long E 5G **63**
  NG13: Bing 5E **51**
  NG15: Huck 4G **7**
Market Side NG6: Bulw 6H **19**
    (off Duke St.)
Market St. DE7: Ilk 1B **40**
  DE75: Hea .3C **14**
  NG1: Nott 3D 4 (4G **45**)
  NG13: Bing 5E **51**
Markham Cres. NG5: Sher 3G **33**
Markham Rd. NG9: Bram 2D **54**
Mark St. NG10: Sand 6E **53**
The Marlborough NG3: Nott 2G **45**
Marlborough Ct. NG2: West Br 4B **58**
  NG9: Bee 3F **55**
Marlborough Rd. NG5: Woodt 2H **33**
  NG9: Bee 3F **55**
  NG10: Long E 4H **63**
Marlborough St. NG7: Lent 2C **56**
Marl Cl. NG11: Rudd 5F **67**
Marldon Cl. NG8: Bilb 4B **42**
Marlow Av. NG6: Bas 5C **32**
Marlow Cres. DE7: West H 1B **38**
MARLPOOL 6D **14**
Marl Rd. NG12: Rad T 6H **49**
Marlwood NG12: Cotg 4G **71**
Marmion Cl. NG3: Nott 3B **46**
Marmion Rd. NG3: Nott 2C **46**
Marnham Dr. NG3: Nott 6A **34**
Marriott Av. NG9: Chil 6A **54**
Marriott Cl. NG9: Chil 6A **54**
Marsant Cl. NG8: Woll 4A **44**
Marsden Cl. NG6: Bulw 2C **32**
Marshall Av. NG14: Calv 3F **11**
Marshall Dr. NG9: Bram 3H **53**
  NG11: Rudd 6F **67**
Marshall Hill Dr. NG3: Mapp 6C **34**
Marshall Rd. NG3: Mapp 6C **34**
Marshall St. DE75: Hea 3D **14**
  NG5: Sher .5G **33**
Marshall Way DE7: Kirk H 3G **39**
Marsham Dr. NG5: Arn 1B **34**
Marsh Av. DE7: Ilk 2A **28**
Marston Rd. NG3: Nott 2D **46**
Martell Cl. NG9: Chil 1A **66**
Martin Cl. NG6: Bulw 5F **19**
Martin Cl. NG6: Bulw 6A **20**
Martin Cres. NG11: Rudd 6F **67**
Martindale Cl. NG2: Gam 4E **59**
Martinmass Cl. NG7: Lent 6C **44**
Martin's Hill NG4: Car 2G **47**
Martin's Pond Nature Reserve 4E **43**
Marton Rd. NG6: Bulw 4A **20**
  NG9: Chil 2C **64**
Marvyn Cl. NG6: Bulw 1C **32**
Marwood Cres. NG4: Car 6E **35**
Marwood Rd. NG4: Car 6A **34**
Mary Cl. NG3: Nott 2G **63**
Maryland Ct. NG9: Stfrd 4D **16**
Mary Rd. NG16: Eastw 6A **36**
Marziale Ct. NG4: Ged 2D **48**
Masonic Pl. NG1: Nott 3C 4 (4F **45**)
Mason Rd. DE7: Ilk 5H **27**
Massey Cl. NG14: Bur J 4E **37**
Massey Gdns. NG3: Nott 3A **46**
Masson Ct. NG5: Top V 4E **21**
Matlock Cl. NG1: Nott 2D 4 (4G **45**)
  NG10: Long E 2B **72**
Matlock St. NG4: Neth 2H **47**
Matthews Cl. NG9: Stfrd 1H **53**
Matthew Thomas Ct. NG9: Bee 5G **55**
Mattingly Rd. NG6: Bulw 1G **31**
Maud St. NG7: Bas 6E **33**

Maun Av. NG7: Radf 3B **44**
Maun Gdns. NG7: Radf 3B **44**
Maurice Dr. NG3: Mapp 5A **34**
Maws La. NG16: Kimb 6G **17**
Maxtoke Rd. NG7: Nott 6A 4 (6E **45**)
Maxwell Cl. NG7: Lent 6D **44**
Maxwell St. DE72: Brea 5B **62**
  NG10: Long E 6G **63**
May Av. NG8: Woll 5E **43**
May Ct. NG5: Sher 6F **33**
Maycroft Gdns. NG3: Nott 2C **46**
Maydene Cl. NG11: Clftn 4B **66**
Mayes Ri. NG6: Bestw V 1C **20**
Mayfair Gdns. NG5: Sher 2D **32**
Mayfield Av. DE75: Hea 4C **14**
  NG14: Bur J 2F **37**
Mayfield Cl. NG3: Nott 1G **57**
Mayfield Dr. NG9: Stfrd 1H **53**
Mayfield Gro. NG10: Long E 4G **63**
Mayfield Rd. NG4: Car 2D **46**
Mayflower Cl. NG2: West Br 4C **58**
Mayflower Rd. NG16: Newth 5D **16**
Maygreen Av. NG12: Cotg 6G **61**
Mayland Cl. NG8: Bilb 3C **42**
Maylands Av. DE72: Brea 5A **62**
Mayo Rd. NG5: Sher 6F **33**
Maypole NG11: Clftn 2C **66**
Maypole Yd. NG1: Nott 3E 5 (4G **45**)
May's Av. NG4: Car 3E **47**
Mays Cl. NG4: Car 3E **47**
May St. DE7: Ilk 3A **28**
Maythorn Cl. NG2: West Br 2G **67**
Maythorne Cl. NG5: Arn 6D **22**
Maythorne Wlk. NG5: Bestw 5G **21**
Maywood Golf Course 5A **52**
Meadowbank Cl. NG16: Eastw 2H **15**
Meadowbank Way NG16: Eastw 2H **15**
Mdw. Brown Rd. NG7: Hys G 1C **44**
Meadow Cl. DE72: Brea 6A **62**
  NG2: Nott 1A **58**
  NG15: Huck 6D **6**
  NG16: Eastw 1B **16**
Meadow Cotts. NG4: Neth 2H **47**
Meadow Cl. NG2: Nott 1B **58**
Meadow Cres. NG12: Cotg 6G **61**
Meadow Cft. Gdns. NG15: Huck 6F **7**
Meadow Dr. NG12: Key 4A **80**
Meadow End NG11: Goth 6H **75**
  NG12: Rad T 6H **49**
Meadow Gdns. DE75: Hea 4F **15**
  NG9: Chil 1E **65**
Meadow Gro. NG2: Nott 1A **58**
Meadow Lane .1A **58**
Meadow La. NG2: Nott 1A **58**
    (not continuous)
  NG9: Chil 6E **55**
  NG10: Long E 6H **63**
    (not continuous)
  NG14: Bur J 3F **37**
Meadow Ri. NG6: Bulw 1F **31**
Meadow Rd. NG4: Neth 3H **47**
  NG9: Bee 6G **55**
  NG16: Aws .2E **29**
MEADOWS 1G **57**
The Meadows DE75: Hea 4C **14**
  NG14: Woodbo 1B **24**
  NG16: Aws .2E **29**
Meadows Embankment Stop (NET) 2F **57**
Meadow St. DE7: Ilk 6B **28**
Meadows Way NG2: Nott 2F **57**
Meadowsweet Hill NG13: Bing 5C **50**
Meadow Trad. Est. NG2: Nott 6A **46**
Meadowvale Cres. NG11: Clftn 4C **66**
Meadowvale Pl. NG11: Clftn 4C **66**
Meadow Vw. NG9: Stfrd 3F **53**
Meadow Vw. Ct. DE72: Ris 1B **62**
Meadow Way West Stop (NET) 1F **57**
Mecca Bingo
  Beeston 5H **55**
Medawar Cl. NG11: Clftn 4A **66**
Medbank Ct. NG11: Wilf 6E **57**
Meden Cl. NG11: Clftn 2C **66**
Meden Gdns. NG7: Hys G 2B **44**
Medina Dr. NG12: Toll 4F **69**
Medway Cl. NG9: Chil 6C **54**
Medway Dr. NG13: Bing 5C **50**
Medway St. NG8: Radf 4B **44**
Meeks Rd. NG5: Arn 5D **22**
Meerbrook Pl. DE7: Kirk H 4G **39**
Meer Rd. NG9: Chil 6A **54**
Melbourne Ct. NG8: Aspl 3B **72**
  NG10: Long E 2B **58**
Melbourne Rd. NG2: West Br 1H **43**
  NG8: Aspl 1G **53**
  NG9: Stfrd .3B **34**
Melbury Rd. NG5: Woodt 1D **42**
  NG8: Bilb 3E **43**
Meldreth Rd. NG8: Bilb 1G **67**
Melford Rd. NG8: Bilb 1D **42**

Melksham Rd. NG5: Bestw 5G **21**
Mellbreak Cl. NG2: West Br 5E **59**
Mellers Ct. NG3: Nott 2C **46**
Mellish Sports Cen. 2B **32**
Mellors Rd. NG2: West Br 6B **58**
  NG5: Arn 4B **22**
Mellors Way NG8: Stre 5C **30**
Melrose Av. NG5: Sher 4G **33**
  NG9: Bee 1H **65**
Melrose Gdns. NG2: West Br 1H **57**
  NG3: Sher .4G **33**
Melton Ct. NG10: Sand 6C **52**
Melton Gdns. NG12: Edwal 1C **68**
Melton Gro. NG2: West Br 1C **68**
Melton Hall NG8: Woll 5A **44**
Melton Rd. NG2: West Br 4A **58**
  NG12: Edwal, Key, Plum, Stant W 4C **68**
Melville Cl. NG3: Mapp P 1G **45**
Melville Gdns. NG3: Nott 1H 5 (3A **46**)
Melville St. NG1: Nott 6E 5 (6G **45**)
Melvyn Dr. NG13: Bing 5E **51**
Mendip Cl. NG10: Long E 4C **62**
Mendip Ct. NG5: Top V 5D **20**
Mensing Av. NG12: Cotg 2E **71**
Merchant St. NG6: Bulw 5H **19**
    (not continuous)
Mercia Cl. NG16: Gilt 5C **16**
Mercian Cl. DE7: Ilk 6A **28**
Mercury Cl. NG6: Bas 2C **32**
Mere Av. NG14: Calv 4H **11**
Mere Cl. NG14: Calv 4H **11**
Meredith Cl. NG2: Nott 2F **57**
Meredith Ct. NG9: Stfrd 1G **53**
Meregill Cl. NG5: Top V 4D **20**
Merevale Av. NG11: Clftn 1D **66**
Mere Way NG11: Rudd 3H **77**
Meriac Cl. NG5: Top V 5D **20**
Meriden Av. NG9: Lent A 3G **55**
Meridian Cl. DE7: Ilk 3A **28**
Meridian Ct. NG5: Sher 5E **33**
Merlin Cl. NG11: Clftn 3C **66**
Merlin Dr. NG15: Huck 1E **19**
Merlin Way DE7: Ilk 5B **40**
Merrivale Cl. NG3: Mapp P 1G **45**
Mersey St. NG6: Bulw 6H **19**
Merton Cl. DE75: Hea 4D **14**
  NG5: Arn 4D **22**
Merton Ct. NG9: Stfrd 2G **53**
Metcalf Rd. NG16: Newth 2D **16**
Meteor Cl. NG13: Newt 2B **50**
Meteor Rd. NG15: Huck 3D **18**
Mettham St. NG7: Lent 6D **44**
Mevell Ct. NG7: Nott 5A 4 (5E **45**)
The Mews NG7: Bas 1E **45**
Mews La. NG14: Calv 4G **11**
Meynell Gro. NG7: Bas 6E **33**
Meynell Rd. NG10: Long E 2F **73**
MFA Bowl
  Ilkeston 2A **40**
Miall Ct. NG7: Lent 4C **44**
Miall St. NG7: Lent 4C **44**
Michael Gdns. NG5: Sher 6F **33**
Michael Rayner Ct. NG6: Bas 4B **32**
Mickleborough Av. NG3: Nott 1B **46**
Mickleborough Way NG2: West Br 2G **67**
Mickledon Cl. NG2: Nott 1G **57**
  NG10: Long E 5D **62**
Micklemoor La. NG13: Car C 1H **51**
Middle Av. NG4: Car 1E **47**
Middlebeck Av. NG5: Arn 5E **23**
Middlebeck Dr. NG5: Arn 5D **22**
Middledale Rd. NG4: Car 3E **47**
Middlefell Cl. NG11: Clftn 4B **66**
Middlefell Way NG11: Clftn 4B **66**
Middle Furlong Gdns. NG2: Nott 1F **57**
Middle Furlong M. NG2: Nott 1F **57**
Middle Hill NG1: Nott 5E 5 (5G **45**)
Middle La. NG9: Chil 6E **55**
Middle Nook NG8: Woll 4E **43**
    (off Cottage Wlk.)
Middle Orchard St. NG9: Stfrd 4F **53**
Middle Pavement NG1: Nott 5E 5 (5G **45**)
Middle St. NG9: Bee 5F **55**
Middle Street Stop (NET) 4G **55**
Middleton Blvd. NG8: Woll 5A **44**
Middleton Cl. NG6: Nuth 1C **30**
Middleton Cl. NG8: Bilb 4D **42**
Middleton Cres. NG9: Bee 2E **55**
Middleton Rd. DE7: Ilk 4C **40**
Middleton St. DE7: Ilk 6C **28**
  NG7: Lent 4C **44**
  NG9: Bee 4E **55**
  NG16: Aws .3E **29**
Midhurst Cl. NG9: Chil 1C **64**
Midhurst Way NG11: Clftn 3C **66**
Midlame Gdns. NG6: Bulw 6F **19**
Midland Av. NG4: Car 2A **48**
  NG7: Lent 6E **44**
  NG9: Stfrd .6E **53**
Midland Cotts. NG2: West Br 4B **58**

Midland Ct. NG7: Radf 3B 44
Midland Cres. NG4: Car 2H 47
Midland Gro. NG4: Neth 1A 48
Midland Rd. DE75: Hea 3C 14
  NG4: Car 2H 47
  NG16: Eastw 3B 16
Midland St. NG10: Long E 5G 63
Midland Way NG7: Radf 3B 44
The Midway NG7: Lent 3C 56
Mikado Rd. NG10: Long E 2E 73
Milburn Gro. NG13: Bing 5C 50
Mildenhall Cres. NG5: Bestw 5G 21
Mile End Rd. NG4: Colw 4G 47
Milford Av. NG10: Long E 2D 62
Milford Cl. NG6: Bulw 5G 19
Milford Ct. NG5: Arn 1H 33
Milford Dr. DE7: Ilk 4H 27
  NG3: Nott 2E 47
Mill Acre Cl. DE7: Ilk 5H 27
Millbank DE75: Hea 4E 15
Millbank Cl. DE7: Ilk 4H 27
Millbank Ct. NG6: Bulw 1G 31
Millbank Pl. NG6: Bestw V 2B 20
Millbeck Av. NG8: Woll 5C 42
Millbeck Cl. NG2: Gam 5E 59
Millbrook Dr. NG4: Car 6E 35
The Mill Cl. NG6: Bas 4C 32
Mill Ct. NG10: Long E 6G 63
Mill Cres. NG5: Arn 5A 22
Milldale Cl. NG11: Clftn 3A 66
Milldale Rd. NG10: Long E 1D 72
Millennium Cl. DE7: Ilk 4A 28
Millennium Ct. NG6: Bulw 2B 32
Millennium Way NG8: Cin 3G 31
Millennium Way E. NG8: Cin 3G 31
Millennium Way W. NG8: Cin 3G 31
Miller Hives Cl. NG12: Cotg 2E 71
Millers Bri. NG12: Cotg 3E 71
Millers Ct. NG7: Radf 3C 44
Millersdale Av. DE7: Ilk 2A 28
Millers Grn. NG2: Nott 5C 46
Millership Way DE7: Ilk 5B 28
Mill Fld. Cl. NG14: Bur J 4E 37
Millfield Cl. DE7: Ilk 3G 27
Millfield Rd. DE7: Ilk 2C 40
  NG16: Kimb 6G 17
Mill Hill La. DE72: Brea 4A 62
Mill Hill Rd. NG13: Bing 6D 50
MILL HILL RDBT. 5A 46
Millicent Gro. NG2: West Br 3B 58
Millicent Rd. NG2: West Br 3A 58
Millidge Cl. NG5: Bestw 2D 32
Mill La. NG4: Lamb 6B 24
  NG5: Arn 5A 22
  NG6: Bestw V 2B 20
  NG10: Sand 5E 53
  NG11: Rudd 3B 78
  NG12: C'ton, Cotg 4D 70
    (not continuous)
  NG12: Cotg 1E 71
  NG16: Coss 1D 40
Mill Rd. DE75: Hea 5E 15
  NG9: Stfrd 3F 53
  NG16: Newth 2C 16
Mills Bldgs. NG1: Nott 5G 5
Mill St. DE7: Ilk 6B 28
  NG6: Bas 4B 32
Mill Vw. Cl. NG2: Nott 6A 46
Millview Ct. NG2: Nott 5H 5 (5A 46)
Mill Yd. NG15: Huck 4G 7
Milner Rd. NG5: Sher 5G 33
  NG10: Long E 5F 63
Milnhay Rd. DE75: Hea 4G 15
  NG16: Lang M 3G 15
Milton Av. DE7: Ilk 3A 28
Milton Cl. NG5: Arn 6D 22
  NG5: Sher 4F 33
Milton Cres. NG9: Atten 3D 64
Milton Ho. NG1: Nott 3E 5 (4G 45)
Milton Ri. NG15: Huck 6D 6
Milton Rd. DE7: Ilk 3A 28
Milton St. DE7: Ilk 3B 28
  NG1: Nott 2E 5 (4G 45)
  NG10: Long E 6F 63
Milton Ter. NG10: Long E 6F 63
Milverton Rd. NG5: Bestw 5G 21
Milward Rd. DE75: Los 3B 14
Mimosa Cl. NG11: Clftn 4A 66
Minerva Gro. NG15: Huck 3A 8
Minerva St. NG6: Bulw 5H 19
    (not continuous)
Minkley Dr. NG16: Lang M 1G 15
MINOR INJURIES UNIT
  (ILKESTON HOSPITAL) 3H 27
Minster Cl. NG15: Huck 3H 7
Minster Ct. NG5: Sher 2F 45
Minster Gdns. NG16: Newth 4D 16
Minstrel Av. NG5: Sher 5E 33
Minstrel Cl. NG15: Huck 6G 7
Mint Gro. NG10: Long E 6C 62

Minton Cl. NG9: Chil 4B 64
Minver Cres. NG8: Aspl 6G 31
Minver Crescent Sports Cen. 6H 31
Mirberry M. NG7: Lent 6C 44
Miriam Ct. NG2: West Br 4A 58
Misk Hollows NG15: Huck 3F 7
Misk Vw. NG16: Eastw 3D 16
Mission St. NG3: Mapp 5A 34
Mitchell Av. NG16: Lang M 1E 15
Mitchell Cl. NG6: Bulw 1G 31
Mitchell St. NG10: Long E 6G 63
Mitchell Ter. DE7: Ilk 4C 40
Mitford Dr. NG5: Arn 3B 22
Moffat Cl. NG3: Nott 2B 46
Mohan Bus. Cen. NG10: Long E 6F 63
Mollington Sq. NG6: Cin 3H 31
Monarch Way DE75: Hea 3B 14
Mona Rd. NG2: West Br 2C 58
Mona St. NG9: Bee 5G 55
Monks Cl. DE7: Ilk 1C 40
Monk's La. NG11: Goth 6H 75
Monksway NG11: Wilf 1E 67
Monkton Cl. DE7: Ilk 4H 27
Monkton Dr. NG8: Bilb 2E 43
Monmouth Cl. NG8: Woll 5B 42
Monroe Wlk. NG5: Bestw 6E 21
Monsaldale Cl. NG10: Long E 1D 72
Monsall Av. DE7: Ilk 2A 28
Monsall St. NG7: Bas 6D 32
Monsell Dr. NG5: Redh 4A 22
Montague Rd. NG15: Huck 3G 7
Montague St. NG6: Bulw 6A 20
Montfort Cres. NG5: Sher 3H 33
Montfort St. NG7: Radf 4E 45
Montgomery Cl. NG9: Chil 3C 64
Montgomery St. NG7: Radf 1A 4 (3E 45)
Montpelier Rd. NG7: Lent 2C 56
Montrose Ct. NG9: Stfrd 2G 53
Monyash Cl. DE7: Ilk 4A 28
Moody Cl. NG9: Chil 3B 64
Moon Cres. NG16: Eastw 4A 16
The Moor DE7: D Ab 6E 39
  NG9: Trow 3A 42
Moorbridge Cvn. Pk. 3B 20
Moorbridge Cotts. NG6: Bulw 3B 20
Moorbridge Ct. NG13: Bing 4E 51
Moorbridge La. NG9: Stfrd 2F 53
Moor Bridge Park & Ride 3B 20
Moorbridge Rd. NG13: Bing 4E 51
Moorbridge Rd. E. NG13: Bing 4E 51
Moor Bridge Stop (NET) 3B 20
Moore Cl. NG2: West Br 2D 58
Moore Ga. NG9: Bee 5F 55
Moore Rd. NG3: Mapp 5C 34
Moores Av. NG10: Sand 4E 53
Moores Pl. NG5: Sher 5E 33
Moore St. NG6: Bulw 2A 32
Moor Farm Holiday & Home Pk. 5C 12
Moor Farm Inn La. NG9: Bram 1A 54
Moorfield Cl. NG9: Stfrd 2G 53
Moorfield Cres. NG10: Sand 6D 52
Moorfields Av. NG16: Eastw 2B 16
Moorgate St. NG7: Radf 2A 4 (4E 45)
MOORGREEN 2F 17
Moorgreen NG16: Newth 1E 17
Moorgreen Dr. NG8: Stre 5D 30
Moorgreen Ind. Pk. NG16: Newth 1D 16
Moorhouse Rd. NG8: Bilb 3E 43
The Moorings NG7: Lent 1D 56
Moorland Av. NG9: Stfrd 5F 53
Moorlands Cl. NG10: Long E 3D 62
Moor La. DE7: D Ab 6D 38
  NG9: Bram 1B 54
  NG11: Bunny 6G 77
  NG11: Goth, Rudd 6H 75
  NG11: Rudd 1G 77
    (Leys Rd.)
  NG11: Rudd 5H 77
    (Littlemoor La.)
  NG13: Bing 4E 51
  NG14: Calv, Epp 5C 12
Moor Rd. NG6: Bestw V 2B 20
  NG8: Stre 6D 30
  NG14: Calv 4A 12
  NG15: Pap 1B 8
Moorsholm Dr. NG8: Woll 5C 42
Moor St. NG4: Neth 2H 47
Moray Ct. NG16: Kimb 6H 17
Morden Cl. NG8: Bilb 1D 42
Morden Rd. NG16: Gilt 5E 17
Moreland Ct. NG2: Nott 6B 46
  NG4: Car 2E 47
Moreland Pl. NG2: Nott 6B 46
Moreland St. NG2: Nott 6B 46
Morello Av. NG4: Car 2H 47
Morello Dr. NG8: Aspl 2A 44

Moreton Rd. NG11: Clftn 6C 66
Morgan M. NG11: Clftn 3B 66
Morkinshire Cres. NG12: Cotg 1F 71
Morkinshire La. NG12: Cotg 1E 71
Morley Av. NG3: Mapp 5A 34
Morley Ct. NG2: Nott 3H 5
Morley Dr. DE7: Ilk 4H 27
Morley Gdns. NG5: Sher 6F 33
  NG12: Rad T 5G 49
Morley Pl. NG2: Nott 1B 46
Morley Rd. NG3: Nott 6C 34
Morley St. NG5: Arn 1H 33
Mornington Cl. NG10: Sand 5E 53
Mornington Cres. NG16: Nuth 4D 30
Morrell Bank NG5: Bestw 1D 32
Morris Av. NG9: Chil 4B 64
Morris Cl. NG4: Colw 4A 48
Morris Rd. NG8: Stre 6D 30
Morris St. NG4: Neth 2A 48
Morton Av. DE7: Ilk 2B 28
Morton Gdns. NG12: Rad T 6H 49
Morval Rd. NG8: Bilb 2E 43
Morven Av. NG15: Huck 5H 7
Mosley St. NG7: Bas 1D 44
  NG15: Huck 5G 7
Mosquito Gro. NG15: Huck 3E 19
Moss Cl. NG5: Arn 5G 21
Mosscroft Av. NG11: Clftn 4B 66
Mossdale Rd. NG5: Sher 2G 33
Moss Dr. NG9: Bram 4B 54
Moss Ri. NG3: Mapp 5D 34
Moss Rd. DE7: Ilk 2A 40
  NG8: Bee 4F 7
Moss Side NG11: Wilf 1E 67
Mosswood Cres. NG5: Bestw 6F 21
Mottram Rd. NG9: Chil 5C 54
The Mount NG3: Mapp 5E 35
  NG5: Redh 4H 21
  NG6: Bestw V 1C 20
  NG8: Stre 6E 31
  NG9: Stfrd 5F 53
Mountain Ash Cres. NG12: Edwal 3C 68
Mountbatten Ct. DE7: Ilk 4B 28
Mountbatten Rd. NG4: Ged 5G 35
Mountbatten Way NG9: Chil 3B 64
Mountfield Av. NG10: Sand 1C 62
Mountfield Dr. NG5: Bestw 6E 21
Mount Hgts. NG7: Bas 6E 33
Mt. Hooton NG1: Nott 3E 45
Mt. Hooton Rd. NG7: Radf 3E 45
Mt. Pleasant DE7: Ilk 3A 28
  NG4: Car 2G 47
  NG6: Bas 5B 32
  NG12: Key 4H 79
  NG12: Rad T 6E 49
Mountsorrel Dr. NG2: West Br 5D 58
Mount St. DE72: Brea 6B 62
  DE75: Hea 4C 14
  NG1: Nott 4C 4 (5F 45)
    (not continuous)
  NG7: Bas 6D 32
  NG9: Stfrd 4G 53
Mount St. Arc. NG1: Nott 4C 4
Mowbray Cl. NG3: Nott 2G 5 (4H 45)
Mowbray Gdns. NG2: West Br 6B 58
Mowbray Ri. NG5: Arn 4B 22
Moyra Dr. NG5: Arn 6G 21
Moyra Ho. NG5: Arn 5H 21
Mozart Cl. NG7: Radf 4C 44
Mudpie La. NG2: West Br 2D 58
Muir Av. NG12: Toll 5F 69
Muirfield Rd. NG5: Arn, Top V 4D 20
Mulberry Cl. NG2: West Br 6F 57
Mulberry Gdns. NG6: Bulw 5G 19
Mulberry Gro. NG15: Huck 1H 19
Mundella Rd. NG2: Nott 2H 57
Mundy's Dr. DE75: Hea 5D 14
Mundy St. DE7: Ilk 5B 28
  DE75: Hea 4C 14
Munford Cir. NG8: Cin 4G 31
Munks Av. NG15: Huck 4F 7
Murby Cres. NG6: Bulw 5H 19
Murden Way NG9: Bee 5H 55
Muriel Gdns. NG6: Bulw 4A 20
Muriel Rd. NG9: Bee 4F 55
Muriel St. NG6: Bulw 4A 20
Murray Cl. NG5: Bestw 2D 32
Mus. of Nottingham Life 6C 4 (6F 45)
Mushroom Farm Ct. NG16: Eastw 2H 15
Muskham Av. DE7: Ilk 4B 28
Muskham St. NG2: Nott 2H 57
Mustang Cl. NG15: Huck 5H 7
Musters Cl. NG2: West Br 3A 58
  NG15: Huck 5A 8
Musters Cres. NG2: West Br 6B 58
Musters Cft. NG4: Colw 6H 47
Musters Rd. NG2: West Br 3A 58
  NG11: Rudd 1F 77
  NG13: Bing 5D 50
Musters Wlk. NG6: Bulw 6G 19

Muston Cl. NG3: Mapp 6B 34
Myrtle Av.
  NG7: Hys G 1F 45
  NG9: Stfrd 5G 53
  NG10: Long E .1E 73
Myrtle Gro. NG9: Bee 4G 55
Myrtle Rd. NG4: Car 1E 47
Myrtus Cl. NG11: Clftn 3A 66
Mytholme Cl. NG10: Long E 3E 63

N

Nabarro Ct. NG14: Calv 4G 11
Nabbs La. NG15: Huck 5D 6
Naburn Cl. NG8: Bas 6B 32
Nairn Cl. NG5: Arn 4D 22
Nairn M. NG4: Car 2G 47
Nansen Gdns. NG5: Bestw 1D 32
Nansen St. NG6: Bulw 1A 32
Naomi Ct. NG6: Bulw 4A 20
Naomi Cres. NG6: Bulw 4A 20
Naranjan M. NG7: Radf 1A 4 (3E 45)
Narrow La. NG16: Want 4H 17
Naseby Cl. NG5: Sher 3D 32
Naseby Dr. NG10: Long E 2G 73
Nathaniel Rd. NG10: Long E 6H 63
Nathans La. NG12: Rad T 4A 60
The National Ice Cen. 4G 5 (5H 45)
National Water Sports Cen. 1G 59
National Water Sports Cen. Holme
  Pierrepont Cvn. & Camping Pk. 2F 59
Natural History Mus. 6G 43
Navdeep Ct. NG2: West Br 4A 58
Navenby Wlk. NG11: Clftn 3C 66
Navigation St. NG2: Nott 1B 58
Naworth Cl. NG6: Bulw 2C 32
Naylor Av. NG11: Goth 6H 75
Naylor Ho. NG5: Arn 1C 34
               (off Derwent Cres.)
Nazareth Ct. NG7: Lent 1C 56
Nazareth Rd. NG7: Lent 1C 56
Neal Ct. NG16: Lang M 2E 15
Neale St. NG10: Long E 6G 63
Near Mdw. NG10: Long E 2G 73
Nearsby Dr. NG2: West Br 5D 58
Needham St. NG13: Bing 5E 51
Needwood Av. NG9: Trow 1F 53
Neeps Cft. NG14: Epp 5G 13
Negus Ct. NG4: Lamb 6B 24
Neighwood Cl. NG9: Toton 3G 63
Nell Gwyn Cres. NG5: Arn 4G 21
Nelper Cres. DE7: Ilk 4C 40
Nelson Rd. NG5: Arn 6A 22
  NG6: Bulw 6A 20
  NG9: Bee 1G 65
Nelson St. DE7: Ilk 3B 28
  DE75: Hea 3B 14
  NG1: Nott 4G 5 (5H 45)
  NG10: Long E 1F 73
Nene Cl. NG15: Huck 2E 19
Nene Way NG13: Bing 6D 50
Nesfield Ct. DE7: Ilk 6A 28
Nesfield Rd. DE7: Ilk 6A 28
Neston Dr. NG6: Cin 3H 31
Nether Cl. NG3: Nott 3C 46
  NG16: Eastw 1B 16
NETHERFIELD 3H 47
Netherfield Rd. NG10: Long E 3D 72
  NG10: Sand .6D 52
Netherfields La. DE72: Shar 1H 59
Netherfield Station (Rail) 3H 47
Nethergate NG11: Clftn 3A 66
NETHER GREEN .1B 16
Nether Grn. NG16: Eastw 2B 16
Nethermere La. NG8: Stre 5C 30
Nether Pasture NG4: Neth 3A 48
Nether Slade Rd. DE7: Ilk 5A 28
Nether St. NG9: Bee 5G 55
Nettlecliff Wlk. NG5: Top V 5C 20
Neville Rd. NG14: Calv 5H 11
Neville Sadler Ct. NG9: Bee 4G 55
The New Alexandra Ct. NG3: Nott 1H 45
Newall Dr. NG9: Chil 3C 64
Newark Av. NG2: Nott 5A 46
Newark Ct. NG5: Bestw 1D 34
Newark Cres. NG2: Nott 5H 5 (5A 46)
Newark Hall NG8: Woll 5B 44
Newark St. NG2: Nott 5H 5 (5A 46)
New Art Exchange 2D 44
NEW BASFORD 6D 32
New Basford Bus. Area NG7: Bas 6D 32
                (off Palm St.)
Newbery Av. NG10: Long E 1H 73
Newbridge Cl. DE7: West H 1B 38
New Brook Ho. NG7: Radf 3D 44
Newbury Cl. NG3: Mapp 3C 34
Newbury Ct. NG5: Sher 1F 45
Newbury Dr. NG16: Nuth 4D 30

Newcastle Av. NG4: Ged 6G 35
  NG9: Bee 5F 55
Newcastle Chambers NG1: Nott 4D 4 (5G 45)
Newcastle Cir. NG7: Nott 5A 4 (5E 45)
Newcastle Ct. NG7: Nott 5A 4 (5E 45)
Newcastle Dr. NG7: Nott 3A 4 (5E 45)
Newcastle Farm Dr. NG8: Aspl 6A 32
Newcastle St. NG6: Bulw 5A 20
  NG8: Aspl 6B 32
Newcastle Ter. NG7: Nott 3A 4 (4E 45)
Newcombe Dr. NG5: Arn 6E 23
New Ct. NG1: Nott 4F 5
New Derby Rd. NG16: Eastw 2H 15
Newdigate Rd. NG16: Want 6A 18
Newdigate St. DE7: Ilk 3C 40
  DE7: West H 1A 38
  NG7: Radf 2A 4 (4E 45)
  NG16: Kimb .1H 29
Newdigate Vs. NG7: Radf 2A 4 (4E 45)
NEW EASTWOOD 4B 16
New Eaton Rd. NG9: Stfrd 5F 53
New Farm La. NG16: Nuth 1C 30
Newfield Rd. NG5: Sher 4D 32
Newgate Cl. NG4: Car 2G 47
Newgate St. NG7: Lent 5D 44
  NG13: Bing .4E 51
Newhall Gro. NG2: West Br 2B 58
Newham Cl. DE75: Hea 4E 15
Newholm Dr. NG11: Wilf 6E 57
Newland Cl. NG8: Aspl 4A 44
  NG9: Toton .3A 64
NEWLANDS 3E 15
Newlands Cl. NG12: Edwal 1E 69
Newlands Dr. DE75: Hea 2C 14
  NG4: Ged 6H 35
New Lawn Rd. DE7: Ilk 1A 40
NEW LENTON 6D 44
Newlyn Dr. NG8: Aspl 1B 44
Newlyn Gdns. NG8: Aspl 1B 44
Newmanleys Rd. NG16: Eastw 5A 16
Newmanleys Rd. Sth. NG16: Eastw 4A 16
New Manor Ground 4C 28
Newmarket Rd. NG6: Bulw 1H 31
Newmarket Way NG9: Toton 4H 63
NEW NUTHALL 1C 30
Newport Dr. NG8: Bas 6B 32
Newquay Av. NG7: Radf 2C 44
New Ri. NG11: Clftn 5A 66
New Rd. NG7: Radf 3B 44
  NG9: Stfrd 2F 53
  NG11: Bart F 1E 75
  NG12: Rad T 6F 49
  NG16: Newth, Want 1F 17, 5A 6
New Row NG4: Car 2F 47
  NG14: Woodbo 1C 24
NEW SAWLEY 2D 72
NEW STANTON 6A 40
NEW STAPLEFORD 2G 53
Newstead Av. NG3: Mapp 5D 34
  NG12: Rad T 5G 49
Newstead Cl. NG5: Woodt 2C 34
Newstead Dr. NG2: West Br 4D 58
Newstead Gro. NG1: Nott 1C 4 (3F 45)
  NG13: Bing .5C 50
Newstead Ind. Est. NG5: Arn 6C 22
Newstead Rd. NG10: Long E 2E 63
Newstead Rd. Nth. DE7: Ilk 4H 27
Newstead Rd. Sth. DE7: Ilk 4H 27
Newstead St. NG5: Sher 4G 33
Newstead Ter. NG15: Huck 3G 7
Newstead Way NG8: Stre 5D 30
New St. DE7: Stly 3A 38
  NG5: Redh 4A 22
  NG5: Sher 6F 33
  NG10: Long E 5G 63
New Ter. NG10: Sand 5D 52
NEWTHORPE 4E 17
NEWTHORPE COMMON 5D 16
Newthorpe Comn. NG16: Newth 4C 16
Newthorpe St. NG2: Nott 1H 57
NEWTON 1B 50
Newton Airfield (disused) 1A 50
Newton Av. NG12: Rad T 5G 49
  NG13: Bing .5D 50
              (not continuous)
Newton Cl. NG5: Arn 1D 34
Newtondale Cl. NG8: Aspl 6B 32
Newton Dr. DE75: Hea 4E 15
  NG2: West Br 1G 67
  NG9: Stfrd 5G 53
Newton Gdns. NG13: Newt 3C 50
Newton Rd. NG4: Ged 4F 35
Newton's La. NG16: Coss 4C 28
              (not continuous)
Newton St. NG7: Lent 3C 56
  NG9: Bee 5E 55
New Tythe St. NG10: Long E 6H 63
New Va. Rd. NG4: Colw 4F 47
New Windmill Ct. NG2: Nott 5B 46

New Works Cotts. NG14: Stoke B 1C 40
ng2 Bus. Pk. NG2: Nott 1E 57
ng2 Stop (NET) 1E 57
Nicholas Cl. DE7: Ilk 3B 40
Nicholas Rd. NG9: Bram 2D 54
Nicker Hill NG12: Key 3H 79
Nicklaus Ct. NG5: Top V 5E 21
             (off Crossfield Dr.)
Nidderdale NG8: Woll 5C 42
Nidderdale Cl. NG8: Woll 6C 42
Nightingale Cl. NG7: Nott 2G 55
  NG16: Nuth .1D 30
Nightingale Ho. NG3: Mapp 5B 34
Nightingale Way NG13: Bing 6G 51
Nile St. NG1: Nott 3G 5 (4H 45)
Nilsson Rd. NG7: Nott 2B 64
Nimbus Way NG16: Want 6H 17
Nine Acre Gdns. NG6: Bulw 6F 19
Nine Corners NG16: Kimb 1H 29
Nixon Ri. NG15: Huck 6D 6
Nobel Rd. NG11: Clftn 5A 66
Noel St. NG7: Bas, Hys G 1D 44
             (not continuous)
  NG16: Kimb .1A 30
Noel Street Stop (NET) 2D 44
No Man's La. DE72: Ris 4A 52
  NG10: Sand .4A 52
The Nook DE75: Los 1A 14
  NG8: Woll 5E 43
  NG9: Bee 4G 55
  NG9: Chil 1E 65
  NG14: Calv 4H 11
  NG16: Kimb .2A 30
Nook End Rd. DE75: Hea 4B 14
Norbett Cl. NG9: Chil 2C 64
Norbett Ct. NG5: Arn 4C 22
Norbett Rd. NG5: Arn 5C 22
Norbreck Cl. NG8: Cin 4H 31
Norburn Cres. NG6: Bas 4D 32
Norbury Way NG10: Sand 5C 52
Nordean Rd. NG5: Woodt 2C 34
Norfolk Av. NG9: Toton 4A 64
Norfolk Cl. NG15: Huck 6D 6
Norfolk Pk. NG5: Arn 2D 34
Norfolk Pl. NG1: Nott 3D 4 (4G 45)
  NG10: Long E 4H 63
Norfolk Wlk. NG10: Sand 6D 52
Norland Cl. NG3: Nott 2A 46
             (not continuous)
Normanby Rd. NG8: Woll 6C 42
Norman Cl. NG3: Nott 1E 5 (3G 45)
  NG9: Chil 6C 54
Norman Cres. DE7: Ilk 4A 28
Norman Dr. NG15: Huck 1E 19
  NG16: Eastw 3D 16
Norman Rd. NG3: Nott 1C 46
Norman St. DE7: Ilk 3A 28
  NG4: Neth 3A 48
  NG16: Kimb .6H 17
Normanton La. NG12: Key 4H 79
NORMANTON-ON-THE-WOLDS 1A 80
Norris Homes NG7: Hys G 1F 45
Northall Av. NG6: Bulw 1H 31
Northampton St. NG3: Nott 3A 46
North Av. NG10: Sand 5C 52
Nth. Church St. NG1: Nott 2D 4 (4G 45)
Nth. Circus St. NG1: Nott 3B 4 (5F 45)
Northcliffe Av. NG3: Mapp 5C 34
Northcote St. NG10: Long E 6G 63
Northcote Way NG6: Bulw 2A 32
Northdale Rd. NG3: Nott 2D 46
Northdown Dr. NG9: Chil 1C 64
Northdown Rd. NG8: Aspl 3B 44
North Dr. NG9: Chil 5E 55
Northern Ct. NG6: Bas 3B 32
Northern Dr. NG6: Bestw V 1D 20
  NG9: Trow 6F 41
Northern Rd. DE75: Hea 3B 14
Northfield Av. DE7: Ilk 5A 28
  NG10: Long E 3D 72
  NG12: Rad T 5H 49
Northfield Cres. NG9: Chil 1H 63
Northfield Rd. NG9: Chil 1A 64
Northfields NG10: Long E 3D 72
North Ga. NG6: Bas 6D 32
North Ga. Pl. NG7: Bas 6D 32
             (off High Chu. St.)
Northgate St. DE7: Ilk 6A 28
North Grn. NG14: Calv 2E 11
North Hill Av. NG15: Huck 4F 7
North Hill Cres. NG15: Huck 4F 7
Northolme Av. NG6: Bulw 6A 20
Northolt Dr. NG16: Nuth 4D 30
North Rd. NG2: West Br 5A 58
  NG5: Sher 3E 33
             (not continuous)
  NG7: Nott 4A 4 (5E 45)
             (Western Ter.)
  NG7: Nott 1B 56
             (West Rd.)

North Rd. NG10: Long E 1E 73
  NG11: Rudd 5F 67
Nth. Sherwood St. NG1: Nott 1D 4 (2F 45)
Northside Wlk. NG5: Arn 3B 22
North St. DE7: Ilk 6B 28
  NG2: Nott 4H 5
  NG9: Bee 5E 55
  NG16: Kimb 2A 30
  NG16: Lang M 2F 15
  NG16: Newth 3E 17
Northumberland Cl. NG3: Nott 1F 5 (3H 45)
Northville Ct. NG3: Nott 2H 45
Northwold Av. NG2: West Br 5H 57
Northwood Cres. NG5: Bestw 1G 33
Northwood Rd. NG5: Bestw 1G 33
Northwood St. NG9: Stfrd 3F 53
Norton Ct. NG7: Radf 3C 44
Norton St. NG7: Radf 3C 44
                 (not continuous)
Norwich Gdns. NG6: Bulw 4H 19
Norwood Cl. DE7: Ilk 2B 28
Norwood Rd. NG7: Radf 4C 44
Noskwith St. DE7: Ilk 4C 40
Notintone Pl. NG2: Nott 5A 46
Notintone St. NG2: Nott 5A 46
NOTTINGHAM 4E 5 (5G 45)
Nottingham Airport 6H 59
Nottingham Arts Theatre 4F 5 (5H 45)
Nottingham Bus. Pk. NG2: Nott 6H 5 (6A 46)
  NG8: Stre 5C 30
Nottingham Castle 6C 4 (5F 45)
Nottingham Castle Caves 6C 4
Nottingham City Golf Course 3G 19
Nottingham Climbing Cen. 1D 44
Nottingham Contemporary 5E 5 (5H 45)
Nottingham Forest FC 2A 58
Nottingham Forest Football Academy 4H 57
Nottingham Greyhound Stadium 5D 46
Nottingham Indoor Bowls Cen. 2G 43
Nottingham Industrial Mus. 6G 43
Nottingham Lakeside Arts 2B 56
Nottingham One NG1: Nott 6F 5 (6H 45)
Nottingham Playhouse 4C 4 (5F 45)
Nottingham Racecourse 6E 47
Nottingham RFC 1A 58
Nottingham Rd. DE7: Ilk 2B 40
  DE72: Dray, Ris 1A 62
  NG5: Arn 1A 34
  NG6: Bas 4C 32
                 (not continuous)
  NG7: Bas 5D 32
  NG8: Cin 3E 31
  NG9: Chil, Toton 5G 63
  NG9: Stfrd 4F 53
  NG9: Trow 5E 41
  NG10: Long E 5G 63
  NG11: Goth 6H 75
  NG12: Key 5G 79
  NG12: Rad T 1D 60
  NG13: Bing 5B 50
  NG14: Bur J 4D 36
  NG14: Woodbo .3F 23
  NG15: Huck 6A 8
  NG16: Cin, Nuth 2D 30
  NG16: Eastw 3B 16
  NG16: Gilt, Newth 4D 16
  NG16: Kimb 1A 30
  NG25: Oxton 1B 12
Nottingham Rd. E.
  NG16: Eastw, Gilt, Newth 4D 16
Nottingham Sailing Club 1F 59
Nottingham St Barnabas' RC Cathedral
  . . . . .3B 4 (5F 45)
Nottingham Science & Technology Pk.
  NG7: Nott 2B 56
Nottinghamshire County Cricket Ground 2A 58
The Nottinghamshire Golf Course 4C 60
NOTTINGHAMSHIRE HOSPICE 1H 45
Nottingham Sth. & Wilford Ind. Est.
  NG11: Wilf 2G 57
Nottingham Station (Rail & NET) 6F 5 (6H 45)
Nottingham Tennis Cen. 2B 56
Nottingham Tourism Centre 4E 5 (5G 45)
Nottingham Trent University
  City Campus 2C 4 (4F 45)
  Clifton Campus .2B 66
  Union Rd. 4G 45
  Waverley St. 1B 4 (3F 45)
Nottingham Trent University Stop
  (NET) 2C 4 (4F 45)
Nottingham University Academy of Science &
  Technology 2C 56
Nottingham Wholesale & Trade Pk.
  NG2: Nott 1A 58
Nottingham Wildcats Arena 4D 46
Notts County FC 1A 58
Notts Gymnastics Academy 1B 68
Nuart Rd. NG9: Bee 5F 55
Nuffield Health
  Nottingham 3D 34

Nugent Gdns. NG3: Nott 1H 5 (3A 46)
Nunn Cl. NG15: Huck 1A 8
The Nurseries NG16: Eastw 3C 16
Nursery Av. DE7: West H 2C 38
  NG9: Chil 6C 54
  NG10: Sand 6B 52
Nursery Cl. NG12: Rad T 6H 49
  NG15: Huck 1G 19
Nursery Dr. NG4: Car 1F 47
Nursery Hollow DE7: Ilk 3A 40
Nursery La. NG6: Bas 3C 32
Nursery Rd. NG5: Arn 6B 22
  NG12: Rad T 6H 49
  NG13: Bing 5H 51
Nutbrook Cres. DE7: Kirk H 5H 39
NUTHALL 2D 30
Nuthall Circ. DE7: Kirk H 5G 39
Nuthall Gdns. NG8: Aspl 1B 44
Nuthall Rd. NG8: Aspl, Cin 4H 31

O

Oak Acres NG9: Chil 6A 54
Oak Apple Cres. DE7: Ilk 3A 40
Oakash Ct. NG16: Nuth 1B 30
Oak Av. NG10: Sand 4C 52
  NG12: Rad T 5E 49
  NG13: Bing 5G 51
  NG16: Lang M 1F 15
Oakdale Dr. NG9: Chil 1C 64
Oakdale Rd. NG3: Nott 3D 46
  NG4: Car 3F 47
  NG5: Arn 5D 22
Oak Dr. NG16: Eastw 3A 16
  NG16: Nuth 1B 30
Oakenhall Av. NG15: Huck 4A 8
Oakfield NG12: Rad T 5G 49
Oakfield Cl. NG8: Woll 6C 42
Oakfield Ct. NG12: Rad T 6H 49
Oakfield Dr. NG10: Sand 2D 62
Oakfield Rd. NG8: Woll 6C 42
  NG9: Stfrd 4F 53
  NG15: Huck 5H 7
Oakfields Rd. NG2: West Br 2C 58
Oak Flatt NG9: Chil 5A 54
Oakford Cl. NG8: Brox 5G 31
Oak Gro. NG15: Huck 1H 19
Oakham Cl. NG5: Top V 6D 20
Oakham Ct. NG4: Ged 4F 35
Oakham Rd. NG11: Rudd 3H 67
Oakham Way DE7: Ilk 4H 27
Oakington Cl. NG5: Bestw 2F 33
Oakland Av. NG10: Long E 2E 73
Oakland Gro. NG14: Calv 4H 11
Oaklands Av. DE75: Hea 3E 15
Oakland St. NG7: Hys G 2C 44
Oakland Ter. NG10: Long E 2E 73
Oakland Way NG8: Bilb 1D 42
Oakleaf Cl. NG6: Bestw V 1C 20
Oakleigh Av. NG3: Mapp 5E 35
Oakleigh St. NG6: Bulw 3B 32
Oakley M. NG6: Bulw 1F 31
Oakley's Rd. NG10: Long E 6G 63
Oakley's Rd. W. NG10: Long E 1F 73
Oak Lodge NG13: Bing 5G 51
Oak Lodge Dr. NG16: Kimb 6H 17
Oakmead Av. NG8: Bilb 1F 43
Oakmere Cl. NG12: Edwal 1F 69
The Oaks NG3: Nott 2H 5 (4H 45)
Oak St. NG5: Sher .6F 33
Oak Tree Av. NG12: Rad T 5F 49
Oak Tree Cl. NG2: West Br 3C 58
  NG15: Huck 1D 18
Oak Tree Ct. NG12: Toll 4E 69
Oak Tree Dr. NG4: Ged 5A 36
Oak Vw. NG7: Radf 3D 44
Oakwell Cres. DE7: Ilk 1A 40
Oakwell Dr. DE7: Ilk 1A 40
Oakwood Dr. NG8: Aspl 2A 44
Oakwood Gdns. NG16: Nuth 4D 30
Oban Rd. NG9: Chil 5C 54
Occupation Rd. NG6: Bulw 2H 31
  NG15: Huck 6G 7
Oceans of Fun 4G 7
Ockbrook Ct. DE7: Ilk 4B 28
Ockbrook Dr. NG3: Mapp 5B 34
Ockerby St. NG6: Bulw 1A 32
Odesa Dr. NG6: Bulw 3H 31
Odin Ct. NG4: Car .1H 47
Ogdon Ct. NG3: Nott 3B 46
Ogle Dr. NG7: Nott 6B 4 (6F 45)
Ogle St. NG15: Huck 4G 7
Okehampton Cres. NG3: Mapp 1E 35
Oldacres NG14: Woodbo 1D 24
Old Bank Cl. NG6: Bas 5B 32
Old Bar Cl. NG6: Bas 5A 32
OLD BASFORD 3C 32
Old Brickyard NG3: Nott 2C 46

Oldbury Cl. NG11: Clftn 6B 66
Old Church St. NG7: Lent 1C 56
Old Coach Rd. NG8: Bilb, Woll 3E 43
Old Coppice Side DE75: Hea 5C 14
                      (Roper Av.)
  DE75: Hea 5D 14
                 (Sunningdale Av.)
Old Derby Rd. NG16: Eastw 2H 15
Old Dr. NG9: Bee 3D 54
Old Epperstone Rd. NG14: Lowd 1G 25
Old Farm Ct. NG11: Bart F 1E 75
Old Farm Rd. NG5: Top V 5D 20
Old Hall Cl. NG14: Calv 4G 11
Old Hall Dr. NG3: Mapp P 6H 33
Oldham Ct. NG9: Chil 1C 64
Old Kiln La. NG5: Arn 4C 16
Oldknow St. NG7: Hys G 3D 44
OLD LENTON 6C 44
Old Lenton St. NG1: Nott 3F 5 (4H 45)
Old Lodge Dr. NG5: Sher 3H 33
Old Main Rd. NG14: Bulc 2G 37
Old Mnr. Cl. NG14: Woodbo 1D 24
Old Market Square Stop (NET) 4D 4 (5G 45)
Old Melton Rd. NG12: Plum 6G 69
                 (not continuous)
Old Mill Cl. NG6: Bestw V 2B 20
  NG7: Radf 4D 44
  NG9: Toton 3A 64
Old Mill Ct. NG13: Bing 4E 51
Old Mission Forge Wlk. NG16: Newth 3E 17
Oldmoor Wood Nature Reserve 1H 41
Old Oak Rd. NG11: Clftn 3E 67
The Old Pk. NG12: Cotg 1F 71
Old Pk. Cl. NG8: Bilb 2E 43
The Old Pond DE75: Hea 5E 15
OLD RADFORD 3B 44
Old Rd. NG2: West Br 2A 68
  NG11: Rudd 4H 67
Old School Cl. NG11: Clftn 5C 66
Old School La. NG16: Aws 2E 29
Old Station Dr. NG11: Rudd 6F 67
Old St. NG1: Nott 2E 5 (4G 45)
Old Tollerton Rd. NG2: Gam 5H 59
Olga Ct. NG3: Nott .3B 46
Olga Rd. NG3: Nott 3B 46
Olive Av. NG10: Long E 4F 63
Olive Gro. NG14: Bur J 2F 37
Oliver Cl. DE72: Brea 5A 62
  DE75: Hea 3F 15
  NG7: Radf 1A 4 (3E 45)
Oliver Rd. DE7: Kirk H 4G 39
Oliver St. NG7: Radf 1A 4 (3E 45)
Ollerton Rd. NG5: Arn 1A 22
                 (not continuous)
  NG14: Calv 1A 22
Olton Av. NG9: Lent A 2F 55
Olympus Ct. NG15: Huck 2D 18
Omer Ct. NG16: Want 6A 18
Onchan Av. NG4: Car 3G 47
Onchan Dr. NG4: Car 3G 47
The Open University
  Nottingham 1F 45
Orange Gdns. NG2: Nott 1H 57
Orby Cl. NG3: Nott .3B 46
Orby Wlk. NG3: Nott 4B 46
The Orchard DE7: Stant D 3B 52
Orchard Av. NG4: Car 2G 47
  NG13: Bing 5D 50
Orchard Bus. Pk. DE7: Ilk 6H 27
Orchard Cl.
  DE7: West H 2C 38
  DE72: Brea 5B 62
  NG11: Clftn 3A 66
  NG12: Rad T 6E 49
  NG12: Toll 5F 69
  NG14: Bur J 2F 37
Orchard Ct.
  NG4: Car 2G 47
  NG4: Ged 5F 35
  NG8: Bas 1C 44
  NG15: Huck 5G 7
  NG16: Lang M 2F 15
Orchard Cres. NG9: Chil 6C 54
Orchard Dr. NG12: Cotg 6G 61
  NG14: Calv 4A 12
Orchard Gro. NG5: Arn 1G 33
Orchard Pk. NG3: Mapp 1E 35
Orchard Pk. Ind. Est. NG10: Sand 5E 53
Orchard Ri. NG6: Bas 5C 30
Orchard Ri. DE75: Hea 3D 14
  NG4: Lamb 6C 24
The Orchards NG4: Ged 6A 36
Orchard St.
  DE7: Ilk 2B 40
  NG10: Long E 6G 63
  NG11: Goth 6H 75
  NG15: Huck 5G 7
  NG16: Kimb 1H 29
  NG16: Lang M 2F 15
  NG16: Newth 4C 16

Orchard Way NG10: Sand 2C 62
Orchid Cl. NG2: West Br 1G 67
Orchid Ct. NG15: Huck 1A 20
Orchil St. NG16: Gilt 5D 16
Ordnance Ct. NG9: Chil 2C 64
Orford Av. NG11: Clftn 1D 66
  NG12: Rad T .1E 61
Orient M. NG16: Want 6A 18
Orion Cl. NG8: Bilb 2E 43
Orion Dr. NG8: Bilb 2E 43
Orlando Dr. NG4: Car 1H 47
Orlock Wlk. NG5: Bestw 2F 33
Ormiston Cl. NG11: Clftn 4D 66
Ormonde St. NG16: Lang M 1F 15
Ormonde Ter. NG5: Sher 5G 33
  NG16: Lang M 1F 15
Ornsay Cl. NG5: Top V 4C 20
Orpean Way NG9: Toton 3G 63
Orston Av. NG5: Arn 6C 22
Orston Dr. NG8: Woll 5A 44
Orston Grn. NG8: Woll 6B 44
Orston Rd. E. NG2: West Br 2B 58
Orston Rd. W. NG2: West Br 2A 58
Orton Av. NG9: Bram 5C 54
Orton Flds. NG9: Bram 5B 54
Ortzen Ct. NG7: Radf 3D 44
Ortzen St. NG7: Radf 3D 44
Orville Rd. NG5: Bestw 2C 32
Osborne Av. NG5: Sher 4G 33
Osborne Cl. NG10: Sand 1D 62
Osborne Gro. NG5: Sher 4G 33
Osborne St. NG7: Radf 3C 44
Osbourne Cl. NG15: Huck 1A 20
  NG16: Want 6B 18
Osgood Rd. NG5: Arn 2E 35
Osier Rd. NG2: Nott 2G 57
Osman Cl. NG2: Nott 2F 57
Osmaston Cl. NG10: Long E 2B 72
Osmaston St. NG7: Lent 6D 44
  NG10: Sand .6E 53
Osprey Cl. NG11: Clftn 4A 66
  NG13: Bing 6F 51
Osprey Gro. NG15: Huck 2B 8
Ossington Cl. NG1: Nott 1D 4 (3G 45)
Ossington St. NG7: Radf 3D 44
Ostara Ho. NG7: Radf 4H 55
Osterley Gro. NG16: Nuth 4D 30
Oulton Cl. NG5: Arn 1B 34
Oulton Lodge NG5: Top V 4B 20
Oundle Dr. DE7: Ilk 2D 40
  NG8: Woll 6A 44
Ousebridge Cres. NG4: Car 1A 48
Ousebridge Dr. NG4: Car 1A 48
The Out Track DE7: Mapp 5C 26
                   (off Church La.)
Oval Gdns. NG8: Aspl 1B 44
Overdale Cl. NG10: Long E 1B 72
Overdale Rd. NG6: Bas 5A 32
Overstrand Cl. NG5: Arn 1B 34
Owen Av. NG10: Long E 1A 74
Owers Av. DE75: Hea 6D 14
Owlston Cl. NG16: Eastw 2B 16
Owsthorpe Cl. NG5: Top V 5E 21
Owthorpe Gro. NG5: Sher 5F 33
Owthorpe Rd. NG12: Cotg 3F 71
Oxborough Rd. NG5: Arn 6G 21
Oxbow Cl. NG2: Nott 2G 57
Oxbury Rd. NG16: Want 5H 17
Oxclose La. NG5: Arn 1F 33
Oxendale Cl. NG2: West Br 5E 59
Oxengate NG5: Arn 1G 33
Oxford Rd. NG2: West Br 4C 58
Oxford St.
  DE7: Ilk 2B 40
  NG1: Nott 4B 4 (5F 45)
  NG4: Car 6G 35
  NG10: Long E 5F 63
  NG16: Eastw 3B 16
Oxgang Cl. NG14: Calv 3E 11
Oxton Av. NG5: Sher 3G 33
Oxton By-Pass NG25: Oxton 1B 12
Oxton Rd.
  NG5: Arn 4B 10
  NG14: Calv 2F 11
  NG14: Epp 1B 12
  NG25: Oxton 1B 12
Ozier Holt NG4: Colw 5G 47
  NG10: Long E 1E 73

P

Packham Ct. NG6: Bas 3C 32
Packman Dr. NG11: Rudd 6A 68
Paddington M. NG3: Nott 2C 46
The Paddock NG9: Atten 3D 64
  NG13: Bing 5E 51
Paddock Cl. NG6: Bulw 2H 31
  NG12: Rad T .1E 61
  NG14: Calv 4H 11

Paddock Dr. DE7: Smal 5A 14
Paddock Farm Cotts. NG14: Epp 6G 13
The Paddocks NG10: Sand 6C 52
  NG12: Edwal .2D 68
  NG14: Bur J .3E 37
  NG16: Nuth .2B 30
Paddocks Vw. NG10: Long E 5C 62
Padge Rd. NG9: Bee 5H 55
Padgham Ct. NG5: Top V 5E 21
Padley Cl. NG6: Bulw 1A 32
Padleys La. NG14: Bur J 2E 37
Padstow Rd. NG5: Bestw 1D 32
Paetina Gro. NG15: Huck 3B 8
Page Av. NG5: Bestw 2E 33
Paget Cres. NG11: Rudd 5G 67
Pagett Cl. NG15: Huck 5A 8
Paige Gdns. NG10: Sand 6C 52
Paignton Cl. NG8: Aspl 5H 31
Paisley Gro. NG9: Chil 4C 64
Palatine St. NG7: Nott 6B 4 (6F 45)
Palin Ct. NG7: Hys G 2D 44
Palin Gdns. NG12: Rad T 6G 49
Palin St. NG7: Hys G 3D 44
Palm Cotts. NG3: Mapp 4H 33
Palm Ct. NG7: Bas 6D 32
Palmer Av. NG15: Huck 3G 7
Palmer Bus. Ct. NG10: Long E 1H 73
Palmer Cres. NG4: Car 2F 47
Palmer Dr. NG9: Stfrd 6F 53
Palmerston Gdns. NG3: Nott 1E 5 (3G 45)
                 (not continuous)
Palmerston Rd. DE7: Ilk 1B 40
Palm St. NG7: Bas 6D 32
Palmwood Ct. NG6: Bulw 2A 32
PAPPLEWICK 1B 8
Papplewick Farm Cl. NG15: Pap 2B 8
Papplewick Grange NG15: Pap 2B 8
Papplewick La. NG15: Huck 4H 7
Parchment M. NG5: Sher 6F 33
THE PARK 4B 4 (5F 45)
The Park NG12: Cotg 1F 71
Park & Ride
  Clifton South .6A 66
  Cotgrave 2F 71
  The Forest 2E 45
  Hucknall 4A 8
  Moor Bridge .3B 20
  Phoenix Park 3G 31
  Queen's Drive 4E 57
  Racecourse .6D 46
  Stragglethorpe 4D 60
  Toton Lane 1H 63
  Wilkinson Street 1C 44
Park Av. DE7: Ilk 1B 40
  DE7: Stly 3A 38
  NG2: West Br 3B 58
  NG3: Mapp P 1G 45
  NG4: Car 1H 47
  NG5: Woodt .2A 34
  NG12: Key 4F 79
                  (Croft Rd.)
  NG12: Key 3H 79
                  (Park Rd.)
  NG14: Bur J .3F 37
  NG14: Woodbo 1B 24
  NG15: Huck 4F 7
  NG16: Aws .2D 28
  NG16: Eastw 2A 16
  NG16: Kimb .3A 30
Park Av. E. NG12: Key 4F 79
Park Av. W. NG12: Key 4F 79
Park Chase NG6: Bulw 2H 31
Park Cl. DE7: Stant D 3B 52
  NG3: Mapp .5A 34
Park Ct. DE75: Hea 4D 14
  NG7: Lent 2C 56
Park Cres. DE7: Ilk 1C 40
  NG8: Woll 5C 42
  NG16: Eastw 1B 16
Parkcroft Rd. NG2: West Br 5B 58
Parkdale Rd. NG3: Nott 3D 46
  NG4: Car 3D 46
Park Dr. DE7: Ilk 2B 40
  NG7: Nott 5A 4 (5E 45)
  NG10: Sand .2C 62
  NG15: Huck 6G 7
Parker Cl. NG5: Arn 5E 23
Parker Gdns. NG9: Stfrd 3H 53
Parker St. NG15: Huck 4H 7
Parkes Bldg. NG9: Bee 4F 55
Parkgate NG15: Huck 2H 7
Park Hall NG7: Nott 6A 4 (6E 45)
Park Hall La. DE7: Mapp, West H 5B 26
Parkham Rd. NG16: Kimb 6H 17
Park Hgts. NG7: Nott 6A 4 (6E 45)
Park Hill NG7: Nott 3A 4 (4E 45)
  NG16: Aws .2D 28
Park Ho. Gates NG3: Mapp P 6H 33
Parkland Cl. NG11: Clftn 2A 66

Parkland M. NG10: Long E 5F 63
                  (off Derby Rd.)
Parklands Cl. NG5: Top V 4F 21
Park La. NG4: Lamb 6C 24
  NG6: Bas, Bulw 3C 32
  NG14: Epp 6G 13
Park La. Bus. Cen. NG6: Bulw 2C 32
Park Lodge Rd. NG16: Gilt 6C 16
Park M. NG3: Mapp P 1G 45
Park Ravine NG7: Nott 6A 4 (6E 45)
Park Rd. DE7: Ilk 2B 40
  NG4: Car 2H 47
  NG5: Woodt .2A 34
  NG6: Bestw V 1C 20
  NG7: Lent 6D 44
  NG9: Bram 3H 53
  NG9: Chil 5E 55
  NG12: Key 3H 79
  NG12: Rad T .5F 49
  NG14: Calv 3F 11
  NG15: Huck 4F 7
Park Rd. E. NG14: Calv 3H 11
Park Rd. Nth. NG9: Chil 5E 55
Park Row NG1: Nott 5C 4 (5F 45)
Park Rock NG7: Lent 6A 4 (6E 45)
Parkside NG8: Woll 6E 43
  NG12: Key 3H 79
Parkside Av. NG10: Long E 5D 62
Parkside Dr. NG10: Long E 5D 62
Parkside Gdns. NG8: Woll 6E 43
Parkside Ri. NG8: Woll 1E 55
Parkstone Cl. NG2: West Br 6G 57
Park St. DE72: Brea 5B 62
  DE75: Hea 3B 14
  NG7: Lent 5D 44
  NG9: Bee 5E 55
  NG9: Stfrd 5E 53
  NG10: Long E 4E 63
Park Ter. NG1: Nott 4B 4 (5F 45)
  NG12: Key 2H 79
Park Vw. NG7: Nott 5B 4 (5F 45)
Park Valley DE75: Hea 4B 14
  NG3: Mapp .5A 34
  NG15: Huck 5H 7
  NG16: Eastw 4B 16
Park Vw. Ct. NG1: Nott 3G 5 (4H 45)
  NG9: Chil 5D 54
Parkview Dr. NG5: Bestw 6E 21
Parkway Ct. NG8: Bilb 4D 42
Park W. NG7: Nott 3A 4
Park Wharf NG7: Nott 6C 4 (6F 45)
Parkwood Ct. NG6: Bulw 2C 32
Parkwood Cres. NG5: Sher 4A 34
Park Yacht Club .1C 58
Parkyn Rd. NG5: Arn 1H 33
Parkyns St. NG11: Rudd 6G 67
Parliament Ter. NG1: Nott 3C 4 (4F 45)
Parr Ct. NG12: Rad T 6F 49
Parr Ga. NG9: Chil 6A 54
The Parrs NG9: Bee 5H 55
Parry Ct. NG3: Mapp 3C 34
  NG3: Nott 3C 46
Parry Way NG5: Arn 5D 22
Parsons Mdw. NG4: Colw 5G 47
Partridge Cl. NG13: Bing 6F 51
Pasteur Ho. NG3: Mapp 5B 34
Pasture Cl. NG4: Colw 5G 47
Pasture La. NG10: Long E 1A 74
  NG11: Rudd .1D 76
Pasture Rd. NG9: Stfrd 2F 53
The Pastures NG8: Bilb 2H 43
  NG14: Calv 4F 11
  NG16: Gilt 5D 16
Pastures Av. NG11: Clftn 5B 66
Pastures Dr. DE7: Smal 5A 14
Patchings Art Cen. 3D 10
Pateley Rd. NG3: Mapp 3C 34
Pates Cl. NG15: Huck 1B 8
Patient Cl. NG9: Chil 6B 54
Paton Cl. NG14: Calv 2G 11
Paton Rd. NG5: Bestw 2C 32
Patricia Dr. NG5: Arn 4C 22
Patrick Rd. NG2: West Br 3A 58
Patriot Cl. NG16: Want 6A 18
Patterdale Cl. NG2: Gam 4E 59
Patterdale Cl. NG9: Chil 6A 54
Patterdale Rd. NG5: Woodt 2B 34
Patterson Rd. NG7: Hys G 2D 44
Paulina Av. NG15: Huck 3A 8
The Pavilion NG7: Hys G 2E 45
Pavilion Cl. NG2: Nott 2H 57
Pavilion Ct. DE7: West H 2B 38
Pavilion Rd. NG2: West Br 2A 58
  NG5: Arn 4F 21
Pavior Rd. NG5: Bestw 2D 32
Paxton Gdns. NG3: Nott 2H 5 (4A 46)
                 (not continuous)
Payne Ho. NG9: Chil 2A 64
Peache Way NG9: Bram 4B 54
Peachey St. NG1: Nott 2D 4 (4G 45)

Peach St. DE75: Hea 4B **14**
Peacock Cl. NG11: Rudd 1F **77**
Peacock Cres. NG11: Clftn 3C **66**
Peacock Dr. NG16: Eastw 4A **16**
Peacock Gdns. NG8: Stre 5C **30**
Peacock Pl. DE7: Ilk 3H **27**
Peakdale Cl. NG10: Long E 1C **72**
Pearmain Dr. NG3: Nott 2B **46**
Pearson Av. NG9: Chil 6B **54**
Pearson Cl. NG9: Chil 6B **54**
Pearson Ct. NG5: Arn 6A **22**
   NG9: Bram 3B **54**
Pearson St. NG4: Neth 3A **48**
   NG7: Bas 5D **32**
Pear Tree Ct. NG6: Bas 3C **32**
Peartree Orchard NG11: Rudd 6G **67**
Pear Tree Yd. NG10: Sand 5D **52**
Peary Cl. NG5: Bestw 1D **32**
Peashill La. NG12: Cotg 6C **60**
Peas Hill Rd. NG3: Nott 3H **45**
Peatburn Av. DE75: Hea 3A **14**
Peatfield Ct. NG9: Stfrd 2F **53**
Peatfield Rd. NG9: Stfrd 2F **53**
Peck La. NG1: Nott 4E **5** (5G **45**)
Pedley St. DE7: Ilk .2B **40**
Pedmore Cl. NG5: Bestw 6F **21**
Pedmore Valley NG5: Bestw 6E **21**
Peel St. NG1: Nott 1C **4** (3F **45**)
   NG10: Long E 5G **63**
   NG16: Lang M 2F **15**
Peel Vs. NG3: Mapp 5A **34**
Pegswood Dr. NG5: Arn 3C **22**
Pelham Av. DE7: Ilk 6A **28**
   NG5: Sher 1F **45**
Pelham Cotts. NG7: Nott 5D **44**
                  (off Pelham Cres.)
Pelham Ct. NG5: Sher 1F **45**
Pelham Cres. NG7: Nott 5D **44**
   NG9: Bee 4H **55**
Pelham Rd. NG5: Sher 1F **45**
Pelham St. DE7: Ilk 6A **28**
   NG1: Nott 4E **5** (5G **45**)
Pemberton St. NG1: Nott 5G **5** (5H **45**)
Pembrey Cl. NG9: Trow 1F **53**
Pembridge Cl. NG6: Bas 5B **32**
Pembroke Dr. NG3: Mapp P 6G **33**
Pembury Rd. NG8: Woll 4E **43**
Penarth Gdns. NG5: Sher 4A **34**
Penarth Ri. NG5: Sher 4A **34**
Pendennis Cl. NG4: Ged 6B **36**
Pendine Cl. NG5: Redh 4H **21**
Pendle Cres. NG3: Nott 6B **34**
Pendock Ct. NG12: Toll 4F **69**
Pendock La. NG11: Rudd 5B **78**
Penhale Dr. NG15: Huck 6C **6**
Penhurst Cl. NG11: Wilf 1E **67**
Penllech Cl. NG5: Bestw 6E **21**
Penllech Wlk. NG5: Bestw 6E **21**
Pen Moor Cl. NG10: Long E 1C **72**
Pennant Rd. NG6: Bas 5B **32**
Pennard Wlk. NG11: Clftn 5B **66**
Penn Av. NG7: Lent .6C **44**
Pennhome Almshouses NG5: Sher 5G **33**
                  (off Haydn Rd.)
Pennhome Av. NG5: Sher 5G **33**
Pennie Cl. NG10: Long E 3F **73**
Pennine Cl. NG5: Arn 4F **21**
   NG10: Long E 4C **62**
Pennyfields Blvd. NG10: Long E 6C **62**
Pennyfoot St. NG1: Nott 5H **5** (5A **46**)
Penrhyn Cl. NG3: Nott 1F **5**
Penrhyn Cres. NG9: Chil 1B **64**
Penrith Av. NG12: Rad T 5G **49**
Penrith Cres. NG8: Aspl 5A **32**
Penshore Cl. NG11: Clftn 4B **66**
Pentland Dr. NG5: Arn 3F **21**
Pentland Gdns. NG10: Long E 4C **62**
Pentrich Rd. NG16: Gilt 6E **17**
Pentridge Dr. DE7: Ilk 4G **27**
Pentwood Av. NG5: Arn 3B **22**
Peoples Hall Cotts. NG1: Nott 4F **5**
Peppercorn Gdns. NG8: Woll 3A **44**
Pepper La. DE7: Stant D 3A **52**
Pepper Rd. NG14: Calv 3G **11**
Pepper St. NG1: Nott 5E **5** (5G **45**)
Percival Rd. NG5: Sher 5F **33**
Percy St. DE7: Ilk 2B **40**
   NG6: Bas 4B **32**
   NG16: Eastw 3C **16**
Peregrine Cl. NG7: Lent 5C **44**
Peregrine Rd. NG15: Huck 2B **8**
Perivale Cl. NG16: Nuth 4D **30**
Perkins Way NG9: Chil 2D **64**
Perlethorpe Av. NG2: Nott 5B **46**
   NG4: Ged 5F **35**
Perlethorpe Cl. NG4: Ged 5G **35**
Perlethorpe Cres. NG4: Ged 5G **35**
Perlethorpe Dr. NG4: Ged 5F **35**
   NG15: Huck 4H **7**

Perry Gro. NG13: Bing 5F **51**
Perry Rd. NG5: Sher 5D **32**
Perth Dr. NG9: Stfrd .2G **53**
Perth St. NG1: Nott 2E **5** (4G **45**)
Peters Cl. NG5: Arn .1E **35**
   NG16: Newth 3E **17**
Petersfield Cl. NG5: Top V 6D **20**
Petersgate NG10: Long E 4C **62**
Petersgate Cl. NG10: Long E 3C **62**
Petersham Ct. NG10: Long E 3D **62**
Petersham M. NG7: Lent 6D **44**
Petersham Rd. NG10: Long E 3C **62**
Petworth Av. NG9: Toton 2H **63**
Petworth Dr. NG5: Sher 3D **32**
Peverell Hall NG11: Clftn 2B **66**
Peverel Rd. NG15: Huck 1F **7**
Peveril Ct. NG2: West Br 4A **58**
Peveril Cres. DE7: West H 1C **38**
   NG10: Long E 2B **72**
Peveril Dr. DE7: Ilk .5H **27**
   NG2: West Br 2A **68**
   NG7: Nott 6B **4** (6F **45**)
Peveril M. NG7: Nott .5A **4**
Peveril Rd. NG9: Bee 3F **55**
Peveril St. NG7: Radf 3D **44**
   NG15: Huck 3G **7**
Pewit Golf Course 1H **39**
Philip Av. NG16: Eastw 4C **16**
   NG16: Nuth 1C **30**
Philip Gro. NG4: Ged 5G **35**
Phoenix Av. NG4: Ged 5G **35**
Phoenix Cen. NG8: Cin 3G **31**
Phoenix Cl. NG2: Nott 1F **57**
Phoenix Ct. NG7: Lent 3D **56**
   NG16: Eastw 3C **16**
Phoenix Park Park & Ride 3G **31**
Phoenix Park Stop (NET) 3G **31**
Phoenix Pl. NG8: Cin 3H **31**
Phoenix Rd. NG16: Newth 1D **16**
Phyllis Cl. NG15: Huck 2F **7**
Phyllis Gro. NG10: Long E 6H **63**
Piccadilly NG6: Bulw 1B **32**
Pickering Av. NG16: Eastw 3B **16**
Pieris Dr. NG11: Clftn 4A **66**
Pierrepont Av. NG4: Ged 6G **35**
Pierrepont Ct. NG2: West Br 2D **58**
Pierrepont Rd. NG2: West Br 3C **58**
Piggott Av. NG4: Ged 4G **35**
Pilcher Ga. NG1: Nott 4E **5** (5H **45**)
Pilkington Rd. NG3: Mapp 6C **34**
Pilkington St. NG6: Bulw 6H **19**
Pilot Dr. NG15: Huck 1E **19**
Pimlico DE7: Ilk 1A **40**
Pimlico Av. NG9: Bram 6B **42**
Pine Av. NG16: Lang M 2E **15**
Pine Gro. NG15: Huck 1H **19**
Pine Hill Cl. NG5: Top V 4D **20**
Pinehurst Av. NG15: Huck 6C **6**
The Pines NG9: Bram 3C **54**
Pines Ct. NG5: Sher .3H **33**
Pine Tree Wlk. NG16: Eastw 3A **16**
Pine Vw. NG7: Radf .3D **44**
Pinewood Av. NG5: Arn 4D **22**
Pinewood Gdns. NG11: Clftn 5B **66**
Pinfold NG13: Bing 5F **51**
Pinfold Cl. NG12: Cotg 1F **71**
   NG14: Woodbo 1C **24**
Pinfold Cres. NG14: Woodbo 1C **24**
Pinfold La.
   NG9: Stfrd 4F **53**
   NG11: Wilf 5F **57**
   NG12: Plum 6H **69**
Pinfold Rd. NG16: Gilt 4E **17**
The Pingle NG10: Long E 4B **62**
Pingle Cres. NG5: Top V 5D **20**
Pintail Cl. NG4: Neth 3B **48**
Pioneer Meadows Local Nature Reserve 5G **39**
Piper Cl. NG15: Huck 2H **7**
Pippin Cl. NG3: Nott .2B **46**
Pitcairn Cl. NG2: Nott 2G **57**
Pitch Cl. NG4: Car 1E **47**
   NG16: Gilt 5E **17**
Pit La. DE7: Ilk 1F **27**
   DE75: Ship 1F **27**
Plackett Cl. DE72: Brea 5A **62**
   NG9: Stfrd 3H **53**
Plains Farm Cl. NG3: Mapp 2E **35**
Plains Gro. NG3: Mapp 3C **34**
Plains Rd. NG3: Mapp 4B **34**
Plane Rd. NG12: Edwal 3C **68**
Plane Tree Cl. NG15: Huck 6H **7**
Plantagenet Ct. NG3: Nott 1G **5** (4H **45**)
Plantagenet St. NG3: Nott 2G **5** (4H **45**)
Plantation Cl. NG5: Arn 4F **21**
Plantation Cotts. NG14: Epp 5F **13**
Plantation Rd. NG8: Woll 5C **42**
   NG12: Key 4G **79**
The Plantations NG10: Long E 5C **62**
Plantation Side NG7: Hys G 2C **44**

Plantin Rd. NG5: Sher 6F **33**
Plant La. NG10: Long E 3C **72**
Platt La. NG12: Key, Norm W 3H **79**
Platts Av. DE75: Hea 4A **14**
Player Cl. NG7: Radf 3C **44**
Player St. NG7: Radf 3C **44**
Plaza Gdns. NG6: Bas 3C **32**
Pleasant Ct. NG7: Hys G 2D **44**
Pleasant Row NG7: Hys G 2D **44**
Plimsoll St. NG7: Hys G 1C **44**
Plough La. NG2: Nott 5H **5** (5A **46**)
Ploughman Av. NG14: Woodbo 1D **24**
Plover Wharf NG7: Lent 1E **57**
Plowman Ct. NG9: Stfrd 5F **53**
Plowright Cl. NG3: Nott 2H **45**
Plowright St. NG3: Nott 2H **45**
Plumb Rd. NG15: Huck 4F **7**
Plumptre Cl. NG16: Eastw 4B **16**
Plumptre Gdns. NG16: Eastw 3B **16**
Plumptre Pl. NG1: Nott 5F **5** (5H **45**)
Plumptre Rd. NG16: Lang M 1F **15**
Plumptre Sq. NG1: Nott 5G **5** (5H **45**)
Plumptre St. NG1: Nott 5F **5** (5H **45**)
Plumptre Way NG16: Eastw 4B **16**
PLUMTREE 6G **69**
Plumtree Cl. NG12: Plum 6G **69**
Plumtree Gdns. NG14: Calv 4H **11**
PLUMTREE PARK 3H **79**
Plumtree Rd. NG12: Cotg 3D **70**
Plungar Cl. NG8: Bilb 3H **43**
Podder La. NG3: Mapp 1E **35**
Poets Cl. NG15: Huck 1E **19**
The Point
   NG1: Nott 5G **5**
   NG2: West Br 4A **58**
             (off Loughborough Rd.)
   NG3: Mapp P 1H **45**
Pointers Ct. NG3: Nott 2C **46**
Pollard Ct. NG9: Bee 4F **55**
Polperro Way NG15: Huck 6C **6**
Pompeia Cl. NG15: Huck 3B **8**
Pond Hills La. NG5: Arn 5B **22**
Poole Av. NG4: Ged .3G **35**
Pool Mdw. NG4: Colw 5H **47**
Popham Ct. NG1: Nott 5F **5** (5H **45**)
Poplar Av. NG5: Sher 5E **33**
   NG10: Sand 4C **52**
Poplar Cl. NG4: Car .3F **47**
   NG12: Cotg 6G **61**
   NG13: Bing 5G **51**
Poplar Cres. NG16: Nuth 1A **30**
Poplar Rd. DE72: Brea 4B **62**
The Poplars
   NG2: West Br 4B **58**
   NG7: Hys G 1C **44**
   NG9: Bee 4F **55**
   NG12: Plum 1G **79**
Poplars Av. NG4: Bur J 2G **37**
Poplars Cl. NG12: Key 3H **79**
Poplars St. NG7: Lent 1D **56**
Poplars Rd. NG7: Lent 1D **56**
Poplar St. NG1: Nott 5G **5** (5H **45**)
                  (not continuous)
Poplar Way DE7: Kirk H 4H **39**
Poppy Cl. NG2: West Br 4H **57**
   NG12: Cotg 1G **71**
Poppy M. NG15: Huck 1B **20**
PORCHESTER 5D **34**
Porchester Cl. NG15: Huck 4A **8**
Porchester St. NG3: Nott 1C **46**
Porchester Rd. NG3: Mapp, Nott 5B **34**
   NG13: Bing 5D **50**
Porlock Cl. NG10: Long E 5C **62**
Portage Cl. NG12: Rad T 1E **61**
Port Arthur Rd. NG2: Nott 5B **46**
Porter Cl. NG11: Clftn 5A **66**
Porters Wlk. NG3: Nott 2C **46**
Portinscale Cl. NG2: West Br 6E **59**
Portland Cl. NG5: Bestw 2F **33**
Portland Cres. NG9: Stfrd 5G **53**
Portland Gdns. NG15: Huck 4F **7**
Portland Grange NG15: Huck 4E **7**
Portland Hill NG7: Nott 2A **56**
Portland Leisure Cen. 2H **57**
Portland Pk. Cl. NG15: Huck 4F **7**
Portland Rd.
   DE7: Ilk 4B **28**
   NG2: West Br 5B **58**
   NG4: Car 5E **35**
   NG7: Radf .2A **4** (4E **45**)
   NG9: Toton 4H **63**
   NG10: Long E 3C **72**
   NG15: Huck 4H **7**
   NG16: Gilt 5E **17**
Portland Sq. NG7: Radf 2A **4** (4E **45**)
Portland St. NG5: Arn 1H **33**
   NG9: Bee 4G **55**
Portree Dr. NG5: Top V 4D **20**
Port Said Vs. NG7: Bas 6D **32**
Portside St. NG2: Nott 1B **58**

Postern St. NG1: Nott 4C **4** (5F **45**)
Pot 'n' Kettle (Ceramic Cafe) *4G 55*
(off High Rd.)
Potomac M. NG7: Nott 5A **4** (5E **45**)
Potters Cl. NG5: Top V 6E **21**
Potters Ct. NG9: Bram 2D **54**
Potters Hill Vw. DE75: Hea 4E **15**
Potters Hollow NG6: Bulw 2A **32**
Potters Way DE7: Ilk 1C **40**
Pottery Cl. NG6: Bulw 6G **19**
Pottery Way NG6: Bulw 6G **19**
Poulter Cl. NG7: Radf 2B **44**
Poulton Dr. NG2: Nott 6B **46**
Poultry NG1: Nott 4E **5** (5G **45**)
Poultry Arc. NG1: Nott 4E **5**
Powerleague
    Nottingham 5C **56**
Powis St. NG6: Bulw 6H **19**
Powtrell Pl. DE7: Ilk 3D **40**
Poynter Cl. DE75: Hea 4A **14**
Poynton St. NG1: Nott 3C **4** (4F **45**)
Poyser Cl. NG7: Bas 6E **33**
Premier Rd. NG7: Hys G 1E **45**
Prendwick Gdns. NG5: Bestw 5F **21**
Prestwick Cl. NG8: Stre 5D **30**
Prestwood Dr. NG8: Aspl 2H **43**
Pretoria Vs. NG8: Aspl 5A **32**
Previn Gdns. NG3: Nott 3B **46**
Primrose Bank NG13: Bing 5D **50**
Primrose Cl. NG3: Nott 2H **45**
Primrose Cotts. DE72: Ris 2A **62**
Primrose Cres. NG4: Car 2H **47**
Primrose Gdns. NG15: Huck 1B **20**
Primrose Hill DE7: Ilk 4A **28**
Primrose Ri. NG16: Newth 5C **16**
Primrose St. DE7: Ilk 4A **28**
    NG4: Car .2H **47**
Primula Cl. NG11: Clftn 3A **66**
Prince Edward Cres. NG12: Rad T 1D **60**
Princess Av. NG9: Bee 5G **55**
Princess Blvd. NG8: Stre 5C **30**
Princess Cl. DE75: Hea 3B **14**
    NG4: Ged .5G **35**
Princess Dr. NG10: Sand 1D **62**
Princess St. NG10: Long E 5F **63**
Princes St. NG16: Eastw 2B **16**
Prince St. DE7: Ilk 3A **28**
    NG10: Long E 5F **63**
Prioridge NG12: Cotg 3G **71**
Prior Rd. NG5: Arn 1H **33**
Priors Cl. NG13: Bing 4G **51**
Priory Av. NG12: Toll 4E **69**
Priory Cir. NG12: Toll 4E **69**
Priory Cl. DE7: Kirk H 3G **39**
Priory Ct.
    NG3: Mapp 6A **34**
    NG4: Ged .6H **35**
    NG7: Lent .6C **44**
Priory Cres. NG4: Ged 6H **35**
PRIORY HOSPITAL NOTTINGHAM 1A **46**
Priory M. NG7: Lent 1C **56**
Priory Rd. NG2: West Br 3B **58**
    NG4: Ged .6H **35**
    NG15: Huck 4E **7**
    NG16: Eastw 4B **16**
Priory St. NG7: Lent 1C **56**
Pritchard Dr. NG3: Mapp 5G **33**
Private Rd. NG3: Mapp 5G **33**
    NG5: Sher .5G **33**
    NG12: Key .4A **80**
    NG14: Woodbo 6B **12**
    NG15: Huck 4E **7**
Private Rd. No. 1 NG4: Colw 3H **47**
Private Rd. No. 2 NG4: Colw 4A **48**
Private Rd. No. 3 NG4: Colw 4A **48**
Private Rd. No. 4 NG4: Colw 4B **48**
Private Rd. No. 5 NG4: Colw 4B **48**
Private Rd. No. 7 NG4: Colw 3H **47**
Private Rd. No. 8 NG4: Colw 4H **47**
Prize Cl. NG11: Clftn 4A **66**
Promenade NG3: Nott 2G **5** (4H **45**)
Prospect Ct. NG4: Car 6C **34**
Prospect Pl. NG7: Lent 6D **44**
Prospect Rd. DE75: Hea 5E **15**
    NG4: Car .6C **34**
Prospect St. NG7: Radf 3C **44**
Prospect Ter. NG7: Radf 6A **28**
Providence Pl. DE7: Ilk 2A **4**
Provident Works NG7: Radf 2H **57**
Prudhoe Ct. NG2: Nott 2H **57**
Pulborough Cl. NG5: Sher 3D **32**
Pullman Rd. NG2: Nott 5B **46**
Pump Works Cl. NG5: Sher 4G **33**
Purbeck Cl. NG10: Long E 5C **62**
Purbeck Dr. NG2: West Br 6G **57**
Purchase Av. DE75: Los 3A **14**
Purdy Mdw. NG10: Long E 2B **72**
Pyatt St. NG2: Nott 2H **57**
Pygall Av. NG11: Goth 6G **75**
Pym Leys NG10: Long E 2B **72**

Pym St. NG3: Nott 3B **46**
Pym Wlk. NG3: Nott 1H **5** (3A **46**)

Q

Quantock Cl. NG5: Arn 3F **21**
Quantock Gro. NG13: Bing 5C **50**
Quantock Rd. NG10: Long E 4C **62**
Quarry Av. NG6: Bulw 1H **31**
Quarrydale NG15: Huck 2F **7**
Quarry Hill DE7: Stant D 3B **52**
Quarry Hill Ind. Est. DE7: Ilk 5B **40**
Quarry Hill Rd. DE7: Ilk 4B **40**
Quasar Elite
    Nottingham 3G **5** (4H **45**)
The Quays NG7: Lent 6E **45**
Quayside Cl. NG2: Nott 2A **58**
Queen Elizabeth Rd. NG9: Chil 1A **64**
Queen Elizabeth Way DE7: Kirk H 4G **39**
Queens Av. DE7: Ilk 3A **38**
    DE7: Stly .3B **14**
    DE75: Hea .5G **35**
    NG4: Ged .3C **32**
Queensberry St. NG6: Bas 5F **21**
Queen's Bower Rd. NG5: Bestw 6G **45**
Queens Bri. Rd. NG2: Nott 2G **67**
Queensbury Av. NG2: West Br 4D **50**
Queen's Ct. NG13: Bing 4E **57**
Queens Ct. NG2: Nott 1A **40**
Queen's Dr. DE7: Ilk 4E **57**
    NG2: Nott .5G **55**
    NG9: Bee .1D **62**
Queens Dr. NG10: Sand 1C **30**
    NG16: Nuth 2E **57**
Queens Dr. Ind. Est. NG2: Nott 4E **57**
Queen's Drive Park & Ride 6G **45**
Queens Gro. NG2: Nott 1B **56**
Queen's Medical Centre Stop (NET) 1B **56**
QUEEN'S MEDICAL CENTRE UNIVERSITY
    HOSPITAL .6G **55**
Queen's Rd. NG9: Bee 6G **45**
    NG12: Rad T 5F **49**
Queens Rd. NG2: Nott 4H **55**
Queen's Rd. E. NG9: Bee 3B **16**
Queens Rd. Nth. NG9: Bee 4B **16**
Queen's Rd. Sth. NG16: Eastw 1D **64**
Queen's Rd. W. NG9: Bee, Chil 3B **16**
Queen's Sq. NG16: Eastw 1A **40**
Queen St. DE7: Ilk 3D **4** (4G **45**)
    NG1: Nott .4B **22**
    NG5: Arn .6G **63**
    NG10: Long E 3F **7**
    NG15: Huck 2G **15**
    NG16: Lang M 2F **57**
Queen's Wlk. NG2: Nott 1G **57**
Queen's Walk Stop (NET) 1A **40**
Queen Ter. DE7: Ilk 5A **34**
Querneby Av. NG3: Mapp 5A **34**
Querneby Rd. NG3: Mapp 6E **57**
Quinton Cl. NG11: Wilf 2E **65**
Quorn Cl. NG9: Atten 2F **73**
Quorndon Cres. NG10: Long E 4E **33**
Quorn Gro. NG5: Sher 4E **33**
Quorn Rd. NG5: Sher . . . .

R

Racecourse Park & Ride 6D **46**
Racecourse Rd. NG2: Colw, Nott 5D **46**
Radbourne Rd. NG2: Nott 6B **46**
Radburn Ct. NG9: Stfrd 2G **53**
Radcliffe Gdns. NG4: Car 1F **47**
Radcliffe Lodge NG12: Rad T 6E **49**
Radcliffe Mt. NG2: West Br 2B **58**
RADCLIFFE ON TRENT 6F **49**
Radcliffe on Trent Golf Course 1H **61**
Radcliffe Rd. NG2: Gam, West Br 2A **58**
    NG12: Hol P 3F **59**
Radcliffe Station (Rail) 6F **49**
Radcliffe St. NG2: Nott 2H **57**
RADFORD 4D **44**
Radford Blvd. NG7: Radf 3C **44**
Radford Bri. Rd. NG8: Aspl, Woll 3A **44**
Radford Ct. *NG7: Bas* *5D 32*
(off Radford Rd.)
    NG7: Radf .4D **44**
Radford Cres. NG4: Ged 5G **35**
Radford Gro. La. NG7: Radf 3C **44**
Radford Rd. NG7: Bas, Hys G 5D **32**
Radford Road Stop (NET) 1D **44**
Radham Ct. NG5: Sher 5G **33**
Radley Sq. NG6: Bulw 6C **44**
Radmarsh Rd. NG7: Lent 1E **73**
Rad Mdws. NG10: Long E 5C **50**
Radnor Gro. NG13: Bing 2C **46**
Radstock Rd. NG3: Nott 6E **57**
Radway Dr. NG11: Wilf 3G **63**
Raeburn Dr. NG9: Toton . . . .

The Rafters NG7: Bas 5D **32**
Ragdale Pl. NG6: Bulw 5A **20**
Ragdale Rd. NG6: Bulw 5H **19**
(not continuous)
Raglan Cl. NG3: Nott 2H **45**
Raglan Ct. NG9: Lent A 2G **55**
Raglan Dr. NG4: Ged 6B **36**
Raglan St. NG16: Eastw 4C **16**
Raibank Gdns. NG5: Woodt 2A **34**
Railway Cotts. NG16: Kimb 1H **29**
Rainham Gdns. NG11: Rudd 1G **77**
Raithby Cl. NG5: Bestw 1E **33**
Raleigh Cl. DE7: Ilk 4B **28**
    NG11: Clftn 4A **66**
Raleigh Ct. NG7: Radf 1A **4** (3E **45**)
Raleigh Pk. NG7: Lent 4B **44**
Raleigh Sq. NG7: Radf 2A **4** (4E **45**)
Raleigh St. NG7: Radf 2A **4** (4E **45**)
Ralf Cl. NG2: West Br 1A **68**
Ralph Way NG5: Sher 2G **33**
Ramblers Cl. NG4: Colw 4G **47**
Ramsdale Av. NG14: Calv 3F **11**
Ramsdale Cres. NG5: Sher 4H **33**
Ramsdale Pk. NG5: Arn 5D **10**
Ramsdale Pk. Golf Cen. 4D **10**
Ramsdale Rd. NG4: Car 6G **35**
Ramsey Cl. NG9: Stfrd 1G **53**
Ramsey Ct. NG5: Sher 6F **33**
Ramsey Dr. NG5: Arn 1D **34**
Ranby Wlk. NG3: Nott 3B **46**
Rancliffe Av. NG12: Key 3F **79**
Randal Gdns. NG7: Hys G 2D **44**
Randal St. NG7: Hys G 2C **44**
(not continuous)
Ranelagh Gro. NG8: Woll 4G **43**
Rani Dr. NG5: Bas 3D **32**
Ranmere Rd. NG8: Bilb 2G **43**
Ranmoor Rd. NG4: Ged 6H **35**
Ranmore Cl. NG9: Bram 1B **54**
Rannerdale Cl. NG2: West Br 5D **58**
Rannoch Ri. NG5: Arn 4B **22**
Rannock Gdns. NG12: Key 4H **79**
Ranskill Gdns. NG5: Top V 5E **21**
Ransom Dr. NG3: Mapp, Nott 6A **34**
Ransom Rd. NG3: Nott 6A **34**
Ranson Rd. NG9: Chil 4B **64**
Ratcliffe St. NG16: Eastw 3B **16**
Rathgar Cl. NG8: Woll 5D **42**
Rathmines Cl. NG7: Lent 6C **44**
Rathvale Ct. NG9: Chil 1A **64**
Raven Av. NG5: Sher 3F **33**
Raven Ct. DE75: Hea 3C **14**
Ravenhill Cl. NG9: Chil 1B **64**
Ravensdale Av. NG10: Long E 3D **62**
Ravensdale Dr. NG8: Woll 6C **42**
Ravensdene Ct. NG3: Mapp P 1G **45**
Ravensmore Rd. NG5: Sher 5F **33**
Ravenstone Ct. NG15: Huck 2D **18**
Ravenswood Rd. NG5: Arn 6B **22**
Ravensworth Rd. NG6: Bulw 5H **19**
Rawson St. NG7: Bas 6D **32**
Raymede Cl. NG5: Bestw 1D **32**
Raymede Dr. NG5: Bestw 1C **32**
Raymond Dr. NG13: Bing 5G **51**
Rayneham Rd. DE7: Ilk 3G **27**
Rayner Ct. NG7: Lent 4D **44**
Raynford Av. NG9: Chil 1D **64**
Raynham Lodge NG5: Top V 4B **20**
Rays Av. DE75: Hea 4C **14**
Ray St. DE75: Hea 4B **14**
Read Av. NG9: Bee 5G **55**
Read Lodge NG9: Bee 5G **55**
Readman Rd. NG9: Chil 2A **64**
Rearsby Cl. NG8: Bilb 4D **42**
Recreation Rd. NG10: Sand 5D **52**
Recreation St. NG10: Long E 5H **63**
Recreation Ter. NG9: Stfrd 5F **53**
Rectory Av. NG8: Woll 5E **43**
Rectory Ct. NG2: West Br 4B **58**
Rectory Dr. NG4: Ged 5H **35**
    NG11: Wilf .3F **57**
Rectory Gdns. NG8: Woll 5F **43**
Rectory Pl. NG11: Bart F 1E **75**
Rectory Rd. DE72: Brea 5A **62**
    NG2: West Br 4A **58**
    NG4: Colw .4G **47**
    NG12: Cotg 2E **71**
Redbourne Dr. NG8: Aspl 3A **44**
Redbridge Cl. DE7: Ilk 2C **40**
Redbridge Dr. NG16: Nuth 4D **30**
Redcar Cl. NG4: Ged 5G **35**
Redcliffe Gdns. NG3: Mapp P 1G **45**
Redcliffe Rd. NG3: Mapp P 1F **45**
The Redens NG10: Long E 3D **72**
Redfield Rd. NG7: Lent 3C **56**
Redfield Way NG7: Lent 2C **56**
Redgates Ct. NG14: Calv 4F **11**
REDHILL 4A **22**
Redhill Leisure Cen. 4A **22**

Redhill Lodge Dr. NG5: Redh 4H 21
Redhill Marina 6G 73
Redhill Rd. NG5: Arn 4A 22
Red Kite Cl. NG15: Huck 3B 8
Redland Av. NG4: Car .1H 47
Redland Cl. DE7: Ilk 4B 28
  NG9: Chil 1C 64
Redland Dr. NG9: Chil .2C 64
Redland Gro. NG4: Car .1G 47
Red Lion Sq. DE75: Hea 3C 14
Red Lion Yd. NG15: Huck 4G 7
  (off High St.)
Redmays Dr. NG14: Bulc 1H 37
Redmile Cl. NG15: Huck .3F 7
Redmile Rd. NG8: Aspl .5A 32
Redoubt St. NG7: Radf .4C 44
Redruth Cl. NG8: Bilb 3C 42
Redwood NG2: West Br .5F 57
Redwood Av. NG8: Woll .6D 42
Redwood Cl. NG8: Bilb .2D 42
Redwood Cft. NG7: Lent .5C 44
  (off Faraday Rd.)
  NG15: Huck 3F 7
Redwood Cres. NG9: Bee 6G 55
Reeders Cft. NG9: Chil .2D 64
Reedham Wlk. NG5: Bestw 5F 21
Reedman Rd. NG10: Long E 3D 72
Reel Cinema 1A 40
Rees Gdns. NG5: Top V .4E 21
Regan Way NG9: Chil 3B 64
Regatta Way NG2: West Br 3E 59
Regency Ct. NG9: Bee 4G 55
Regency Point NG2: West Br 3B 58
Regent M. NG1: Nott 3B 4 (4F 45)
Regents Pk. Cl. NG2: West Br 6G 57
Regents Pl. NG11: Wilf .5F 57
Regent St. DE7: Ilk 2B 40
  NG1: Nott .4B 4 (5F 45)
  NG7: Bas 6E 33
  NG9: Bee 4G 55
  NG10: Long E 5F 63
  NG10: Sand 6E 53
  NG16: Kimb 1H 29
  NG16: Lang M 2F 15
Regina Cl. NG12: Rad T .1E 61
Reid Gdns. NG16: Want .1B 30
Reigate Cl. NG9: Atten .3E 65
Reigate Dr. NG9: Atten .3E 65
Reigate Rd. NG7: Bas 5D 32
Remembrance Way NG11: Clftn 4A 66
Rempstone Dr. NG6: Bulw 2B 32
Renals Way NG14: Calv .5H 11
Renfrew Dr. NG8: Woll .5E 43
Rennie Hogg Rd. NG2: Nott 2D 56
Renshaw Dr. NG4: Ged .4G 35
Repton Dr. DE7: Ilk 2D 40
Repton Rd. NG2: West Br 6A 58
  NG6: Bulw 1B 32
  NG10: Long E 3B 72
Retford Rd. NG5: Sher .4E 33
Retlaw Ct. NG9: Chil 6D 54
Revelstoke Av. NG5: Top V 4B 20
Revelstoke Way NG5: Top V 4B 20
Revena Cl. NG4: Colw 3H 47
Revesby Gdns. NG8: Aspl 2A 44
Revesby Rd. NG5: Woodt 2B 34
Revill Cl. DE7: Ilk 5G 27
Revill Cres. NG9: Stfrd .3H 53
Reydon Dr. NG8: Bas 6B 32
Reynolds Dr. NG8: Woll .4F 43
Rhodes Way NG6: Bestw V 5F 9
Rhyl Cres. NG4: Ged 5H 35
Ribblesdale DE7: Kirk H .4G 39
Ribblesdale Ct. NG9: Chil 1A 64
Ribblesdale Rd. NG5: Sher 2G 33
  NG10: Long E 2C 72
Riber Cl. DE7: West H 1C 38
  NG10: Long E 2F 73
Riber Cres. NG5: Bestw .2D 32
Richard Herrod Cen. 1E 47
Richardson Cl. NG11: Clftn 4A 66
Richborough Pl. NG8: Woll 1D 54
Richey Cl. NG5: Arn 6D 22
Richmond Av. DE7: Ilk 3B 28
  DE72: Brea 5C 62
  NG3: Nott 2B 46
  NG10: Sand 1C 62
  NG14: Calv 3A 12
  NG16: Newth 3D 16
Richmond Cl. DE7: West H 1B 38
Richmond Ct. NG9: Chil .6E 55
Richmond Dr. NG3: Mapp P 5H 33
  NG9: Chil 6E 55
  NG12: Rad T 5F 49
Richmond Gdns. NG5: Redh 4A 22
Richmond Rd. NG2: West Br 2B 58
Richmond Ter. NG12: Rad T 6F 49
Ricklow Ct. NG5: Top V .5E 21
  (off Gautries Cl.)
Rick St. NG1: Nott 3F 5 (4H 45)

The Riddings NG4: Neth 2A 48
  (off Morris St.)
Ridding Ter. NG3: Nott 1E 5 (3G 45)
Riddles Ct. NG16: Want .5A 18
Ridge La. NG12: Rad T .4G 49
  NG5: Top V 6C 20
Ridgeway DE75: Hea 5D 14
Ridgeway Dr. DE7: Kirk H 4F 39
Ridgeway Wlk. NG5: Top V 5E 21
Ridgewood Dr. NG9: Chil 1C 64
Ridgmont Wlk. NG11: Clftn 5B 66
Ridgway Cl. NG2: West Br 6E 59
Ridgway St. NG3: Nott 3A 46
The Ridings NG12: Key .4A 80
  NG14: Bulc 2G 37
Ridsdale Rd. NG5: Sher .2G 33
Rifle St. NG7: Radf 4C 44
Rigg La. NG5: Arn 1A 10
Rigley Av. DE7: Ilk 6B 28
Rigley Dr. NG5: Top V 6C 20
Ring Leas NG12: Cotg 3F 71
Ringstead Cl. NG2: West Br 6G 57
Ringstead Wlk. NG5: Bestw 5F 21
Ringwood Cres. NG8: Woll 4A 44
Ringwood Rd. NG13: Bing 5C 50
Ripon Rd. NG3: Nott 4D 46
The Rise NG5: Sher 4H 33
Riseborough Wlk. NG6: Bulw 4H 19
  (not continuous)
Rise Ct. NG5: Sher 1F 45
Risegate NG12: Cotg 2F 71
Risegate Gdns. NG12: Cotg 2F 71
Riseholme Av. NG8: Woll 6C 42
RISE PARK 4C 20
Rise Pk. Rd. NG5: Top V 4B 20
Rise Pk. Shop. Cen. 4D 20
RISLEY 1A 62
Risley Ct. DE7: Ilk 4B 28
Risley Dr. NG2: Nott 1F 57
Risley La. DE72: Brea, Ris 2A 62
Riste's Pl. NG1: Nott 4F 5 (5H 45)
Ritchie Cl. NG12: Cotg 3G 71
Ritson Cl. NG3: Nott 1G 5 (3H 45)
River Cres. NG2: Nott 1C 58
Riverdale Rd. NG9: Chil .3D 64
Rivergreen NG11: Clftn .2C 66
Rivergreen Cl. NG9: Bram 1C 54
Rivergreen Cres. NG9: Bram 1C 54
Rivermead Stop (NET) 3D 66
Rivermead NG2: West Br 4H 57
  NG12: Cotg 2F 71
River Rd. NG4: Colw 5G 47
Riverside NG14: Stoke B .1F 49
Riverside Cl. NG9: Bee .2H 65
Riverside Family Golf Centre 5D 56
Riverside Golf Course 5D 56
Riverside Point NG7: Lent 6C 44
Riverside Retail Pk.
  Nottingham 3E 57
Riverside Rd. NG9: Bee .2G 65
Riverside Way NG2: Nott 2F 57
River Vw. NG2: Nott 2H 57
  NG10: Long E 4C 72
Riverway Gdns. NG2: Nott 1H 57
Rivington Rd. NG9: Toton 3G 63
Robbie Burns Rd. NG5: Bestw 5G 21
Robbinetts La. NG8: Stre 6H 29
  NG16: Babb, Coss 6F 29
  (not continuous)
Roberts La. NG15: Huck .4F 7
Roberts St. DE7: Ilk 3C 40
  NG2: Nott 5A 46
Roberts Yd. NG9: Bee 4G 55
Robert Wilkinson Smith Homes 2G 45
Robey Cl. NG15: Lin 2H 7
Robey Dr. NG16: Eastw .2B 16
Robey Ter. NG7: Hys G .2D 44
Robina Dr. NG16: Gilt 5E 17
Robin Bailey Way NG15: Huck 5A 8
Robinet Rd. NG9: Bee 6F 55
Robin Hood Chase NG3: Nott 2H 45
Robin Hood Cl. NG16: Eastw 4B 16
Robin Hood Cl. NG15: Huck 1E 19
Robin Hood Ind. Est. NG3: Nott 2H 5 (4A 46)
Robin Hood Rd. NG5: Arn 4G 21
Robin Hood Statue 5C 4
Robin Hood St. NG3: Nott 3H 5 (4A 46)
Robin Hood Ter. NG3: Nott 2G 5 (4H 45)
Robin Hood Way NG2: Nott 2F 57
Robinia Ct. NG2: West Br 6C 58
Robinson Ct. NG9: Chil .3B 64
Robinson Gdns. NG11: Clftn 4A 66
Robinson Rd. NG3: Mapp 4B 34
Robinsons Hill NG6: Bulw 6H 19
Robin's Row NG15: Huck 6E 7
  (off Knoll Av.)
Robins Wood House 2H 43
Robins Wood Rd. NG8: Aspl 3H 43
Rob Roy Av. NG7: Lent .6D 44
Roche Cl. NG5: Arn 6E 23

Rochester Av. NG4: Neth 2A 48
Rochester Cl. NG10: Long E 6C 62
Rochester Ct. NG6: Bulw 1F 31
Rochester Wlk. NG11: Clftn 4D 66
Rochford Ct. NG12: Edwal 2E 69
Rock City 3C 4
Rock Ct. NG6: Bas 4D 32
Rock Dr. NG7: Nott 6A 4 (6E 45)
Rocket Cl. NG16: Want .6A 18
Rockford Ct. NG9: Stfrd .2G 53
Rockford Rd. NG5: Sher .4D 32
Rockingham Gro. NG13: Bing 5C 50
Rockley Av. NG12: Rad T 5F 49
  NG16: Newth 4C 16
Rockley Cl. NG15: Huck .6D 6
Rockleys Vw. NG14: Lowd 3G 25
Rock Side NG16: Kimb .1H 29
  (off Edgwood Rd.)
Rockside Gdns. NG15: Huck 4E 7
Rock St. NG6: Bulw 5G 19
Rockwood Ct. NG9: Stfrd 4G 53
Rockwood Cres. NG15: Huck 5D 6
Rockwood Wlk. NG15: Huck 5E 7
Rodel Ct. NG3: Nott 1F 5 (3H 45)
Roden St. NG3: Nott 3H 5 (4A 46)
Roderick St. NG6: Bas 3B 32
Rodice Ct. NG7: Lent 4C 44
Rodney Rd. NG2: West Br 5C 58
Rodney Way DE7: Ilk 4B 28
Rodwell Cl. NG8: Aspl 3A 44
Roebuck Cl. NG5: Arn 5F 21
Roecliffe NG2: West Br .1A 68
Roe Gdns. NG11: Rudd 6F 67
Roehampton Dr. NG9: Trow 1F 53
Roe Hill NG14: Woodbo .5C 12
Roe La. NG14: Woodbo 1C 24
Roes La. NG14: Calv 4A 12
Roker Cl. NG8: Aspl 6G 31
Roland Av. NG11: Wilf 4F 57
  NG16: Nuth 3E 31
Rolleston Cl. NG15: Huck .6D 6
Rolleston Cres. NG16: Want 4H 17
Rolleston Dr. NG5: Arn 6C 22
  NG7: Lent 5D 44
  NG16: Newth 5C 16
Rolls Royce Leisure 2E 19
Roman Cres. NG15: Huck 3B 8
Roman Dr. NG6: Bas 3C 32
Romans Ct. NG6: Bas 5C 32
Romilay Cl. NG9: Lent A .2G 55
Romney Av. NG8: Woll 1D 54
Romorantin Pl. NG10: Long E 6G 63
Rona Cl. NG6: Bulw 2C 32
Ronald St. NG7: Radf 4D 44
Rookery Gdns. NG5: Arn .5B 22
Rookwood Cl. NG9: Bee .5E 55
Roosa Cl. NG6: Bulw 2F 31
Roosevelt Av. NG10: Long E 2E 73
Roper Av. DE75: Hea 5C 14
The Ropewalk DE7: Ilk 6C 28
  DE7: Stan C 6A 26
  DE75: Hea 5D 14
  NG1: Nott .3A 4 (4E 45)
Ropewalk Ct. NG1: Nott 3B 4 (4F 45)
ROPEWALK HOUSE 4B 4
Ropewalk Ind. Est. DE7: Ilk 6C 28
Ropsley Cres. NG2: West Br 2C 58
Rosa Ct. NG4: Ged 6A 36
Roscoe Av. NG5: Redh 3A 22
Roseacre NG9: Bee 6G 55
Rose Ash La. NG5: Bestw 5F 21
Rose Av. DE7: Ilk 5A 28
Rosebank Dr. NG5: Arn .4D 22
Rosebay Av. NG7: Hys G 1C 44
Roseberry Gdns. NG15: Huck 5A 8
Rosebery Av. NG2: West Br 2A 58
Rosebery St. NG6: Bas 3C 32
Rose Cl. NG3: Nott 2H 45
Rose Cotts. NG14: Bur J .2E 37
Rose Ct. NG10: Long E 4D 62
Rosecroft Dr. NG5: Bestw 1G 33
Rosedale Cl. NG10: Long E 1D 72
Rosedale Dr. NG8: Woll .5B 42
Rosedale Gdns. NG15: Huck 4E 7
Rosedale Rd. NG3: Nott .3E 47
Rose Flower Gro. NG15: Huck 1A 20
Rosegarth Wlk. NG6: Bas 3B 32
Rose Gro. NG9: Bee 6H 55
  NG12: Key 3H 79
Rosegrove Av. NG5: Arn .4B 22
Rose Hill NG12: Key 4G 79
Roseland Cl. NG12: Key .5G 79
Roseleigh Av. NG3: Mapp 5D 34
Rosemary Cl. NG8: Brox .6E 31
Rose M. NG3: Nott 2H 45
Roseneath Av. NG5: Top V 4C 20
Rosetta Rd. NG7: Bas 6D 32
  (not continuous)
Rosewall Ct. NG5: Arn 6D 22
Rose Way NG12: Edwal .3C 68

Rosewood Cres. DE75: Hea 3F 15
Rosewood Gdns. NG2: West Br 2G 67
  NG6: Bulw 6F 19
Roslyn Av. NG4: Ged 5G 35
Roslyn Ct. NG14: Bur J 2F 37
Rossell Dr. NG9: Stfrd 6G 53
Rossendale DE7: Ilk 3A 28
Rossett Cl. NG2: Gam 5F 59
Rossington Rd. NG2: Nott 4B 46
Ross La. NG4: Lamb 6C 24
Rosslyn Dr. NG8: Aspl 5G 31
  NG15: Huck 3A 8
Rosthwaite Cl. NG2: West Br 6E 59
Rothbury Av. NG9: Trow 1F 53
Rothbury Cl. NG5: Arn 3B 22
Rothbury Gro. NG13: Bing 4C 50
Rothesay Av. NG7: Lent 4D 44
Rothley Av. NG3: Nott 4B 46
Rothwell Cl. NG11: Huck 1D 18
Roughs Wood La. NG15: Huck 1D 18
Round Ho. Cl. DE75: Hea 5A 14
Roundwood Rd. NG5: Arn 6G 21
Rowan Av. NG9: Stfrd 1G 53
Rowan Cl. DE7: Ilk 4B 40
  NG12: Cotg 6G 61
  NG13: Bing 5G 51
  NG14: Calv 4F 11
Rowan Ct. NG15: Huck 3A 8
  NG16: Nuth 1B 30
Rowan Dr. NG11: Wilf 1E 67
  NG12: Key 5A 80
Rowan Gdns. NG6: Bulw 6F 19
Rowans Cres. NG6: Cin 3H 31
Rowan Wlk. NG3: Nott 1C 46
Rowe Ct. NG10: Long E 6G 63
Rowe Gdns. NG6: Bulw 1B 32
Rowland Av. NG3: Mapp 5C 34
Rowland M. NG3: Nott 2A 46
Rowley Ct. NG5: Sher 5E 33
Rowley Dr. NG5: Sher 5E 33
Rowsley Av. NG10: Long E 2C 72
Roxburgh Cl. NG5: Arn 5E 23
Roxby Ho. NG5: Arn 1C 34
Roxley Ct. NG9: Bee 4E 55
Roxton Ct. NG16: Kimb 6H 17
Royal Albert Ct. NG7: Radf 3E 45
                    (off Russell St.)
Royal Av. NG10: Long E 4F 63
Royal Cen. NG1: Nott 3D 4
Royal Centre Stop (NET) 3D 4 (4F 45)
Royal Concert Hall 3D 4 (4G 45)
Royal Ct. NG5: Sher 5G 33
                    (off Haydn Rd.)
Royal M. NG9: Chil 2C 64
Royal Standard Ho. NG1: Nott . .5C 4 (5F 45)
Royal Standard Pl. NG1: Nott 5C 4
Royal Victoria Ct. NG7: Radf 1A 4 (3E 45)
Roy Av. NG9: Bee 1H 65
Royce Av. NG15: Huck 1E 19
Royston Cl. NG2: Nott 2F 57
Royston Ct. NG4: Car 1E 47
Ruby Paddocks NG16: Kimb 2H 29
RUDDINGTON .6G 67
Ruddington Flds. Bus. Pk. NG11: Rudd . .2H 77
Ruddington Framework Knitters Mus. . .1G 77
Ruddington Gdns. NG11: Wilf 2F 67
Ruddington Grange Golf Course 3G 67
Ruddington La. NG11: Wilf 5F 57
Ruddington Station
  Great Central Railway 2G 77
Ruddington Village Mus. 6G 67
Rudge Cl. NG8: Woll 4F 43
Ruffles Av. NG5: Arn 2D 34
Rufford Av. NG4: Ged 5F 35
  NG9: Bram 3A 54
Rufford Cl. NG15: Huck 5A 8
Rufford Gro. NG13: Bing 5D 50
Rufford Hall NG7: Nott 1C 58
Rufford Rd. NG5: Sher 4G 33
  NG10: Long E 3D 72
  NG11: Rudd 6H 67
Rufford Wlk. NG6: Bulw 6H 67
  NG11: Rudd 6H 67
Rufford Way NG2: West Br 6E 7
RUFFS 6E 7
Ruffs Dr. NG15: Huck 6E 7
Rugby Cl. NG5: Top V 6C 20
Rugby Ct. NG2: West Br 6A 58
Rugby Rd. NG2: West Br 6G 57
Rugby Ter. NG7: Hys G 2D 44
Rugeley Av. NG10: Long E 6G 17
Ruislip Cl. NG16: Kimb 6H 63
Runcie Cl. NG12: Cotg 3F 71
Runnymede Ct. NG7: Radf 2A 4 (4E 45)
  NG9: Bee 6G 55
                    (off Grove St.)
Runswick Dr. NG5: Arn 5B 22
  NG8: Woll 4G 43
Runton Dr. NG6: Bas 3D 32
Rupert Rd. NG13: Bing 5D 50

Rupert St. DE7: Ilk 6C 28
Ruscombe Pl. NG3: Nott 3H 45
Rushcliffe Arena 5H 57
Rushcliffe Av. NG4: Car 1F 47
  NG12: Rad T .6F 49
Rushcliffe Country Pk. 2G 77
Rushcliffe Ct. NG6: Bulw 1B 32
Rushcliffe Ri. NG5: Sher 2H 33
Rushcliffe Rd. NG15: Huck 6E 7
The Rushes NG11: Goth 6H 75
Rushes Cl. NG9: Bee 5G 55
Rushford Dr. NG8: Woll 5C 42
Rush Leys NG10: Long E 2F 73
Rushmere Wlk. NG5: Woodt 2B 34
Rushton Gdns. NG3: Nott 2A 46
Rushworth Av. NG2: West Br 3A 58
Rushworth Cl. NG3: Nott 2A 46
Rushworth Ct. NG2: West Br 3A 58
Rushy Cl. NG8: Bilb 4D 42
Rushy La. DE72: Ris 6A 52
  NG10: Sand 5A 52
Ruskin Av. NG9: Chil 1D 64
  NG10: Long E 2D 72
Ruskin Cl. NG5: Arn 6H 21
Ruskin St. NG7: Radf 4C 44
Russell Av. NG8: Woll 4F 43
Russell Cl. NG10: Long E 4F 63
Russell Cres. NG8: Woll 4E 43
Russell Dr. NG8: Woll 4E 43
Russell Farm Cl. NG12: Toll 4F 69
Russell Gdns. NG9: Chil 3C 64
Russell Pl. NG1: Nott 3C 4 (4F 45)
Russell Rd. NG7: Hys G 1D 44
Russell St. NG7: Radf 1A 4 (3E 45)
                 (not continuous)
  NG10: Long E 4F 63
Russet Av. NG4: Car 2G 47
Russett Way NG8: Aspl 2H 43
Russley Rd. NG9: Bram 3A 54
Ruth Dr. NG5: Arn 4C 22
Rutherford Ho. NG7: Nott 2B 56
Ruthwell Gdns. NG5: Top V 3E 21
Rutland Av. NG9: Toton 3A 64
Rutland Cl. NG2: Nott 1F 57
  DE7: Ilk 6H 27
Rutland Gro. NG10: Sand 6E 53
Rutland Rd. NG2: West Br 2B 58
  NG4: Ged 4F 35
  NG13: Bing 5F 51
Rutland St. DE7: Ilk 5B 28
  NG1: Nott 5C 4 (5F 45)
Rutland Ter. DE7: Ilk 5B 28
Rutland Vs. NG2: Nott 5B 46
Ryan Way NG9: Bee 2G 65
Rydal Av. NG10: Long E 3D 62
Rydal Dr. NG9: Bram 3D 54
  NG15: Huck 3F 7
Rydale Rd. NG5: Sher 2G 33
Rydal Gdns. NG2: West Br 6C 58
Rydal Gro. NG6: Bas 4C 32
Ryder St. NG6: Bas 3B 32
Ryecroft St. NG9: Stfrd 2G 53
Ryefield Av. DE7: Ilk 2B 28
Ryehill Cl. NG2: Nott 1H 57
Ryehill St. NG2: Nott 1H 57
Ryeland Gdns. NG2: Nott 1G 57
Ryemere Cl. NG16: Eastw 3A 16
Ryemere Cl. NG16: Eastw 3A 16
              (off Bailey Gro. Rd.)
Rye St. NG7: Bas 6D 32
Rykneld Rd. NG15: Huck 3A 8
RYLANDS 6H 55
Rylands Cl. NG9: Bee 1H 65
Rylands Ct. NG9: Bee 6G 55
Ryton St. DE7: Ilk 2H 57
Ryton Sq. NG8: Aspl 6H 31

S

Sabina Rd. NG15: Huck 3A 8
Saco Ho. NG1: Nott 4B 4 (5F 45)
Saddlers Ga. NG12: Rad T 6F 49
Saddlers Yd. NG12: Plum 6G 69
Saddleworth Ct. NG3: Nott 2G 45
Saffron Gdns. NG2: Nott 1F 57
St Agnes Cl. NG8: Bilb 1D 42
St Aidans Ct. NG6: Bas 3C 32
St Albans Cl. NG10: Long E 2G 73
St Albans M. NG6: Bulw 1B 32
St Albans Rd. NG5: Arn 6H 21
  NG6: Bestw V 1C 20
  NG6: Bulw 5A 20
St Albans St. NG5: Sher 4G 33
St Andrew Cl. NG11: Goth 6H 75
St Andrews Cl. NG6: Bulw 6A 20
  NG15: Huck 3F 7
St Andrew's Ct. DE7: Ilk 6H 27
St Andrews Ct. NG6: Bulw 6B 20
St Andrew's Dr. DE7: Ilk 1A 40

St Andrews Ho. NG3: Mapp 4E 35
St Andrew's M. DE7: Stly 4A 38
St Andrews Rd. NG3: Mapp P 2F 45
ST ANN'S 3H 45
St Ann's Gdns. NG3: Nott 2A 46
St Ann's Hill NG3: Nott 2G 45
St Ann's Hill Rd. NG3: Nott 2G 45
St Ann's St. NG1: Nott 2E 5 (4G 45)
St Ann's Valley NG3: Nott 3A 46
St Ann's Way NG3: Nott 1E 5 (3G 45)
St Ann's Well Rd. NG3: Nott 2F 5 (4H 45)
St Anthony Ct. NG7: Lent 1C 56
St Augustines Cl. NG7: Bas 6E 33
St Austell Dr. NG11: Wilf 6F 57
St Austins Ct. NG4: Car 1H 47
St Austins Dr. NG4: Car 1H 47
St Bartholomews Rd. NG3: Nott 2B 46
St Bartholomew's Rd. NG3: Nott 2B 46
St Catherines St. NG12: Rad T 1E 61
St Cecilia Gdns. NG3: Nott 3H 45
St Chads Rd. NG4: Car 2H 47
St Chad's Rd. NG3: Nott 4A 46
St Christopher St. NG2: Nott 5B 46
St Cuthbert's Rd. NG3: Nott 4A 46
St Emmanuel Vw. NG5: Arn 4F 21
St Ervan Rd. NG11: Wilf 5F 57
St Francis Dr. NG11: Rudd 5G 67
St George's Dr. NG2: Nott 1G 57
St Georges Dr. NG9: Toton 3H 63
St Helen's Cres. NG14: Bur J 3F 37
St Helens Cres. NG9: Trow 5E 41
St Helen's Gro. NG14: Bur J 4E 37
St Helens Rd. NG2: West Br 5B 58
St Helen's St. NG7: Nott 3A 4 (4E 45)
St Helier NG2: Nott 5A 4 (5E 45)
St James Av. DE7: Ilk 2C 40
St James Cl. NG3: Mapp 5D 34
  NG10: Sand 2D 62
St James's St. NG1: Nott 5C 4 (5F 45)
St James's Ter. NG1: Nott 5C 4 (5F 45)
St James St. NG9: Stfrd 5E 53
St James Ter. NG9: Stfrd 5E 53
St John's Ct. NG4: Car 2F 47
St John's Cres. NG15: Huck 6A 8
St John's Rd. DE7: Ilk 2C 40
  NG11: Rudd 6G 67
St Johns St. NG10: Long E 6F 63
St Jude's Av. NG3: Mapp 5H 33
St Laurence Ct. NG10: Long E 1G 73
St Lawrence Blvd. NG12: Rad T 1D 60
St Lawrence Cl. DE75: Hea 3D 14
St Leodegar's Dr. NG8: Woll 5F 43
St Leven Cl. NG8: Bilb 1D 42
St Lukes Cl. NG2: West Br 6D 58
St Lukes St. NG3: Nott 3H 5 (4A 46)
St Lukes Way NG14: Stoke B 1F 49
St Margaret's Av. NG8: Aspl 1A 44
St Mark's St. NG3: Nott 2F 5 (4H 45)
St Martins Cl. NG8: Stre 1E 43
St Martin's Gdns. NG8: Stre 1D 42
St Martin's Rd. NG8: Stre 1E 43
St Mary Ct. DE7: Ilk 1A 40
                (off St Mary St.)
St Mary's Av. NG4: Ged 5G 35
St Mary's Church
  Nottingham 5F 5 (5H 45)
St Mary's Cl. NG5: Arn 4B 22
  NG9: Atten 4D 64
St Mary's Cres. NG11: Rudd 6G 67
St Mary's Ga. NG1: Nott 4F 5 (5H 45)
St Mary's Pl. NG1: Nott 4F 5 (5H 45)
St Marys Rd. NG13: Bing 4F 51
St Marys St. DE7: Ilk 1A 40
St Marys Vw. NG15: Huck 4G 7
                  (off Ogle St.)
St Marys Way NG15: Huck 3F 7
St Matthias Rd. NG3: Nott 3A 46
St Mawes Av. NG11: Wilf 5F 57
St Michael's Av. NG4: Ged 5G 35
  NG8: Bilb 1D 42
St Michaels Sq. NG9: Bram 3B 54
St Michaels Vw. NG15: Huck 2H 7
St Nicholas Cl. NG5: Arn 6A 22
St Nicholas St. NG1: Nott 5D 4 (5G 45)
St Norbert Dr. DE7: Kirk H 4G 39
St Patrick's Rd. NG15: Huck 4F 7
  NG16: Nuth 1B 30
St Paul's Av. NG7: Hys G 2D 44
St Pauls Ct. NG16: Kimb 1H 29
St Paul's St. NG8: Radf 4B 44
St Paul's Ter. NG7: Hys G 2D 44
St Peters Chambers NG1: Nott 4E 5
                (off Bank Pl.)
St Peter's Chu. Wlk. NG1: Nott . .4E 5 (5G 45)
St Peters Ct. NG7: Radf 4B 44
St Peters Cres. NG11: Rudd 6G 67
St Peter's Ga. NG1: Nott 4E 5 (5G 45)
St Peter's Sq. NG1: Nott 4E 5
St Peter's St. NG7: Radf 4C 44

St Saviours Gdns. NG2: Nott 1H 57
St Stephen's Av. NG2: Nott 5B 46
St Stephen's Rd. NG2: Nott 5A 46
St Thomas More Cl. NG8: Woll 5D 42
St Vincent Cl. NG10: Long E 1G 73
St Wilfrids Chu. Dr. NG11: Wilf 3F 57
St Wilfrid's Rd. DE7: West H 2C 38
St Wilfrid's Sq. NG14: Calv 4H 11
Salamander Cl. NG4: Car 5F 35
Salcey Dr. NG9: Trow 1F 53
Salcombe Cir. NG5: Redh 4H 21
Salcombe Cl. NG16: Newth 4E 17
Salcombe Cres. NG11: Rudd 5H 67
Salcombe Dr. NG5: Redh 4H 21
Salcombe Rd. NG5: Sher 4D 32
Salford Gdns. NG3: Nott 2G 5 (4H 45)
                                    (not continuous)
Salisbury Ct. NG3: Mapp 5A 34
Salisbury Sq. NG7: Lent 5C 44
Salisbury St. NG7: Lent 4C 44
  NG9: Bee 4G 55
  NG10: Long E 6G 63
Salmon Cl. NG6: Bulw 6F 19
Salop St. NG5: Arn 6H 21
Saltburn Rd. NG8: Bilb 3G 43
Saltby Grn. NG2: West Br 2F 67
Salterford Av. NG14: Calv 3H 11
Salterford Rd. NG15: Huck 6E 7
Saltford Cl. NG4: Ged 5H 35
Salthouse Cl. NG9: Bee 3G 55
Salthouse Ct. NG9: Bee 3G 55
Salthouse La. NG9: Bee 3G 55
Saltney Way NG11: Wilf 2E 67
Samson Ct. NG11: Rudd 5F 67
Sandale Cl. NG2: Gam 5E 59
Sandays Cl. NG2: Nott 2G 57
Sandby Cl. NG1: Nott 2C 4
Sandby Ct. NG9: Chil 6C 54
Sanders Cl. DE7: Ilk 5G 27
Sanderson Dr. NG3: Mapp 1F 35
Sandfield Cl. NG6: Bulw 1G 31
Sandfield Rd. NG5: Arn 1B 34
  NG7: Lent 5D 44
  NG9: Toton 3G 63
Sandford Av. NG10: Long E 6G 63
Sandford Rd. NG3: Mapp 5B 34
Sandgate NG9: Bram 2D 54
Sandham Wlk. NG11: Clftn 2C 66
Sandhurst Dr. NG9: Chil 3C 64
  NG11: Rudd 1F 77
Sandhurst Rd. NG6: Bulw 4H 19
SANDIACRE 6D 52
Sandiacre Friesland Sports Cen. 6B 52
Sandiacre Rd. NG9: Stfrd 5E 53
Sandon St. NG7: Bas 6E 33
Sandown Rd. NG9: Toton 2H 63
Sandpiper Cl. NG13: Bing 6F 51
Sandpiper Way NG7: Lent 5C 44
Sandringham Av. NG2: West Br 3A 58
Sandringham Cres. NG8: Woll 4C 42
Sandringham Dr. DE75: Hea 3A 14
  NG9: Bram 2C 54
Sandringham Pl. DE7: Kirk H 4H 39
  NG15: Huck 3H 7
Sandringham Rd. NG2: Nott 5B 46
  NG10: Sand 2D 62
Sands Cl. NG4: Colw 4G 47
Sandside NG12: Cotg 3F 71
Sandstone Ct. NG6: Bulw 5G 19
Sandwell Cl. NG10: Long E 1C 72
Sandyford Cl. NG6: Bas 4A 32
Sandy La. NG9: Bram 1D 54
  NG12: Hol P 1B 60
  NG15: Huck 4G 7
Sanger Cl. NG11: Clftn 5A 66
Sanger Gdns. NG11: Clftn 5A 66
Sankey Dr. NG6: Bulw 6G 19
Sapele Cl. NG4: Ged 5A 36
Sarah Av. NG5: Sher 5E 33
Sargent Gdns. NG3: Nott 3B 46
Saskatoon Cl. NG12: Rad T 1E 61
Saunby Cl. NG5: Arn 6D 22
Saunton Cl. NG12: Edwal 1E 69
Savages Rd. NG11: Rudd 5G 67
Savages Row NG11: Rudd 5G 67
Saville Cl. NG9: Stfrd 3G 53
Saville Rd. NG5: Woodt 2B 34
Savoy Cinema 5D 44
SAWLEY 3C 72
Sawley Rd. DE72: Brea, Dray 6A 62
  DE72: Dray 2A 72
Sawmand Cl. NG10: Long E 1E 73
Sawmills Ind. Pk. DE75: Los 2B 14
Saxby Cl. NG11: Rudd 6H 67
Saxelby Gdns. NG6: Bulw 5H 19
SAXONDALE 5A 50
Saxondale Ct. NG6: Bulw 4A 20
Saxondale Dr. NG6: Bulw 2B 32
Saxon Grn. NG7: Lent 6C 44
Saxon Way NG12: Cotg 4F 71

Saxton Av. DE75: Hea 3D 14
Saxton Av. NG8: Stre 6C 30
Saxton Cl. NG9: Bee 4H 55
Saxton Cl. NG5: Arn 6E 23
Scafell Cl. NG2: West Br 6E 59
Scafell Way NG11: Clftn 6B 66
Scalby Cl. NG16: Eastw 3H 15
Scalford Dr. NG8: Woll 5A 44
Scarborough Av. DE7: Ilk 1H 39
Scarborough St. NG3: Nott 2G 5 (4H 45)
Scargill Av. NG16: Newth 4D 16
Scargill Cl. NG16: Newth 4D 16
Scargill Rd. DE7: West H 1C 38
Scargill Wlk. NG16: Eastw 2B 16
Scarrington Rd. NG2: West Br 2B 58
Sceptre St. NG5: Sher 5G 33
Scholar Cl. DE7: Ilk 3B 40
School Av. NG15: Huck 1D 18
School Cl. NG2: Nott 2H 57
School Gdns. NG25: Oxton 1B 12
School La. DE7: Stant D 4B 52
  NG9: Chil 1C 64
  NG13: Bing 4E 51
School Sq. DE7: West H 2C 38
School Wlk. NG6: Bestw V 1C 20
School Way NG2: Nott 2H 57
School Woods Cl. DE75: Ship 1E 27
Science Rd. NG7: Nott 2B 56
Scollins Ct. DE7: Ilk 5A 28
Scotholme Av. NG7: Hys G 1D 44
Scotland Bank NG12: Cotg 2F 71
Scotland Rd. NG5: Bas 4D 32
Scott Av. NG9: Bee 5F 55
Scott Cl. NG6: Bulw 2F 31
Scrimshire La. NG12: Cotg 2E 71
Script Dr. NG6: Bas 3C 32
Scrivelsby Gdns. NG9: Chil 1D 64
Scrooby Row NG5: Top V 5E 21
Seaburn Rd. NG9: Toton 2G 63
Seaford Av. NG8: Woll 4H 43
Seagrave Ct. NG5: Arn 6A 22
  NG8: Stre 6D 30
Seagrave Rd. NG8: Stre 6D 30
Seamer Rd. NG16: Kimb 6H 17
Sean Upton Cl. NG9: Chil 2D 64
Seatallan Cl. NG2: West Br 5E 59
Seathwaite Cl. NG2: West Br 1E 69
Seatoller Cl. NG2: West Br 6E 59
Seaton Cres. NG8: Aspl 6G 31
Seaton Way NG3: Ged 2G 35
Second Av. DE7: Ilk 2B 40
  DE72: Ris 1B 62
  NG4: Car 2E 47
  NG4: Ged 6H 35
  NG6: Bulw 6H 19
  NG7: Hys G 1F 45
  NG7: Nott 5A 56
Sedgebrook Cl. NG6: Bas 4A 32
Sedgemoor Rd. NG10: Long E 2G 73
Sedgewood Gro. NG11: Clftn 2C 66
Sedgley Av. NG2: Nott 4B 46
Sedgley Rd. NG12: Toll 5F 69
Sedgwick St. NG16: Lang M 2F 15
Sedley Av. NG16: Nuth 1C 30
Seeley Ho. NG1: Nott 5G 5
                                    (off Malin Hill)
Seely Av. NG14: Calv 3F 11
Seely Rd. NG7: Lent, Radf 4D 44
Sefton Av. NG9: Stfrd 3G 53
Sefton Dr. NG3: Mapp P 6H 33
Selbourne Gdns. NG3: Nott 1H 5 (3A 46)
Selby Cl. NG9: Toton 2G 63
Selby La. NG12: Key 5G 79
Selby Rd. NG2: West Br 5B 58
Selhurst Ct. NG7: Hys G 2D 44
Selhurst St. NG7: Hys G 2D 44
Selkirk Way NG5: Sher 6F 33
Sellars Av. NG11: Rudd 1G 77
Sellers Wood Dr. NG6: Bulw 5F 19
Sellers Wood Dr. W. NG6: Bulw 6E 19
Seller's Wood Nature Reserve 6E 19
Selsby Cl. NG8: Stre 5C 30
Selside Ct. NG9: Chil 1A 64
Selston Dr. NG8: Woll 6A 44
Selwyn Cl. NG6: Bulw 2C 32
Senator Cl. NG15: Huck 3A 8
Senso Ct. NG4: Ged 6B 36
Serif Cl. NG5: Sher 6F 33
Serina Ct. NG2: West Br 4A 58
  NG9: Bee 4H 55
Serlby Ri. NG3: Nott 3B 46
Serlby Rd. NG16: Newth 2C 16
Seven Oaks Cres. NG9: Bram 2B 54
Seven Oaks Rd. DE7: Stant D 2B 52
Severals NG9: Stfrd 4H 53
Severn Ind. Est. NG6: Bulw 6H 19
Severn St. NG6: Bulw 6H 19
Seymour Cl. DE7: Ilk 2B 28
Seymour Ct. NG7: Radf 1A 4 (3E 45)

Seymour Pl. NG2: West Br 2D 58
Seymour Rd. NG2: West Br 3D 58
  NG15: Huck 6E 7
  NG16: Eastw 4B 16
Seymour St. NG3: Nott 4A 46
Shackleton Cl. NG8: Stre 5D 30
Shacklock Cl. NG5: Arn 3E 21
Shadwell Gro. NG12: Rad T 6E 49
Shady La. NG9: Atten 3D 64
Shaftesbury Av. NG10: Long E 3D 72
  NG10: Sand 6C 52
  NG14: Bur J 2G 37
Shaftesbury St. NG7: Bas 6E 33
Shakespeare Cl. NG4: Colw 4G 47
Shakespeare Ho. NG1: Nott 2E 5 (4G 45)
Shakespeare Rd. NG16: Aws 2E 29
Shakespeare St. NG1: Nott 2C 4 (4F 45)
  NG10: Long E 4E 63
Shakespeare Vs. NG1: Nott 2D 4 (4G 45)
Shakir Ct. NG7: Bas 6E 33
Shaldon Cl. NG3: Ged 2F 35
  NG5: Top V 4D 20
Shandwick Cl. NG5: Arn 4D 22
Shanklin Dr. NG9: Stfrd 4F 53
Shanwell Cl. NG8: Stre 5D 30
Shardale Gdns. NG6: Bas 3B 32
Sharnford Way NG9: Bram 5B 42
Sharp Cl. DE7: Kirk H 3G 39
  NG10: Long E 1E 73
Sharpes Way NG6: Bestw V 6F 9
Sharphill Rd. NG12: Edwal 1D 68
Shaw Cres. NG15: Huck 1E 19
Shaw Gdns. NG4: Ged 1B 48
  NG11: Clftn 5A 66
Shaw Rd. NG9: Chil 3B 64
Shaw St. NG11: Rudd 6G 67
Shaw St. E. DE7: Ilk 3C 40
Shaw St. W. DE7: Ilk 3C 40
Shearing Cl. NG4: Ged 6A 36
Shearing Hill NG4: Ged 6A 36
Sheepfold La. NG11: Rudd 1G 77
Sheerness Cl. NG16: Gilt 6D 16
Sheets Stores Ind. Est. NG10: Long E 2F 73
Shelby Cl. NG7: Lent 5C 44
Sheldon Cl. NG10: Long E 2D 62
Sheldon Rd. DE75: Los 1A 14
SHELFORD 6H 37
Shelford Cl. NG9: Chil 1D 64
  NG12: Rad T 5G 49
Shelford Cres. NG14: Bur J 2G 37
Shelford Dr. NG13: Bing 5D 50
Shelford Ri. NG3: Nott 3C 46
Shelford Rd. NG4: Ged 4E 35
  NG12: Rad T, S'frd 6F 49
  NG13: Newt 1A 50
Shellburne Cl. NG5: Top V 5C 20
Shelley Av. NG11: Clftn 2C 66
Shelley Cl. NG15: Huck 5D 6
  NG16: Nuth 1B 30
Shelley Rd. NG5: Arn 6H 21
Shelt Hill NG14: Woodbo 1D 24
Shelton Av. NG15: Huck 1A 20
Shelton Gdns. NG11: Rudd 6F 67
Shelton St. NG3: Nott 1E 5 (3G 45)
Shenfield Gdns. NG5: Top V 4B 20
Shepard Cl. NG6: Bulw 1F 31
Shepherd Cl. NG15: Huck 1D 18
Shepherd Ho. NG5: Bestw 2E 33
Shepherds Cl. NG8: Bilb 2G 43
Shepherds Wood Dr. NG8: Aspl 2A 44
Shepton Cl. DE7: Ilk 4H 27
Shepton Cres. NG8: Aspl 5H 31
Sheraton Dr. NG8: Woll 6E 43
Sherborne Rd. NG2: West Br 6B 58
  NG8: Aspl 6G 31
Sherbrook Av. NG5: Arn 1H 33
Sherbrook Bus. Cen. NG5: Arn 1H 33
Sherbrooke Cl. NG14: Calv 3G 11
Sherbrooke Rd. NG5: Sher 6F 33
Sherbrooke Ter. NG5: Sher 6F 33
Sherbrook Rd. NG5: Arn 1G 33
Sherbrook Ter. NG5: Arn 1H 33
Sheridan Ct. NG1: Nott 1D 4
  NG9: Stfrd 2H 53
Sheridan Way NG5: Sher 4E 33
  NG15: Huck 6G 7
Sheriffs Lea NG9: Toton 3G 63
Sheriffs Way NG2: Nott 6G 45
Sheringham Cl. NG5: Arn 1B 34
Sherman Dr. NG9: Chil 3C 64
Sherrington Cl. NG11: Clftn 4A 66
Sherwin Gro. NG7: Lent 6C 44
Sherwin Rd. NG7: Lent 6C 44
  NG9: Stfrd 2H 53
Sherwin Wlk. NG3: Nott 1D 4 (3G 45)
SHERWOOD 4E 33
Sherwood Av. NG5: Sher 4H 33
  NG14: Calv 3F 11
Sherwood Cl. NG9: Chil 2C 64
  NG14: Calv 3H 11

Sherwood Gro. NG13: Bing 5D 50
  NG14: Calv 3H 11
Sherwood Lodge Dr. NG5: Arn 1G 9
SHERWOOD RISE 1E 33
Sherwood Ri. NG7: Sher 6E 33
  NG16: Eastw 4B 16
Sherwood St. NG15: Huck 5A 8
Sherwood Va. NG5: Sher 4A 34
Sherwood Wlk. NG15: Lin 1G 7
Shilling Way NG10: Long E 6C 62
Shilo Way NG16: Aws 3D 28
SHIPLEY .1F 27
SHIPLEY COMMON 4G 27
Shipley Comn. La. DE7: Ilk 3G 27
Shipley Country Pk. 3D 26
Shipley Country Pk. Vis. Cen. 6C 14
Shipley Ct. DE7: Ilk 6H 27
  DE75: Hea 5B 14
Shipley Ga. NG16: Eastw 6A 16
Shipley La. DE75: Hea, Ship 2D 26
Shipley Pk. Gdns. DE75: Hea 6C 14
Shipley Ri. NG4: Car 2G 47
Shipley Rd. NG8: Brox 5F 31
Shipstones Bus. Cen. NG7: Bas 6D 32
Shipstone St. NG7: Bas 1D 44
Shipstone Street Stop (NET) 1D 44
Shipstones Yd. NG6: Bulw 5A 20
Shirebrook Cl. DE7: Ilk 1B 28
Shirebrooke Cl. NG6: Bas 4A 32
Shire Hall & Galleries of Justice Mus.
. . . . .5F 5 (5H 45)
Shires Dr. NG3: Mapp 5A 34
Shirland Cl. DE7: Ilk 2B 28
Shirley Ct. NG9: Toton 3A 64
Shirley Cres. DE72: Brea 5A 62
Shirley Dr. NG5: Arn 6D 22
Shirley Rd. NG3: Mapp P 1G 45
Shirley St. NG10: Long E 3C 72
Shoreswood Cl. NG5: Bestw 5F 21
Shortcross Av. NG3: Mapp 3B 34
Short Hill NG1: Nott 5G 5 (5H 45)
Short Stairs NG1: Nott 5G 5
Shortwood Av. NG15: Huck 6F 7
Shortwood Cl. NG1: Nott 5F 5 (5H 45)
Shorwell Rd. NG3: Nott 2E 47
Shotton Dr. NG5: Arn 3C 22
Showcase Cinema 3C 56
Shrewsbury Rd. NG2: Nott 5C 46
Shrimpton Ct. NG11: Rudd 1H 77
The Shrubberies NG5: Sher 4F 33
Sibson Wlk. NG5: Arn 3B 22
Sidbury Cl. NG3: Ged 1G 35
The Sidings NG16: Kimb 1H 29
Sidings La. NG9: Bram 6A 42
Sidlaw Ri. NG5: Arn 3F 21
Sidmouth Cl. NG12: Key 3G 79
Sidney Rd. NG9: Bee 4E 55
Sidney St. NG10: Long E 1F 73
  NG16: Kimb 1H 29
Silbury Cl. NG11: Clftn 6B 66
Sillitoe Ct. NG7: Lent 4B 44
Sillitoe Way NG7: Lent 5B 44
Silver Birch Cl. NG6: Cin 3H 31
SILVERDALE 1E 67
Silverdale NG9: Stfrd 6G 53
Silverdale Rd. NG7: Bas 5D 32
Silverdale Wlk. NG11: Clftn, Wilf 2E 67
Silverhill Cl. NG8: Stre 5D 30
Silverhow Cl. NG2: West Br 6E 59
Silverwood Rd. NG9: Bee 5A 54
Simkin Av. NG3: Mapp 6C 34
Simkin Wlk. NG10: Long E 6D 62
Simone Gdns. NG11: Clftn 3C 66
Simons Ct. NG9: Bram 2D 54
Sinclair Cl. DE75: Hea 6H 21
Siskin Cl. NG9: Bram 5B 14
Sir John Robinson Way NG5: Arn 5C 54
Sisley Av. NG9: Stfrd 5G 53
Sixth Av. NG7: Nott 6A 56
Skeavingtons La. DE7: Ilk 2A 28
Skelwith Cl. NG2: West Br 6E 59
Sketchley Ct. NG6: Bulw 6G 19
Sketchley St. NG3: Nott 6E 59
Skiddaw Cl. NG2: West Br 6E 59
Skipton Cir. NG3: Nott 3C 46
Skipton Cl. DE7: Ilk 4H 27
Skylark Cl. NG13: Bing 6F 51
Skylark Dr. NG6: Bas 3B 32
Slack La. DE75: Hea 5C 14
Slack Rd. DE7: Mapp 4D 26
Slade Cl. DE7: Ilk 4C 40
Slade Rd. NG9: Chil 6B 54
Slaidburn Av. NG11: Wilf 6E 57
Slalom Run NG4: Car 6E 35
Slaters Way NG5: Bestw 2D 32
Sloan Dr. NG9: Bram 6B 42
Sloane Ct. NG2: West Br 2G 67
Sloethorne Gdns. NG5: Arn 5H 21
Smalley Farm Cl. DE75: Hea 5A 14
Smalley Mnr. Dr. DE7: Smal 5A 14

Small's Cft. NG14: Woodbo 1C 24
Smedley Av. DE7: Ilk 2C 40
Smedley Cl. NG8: Aspl 5H 31
Smedley's Av. NG10: Sand 6D 52
Smeeton St. DE75: Hea 4F 15
Smite Ct. NG7: Radf 2B 44
Smith Dr. NG16: Lang M 2E 15
Smithurst Rd. NG16: Gilt 5C 16
Smithy Cl. NG11: Clftn 3B 66
  NG14: Woodbo 2C 24
Smithy Cres. NG5: Arn 5B 22
Smithy Row NG1: Nott 4E 5 (5G 45)
Smithy Vw. NG6: Bestw V 6F 9
  NG14: Calv 4G 11
Smythson Dr. NG8: Woll 5E 43
Snape Nook Ct. NG6: Bulw 6F 19
Snape Wood Rd. NG6: Bulw 6F 19
Snead Ct. NG5: Top V 4E 21
SNEINTON 5B 46
Sneinton Blvd. NG2: Nott 5B 46
Sneinton Dale NG2: Nott 5B 46
  NG3: Nott 4C 46
Sneinton Hermitage NG2: Nott 6H 5 (6A 46)
Sneinton Hollows NG2: Nott 5B 46
Sneinton Mkt. Sq. NG1: Nott 3H 5
Sneinton Rd. NG2: Nott 4H 5 (5A 46)
Snowdon Cl. NG5: Top V 4F 21
Snowdrop Cl. NG15: Huck 1A 20
Soarbank Cl. NG16: Kimb 6G 17
Sobers Gdns. NG5: Arn 1D 34
Softwood Cl. NG6: Bulw 6F 19
Soloman Pk. DE7: Ilk 5D 28
Soloman Rd. DE7: Ilk 5D 28
Solway Cl. NG9: Chil 6E 55
Somerby Cl. NG9: Bram 5B 42
Somerley Dr. DE7: Ilk 5C 40
Somersby Rd. NG3: Mapp 2B 34
  NG5: Woodt 2B 34
Somerset Ct. NG10: Long E 5A 64
Somerton Av. NG11: Wilf 1E 67
Songthrush Av. NG6: Bas 3B 32
Sophie Rd. NG7: Hys G 3D 44
Sorrel Dr. NG13: Bing 5C 50
Soudan Dr. NG2: Nott 2F 57
Sough Wood Cl. DE75: Los 3A 14
Southampton St. NG3: Nott 3A 46
South Av. NG12: Rad T 5H 49
Southchurch Ct. NG11: Clftn 2D 66
Southchurch Dr. NG11: Clftn 5C 66
Southchurch Drive North Stop (NET) 2D 66
Southcliffe Rd. NG4: Car 2F 47
South Ct. NG9: Bee 1H 65
Southdale Dr. NG4: Car 2F 47
Southdale Rd. NG4: Car 2F 47
Sth. Devon Av. NG3: Mapp 5D 34
Southey St. NG7: Radf 3D 44
Southfield Gro. NG13: Bing 6E 51
Southfield Rd. NG8: Aspl 3B 44
Southfields NG10: Long E 6G 63
Southfields Ct. NG9: Chil 5B 54
Southglade Food Pk. NG5: Bestw 1C 32
Southglade Leisure Cen. 6D 20
Southglade Rd. NG5: Bestw 1C 32
Southlea Rd. NG4: Car 2F 47
South Pde. NG1: Nott 4D 4 (5G 45)
Southport Ter. NG7: Hys G 2C 44
South Rd. NG2: West Br 5A 58
  NG5: Sher 3F 33
  NG7: Nott 5A 4 (6E 45)
    (Newcastle Cir.)
  NG7: Nott 1B 56
    (West Rd.)
  NG9: Bee 1G 65
Sth. Sherwood St. NG1: Nott 2D 4 (4G 45)
Southside NG5: Arn 5E 23
Sth. Snape Cl. NG6: Bulw 6F 19
South St. DE7: Ilk 1A 40
  NG10: Long E 6G 63
  NG15: Huck 4G 7
  NG16: Eastw 3A 16
  NG16: Gilt 5E 17
South Vw. Rd. NG4: Car 5F 35
Southwark St. NG6: Bas 4C 32
Southwell Hall NG8: Woll 5B 44
Southwell Ri. NG16: Gilt 5D 16
Southwell Rd. NG1: Nott 4H 5 (5H 45)
  NG25: Oxton, S'well 1C 12
    (not continuous)
Southwold Dr. NG8: Aspl 4A 44
Sovereign Cl. NG9: Bee 6G 55
Sovereign Gro. NG10: Long E 6D 62
Sovereign Way DE75: Hea 4B 14
Sowbrook La. DE7: D Ab, Stant D 5H 39
Spalding Rd. NG3: Nott 4A 46
Spaniel Row NG1: Nott 5D 4 (5G 45)
Sparrow Cl. DE7: Ilk 4C 40
Spean Ct. NG8: Woll 4G 43
Spean Dr. NG8: Aspl 2H 43
Speedway Cl. NG10: Long E 5H 63

Speedwell Cl. NG13: Bing 5C 50
Speedwell La. NG16: Kimb 1G 29
Spencer Av. NG3: Mapp 2E 35
  NG10: Sand 4D 52
Spencer Cl. NG11: Rudd 6F 67
Spencer Ct. NG7: Hys G 1F 45
Spencer Cres. NG9: Stfrd 3H 53
Spencer Dr. NG16: Nuth 1C 30
Spey Cl. NG15: Huck 2D 18
Spicer Cl. NG9: Chil 3C 64
Spindle Gdns. NG6: Bulw 6G 19
Spindle La. NG14: Calv, Woodbo 6E 11
Spindle Vw. NG14: Calv 5H 11
The Spinney DE7: Ilk 3A 40
  DE7: Stant D 3B 52
  NG5: Woodt 3A 34
  NG6: Bestw V 6C 8
  NG14: Bulc 2H 37
  NG16: Nuth 4F 31
    (Harcourt Cres.)
  NG16: Nuth 1B 30
    (Keats Cl.)
Spinney Cl. NG2: West Br 1D 68
  NG12: Cotg 3F 71
Spinney Cres. NG9: Toton 2H 63
Spinney Dr. NG10: Long E 1E 63
Spinney Hill NG2: West Br 3A 68
Spinney Ri. NG9: Toton 2G 63
Spinney Rd. DE7: Ilk 3E 63
  NG10: Long E 2G 63
  NG12: Key 4F 79
  NG13: Bing 5D 50
Spinney Way NG11: Wilf 1E 67
Sinningdale NG5: Arn 4D 22
Spinning Dr. NG5: Top V 3A 68
SPIRE NOTTINGHAM HOSPITAL 6H 59
Spire Vw. NG10: Long E 3D 72
Spitfire Way NG15: Huck 2D 18
Spondon Rd. DE7: D Ab 6B 38
Spondon St. NG5: Sher 5G 33
Spray Cl. NG4: Colw 4G 47
Spridgeon Cl. NG10: Long E 3D 62
The Spring NG10: Long E 2F 73
Spring Cl. NG16: Want 3D 58
Spring Ct. NG2: West Br 4G 53
  NG9: Stfrd . . . .
Springdale Gdns. NG9: Trow 1F 53
Springfield Av. NG10: Long E 5H 63
  NG10: Sand 2C 62
  NG16: Eastw 3C 16
Springfield Ct. NG9: Stfrd 2H 53
Springfield Dr. NG6: Bulw 1F 31
Springfield Gdns. DE7: Ilk 5B 28
Springfield Mill NG10: Sand 5D 52
SPRINGFIELD PARK 2D 62
Springfield Pastures NG3: Nott 1H 45
Springfield Retail Pk. 5A 20
Springfield Rd. NG5: Redh 4A 22
  NG15: Huck 5D 6
Springfields NG2: West Br 5H 57
Springfield St. NG7: Bas 6D 32
Spring Gdns. NG8: Bilb 2C 42
Spring Gdn. Ter. DE7: Ilk 5B 28
Spring Grn. NG11: Clftn 6C 66
Springhead Ct. NG6: Bulw 1G 31
Spring Hill NG16: Kimb 2H 29
Springhill Cl. NG6: Bulw 4H 19
Springland Farm Cotts. NG16: Nuth 1D 30
    (off Watnall Rd.)
Spring La. DE75: Hea 4C 14
  NG3: Mapp 1E 35
  NG4: Lamb 1E 35
Spring Mdw. NG12: Cotg 2G 71
Spring Moor NG2: Colw 4F 47
Spring Rd. NG6: Bulw 6A 20
Spring St. NG15: Huck 3G 7
Spring Ter. NG16: Nuth 2D 30
Spring Ter. Gdns. NG16: Nuth 1D 30
Springwater Golf Course 5C 12
Springwood Cl. NG14: Calv 4A 12
Springwood Gdns. NG5: Woodt 4B 34
Spruce Gdns. NG6: Bulw 6G 19
Spruce Gro. NG15: Huck 6H 7
Sprydon Wlk. NG11: Clftn 6D 66
The Square NG6: Bestw V 1C 20
  NG8: Woll 5E 43
  NG9: Bee 5F 55
  NG11: Goth 6H 75
  NG12: Key 5G 79
Squires Av. NG6: Bulw 4H 19
Squires Cl. NG6: Bestw V 5F 9
Squires Way NG2: West Br 5H 57
Stacey Av. NG5: Top V 6D 20
Stafford Av. NG6: Bulw 1H 31
Stafford Ct. NG6: Bulw 2F 31
Staffords Cl. NG4: Neth 2A 48
Stafford St. NG10: Long E 5H 63
Stagsden Cres. NG8: Bilb 4C 42
Staindale Cl. NG5: Bas 6A 32
Staindale Dr. NG8: Aspl 6A 32

Stainmore Gro. NG13: Bing 5C **50**
Stainsborough Rd. NG15: Huck 5C **6**
Stainsby Av. DE75: Hea 4C **14**
Stakeford Ct. NG5: Arn 3B **22**
Stamford Cl. NG10: Long E 3G **73**
Stamford Ct. DE75: Hea 3C **14**
(off Nelson St.)
NG5: Bestw 5F **21**
Stamford Rd. NG2: West Br 6B **58**
Stamford St. DE7: Ilk 6A **28**
DE75: Hea 3C **14**
NG16: Aws 3E **29**
NG16: Newth 4E **17**
Stancliffe Av. NG6: Bulw 6A **20**
Standard Ct. NG1: Nott 5C **4** (5F **45**)
STANDARD HILL 5C **4** (5F **45**)
Standard Hill NG1: Nott 5C **4** (5F **45**)
Standhill Av. NG4: Car 1D **46**
Standhill Rd. NG4: Car 6C **34**
Stanesby Ri. NG11: Clftn 4C **66**
Stanford Gdns. NG12: Rad T 1H **63**
Stanford St. NG1: Nott 5D **4** (5G **45**)
Stanhome Cl. NG2: West Br 1H **67**
Stanhome Dr. NG2: West Br 1H **67**
Stanhome Sq. NG2: West Br 1H **67**
Stanhope Av. NG5: Sher 6F **33**
Stanhope Cl. NG16: Newth 3D **16**
Stanhope Cres. NG5: Arn 5A **22**
NG14: Stoke B 2F **49**
Stanhope Rd. NG4: Ged 3F **35**
NG5: Arn 5A **22**
Stanhope St. DE7: Ilk 3C **40**
DE7: Stant D 3B **52**
NG1: Nott 4G **5** (5H **45**)
NG10: Long E .5C **72**
Stanhope Way NG13: Bing 5E **51**
Staniland Cl. NG9: Chil 3C **64**
STANLEY 3A **38**
Stanley Av. NG7: Hys G 1E **45**
Stanley Cl. DE7: Ilk 2A **40**
Stanley Cl. NG16: Eastw 4B **16**
Stanley Dr. NG9: Bram 3A **54**
Stanley M. NG16: Kimb 6F **17**
Stanley Pl. NG1: Nott 3C **4** (4F **45**)
Stanley Rd. NG2: West Br 5B **58**
NG3: Mapp 5C **34**
NG7: Hys G 1E **45**
(not continuous)
Stanley St. DE7: Ilk 2B **40**
NG10: Long E .6G **63**
Stanmore Cl. NG16: Nuth 4E **31**
Stanmore Gdns. NG5: Arn 1A **34**
(not continuous)
Stannier Way NG16: Want 6A **18**
Stansfield St. NG7: Lent 4C **44**
Stanstead Av. NG5: Top V 5B **20**
NG12: Toll 5F **69**
Stanthorne Cl. NG11: Wilf 1E **67**
STANTON-BY-DALE 3B **52**
STANTON GATE 2E **53**
Stanton Ga. DE7: Stant D 2E **53**
Stanton La. NG12: Stant W 5B **80**
Stanton M. NG12: Stant W 5C **80**
STANTON-ON-THE-WOLDS 6B **80**
Stanton-on-the-Wolds Golf Course 5B **80**
Stanton St. DE7: Ilk 3B **40**
NG10: Sand 4B **52**
Stanway Cl. NG3: Nott 3E **47**
Stanwick Cl. NG8: Bilb 1E **43**
STAPLEFORD 4F **53**
Stapleford By-Pass NG10: Sand 1C **62**
Stapleford La. NG9: Toton 1H **63**
Stapleford Rd. NG9: Trow 5E **41**
Staplehurst Dr. NG5: Sher 3E **33**
Staples St. NG3: Mapp 5A **34**
Stapleton Rd. DE7: Ilk 3A **28**
Starch La. NG10: Sand 4D **52**
Starnhill Way NG13: Bing 6E **51**
Starthe Bank DE75: Hea 3D **14**
Starthe Vw. DE75: Hea 4E **15**
Starth Wood Rd. NG15: Huck 1D **18**
Stathern Wlk. NG5: Bestw 6F **21**
Station Av. NG4: Ged 6A **36**
Station Ct. DE7: Ilk 6A **28**
(off Bath Rd.)
Station Rd. DE7: Ilk 6B **28**
DE7: Stly, West H 1A **38**
NG4: Car 2G **47**
NG6: Bulw 1A **32**
NG9: Bee 5F **55**
(not continuous)
NG10: Long E .5H **63**
NG10: Sand 6E **53**
NG12: Key, Plum 1G **79**
NG14: Bur J 4F **37**
NG15: Huck 4H **7**
NG16: Aws 2E **29**
NG16: Kimb 1H **29**
NG16: Lang M .3E **15**

Station St. DE7: Ilk 5C **28**
NG2: Nott 6E **5** (6G **45**)
NG10: Long E .6G **63**
NG13: Bing 4F **51**
Station Ter.
NG12: Rad T 6F **49**
NG15: Huck 4H **7**
Station Vs. NG9: Bee 6G **55**
Staunton Dr. NG5: Sher 3G **33**
Stavely Way NG2: Gam 4E **59**
Staverton Rd. NG8: Bilb 3D **42**
Steadfold Cl. NG6: Bulw 1H **31**
Steads Cl. NG4: Car 2H **47**
Steedman Av. NG3: Mapp 3C **34**
Steeles Way NG4: Lamb 6B **24**
Steinbeck Rd. NG4: Car 2E **47**
Stella Av. NG12: Toll 5F **69**
Stella Gro. NG12: Toll 5F **69**
Stepney Ct. NG8: Brox 6F **31**
Sterndale Rd. NG10: Long E 1D **72**
Steven Cl. NG9: Toton 1H **63**
Stevenholme Cres. NG5: Bestw 1E **33**
Steven's La. DE72: Brea 5A **62**
Stevenson Gdns. NG11: Rudd 1H **77**
Stevens Rd. NG10: Sand 6C **52**
Stewarton Cl. NG5: Arn 4D **22**
Stiles Rd. NG5: Arn 1E **35**
Stinsford Cl. NG5: Bestw 5G **21**
Stirling Gdns. NG9: Chil 3B **64**
Stirling Gro. NG11: Clftn 5D **66**
NG16: Kimb 6G **17**
Stockdale Cl. NG5: Arn 3E **21**
Stockgill Cl. NG2: West Br 5E **59**
Stockhill Cir. NG6: Bas 4A **32**
Stockhill La. NG6: Bas 4A **32**
Stocks Rd. NG16: Kimb 6G **17**
Stockton St. NG6: Bulw 6H **19**
Stock Well NG6: Bulw 1H **31**
Stoddard Dr. DE75: Hea 3D **14**
STOKE BARDOLPH 1F **49**
Stoke Ferry La. NG12: S'frd 6F **37**
Stoke La. NG4: Ged 6B **36**
NG14: Stoke B 1D **48**
(not continuous)
Stokesay Wlk. NG2: West Br 6B **58**
Stolle Cl. NG5: Arn 6E **23**
Stoneacre NG5: Bestw 5F **21**
Stone Av. DE75: Hea 4E **15**
Stonebridge City Farm 2H **5** (4A **46**)
Stonebridge Ct. NG3: Nott 2H **5** (4A **46**)
Stonebridge Rd. NG3: Nott 2H **5** (4A **46**)
Stonebridge Way NG14: Calv 3E **11**
Stonehaven Cl. NG5: Arn 4D **22**
Stoneleigh Cl. NG9: Chil 5C **54**
Stoneleigh St. NG7: Radf 2A **4** (4E **45**)
Stone Mdws. NG10: Long E 2G **73**
Stonepit Cl. NG3: Nott 6B **34**
Stonesby Va. NG2: West Br 2F **67**
Stones Cl. NG16: Eastw 3C **16**
Stonesdale Cl. NG5: Sher 2G **33**
Stoney Houghton Gdns. NG6: Bulw 5F **19**
Stoney La. NG9: Trow 3D **40**
Stoney St. NG1: Nott 4F **5** (5H **45**)
NG9: Bee 4F **55**
Stony Clouds Local Nature Reserve 3D **52**
Stoppard Cl. DE7: Ilk 5H **27**
Storey Av. NG4: Ged 5G **35**
Stornoway Ct. NG9: Bee 6G **55**
Storth Av. NG15: Huck 5G **7**
Story Gdns. NG15: Huck 6A **8**
Stotfield Rd. NG8: Bilb 4B **42**
Stourdale Cl. NG10: Long E 1C **72**
Stowe Av. NG2: West Br 6H **57**
STRAGGLETHORPE 4G **61**
Stragglethorpe La. NG12: Rad T 2C **60**
Stragglethorpe Park & Ride 4D **60**
The Strand NG9: Atten 4D **64**
Stratford Cl. NG4: Colw 4G **47**
Stratford Rd. NG2: West Br 4B **58**
Stratford St. DE7: Ilk 3B **28**
Strathglen Cl. NG16: Nuth 6G **17**
Strathmore Cl. NG15: Huck 6E **7**
Strathmore Rd. NG5: Arn 4D **22**
STRELLEY 1D **42**
Strelley Cl. NG15: Huck 1F **7**
Strelley La. NG8: Stre 1B **42**
Strelley Rd. NG8: Bilb, Stre 1C **42**
Strelley St. NG6: Bulw 6H **19**
The Stretton NG7: Lent 1C **56**
(off Leen Ct.)
Stretton St. NG3: Nott 1F **5** (3H **45**)
Striding Edge Cl. NG10: Long E 3D **62**
Stripes Vw. NG14: Calv 5H **11**
Strome Cl. NG2: Nott 1G **57**
Strome Ct. NG2: Nott 1G **57**
Stuart Cl. NG5: Arn 5D **22**
The Studio Theatre 5D **58**
Studland Way NG2: West Br 6G **57**
Sturgeon Av. NG11: Clftn 1D **66**

Sturmer Way NG8: Aspl 2H **43**
Sturton St. NG7: Hys G 1E **45**
Styring St. NG9: Bee 5F **55**
Sudbury Av. DE7: Ilk 2C **40**
NG10: Sand 4C **52**
Sudbury Cl. NG3: Ged 2G **35**
Sudbury Ct. NG10: Long E 3B **72**
Suez St. NG7: Bas 6D **32**
Suffolk Av. NG9: Bee 1A **66**
NG15: Huck 6C **6**
Sullivan Cl. NG3: Nott 2B **46**
Sullivan St. NG7: Radf 4C **44**
Sumburgh Rd. NG11: Clftn 4E **67**
Summer Cres. NG9: Bee 4H **55**
Summer Dr. NG2: West Br 6H **57**
Summerfields Way DE7: Ilk 3G **27**
Summerfields Way Sth. DE7: Ilk 5H **27**
Summer Leys Rd. NG2: Nott 6H **45**
Summerwood La. NG11: Clftn 5B **66**
Summerwood Lane Stop (NET) 5B **66**
Sunbourne Ct. NG7: Radf 3E **45**
Sunbury Gdns. NG5: Arn 4C **22**
Sunderland Gro. NG8: Stre 5D **30**
Sundown Dr. NG12: Cotg 6G **61**
Sundridge Pk. Cl. NG2: West Br 6G **57**
Sunflower Dr. NG12: Edwal 3C **68**
Sunlea Cres. NG9: Stfrd 6H **53**
Sunnindale Dr. NG12: Toll 4F **69**
Sunningdale Av. DE75: Hea 5D **14**
Sunningdale Dr. DE7: Kirk H 4F **39**
NG14: Woodbo .6C **12**
Sunninghill Cl. DE7: West H 1B **38**
Sunninghill Dr. NG11: Clftn 2C **66**
Sunninghill Ri. NG5: Arn 4C **22**
Sunnydale Rd. NG3: Nott 3D **46**
Sunny Row NG8: Woll 4E **43**
Sunnyside Rd. NG9: Chil 5C **54**
Sunridge Ct. NG3: Mapp P 1G **45**
Sunrise Av. NG5: Bestw 2D **32**
NG6: Bestw V 6G **9**
Surbiton Ct. DE7: West H 1B **38**
NG3: Mapp 6A **34**
Surbiton Sq. NG8: Cin 4H **31**
Surfleet Cl. NG8: Woll 6C **42**
Surgey's La. NG5: Arn 4B **22**
Surrey Ct. NG3: Mapp 6A **34**
Susan Cl. NG15: Huck 2H **7**
Susan Dr. NG6: Bulw 3B **32**
Sussex Cl. NG16: Gilt 5C **16**
Sussex St. NG1: Nott 5E **5** (5G **45**)
Sutherland Cl. NG10: Sand 6D **52**
Sutherland Dr. NG2: West Br 1C **68**
Sutherland Rd. NG3: Nott 2D **46**
Sutton Cl. NG16: Eastw 3B **16**
Sutton Gdns. NG11: Rudd 1G **77**
Sutton Gro. NG9: Chil 5D **54**
Sutton Passeys Cres. NG8: Woll 5H **43**
Sutton Rd. NG5: Arn 3B **22**
Swain's Av. NG3: Nott 3C **46**
Swale Cl. NG6: Bulw 6B **20**
Swaledale Cl. NG8: Aspl 6B **32**
Swale Gro. NG13: Bing 6D **50**
Swallow Cl. NG6: Bas 3B **32**
Swallow Dr. NG13: Bing 6F **51**
Swallow Gdns. NG4: Car 6D **34**
Swan Mdw. NG4: Colw 5G **47**
Swansdowne Dr. NG11: Clftn 3D **66**
Swanwick Dr. DE7: Ilk 2B **28**
Sweeney Ct. NG5: Top V 5E **21**
Sweet Leys Rd. NG2: Nott 2G **57**
Swenson Av. NG7: Lent 6C **44**
Swift Cl. NG16: Eastw 3B **16**
Swigert Cl. NG6: Bulw 2F **31**
Swildon Wlk. NG5: Top V 5D **20**
Swinburne St. NG3: Nott 3B **46**
Swinburne Way NG5: Arn 6B **22**
Swindale Cl. NG2: Gam 4D **58**
Swindell Cl. NG3: Mapp 2D **34**
Swindon Cl. NG16: Gilt 6E **17**
Swiney Way NG9: Chil, Toton 3H **63**
SWINGATE 2A **30**
Swingate NG16: Kimb 1H **29**
Swinley Ct. NG13: Bing 5C **50**
Swinscoe Gdns. NG5: Top V 5D **20**
Swinstead Cl. NG8: Bilb 3F **43**
Swithland Dr. NG2: West Br 1A **68**
Sycamore Cl. DE7: Mapp 4D **26**
NG11: Rudd 6H **67**
NG12: Rad T 1F **61**
NG13: Bing 5C **50**
NG15: Huck 6E **7**
Sycamore Ct. NG9: Bee 4G **55**
Sycamore Cres. NG10: Sand 4C **52**
Sycamore Dr. DE7: Ilk 2D **40**
Sycamore Gdns. DE75: Hea 4B **14**
Sycamore Pl. NG3: Mapp P 1G **45**
Sycamore Ri. NG6: Cin 3H **31**

Sycamore Rd. NG10: Long E 2E 73
   NG16: Aws 2D 28
The Sycamores NG16: Eastw 4A 16
Syderstone Wlk. NG5: Arn 2B 34
Sydney Gro. NG12: Rad T 6E 49
Sydney Rd. NG8: Woll 4H 43
Syke Rd. NG5: Top V 5D 20
Synge Cl. NG11: Clftn 5A 66
Syon Pk. Cl. NG2: West Br 6G 57

T

Taft Av. NG10: Sand .5D 52
Talbot Ct. NG12: Rad T 6E 49
Talbot Dr. NG9: Stfrd 1F 53
Talbot St. NG1: Nott 3B 4 (4F 45)
Tamarix Cl. NG4: Ged 5A 36
Tambling Cl. NG5: Arn 1D 34
Tame Cl. NG11: Clftn 1C 66
Tamworth Gro. NG11: Clftn 3D 66
Tamworth Rd. DE72: Shar 6A 72
   NG10: Long E 4C 72
Tangmere Cres. NG8: Stre 6H 31
Tanners Wlk. NG1: Nott 5E 5 (5G 45)
Tannery Rd. NG16: Gilt 6E 17
Tannin Cres. NG6: Bulw 2A 32
Tansy Way NG13: Bing 6C 50
Tantum Av. DE75: Los 1A 14
Tanwood Rd. NG9: Toton 4B 64
Tarbert Cl. NG2: Nott 1F 57
Target St. NG7: Radf .4C 44
Tarn Cl. NG16: Lang M 1F 15
Tarrat St. DE7: Ilk 5A 28
Tasmania Cl. NG2: Nott 2G 57
Tatham's La. DE7: Ilk 5A 28
Tattershall Dr. NG7: Nott 4A 4 (5E 45)
   NG9: Bee 4H 55
Taunton Rd. NG2: West Br 5B 58
Taupo Dr. NG15: Huck 6C 6
Tavern Av. NG8: Aspl 5A 32
Tavistock Av. NG3: Mapp P 6G 33
Tavistock Cl. NG15: Huck 6D 6
Tavistock Ct. NG5: Sher 6G 33
Tavistock Dr. NG3: Mapp P 6G 33
Tavistock Rd. NG2: West Br 5B 58
Taylor Cl. NG2: Nott .5C 46
Taylor Cres. NG9: Stfrd 3H 53
Taylor La. DE75: Los 2B 14
Taylor La. Ind. Est. DE75: Los 2B 14
Taylor Pl. NG3: Nott .1B 46
Taylors Cft. NG14: Woodbo 1B 24
Taylor St. DE7: Ilk 6B 28
Teak Cl. NG3: Nott 2H 45
Tealby Cl. NG6: Bulw 6F 19
Teal Cl. NG4: Neth 2B 48
Teal Wharf NG7: Lent 1E 57
The Teasels NG13: Bing 6D 50
Technology Dr. NG9: Bee 6G 55
Teesbrook Dr. NG8: Woll 5B 42
Tees Ct. NG13: Bing .6D 50
Teesdale Ct. NG9: Chil 1A 64
Teesdale Rd. NG5: Sher 5E 33
   NG10: Long E 2D 16
Telford Dr. NG16: Newth 5D 16
Teme Ct. NG2: West Br 5H 55
Templar Lodge NG9: Bee 5H 55
Templar Rd. NG9: Bee 5H 55
Templars Ct. NG7: Radf 3B 44
                    (off New Rd.)
Temple Cres. NG16: Nuth 3D 30
Temple Dr. NG16: Nuth 3E 31
Templeman Cl. NG11: Rudd 5F 67
Templeoak Dr. NG8: Woll 6C 42
Tenants Hall Cl. NG9: Lent A 2G 55
Tenbury Cres. NG8: Aspl 6H 31
Tene Cl. NG5: Arn 3B 22
Tennis Ct. Ind. Est. NG2: Nott 6C 46
Tennis Dr. NG7: Nott 4A 4 (5E 45)
Tennis M. NG7: Nott 4A 4 (5E 45)
Tennis Vw. NG7: Nott 4A 4 (5E 45)
Tennyson Av. NG4: Ged 6H 35
Tennyson Ct. NG5: Sher 4F 33
   NG15: Huck 5D 6
Tennyson Dr. NG9: Atten 3D 64
Tennyson Grange NG4: Ged 6A 36
Tennyson Rd. NG5: Woodt 3A 34
Tennyson Sq. NG16: Aws 3E 29
Tennyson St. DE7: Ilk 4A 28
   NG7: Radf .1A 4 (3E 45)
              (not continuous)
Tenpin
   Nottingham 2C 56
Tenter Cl. NG5: Top V 5D 20
   NG10: Long E 2F 73
Terrace St. NG7: Hys G 2D 44
Terrian Cres. NG2: West Br 4B 58
Terton Rd. NG5: Top V 5D 20
Tetney Wlk. NG8: Bilb 2G 43
Tettenbury Rd. NG5: Sher 4D 32

Teversal Av. NG7: Lent 5D 44
Tevery Cl. NG9: Stfrd 3G 53
Teviot Rd. NG5: Bestw 2D 32
Tewkesbury Av. NG2: West Br 5C 58
Tewkesbury Cl. NG2: West Br 3C 32
Tewkesbury Dr. NG6: Bas 6G 17
   NG16: Kimb 1A 30
Tewkesbury Rd. NG10: Long E 3G 73
Thackeray's La. NG5: Woodt 2H 33
Thackeray St. NG7: Radf 4D 44
Thales Dr. NG5: Arn .6E 23
Thames St. NG6: Bulw 6H 19
Thane Rd. NG7: Lent, Nott 5B 56
Thatcham Cl. NG8: Aspl 2B 44
Thatchmarsh Cl. DE7: Ilk 1B 28
Thaxted Cl. NG8: Bilb 3D 42
Theatre Royal 3D 4 (4G 45)
Theatre Sq. NG1: Nott 3D 4
Thelda Av. NG12: Key 4G 79
Thetford Cl. NG5: Arn 1C 34
Third Av.
   DE7: Ilk 2B 40
   NG4: Car 1D 46
               (not continuous)
   NG4: Ged 6H 35
   NG6: Bulw 6H 19
   NG7: Hys G 1F 45
   NG7: Nott 5A 56
Thirlmere NG2: West Br 6E 59
Thirlmere Cl. NG3: Nott 2B 46
   NG10: Long E 3D 62
Thirlmere Rd. NG10: Long E 3D 62
Thirston Cl. NG6: Bulw 6F 19
Thistle Cl. NG16: Newth 5D 16
Thistledown Rd. NG11: Clftn 6C 66
Thistlegreen Cl. DE75: Hea 4F 15
Thistle Rd. DE7: Ilk 5C 40
Thomas Av. NG12: Rad T 5H 49
Thomas Cl. NG3: Nott 1G 5 (3H 45)
Thomas Forman Ct. NG5: Sher 6F 33
Thompson Cl. NG9: Chil 2C 64
Thompson Ct. NG9: Chil 4B 64
Thompson Gdns. NG5: Top V 4E 21
Thompson St. NG16: Lang M 2F 15
Thoresby Av. NG2: Nott 6B 46
   NG4: Ged 5F 35
Thoresby Cl. NG12: Rad T 5G 49
Thoresby Ct. NG3: Mapp P 1H 45
Thoresby Dale NG15: Huck 4H 7
Thoresby Rd. NG9: Bram 2C 54
   NG10: Long E 1D 72
   NG13: Bing 5C 50
Thoresby St. NG1: Nott 5H 5 (5A 46)
Thor Gdns. NG5: Top V 4D 20
Thornbury Way NG5: Top V 6D 20
Thorncliffe Ho. NG5: Top V 5C 20
Thorncliffe Ri. NG3: Mapp P 1G 45
Thorncliffe Rd. NG3: Mapp P 1G 45
Thorndale Rd. NG6: Bas 5A 32
   NG14: Calv 4H 11
Thorn Dr. NG16: Newth 5D 16
Thorndyke Cl. NG9: Bee 1H 65
Thorner Cl. NG6: Bulw 2C 32
Thorney Hill NG3: Nott 2B 46
THORNEYWOOD 1C 46
Thorneywood Mt. NG3: Nott 2B 46
Thorneywood Ri. NG3: Nott 2B 46
Thorneywood Rd. NG10: Long E 5H 63
Thornfield Ind. Est. NG3: Nott 4B 46
Thornfield Sq. NG10: Long E 5H 63
Thorn Gro. NG15: Huck 1H 19
Thornhill Cl. NG9: Bram 1B 54
Thornley St. NG7: Hys G 2C 44
Thornthwaite Cl. NG2: West Br 5E 59
Thornton Av. NG5: Redh 4H 21
Thornton Cl. NG8: Woll 5E 43
Thorntons Cl. NG12: Cotg 2G 71
Thornton's Holt Camping Pk. 3D 60
Thorntree Cl. DE72: Brea 4B 62
Thorn Tree Gdns. NG16: Eastw 1B 16
Thoroton Rd. NG2: West Br 3C 66
Thoroton St. NG7: Radf 2B 58
Thorpe Cl. NG5: Top V 4E 45
   NG9: Stfrd 4E 53
Thorpe Cres. NG3: Mapp 5D 34
Thorpe Hill Dr. DE75: Hea 6C 14
Thorpe Leys NG10: Long E 2F 73
Thorpe Rd. NG16: Eastw 1B 16
Thorpe's Rd. DE75: Hea 4B 14
Thorpes Rd. Ind. Est. DE75: Hea 4A 28
Thorpe St. DE7: Ilk 3B 22
Thrapston Av. NG5: Arn 6E 49
Thraves Yd. NG12: Rad T 6E 49
Threeleys Cl. DE7: Ilk 4B 40
Three Tuns Rd. NG16: Eastw 3C 16
Threlkeld Cl. NG2: West Br 5E 59
THRUMPTON 4B 74
Thrumpton Av. NG10: Long E 6H 63
Thrumpton Dr. NG2: Nott 2F 57
Thrumpton La. NG11: Bart F 3F 75

Thurgarton Av. NG2: Nott 5B 46
Thurgarton St. NG2: Nott 5B 46
Thurland St. NG1: Nott 4E 5 (5G 45)
Thurlbeck NG12: Cotg 4G 71
Thurlby La. NG12: Stant W 6B 80
Thurlestone Dr. NG3: Mapp 1E 35
Thurloe Ct. NG2: West Br 2G 67
Thurman Dr. NG12: Cotg 2F 71
Thurman St. DE7: Ilk .3C 40
   NG7: Hys G 3D 44
Thursby Rd. NG11: Clftn 2C 66
Thymus Wlk. NG11: Clftn 4A 66
Thyra Ct. NG3: Nott 6H 33
Thyra Gro. NG3: Nott 6H 33
   NG9: Bee 5G 55
Tiberius Gdns. NG15: Huck 3A 8
Tidworth Cl. NG8: Bilb 3G 43
Tilberthwaite Cl. NG2: Gam 5E 59
Tilbury Ri. NG8: Cin 4G 31
Tilford Gdns. NG9: Stfrd 5G 53
Tilstock Ct. NG16: Want 5A 18
Tilton Gro. DE7: Kirk H 4G 39
Tim La. NG14: Bur J 3F 37
Tindall Cl. NG9: Chil .3B 64
Tinker Cft. DE7: Ilk 2A 40
Tinkers Way NG7: Lent 6F 45
Tinsley Rd. NG16: Eastw 4A 16
Tintagel Grn. NG11: Clftn 4C 66
Tintern Dr. NG8: Bas .5B 32
Tippett Ct. NG3: Nott .3B 46
Tip Tree Cl. NG16: Kimb 6H 17
Tiree Cl. NG9: Trow 1F 53
Tishbie St. NG6: Bulw 6H 19
Tissington Cl. NG7: Hys G 1E 45
   NG9: Chil 4C 64
Tissington Rd. NG7: Hys G 1E 45
Titchfield Av. NG15: Huck 5G 7
Titchfield St. NG15: Huck 4G 7
Titchfield Ter. NG15: Huck 4H 7
Tithby Rd. NG5: Sher 3H 33
Tithby Rd. NG13: Bing 6E 51
              (not continuous)
Tithe Gdns. NG5: Top V 4E 21
Tithe La. NG14: Calv .4H 11
Tiverton Cl. NG8: Aspl 5H 31
   NG15: Huck 6D 6
Toad Hole Cl. DE7: Kirk H 3G 39
Toad La. NG14: Epp .6G 13
Tobias Cl. NG5: Top V 5D 20
Todd Cl. NG11: Clftn .5A 66
Todd Ct. NG11: Clftn .5A 66
Toft Cl. NG12: Cotg 3E 71
Toft Rd. NG9: Chil 2A 64
Token Ho. Yd. NG1: Nott 4E 5
TOLLERTON 4F 69
Tollerton Grn. NG6: Bulw 2B 32
Tollerton La. NG12: Toll 5F 59
Tollerton Pk. Cvn. Pk. 5C 20
Tollhouse Hill NG1: Nott 3C 4 (4F 45)
Tom Blower Cl. NG8: Woll 4G 43
Tomlinson Av. NG11: Goth 6G 75
Tonbridge Mt. NG8: Woll 1D 54
Tongue Way NG11: Rudd 6E 67
Tonnelier Rd. NG7: Lent 2C 56
Toothill Ct. NG14: Calv 3E 11
Topliff Rd. NG9: Chil .3C 64
Top Rd. NG11: Rudd .1G 77
Top Row NG14: Stoke B 2D 48
TOP VALLEY 5C 20
Top Valley Dr. NG5: Top V 5C 20
Top Valley Way NG5: Top V 6C 20
Torbay Cres. NG5: Bestw 1F 33
Torkard Ct. NG15: Huck 6G 7
Torkard Dr. NG5: Top V 5D 20
Torkard Way NG15: Huck 4H 7
Torrington Ct. NG5: Sher 5H 33
Torvill Dr. NG8: Woll .4E 43
Torvill Hgts. NG8: Woll 4E 43
Toston Dr. NG8: Woll .5A 44
Totland Dr. NG8: Bas .5B 32
Totland Rd. NG9: Bram 1C 54
Totley Cl. NG6: Bulw .3A 20
Totnes Cl. NG15: Huck 5D 6
Totnes Rd. NG3: Nott 4D 46
TOTON 3A 64
Toton Cl. NG6: Bulw .2B 32
Toton La. NG9: Stfrd .4F 53
Toton Lane Park & Ride 1H 63
Toton Lane Stop (NET) 1H 63
Toton Sidings NG9: Toton 2F 63
Tottle Gdns. NG7: Radf 3B 44
Tottle Rd. NG2: Nott 3E 57
Tower Cres. NG16: Kimb 3A 30
Towe's Mt. NG4: Car .2G 47
Towlson Ct. NG9: Chil 3C 72
Towlsons Cft. NG6: Bas 4B 32
Town End Cotts. NG12: Plum 6G 69
Townsend Ct. NG5: Top V 4E 21
Townside Cl. NG10: Long E 3D 72

Town St. NG9: Bram 3B **54**
NG10: Sand 6D **52**
Town Vw. NG16: Kimb 6H **17**
Towson Av. NG16: Lang M 3G **15**
Towyn Cl. NG5: Bestw 6E **21**
Tracy Cl. NG9: Bram 2E **55**
Trafalgar Cl. NG7: Radf 3D **44**
Trafalgar Rd. NG9: Bee 1G **65**
NG10: Long E 1F **73**
Trafalgar Sq. NG10: Long E 6H **63**
Trafalgar Ter. NG10: Long E 6G **63**
Traffic St. NG2: Nott 6G **45**
Trafford Gdns. NG8: Aspl 2B **44**
Tranby Gdns. NG8: Woll 5F **43**
Travers Rd. NG10: Sand 5C **52**
Treegarth Sq. NG5: Top V 4F **21**
TREETOPS HOSPICE 1A **62**
Tree Vw. Cl. NG5: Arn 4G **21**
Trefan Gdns. NG5: Bestw 6E **21**
Trefoil Cl. NG13: Bing 6D **50**
Trelawn Cl. NG5: Sher 5H **33**
Tremadoc Ct. NG5: Sher 1F **45**
Tremayne Rd. NG8: Bilb 3C **42**
Trenchard Cl. NG13: Newt 2B **50**
Trent Av. NG11: Rudd 5G **67**
Trent Blvd. NG2: West Br 2B **58**
Trent Bridge 2A **58**
Trent Bri. NG2: Nott, West Br 2A **58**
Trent Bri. Bldgs. NG2: West Br 2A **58**
Trent Bus. Cen. NG10: Long E 3E **63**
Trent Cotts. NG10: Long E 1H **73**
Trent Cl. NG2: West Br 2C **58**
Trent Cres. NG9: Atten 2E **65**
Trentdale Rd. NG4: Car 3F **47**
Trent Dr. NG15: Huck 2D **18**
Trent Gdns. NG14: Bur J 3G **37**
Trentham Dr. NG8: Aspl 2A **44**
Trentham Gdns. NG8: Aspl 2A **44**
NG14: Bur J 4D **36**
Trent Ho. NG10: Long E 3C **72**
Trent La. NG2: Nott 6B **46**
(not continuous)
NG10: Long E 3G **73**
NG14: Bur J 3G **37**
TRENTLOCK 4G **73**
Trent Lock Golf Course 3F **73**
Trenton Cl. NG9: Bram 2A **54**
Trenton Dr. NG10: Long E 5A **64**
Trent Rd. DE7: Kirk H 5H **39**
NG2: Nott 5B **46**
NG9: Bee 1G **65**
Trent Side NG11: Bart F 6C **64**
Trentside NG2: West Br 3A **58**
Trent Side NG9: Bee 2G **65**
(off Riverside Rd.)
Trent Side Nth. NG2: West Br 2A **58**
Trent Sth. Ind. Pk. NG2: Nott 6C **46**
Trent St. NG2: Nott 6F **5** (6H **45**)
NG10: Long E 5G **63**
Trent Va. Rd. NG9: Bee 1G **65**
Trent Valley Rd. NG4: Ged, Neth 2B **48**
NG14: Bur J 2B **48**
Trent Valley Sailing Club 4G **73**
Trent Valley Vw. NG3: Mapp 6C **34**
(off Hickling Rd.)
Trentview Ct. NG2: Nott 1B **58**
Trent Vw. Gdns. NG12: Rad T 4G **49**
Tressall Cl. DE7: Ilk 1C **40**
Trevelyan Rd. NG2: West Br 3B **58**
Trevino Gdns. NG5: Top V 4E **21**
Trevone Av. NG9: Stfrd 5G **53**
Trevor Rd. NG2: West Br 5C **58**
NG9: Bee 6F **55**
Trevose Gdns. NG5: Sher 4H **33**
Treyford Cl. NG11: Wilf 1E **67**
The Triangle DE7: Ilk 3C **40**
NG2: Nott 1E **57**
Tricornia Dr. NG6: Cin 3H **31**
Tring Va. NG5: Sher 3E **33**
Trinity Av. NG7: Lent 6C **44**
Trinity Cl. DE7: Ilk .4A **28**
Trinity Cres. NG4: Lamb 6C **24**
Trinity Row NG1: Nott 3D **4** (4G **45**)
Trinity Sq. NG1: Nott 3D **4** (4G **45**)
Trinity Vw. NG10: Long E 5C **14**
Trinity Wlk. NG1: Nott 3E **5** (4G **45**)
Trinity Way DE75: Hea 5C **14**
Trinstead Way NG5: Bestw 6G **21**
Triumph Rd. NG7: Lent 5B **44**
NG8: Lent 5B **44**
Trivett Sq. NG1: Nott 5G **5**
Troon Cl. NG16: Kimb 6G **17**
Trough La. NG16: Want 5H **17**
Trough Rd. NG16: Want 5H **17**
Troutbeck NG12: Cotg 2G **71**
Troutbeck Cres. NG9: Bram 3C **54**
TROWELL 5E **41**
Trowell Av. DE7: Ilk 4C **40**
NG8: Woll 4B **42**
Trowell Gdns. NG8: Bilb 4C **42**

Trowell Gro. NG9: Trow 6F **41**
NG10: Long E 3D **62**
TROWELL MOOR 4B **42**
Trowell Pk. Dr. NG9: Trow 1F **53**
Trowell Rd. NG8: Woll 5B **42**
NG9: Stfrd 1G **53**
TROWELL SERVICE AREA 3G **41**
Trueman Gdns. NG5: Arn 1D **34**
Trueman St. DE7: Ilk 3B **28**
Truman Cl. NG3: Nott 1F **5** (3H **45**)
Truman Dr. NG15: Huck 5G **7**
Trumans Rd. NG2: Nott 2H **57**
Truman St. NG16: Kimb 6F **17**
Truro Cres. NG7: Radf 2C **44**
Tudor Cl. NG4: Colw 4G **47**
NG9: Bee 4G **63**
Tudor Ct. NG9: Stfrd 6F **53**
NG15: Huck 6C **6**
Tudor Falls DE75: Hea 2C **14**
Tudor Gro. NG1: Nott 2F **45**
Tudor Pl. DE7: Kirk H 4G **39**
Tudor Rd. NG2: West Br 4B **58**
Tudor Sq. NG2: West Br 4B **58**
Tudwal Cl. NG5: Bestw 6E **21**
Tudwal Wlk. NG5: Bestw 6E **21**
Tulip Av. NG3: Nott .2H **45**
Tulip Cl. NG12: Cotg 6G **61**
Tulip Rd. NG16: Aws 2D **28**
Tumble Town Play Cen. 5A **22**
Tunnel Rd. NG7: Nott 5A **4** (5E **45**)
Tunnicliffe Cl. DE7: Ilk 5A **28**
Tunnicliffe Ct. DE7: Ilk 3B **28**
Tunstall Cres. NG8: Aspl 6G **31**
Tunstall Dr. NG5: Sher 3D **32**
Tunstall Rd. NG5: Woodt 3B **34**
Turnberry Cl. DE7: Ilk 5G **27**
NG9: Bram 5C **54**
Turnberry Ct. NG12: Edwal 2E **69**
Turnberry Rd. NG6: Bulw 1B **32**
Turner Av. NG16: Lang M 2E **15**
Turner Cl. NG5: Sher 2F **33**
NG9: Stfrd 5G **53**
Turner Dr. NG16: Gilt 6D **16**
Turner Rd. NG10: Long E 3E **73**
Turner St. NG15: Huck 4G **7**
Turneys Ct. NG2: Nott 2A **58**
Turney St. NG2: Nott 2H **57**
Turnoak Av. DE7: Ilk 2B **28**
Turnpike La. NG9: Bee 3G **55**
Turnpike Village NG9: Bee 3G **55**
Turnpike Village Halls of Residence 4G **55**
Turnstone Wharf NG7: Lent 1D **56**
Turpin Av. NG4: Ged 4F **35**
Turton Cl. NG16: Lang M 2E **15**
Turton Dr. NG5: Arn 6A **22**
Tuxford Wlk. NG3: Nott 3B **46**
Twells Cl. NG3: Nott 2B **46**
Twelve Ho's. DE7: Stant D 6A **40**
The Twitchell NG9: Chil 1E **65**
Twycross Rd. NG5: Bestw 6F **21**
Twyford Cl. DE7: West H 1B **38**
DE75: Hea 5A **14**
Twyford Gdns. NG11: Clftn 1C **66**
Twyford Rd. NG10: Long E 3B **72**
Tyburn Cl. NG5: Arn 4E **21**
Tyne Cl. NG2: Nott 5A **32**
Tynedale Cl. NG8: Aspl 6B **32**
NG10: Long E 1C **72**
Tyne Gdns. NG15: Huck 2D **18**
Tyrian St. NG16: Gilt 5D **16**

U

Ulgham Cl. NG5: Arn 3B **22**
Ulldale Ct. NG5: Chil 1B **64**
Ullscarf Cl. NG2: West Br 6E **59**
Ullswater Cl. NG2: Gam 5F **59**
NG4: Ged 5H **35**
Ullswater Cres. NG9: Bram 2C **54**
Ullswater Dr. NG15: Huck 4F **7**
Underwood M. NG8: Stre 6C **30**
Union Cl. NG15: Lin .1G **7**
Union Rd. DE7: Ilk 2A **40**
NG1: Nott 2E **5** (4G **45**)
NG3: Nott 2F **5** (4H **45**)
Union St. NG9: Bee .4G **55**
NG10: Long E 5G **63**
NG13: Bing 5E **51**
Unity Cres. NG3: Mapp 5E **35**
University Blvd. NG7: Nott 3H **55**
NG9: Bee 3H **55**
University Boulevard Stop (NET) 4H **55**
University Library
Nottingham 4F **45**
University of Nottingham
Jubilee Campus 5B **44**
King's Meadow Campus 2D **56**
Medical School 1B **56**
University Pk. Campus 1A **56**

University of Nottingham Stop (NET) 2B **56**
University Pk. NG7: Nott 2H **55**
Uplands Ct. NG8: Woll 3F **43**
Upminster Dr. NG5: Arn 4B **22**
NG16: Nuth 3D **30**
Up. Barn Cl. DE75: Hea 3D **14**
Up. Canaan NG11: Rudd 5H **67**
Up. College St. NG1: Nott 3B **4** (4F **45**)
Up. Dunstead Rd. NG16: Lang M 2F **15**
Up. Eldon St. NG2: Nott 4H **5** (5A **46**)
Up. Orchard St. NG9: Stfrd 4G **53**
Up. Parliament St. NG1: Nott 3C **4** (4F **45**)
Up. Wellington St. NG10: Long E 4E **63**
Uppingham Cres. NG2: West Br 6H **57**
Uppingham Gdns. NG2: Nott 1H **57**
Upton Cl. DE75: Hea 4E **15**
Upton Dr. NG5: Sher 2H **33**
Upton M. NG3: Nott 1D **46**
URGENT CARE CENTRE (CITY LINK)
NOTTINGHAM 6G **5** (5H **45**)
Utile Gdns. NG6: Bulw 6G **19**

V

The Vale DE7: Ilk 4A **28**
Valebrook Rd. NG5: Sher 2G **33**
Vale Cl. NG5: Eastw 3D **16**
Vale Cres. Nth. NG8: Aspl 3B **44**
Vale Cres. Sth. NG8: Aspl 3B **44**
Vale Gdns. NG4: Colw 4F **47**
Valerian Gro. NG15: Huck 3A **8**
Valerian Way NG13: Bing 5C **50**
Valeside Gdns. NG4: Colw 4G **47**
Valetta Rd. NG5: Arn 6D **22**
Valeview Ho. NG12: Cotg 2F **71**
Valley Cl. NG4: Car .6D **34**
NG5: Sher 2H **33**
Valley Dr. NG16: Newth 3D **16**
Valley Farm Ct. NG5: Top V 5E **21**
Valley Gdns. NG2: West Br 6E **59**
Valley Ho. NG1: Nott 5C **4**
Valley Rd. DE7: Kirk H 4A **40**
NG2: West Br 6C **58**
NG4: Car 6D **34**
NG5: Bas, Sher 5D **32**
NG9: Chil 6A **54**
NG12: Rad T 4G **49**
NG16: Kimb 6F **17**
Valley Vw. DE7: Kirk H 4A **40**
Valmont Rd. NG5: Sher 4E **33**
NG9: Bram 3A **54**
Vancouver Av. NG12: Rad T 1E **61**
Vanguard Rd. NG10: Long E 2F **73**
The Vantage NG7: Hys G 1F **45**
Varden Av. NG9: Lent A 2G **55**
Varley Cl. DE75: Hea 3E **15**
Varney Rd. NG11: Clftn 2D **66**
Vaughan Av. NG15: Huck 2H **7**
Vaughan Rd. NG9: Chil 1A **64**
Vedonis Pk. NG15: Huck 6G **7**
Venn Ct. NG9: Bee 5F **55**
Ventnor Ri. NG5: Sher 3D **32**
Ventura Dr. NG6: Bulw 4A **20**
Venus Cl. NG6: Bas .2C **32**
Verbena Cl. NG3: Nott 2H **45**
Verden Way NG8: Stre 5C **30**
Verder Gro. NG5: Top V 5C **20**
Vere St. NG6: Bulw .6H **19**
Verne Cl. NG4: Car .2E **47**
Vernon Av. NG4: Car 1H **47**
NG6: Bas 3D **32**
NG9: Bee 5F **55**
NG11: Wilf 3F **57**
Vernon Ct. NG12: Rad T 6F **49**
NG16: Nuth 4F **31**
Vernon Dr. NG16: Nuth 4F **31**
Vernon Pk. Dr. NG6: Bas 4C **32**
Vernon Pk. Trad. Est. NG6: Bas 4C **32**
Vernon Pl. NG6: Bas 3B **32**
Vernon Rd. NG6: Bas 3B **32**
Vernon St. DE7: Ilk .3B **28**
NG1: Nott 3B **4** (4F **45**)
Vernon Works NG6: Bas 4C **32**
Verona Av. NG4: Colw 3H **47**
Veronica Dr. NG4: Car 6F **35**
NG16: Gilt 5E **17**
Veronica Wlk. NG11: Clftn 4A **66**
Versailles Gdns. NG15: Huck 6G **7**
Vicarage Av. DE7: Ilk 3H **27**
Vicarage Cl. NG5: Sher 4D **32**
Vicarage Dr. NG14: Bur J 3E **37**
Vicarage Gdns. DE75: Hea 4D **14**
Vicarage Grn. NG12: Edwal 2D **68**
Vicarage La. NG11: Rudd 6G **67**
NG12: Rad T 6E **49**
Vicarage St. DE7: Ilk 3H **27**
NG9: Bee 5E **55**
Vickers Cl. NG4: Ged 4G **35**

Vickers St. NG3: Mapp P 1H 45
Vickery Way NG9: Chil 3B 64
The Victor NG7: Lent 1C 56
  (off Leen Ct.)
Victor Cres. NG10: Sand 1E 63
Victoria Av. DE75: Hea 4B 14
  NG2: Nott 5B 46
Victoria Bus. Pk. NG4: Neth 3B 48
Victoria Bus Station 1E 5 (3G 45)
Victoria Centre Clock Tower 3C 44
Victoria Cen. Sth. 3E 5
  (within Victoria Cen.)
Victoria Cl. NG5: Arn 3B 22
Victoria Ct. DE7: Ilk 6A 28
  NG7: Lent 5D 44
  NG10: Long E 5G 63
Victoria Cres. NG5: Sher 5H 33
Victoria Emb. NG2: Nott 2G 57
Victoria Gdns. NG16: Want 4A 18
Victoria Gro. NG15: Lin 1H 7
Victoria Hall NG3: Nott 2F 5 (4H 45)
  (not continuous)
Victoria Leisure Cen. 3G 5 (4H 45)
Victoria Mkt. NG1: Nott 3E 5 (4G 45)
Victoria Pk. NG11: Nott 6G 67
Victoria Pk. Leisure Cen. 6A 28
Victoria Pk. Way NG4: Neth 3B 48
Victoria Rd. NG2: West Br 4A 58
  NG4: Neth 2H 47
  NG5: Sher 4F 33
  NG10: Sand 6D 52
  NG11: Bunny 6A 78
  NG13: Bing 4G 51
Victoria St. DE7: Ilk 4B 28
  NG1: Nott 4E 5 (5G 45)
  NG4: Ged 6H 35
  NG9: Stfrd 4F 53
  NG10: Long E 2D 72
  NG12: Rad T 6F 49
  NG15: Huck 3F 7
  NG16: Eastw 2B 16
  NG16: Kimb 1A 30
  NG16: Lang M 2G 15
Victoria Ter. NG2: Nott 1A 46
Victoria Way NG15: Huck 5A 8
Victor Ter. NG5: Sher 2F 73
Victory Cl. NG10: Long E 1G 65
Victory Rd. NG9: Bee 4B 54
The View NG9: Bram 6D 38
The Village DE7: D Ab 2C 38
  DE7: West H 2D 68
Village Cl. NG12: Edwal 3A 66
Village Rd. NG11: Clftn 2C 68
Village St. NG12: Edwal 2G 45
Villa Rd. NG3: Mapp P 3H 79
  NG12: Key 4F 55
Villa St. NG9: Bee 5C 58
Villiers Rd. NG2: West Br 3H 33
  NG5: Woodt 1B 40
Vincent Av. DE7: Ilk 6F 55
Vincent Cl. NG15: Huck 2A 8
Vincent Gdns. NG7: Hys G 2C 44
Vine Cres. NG10: Sand 5D 52
Vine Farm Cl. DE7: Kirk H 3H 39
  NG12: Cotg 2E 71
Vines Cross NG8: Woll 1E 55
Vine Ter. NG15: Huck 4H 7
Violet Av. NG16: Newth 5D 16
Violet Cl. NG6: Bas 4B 32
Violet Gro. NG15: Huck 4A 8
Violet Rd. NG2: West Br 3C 58
  NG4: Car 5F 35
Virgin Active
  Nottingham 6G 5 (6H 45)
Vision Bus. Pk. NG6: Bulw 4G 19
The Vista NG9: Stfrd 6G 53
Vivian Av. NG5: Sher 1F 45
Vivian Ct. NG5: Sher 1F 45
Viyella Gdns. NG15: Huck 6G 7
Viyella M. NG15: Huck 5G 7
Voce Gdns. NG15: Huck 5A 8
Vulcan Cl. NG6: Bas 3C 32
Vyse Dr. NG10: Long E 1D 72

W

Waddington Dr. NG2: West Br 6H 57
Wade Av. DE7: Ilk 2C 40
Wades Av. NG7: Hys G 1C 44
Wades Way NG13: Bing 6G 51
Wadham Rd. NG5: Woodt 2A 34
Wadhurst Gdns. NG3: Nott 1G 5 (3H 45)
Wadhurst Gro. NG8: Woll 1D 54
Wadsworth Rd. NG9: Stfrd 3H 53
Wainfleet Cl. DE7: Ilk 4G 27
Wainfleet Cl. NG5: Arn 3C 22
Waingrove NG11: Wilf 2E 67
Wainwright Ho. NG3: Nott 3A 46

Wakefield Av. NG12: Rad T 5G 49
Wakefield Cl. NG11: Wilf 6E 57
Wakefield Cft. DE7: Ilk 4G 27
Walbrook Cl. NG8: Cin 4G 31
Walcote Dr. NG2: West Br 1G 67
Walcott Grn. NG11: Clftn 4B 66
Waldeck Rd. NG5: Sher 6F 33
Waldemar Gro. NG9: Bee 5G 55
Waldron Rd. NG4: Ged 4G 35
Waldron Cl. NG2: Nott 1H 57
Walesby Cres. NG8: Aspl 3A 44
Walgrave Wlk. NG5: Bestw 6F 21
Walker Cl. DE7: Ilk 5C 40
Walker Gro. NG9: Stfrd 5G 53
Walkers Cl. NG13: Bing 5E 51
Walker St. NG2: Nott 3H 5 (5A 46)
  NG16: Eastw 3C 16
Walker's Yd. NG12: Rad T 6F 49
Wlk. Mill Dr. NG15: Huck 2H 7
Wallace Av. NG4: Car 2H 47
Wallace Gdns. NG9: Toton 3H 63
Wallace St. NG11: Goth 5H 75
Wallet Cl. DE7: Ilk 3C 44
Wallet St. NG4: Neth 2A 48
Wallett Av. NG9: Bee 3F 55
Wallett St. NG2: Nott 1H 57
Wallis St. NG6: Bas 3C 32
Wallsend Cl. DE7: Ilk 3B 28
Walnut Cl. DE7: Ilk 2C 40
  NG2: West Br 2E 59
Walnut Ct. NG12: Rad T 6F 49
  (off Walnut Gro.)
Walnut Cft. NG11: Rudd 1H 77
Walnut Dr. NG9: Bram 3B 54
Walnut Gro. NG12: Cotg 2F 71
  NG12: Rad T 6F 49
  NG14: Calv 3H 11
Walnut Tree Gdns. NG6: Bulw 6F 19
Walsham Cl. NG9: Chil 3C 64
Walsingham Rd. NG5: Woodt 2C 34
Walter St. NG7: Radf 1A 4 (3E 45)
Waltham Cl. NG2: West Br 5D 58
Walton Av. NG3: Nott 4B 46
Walton Ct. DE7: West H 1B 38
  NG4: Car 2G 47
  NG12: Key 4H 79
Walton Cres. NG4: Car 2G 47
Walton Dr. NG12: Key 4H 79
Walton M. NG3: Nott 2B 46
Walton Rd. NG5: Arn 4C 22
Walton St. NG10: Long E 5F 63
Walton Ter. NG3: Nott 4B 46
Wansbeck Cl. NG5: Arn 3B 22
  NG7: Radf 4E 45
Wansford Av. NG5: Arn 3B 22
Wanstead Way NG5: Top V 4C 20
Warburton Ct. NG15: Huck 5H 7
Ward Av. NG3: Mapp 4D 34
  NG15: Huck 2F 7
Wardle Gro. NG5: Arn 5C 22
Wardlow Rd. DE7: Ilk 4A 28
Ward's La. DE72: Brea 5A 62
Ward St. NG7: Bas 1D 44
Wareham Cl. NG2: West Br 6G 57
  NG8: Cin 4G 31
The Warehouse NG1: Nott 5F 5
Warkton Cl. NG9: Chil 6C 54
Warner St. NG7: Radf 4C 44
The Warren NG12: Cotg 3F 71
Warren Av. NG5: Sher 5E 33
  NG9: Stfrd 4F 53
Warren Ct. NG9: Stfrd 4F 53
Warrender Cl. NG9: Bram 2C 54
Warrener Gro. NG5: Top V 5C 20
Warren Hill Cl. NG5: Arn 6G 21
Warren La. DE74: Lock 5C 72
  NG10: Long E 5C 72
Warren Rd. NG15: Huck 6D 6
Warrington Rd. NG6: Bulw 6A 20
Warser Ga. NG1: Nott 4F 5 (5H 45)
Warsop Cl. NG8: Stre 5D 30
Warton Av. NG3: Nott 1B 46
Warwick Av. NG5: Woodt 2A 34
  NG9: Bee 3F 55
Warwick Dr. DE7: Ilk 4G 27
Warwick Gdns. NG12: Cotg 4F 71
Warwick Rd. NG3: Mapp P 5H 33
  NG10: Long E 6H 63
Warwick St. NG7: Lent 1C 56
Wasdale Cl. NG2: West Br 6E 59
Washdyke La. NG15: Huck 2E 7
Washington Ct. NG5: Arn 6B 22
Washington Dr. NG9: Stfrd 2H 53
Wasnidge Cl. NG3: Nott 2G 5 (4H 45)
Wasnidge Wlk. NG3: Nott 1G 5
Watchwood Gro. NG14: Calv 3H 11
Watcombe Cir. NG5: Sher 5F 33
Watcombe Rd. NG5: Sher 6G 33
Watendlath Cl. NG2: West Br 6E 59
Waterdown Rd. NG11: Clftn 4B 66

Waterford St. NG6: Bas 4C 32
Waterfront Plaza NG2: Nott 6G 5 (6H 45)
Waterhouse La. NG4: Ged 5A 36
Water La. NG12: Rad T 6E 49
  NG25: Oxton 1B 12
Waterloo Cres. NG7: Radf 3E 45
Waterloo La. NG9: Trow 3G 41
Waterloo Prom. NG7: Radf 3E 45
  (not continuous)
Waterloo Rd. NG7: Radf 3E 45
  NG9: Bee 6G 55
  NG15: Lin 1G 7
Watermark Cl. NG5: Sher 5F 33
Watermark Ho. NG5: Sher 5F 33
The Watermeadows NG10: Long E 5C 62
Water Orton Cl. NG9: Toton 2G 63
Waters Edge NG11: Wilf 4F 57
Waterside Cl. NG2: Gam 5E 59
  NG10: Sand 2D 62
Waterside Gdns. NG7: Lent 2C 56
Waterside Retail Pk.
  Ilkeston Junction 6C 28
Waterside Way NG2: Colw, Nott 1C 58
The Waterway NG10: Sand 1E 63
Waterway St. NG2: Nott 1H 57
  (Newthorpe St.)
  NG2: Nott 1H 57
  (Wallet St.)
Waterway St. W. NG2: Nott 1G 57
Watford Rd. NG8: Aspl 5H 31
Watkinson St. DE75: Hea 3B 14
Watkin St. NG3: Nott 1E 5 (3G 45)
WATNALL 5A 18
WATNALL CANTELUPE 5H 17
WATNALL CHAWORTH 4A 18
Watnall Rd. NG15: Huck 3D 18
  NG16: Nuth 1C 30
Watnall Rd. Factory Units NG15: Huck 6F 7
Watson Av. DE75: Hea 3D 14
  NG3: Nott 3D 46
Watson Rd. DE7: Ilk 5G 27
Waveney Cl. NG5: Arn 1C 34
Waverley Av. NG4: Ged 6A 36
  NG9: Bee 5G 55
Waverley Mt. NG7: Nott 3E 45
Waverley St. NG1: Nott 1A 4 (3E 45)
  NG7: Nott 1A 4 (3E 45)
  NG10: Long E 5G 63
Waverley Ter. NG1: Nott 2C 4 (4F 45)
Wayford Wlk. NG6: Bulw 5H 19
Wayne Cl. NG11: Clftn 4C 66
Wayte Ct. NG11: Rudd 4A 68
Weardale Rd. NG5: Sher 5E 33
Wearmouth Gdns. NG5: Top V 4E 21
Weave Cl. NG6: Bas 3C 32
Weaver Row DE7: Ilk 1B 40
Weaverthorpe Rd. NG5: Woodt 2C 34
Weaving Gdns. NG5: Bestw 2G 33
Webb Rd. NG8: Bilb 2H 43
Webster Av. NG16: Eastw 4B 16
Webster Cl. NG15: Huck 1A 8
Weedon Cl. NG3: Nott 3C 46
Weekday Cross NG1: Nott 5E 5 (5G 45)
Weetman Gdns. NG5: Top V 5E 21
Weightman Av. NG4: Ged 4G 35
Weightman Dr. NG16: Gilt 6D 16
Welbeck Av. DE7: Kirk H 4H 39
  NG4: Ged 5F 35
Welbeck Ct. NG5: Woodt 3C 34
Welbeck Gdns. NG5: Woodt 3C 34
  NG9: Toton 2H 63
Welbeck Gro. NG13: Bing 5C 50
Welbeck Rd. NG2: West Br 3A 58
  NG10: Long E 2E 72
  NG12: Rad T 5G 49
Welbeck Wlk. NG3: Nott 3G 45
Welbeck Workshops NG3: Nott 3G 45
  (off Alfred Cl.)
Welby Av. NG7: Lent 5D 44
Welch Av. NG9: Stfrd 3H 53
Weldbank Cl. NG9: Chil 1B 64
Welham Cres. NG5: Arn 6C 22
Welland Cl. NG3: Nott 3B 46
Welland Gdns. NG13: Bing 6D 50
Wellesley Cres. NG8: Stre 5D 30
Wellin Cl. NG12: Edwal 2D 68
Wellin Ct. NG12: Edwal 2D 68
Wellington Cir. NG1: Nott 4B 4 (5F 45)
Wellington Ct. NG1: Nott 4C 4
  NG16: Eastw 3B 16
Wellington Cres. NG2: West Br 4B 58
Wellingtonia Cres. NG12: Edwal 3D 68
Wellington Pl. NG16: Eastw 3B 16
Wellington Rd. NG14: Bur J 2G 37
Wellington Sq. NG7: Nott 3A 4 (4E 45)
Wellington St. DE75: Hea 3B 14
  NG3: Nott 1E 5 (3G 45)
  NG9: Stfrd 5E 53
  NG10: Long E 2E 63
  NG16: Eastw 2B 16

Wellington Ter. NG7: Radf 4E 45
Wellington Vs. NG7: Lent 4E 45
Wellin La. NG12: Edwal 2D 68
Wells Gdns. NG3: Nott 1B 46
Wellspring Dale NG9: Stfrd 6G 53
The Wells Rd. NG3: Mapp, Nott 5A 34
THE WELLS ROAD CENTRE 5B 34
Welstead Av. NG8: Aspl 5G 31
Welton Gdns. NG6: Bulw 5G 19
Welwyn Rd. NG8: Woll 4E 43
Wembley Gdns. NG9: Bram 1B 54
Wembley Rd. NG5: Arn 1D 34
Wemyss Gdns. NG8: Woll 6B 44
Wendling Gdns. NG5: Bestw 6F 21
Wendover Dr. NG8: Aspl 5H 31
Wenlock Cl. NG16: Gilt 5E 17
Wenlock Dr. NG2: West Br 6B 58
 NG15: Huck 4A 8
Wensleydale Cl. NG8: Aspl 6B 32
Wensleydale Rd. NG10: Long E 1D 72
Wensley Rd. NG5: Woodt 2A 34
Wensor Av. NG9: Lent A 3F 55
Wentworth Cl. NG16: Kimb 5E 17
Wentworth Cft. DE75: Hea 2E 15
Wentworth Rd. NG5: Sher 5F 33
 NG9: Chil 5C 54
Wentworth St. DE7: Ilk 5C 28
Wentworth Way NG12: Edwal 2D 68
Wesleyan Chapel Wlk. NG9: Stfrd 4F 53
Wesley Av. NG9: Bee 5F 55
Wesley Ct. NG5: Sher 5G 33
 (off Drayton St.)
Wesley Gro. NG5: Sher 6F 33
Wesley Pl. NG9: Stfrd 6G 53
Wesley St. DE7: Ilk 3A 28
 NG5: Sher 6F 33
 NG16: Lang M 2F 15
Wesley Way NG11: Rudd 1H 77
Wessex Dr. NG16: Gilt, Newth 5C 16
West Av. NG2: West Br 4A 58
 NG9: Stfrd 3G 53
 NG10: Sand 5C 52
Westbourne Ct. NG9: Bram 2H 53
WEST BRIDGFORD 5A 58
Westbury Cl. NG9: Chil 1C 64
Westbury Rd. NG5: Sher 5D 32
Westby La. NG16: Babb, Coss 3E 29
Westcliffe Av. NG4: Ged 4F 35
 NG12: Rad T 5G 49
Westcliffe Ct. NG12: Rad T 5G 49
West Cl. NG12: Key 5G 79
West Cres. NG9: Bee 1H 65
W. Cross Av. NG9: Stfrd 3G 53
Westdale Cl. NG10: Long E 2C 72
Westdale Ct. NG4: Car 5F 35
Westdale Cres. NG4: Car 6G 35
Westdale La. E. NG4: Car 5E 35
Westdale La. W. NG3: Mapp 4C 34
West Dr. NG7: Nott 3H 55
West End NG9: Bee 6F 55
 NG14: Calv 3E 11
West End Arc. NG1: Nott 4C 4 (5F 45)
West End Cres. DE7: Ilk 1H 39
W. End Dr. DE7: Ilk 1H 39
W. End St. NG9: Stfrd 5E 53
West End Vs. NG12: Rad T 6E 49
 (off Main Rd.)
 NG14: Lowd 2H 25
Westerfield Way NG11: Wilf 1E 67
Westerham Cl. NG8: Bilb 2D 42
Westerham Rd. NG11: Rudd 1F 77
Westerhope Cl. NG12: Edwal 1E 69
Westerlands NG9: Stfrd 5G 53
Western Av. NG13: Bing 4D 50
Western Blvd. NG8: Aspl, Bas 1A 44
Western Dr. DE75: Hea 5D 14
Western Fids. NG11: Rudd 1F 77
Western Gdns. NG8: Aspl 1A 44
Western St. NG1: Nott 3F 5 (4H 45)
Western Ter. NG7: Nott 4A 4 (4H 45)
Westfield Av. DE75: Hea 5D 14
Westfield Cl. DE7: Kirk H 3G 39
Westfield Dr. DE7: Ilk 5H 27
Westfield La. NG14: Woodbo 1A 24
Westfield Rd. NG13: Bing 5D 50
West Furlong NG12: Cotg 3G 71
West Ga. NG10: Long E 6G 63
Westgate Ct. NG9: Chil 6E 55
Westgate St. NG3: Nott 3A 46
WEST HALLAM 1B 38
WEST HALLAM COMMON 1A 38
West Hallam Storage Dpt. DE7: West H 3C 38
Westhay Ct. NG8: Woll 4A 44
Westholme Gdns. NG8: Aspl 3A 44
Westhorpe Av. NG3: Nott 4B 46
Westhorpe Dr. NG10: Long E 5E 63
Westland Av. NG15: Huck 1D 18
W. Leake La. NG11: King 6C 74
Westleigh Rd. NG8: Brox 5E 31
Westmaner Ct. NG9: Chil 6D 54

West Mnr. Pk. NG14: Epp 5F 13
Westminster Av. NG10: Sand 6E 53
Westminster Cl. NG3: Nott 2A 46
West Moor NG2: Colw 5F 47
Westmoore Cl. NG3: Mapp 4D 34
Westmoore Ct. NG3: Mapp 4D 34
Westmoreland Ct. NG5: Sher 6F 33
 (off Ebury Rd.)
Weston Av. NG7: Radf 3E 45
Weston Cl. NG5: Woodt 3A 34
Weston Cotts. NG7: Radf 3C 44
Weston Cres. NG10: Long E 3B 72
Weston St. DE75: Hea 5E 15
Weston Ter. NG5: Sher 4G 33
West Pk. NG10: Long E 6F 63
West Park Leisure Cen. 6D 62
Westpoint NG2: West Br 4H 57
Westray Cl. NG9: Bram 6B 42
West Rd. NG7: Nott 1B 56
West St. DE7: Ilk 2A 40
 DE75: Hea 3B 14
 NG2: Nott 4H 5 (5A 46)
 NG5: Arn 6A 22
 NG12: S'frd 6H 37
 NG15: Huck 4G 7
 NG16: Kimb 3A 30
 NG16: Lang M 2F 15
West Ter. DE7: Ilk 6B 28
 NG15: Huck 4G 7
West Vw. NG2: West Br 6H 57
Westview Ct. NG4: Car 1H 47
West Vw. Rd. NG4: Car 1H 47
WESTVILLE 1D 18
Westville Dr. NG15: Huck 2E 19
Westville Gdns. NG3: Nott 2H 45
West Wlk. NG2: Nott 4H 5 (5A 46)
Westward Av. NG9: Bee 5G 55
Westway NG12: Cotg 3F 71
Westwick Rd. NG8: Bilb 3C 42
Westwick St. DE7: Ilk 3C 40
Westwood Rd. NG2: Nott 5B 46
Wetherby Cl. NG8: Aspl 6H 31
 NG16: Kimb 6G 17
Wetherlam Cl. NG2: Nott 1G 57
Weybridge Cl. DE7: West H 1B 38
Wharfedale NG8: Woll 6B 42
Wharfedale Rd. NG10: Long E 1C 72
Wharf Gdns. NG13: Bing 6C 50
Wharf La. NG12: Rad T 6E 49
Wharf Rd. NG7: Nott 6C 4 (6F 45)
Wharncliffe Rd. DE7: Ilk 1A 40
Wharton Cres. NG9: Bee 1F 65
Whatton Dr. NG2: West Br 2F 67
Whatton Ri. NG5: Sher 3F 33
Wheatacre Rd. NG11: Clftn 4D 66
Wheat Cl. NG8: Bilb 4D 42
Wheatcroft Bus. Cen. NG12: Edwal 4B 68
Wheatcroft Vw. NG2: West Br 2G 67
Wheatfields Rd. NG3: Nott 2C 46
Wheatgrass Rd. NG9: Chil 6B 54
Wheatley Cl. NG11: Rudd 2G 77
Wheatley Dr. NG4: Car 2E 47
Wheatley Gro. NG9: Chil 1F 65
Wheatsheaf Ct. NG14: Bur J 3F 37
Wheeldale Cl. NG8: Woll 5B 42
Wheeldon Cl. DE7: Ilk 1B 28
Wheeldon Ct. NG7: Bas 6D 32
Wheeler Av. NG16: Eastw 4D 16
Wheeler Ga. NG1: Nott 4D 4 (5G 45)
Wheldon Av. NG4: Car 6E 35
Whernside Rd. NG5: Woodt 2A 34
Whetstone Cl. NG16: Nuth 5D 30
Whickham Ct. NG2: Nott 2H 57
Whilton Cres. DE7: West H 1B 38
Whimsey Pk. NG4: Car 3H 47
Whinbush La. NG14: Calv 1G 11
Whinfell Cl. NG11: Clftn 3D 66
Whinlatter Dr. NG2: West Br 5E 59
Whiston Cl. NG5: Bestw 1E 33
Whitbread St. NG7: Bas 1D 44
Whitburn Rd. NG9: Toton 2G 63
Whitby Cl. NG8: Woll 5B 42
Whitby Cres. NG5: Woodt 2C 34
Whitby Rd. NG16: Newth 2C 16
Whitchurch Cl. NG5: Top V 5D 20
Whitcliffe Gdns. NG2: West Br 6B 58
Whitcombe Gdns. NG5: Top V 5E 21
Whiteacre NG14: Bur J 2E 37
Whitebeam Cl. NG12: Edwal 4C 68
Whitebeam Gdns. NG6: Bulw 6F 19
Whitechapel St. NG6: Bas 5B 32
White City Trad. Est. NG2: Nott 6C 46
Whitedale Rd. NG14: Calv 3E 11
White Furrows NG12: Cotg 3E 71
Whitegate Va. NG11: Clftn 4B 66
Whitehead Cl. DE7: Ilk 5H 27
Whitelands NG12: Cotg 3G 71
White Lodge Gdns. NG8: Bilb 2D 42
Whitely Av. DE7: Ilk 2B 28

Whitely Cl. NG9: Stfrd 3G 53
WHITEMOOR 1B 44
Whitemoor Av. NG8: Aspl, Bas 1B 44
Whitemoor Ct. NG8: Aspl 1B 44
Whitemoor Ct. Ind. Est. NG8: Aspl 1B 44
Whitemoor Rd. NG6: Bas 5B 32
Whitemoss Cl. NG8: Woll 6E 43
White Rd. NG5: Bas 4C 32
White's Av. NG3: Nott 3D 46
Whites Cft. NG14: Woodbo 1B 24
Whiteways Ct. NG11: Clftn 4C 66
Whitfield Cl. NG11: Wilf 5F 57
Whiting Av. NG9: Toton 3H 63
Whiting Cl. NG15: Huck 1A 8
Whittaker Rd. NG9: Chil 2A 64
Whittier Rd. NG2: Nott 6C 46
Whittingham Ct. NG3: Mapp 4C 34
Whittingham Rd. NG3: Mapp 4C 34
Whitton Cl. NG5: Top V 4F 21
 NG9: Chil 3C 64
Whitwell Cl. DE7: Ilk 1A 28
 NG8: Brox 6F 31
Whitwell Rd. NG8: Brox 6E 31
Whitworth Dr. NG12: Rad T 1E 61
 NG14: Bur J 5C 36
Whitworth Ri. NG5: Top V 5D 20
Whitworth Rd. DE7: Ilk 3B 40
Whyatt Cl. NG5: Arn 1H 33
Whyburn Ct. NG15: Huck 1A 20
Whyburn La. NG15: Huck 4C 6
Whyburn Pct. NG15: Huck 6E 7
Whyburn St. NG15: Huck 5A 8
Whysall Rd. NG10: Long E 6D 62
Whysall St. DE75: Hea 3C 14
Whyston Ct. NG15: Huck 6C 6
Whytehall Ct. NG10: Long E 2E 73
Wibberley Dr. NG11: Rudd 6F 67
Wichal Cl. NG5: Bestw 2G 33
Wichnor Cl. NG11: Clftn 1C 66
Wickens Wlk. NG3: Nott 3A 46
Wicker Cl. NG6: Bas 3C 32
Wicket Gro. NG7: Lent 5C 44
The Wickets NG2: West Br 2B 58
Wickstead Cl. NG5: Woodt 4B 34
Widdington Cl. NG5: Arn 3B 22
Widdowson Cl. NG6: Bulw 5F 19
Widdowson Dr. NG10: Long E 2D 72
Widdowson's Row NG11: Rudd 6G 67
 (off Easthorpe St.)
Widecombe La. NG11: Clftn 5B 66
Widmerpool La. NG12: Key, Widm 5A 80
WIGHAY 2F 7
Wighay Rd. NG15: Huck, Lin 2F 7
Wigley Cl. NG3: Nott 3A 46
Wigman Ct. NG15: Huck 5B 8
Wigman Rd. NG8: Bilb 1D 42
Wigwam Gro. NG15: Huck 4A 8
Wigwam La. NG15: Huck 4A 8
Wilberforce Rd. NG11: Wilf 6E 57
Wilcocksons Yd. NG15: Huck 4G 7
 (off Baker St.)
Wilden Cres. NG11: Clftn 2C 66
Wildman St. NG7: Radf 1A 4 (3E 45)
WILFORD 5F 57
Wilford Bri. NG2: Nott 2F 57
Wilford Cres. NG11: Rudd 5G 67
Wilford Cres. E. NG2: Nott 2H 57
Wilford Cres. W. NG2: Nott 1G 57
Wilford Gro. NG2: Nott 1G 57
 (not continuous)
WILFORD HILL 1A 68
Wilford Hill Crematorium 2H 67
Wilford La. NG2: West Br 5F 57
 NG11: West Br, Wilf 5F 57
Wilford Rd. NG2: Nott 1F 57
 (not continuous)
 NG11: Rudd 6D 4 (6G 45)
Wilford Village Stop (NET) 3F 57
Wilfrid Gro. NG2: West Br 2A 68
Wilkins Gdns. NG11: Clftn 4A 66
Wilkinson Av. NG9: Bee 5F 55
Wilkinson Cl. NG9: Chil 3B 64
Wilkinson St. NG7: Bas 6B 32
 NG8: Bas 6B 32
Wilkinson Street Park & Ride 1C 44
Wilkinson Street Stop (NET) 1C 44
Willaston Cl. NG6: Cin 3A 32
Wilbert Rd. NG5: Arn 5C 22
Willerby Rd. NG5: Woodt 2C 34
Willersley Dr. NG2: Nott 1G 57
Willesden Grn. NG16: Nuth 4D 30
William Av. NG16: Eastw 3B 16
William Bancroft Bldg. NG3: Nott 2H 5
William Booth Birthplace Mus. 5A 46
William Booth Rd. NG2: Nott 5C 46
William Cl. NG4: Ged 1B 48
William Gregg VC Leisure Cen. 4D 14
William Lee Bldgs. NG7: Nott 3B 56
William Olds Ct. NG8: Woll 4G 43

William Rd. NG2: West Br 3A 58
NG9: Stfrd 4F 53
Williams Dr. NG14: Calv 2G 11
Williamson Gdns. NG16: Lang M 2E 15
Williamson Row NG5: Bestw 2E 33
(off Arnold Rd.)
Williams Rd. NG9: Chil 2A 64
William St. NG10: Long E 3E 63
NG15: Huck 4G 7
Willoughby Av. NG4: Lent 5D 44
NG10: Long E 3E 63
Willoughby Cl. DE72: Brea 5B 62
NG7: Nott 3H 55
Willoughby Rd. NG2: West Br 5B 58
Willoughby St. NG7: Lent 6D 44
NG9: Bee 4F 55
Willow Av. NG4: Car 1A 48
NG9: Stfrd 5F 53
NG10: Long E 4F 63
NG15: Huck 1D 18
Willow Brook NG12: Key 5A 80
Willowbrook Ct. NG2: Nott 2G 57
Willow Cl. NG2: West Br 2F 59
NG12: Rad T .1F 61
NG14: Bur J 2F 37
NG16: Lang M 2F 15
Willow Cotts. NG8: Bilb 2G 43
Willow Ct. NG2: West Br 6H 57
Willow Cres. NG4: Ged 5A 36
NG4: Lamb 6B 24
Willowdene NG12: Cotg 2G 71
Willow Hill Cl. NG6: Bulw 1G 31
Willow La. NG4: Ged 5H 35
Willow Ri. NG10: Sand 6D 52
Willow Rd. NG2: West Br 1A 68
NG4: Car 2C 56
NG7: Lent 6G 61
NG12: Cotg 5G 51
NG13: Bing 2G 43
The Willows NG8: Bilb 5F 55
NG9: Bee 3D 44
Willow Vw. NG7: Radf 3D 44
Willow Wong NG14: Bur J 2F 37
Willow Wong Cotts. NG14: Bur J 2G 67
Willwell Dr. NG2: West Br 1H 33
Wilmington Gdns. NG5: Arn 1D 64
Wilmore Cl. NG9: Chil 6F 55
Wilmot La. NG9: Bee 6A 28
Wilmot St. DE7: Ilk 4C 14
DE75: Hea 2C 72
NG10: Long E 3C 72
Wilne Av. NG10: Long E 3B 72
Wilne Cl. NG10: Long E 3A 72
Wilne La. DE72: Dray 3A 72
NG10: Long E 3A 72
Wilne Rd. NG10: Long E 3B 72
Wilson Av. DE75: Los 1A 14
Wilson Cl. NG5: Arn 1D 34
Wilson Rd. NG16: Eastw 4B 16
Wilsons Ct. NG11: Rudd 6G 67
WILSTHORPE .5D 62
Wilsthorpe Rd. DE72: Brea 5A 62
NG10: Long E 5D 62
Wilton Pl. DE7: Ilk 6B 28
Wilton Rd. NG7: Radf 3C 44
Wilton St. DE7: Ilk 6B 28
NG6: Bas 3C 32
Wilton Ter. NG6: Bas 3C 32
Wimbledon Dr. NG16: Nuth 4E 31
Wimbledon Rd. NG5: Sher 4E 33
Wimborne Cl. NG2: West Br 6G 57
Wimbourne Rd. NG7: Radf 3D 44
Wimpole Rd. NG9: Bram 2D 54
Winchester Av. NG9: Bee 3E 55
Winchester Ct. NG5: Sher 4A 34
Winchester Cres. DE7: Ilk 1C 40
Winchester St. NG5: Sher 4G 33
Winchester Ter. NG5: Sher 4G 33
Windermere Av. DE7: Kirk H 4G 39
Windermere Cl. NG2: Gam 4F 59
NG4: Ged 5H 35
Windermere Gdns. NG10: Long E 3D 62
Windermere Rd.
NG7: Hys G 1E 45
NG9: Bram 2D 54
NG10: Long E 3C 62
NG15: Huck 4F 7
The Windings NG4: Car 2F 47
(off Chesterfield St.)
Windles Sq. NG14: Calv 4A 12
Windley Dr. DE7: Ilk 4H 27
Windmill Av. NG15: Huck 5G 7
Windmill Cl. NG3: Nott 4B 46
NG11: Goth 6H 75
Windmill Ct. NG12: Key 5H 79
Windmill Gro. NG15: Huck 4G 7
Windmill La. NG2: Nott 5A 46
NG3: Nott 5A 46
Windmill Vw. NG2: Nott 5C 46
Windrush Cl. NG9: Bram 2D 54

Windsor Cl. DE75: Hea 2C 14
NG8: Aspl 2B 44
NG9: Trow 4D 40
NG15: Huck 3H 7
Windsor Ct.
DE7: West H .1B 38
NG10: Long E 6G 63
NG10: Sand 1D 62
NG13: Bing 5C 50
Windsor Cres. DE7: Kirk H 4H 39
NG5: Woodt .1C 34
NG9: Stfrd 4G 53
Windsor Ho. NG3: Mapp P 1G 45
Windsor St. NG9: Bee 5G 55
NG9: Stfrd 4G 53
Wing All. NG1: Nott 4F 5 (5H 45)
Wingate Cl. NG8: Bilb 3F 43
Wingbourne Wlk. NG6: Bulw 4A 20
(not continuous)
Wingfield Dr. DE7: Ilk 4H 27
NG9: Lent A 2G 55
Wings Dr. NG15: Huck 1D 18
Winifred Cl. NG11: Wilf 5E 57
Winifred Cres. NG14: Bur J 3F 37
Winifred St. NG15: Huck 5H 7
Winrow Gdns. NG6: Bas 4A 32
Winscale Av. NG5: Top V 5E 21
Winscale Gdns. NG5: Top V 5E 21
Winscombe Mt. NG11: Clftn 5B 66
Winsford Cl. NG8: Aspl 5H 31
Winster Av. NG4: Car 6F 35
Winster Cl. NG9: Lent A 2F 55
Winster Pk. DE7: Ilk 4C 40
Winster Way NG10: Long E 2B 72
Winston Cl. NG3: Mapp 2E 35
NG9: Stfrd 3G 53
Winterbourne Dr. NG9: Stfrd 2G 53
Winterton Cl. NG5: Arn 1B 34
Winterton Gdns. NG5: Bestw 6F 21
Winterton Ri. NG5: Bestw 6F 21
Winthorpe Rd. NG5: Arn 6C 22
Wintringham Cres. NG5: Woodt 2C 34
Wirksworth Rd. DE7: Kirk H 4F 39
Wisa Ter. NG5: Sher 4H 33
Wishford Av. NG7: Lent 6C 44
Wisley Cl. NG2: West Br 2G 67
Wisteria Rd. NG4: Neth, Stoke B 2C 48
Wistow Cl. NG8: Bas 1C 44
Withern Rd. NG8: Brox 6F 31
Witney Cl. NG5: Top V 5C 20
Wittering Cl. NG10: Long E 2G 73
Wiverton Rd. NG7: Hys G 1E 45
NG13: Bing 5E 51
Woburn Cl. NG12: Edwal 1E 69
Woburn Cft. NG10: Sand 1C 62
Woburn Ri. NG5: Woodt 2D 34
Wodehouse Av. NG11: Goth 5H 79
Wolds Dr. NG12: Key 2D 80
Wolds Farm Cotts. NG12: Stant W 5D 70
Wolds La. NG12: C'ton 6G 79
NG12: Key 6B 70
NG12: Norm W 4H 79
Wolds Ri. NG12: Key 2F 71
Woldsview Ho. NG12: Cotg 6D 42
WOLLATON 4F 35
Wollaton Av. NG4: Ged 1C 32
Wollaton Ct. NG6: Bulw 3E 55
Wollaton Cres. NG9: Bee 6G 43
Wollaton Hall 6B 44
Wollaton Hall Dr. NG8: Woll 5C 42
Wollaton Paddocks NG8: Woll 6H 43
Wollaton Pk. Golf Course 1E 55
Wollaton Ri. NG8: Woll 5E 43
Wollaton Rd. NG8: Radf, Woll 2E 55
NG9: Bee 3B 4 (4F 45)
Wollaton St. NG1: Nott 4H 7
NG15: Huck . . . .
(not continuous)
Wollaton Va. NG8: Woll 5B 42
Wolsey Av. NG7: Radf 4D 44
Wood Av. NG10: Sand 5C 52
Woodbank Dr. NG8: Woll 1D 54
WOODBOROUGH 1C 24
Woodborough La. NG3: Mapp 2D 22
NG5: Arn 2D 22
Woodborough Rd. NG1: Nott 1E 5 (3G 45)
NG3: Mapp, Nott 1E 5 (3G 45)
Woodbridge Av. NG11: Clftn 2C 66
Woodbridge Cl. DE75: Hea 4F 15
Woodbridge Gro. NG7: Hys G 2D 44
(off St Paul's Av.)
Woodchurch Rd. NG5: Arn 4F 21
Wood Cl. NG11: Rudd 1F 77
Wood End Rd. DE75: Hea 3C 14
Wood Farm Cl. NG11: Thru 5C 74
Woodfield Rd. NG8: Brox 6E 31
Woodford Cl. NG5: Top V 4C 20
Woodford Rd. NG5: Woodt 2C 34
NG15: Huck 5H 7
Woodgate Cl. NG12: Cotg 2E 71

Woodgate Ct. NG7: Radf 3A 4 (4E 45)
Woodgate La. NG12: Cotg 1D 70
Wood Gro. NG14: Calv 3H 11
Woodhall Rd. NG8: Woll 4H 43
Woodhedge Dr. NG3: Nott 1C 46
Woodhorn Cl. NG5: Arn 3B 22
Woodhouse Gdns. NG11: Rudd 5F 67
Woodhouse St. NG3: Nott 4B 46
Woodhouse Way NG8: Stre 1D 42
NG16: Nuth 1D 42
Woodkirk Rd. NG11: Clftn 3D 66
Woodland Av. DE7: Ilk 3H 27
DE72: Brea 5B 62
NG6: Bulw 2A 32
Woodland Cl. NG12: Cotg 3F 71
NG12: Rad T .6H 49
NG16: Want 6A 18
Woodland Dr. NG3: Mapp P 6H 33
NG16: Nuth 3F 31
Woodland Gro. NG4: Colw 3H 47
NG5: Sher 3H 33
NG9: Chil 6D 54
Woodlands NG2: West Br 2B 58
The Woodlands DE7: Kirk H 6E 49
Woodlands Farm Cl. NG15: Huck 1D 18
Woodlands Gro. NG15: Huck 1D 18
Woodland Way NG16: Eastw 3A 16
Wood La. NG4: Ged 6A 36
NG15: Huck 4E 7
Woodlane Gdns. NG3: Nott 2B 46
Woodlark Ho. NG3: Nott 2B 46
Woodleigh NG12: Key 5G 79
Woodleigh Gdns. NG3: Mapp 5D 34
Woodley Sq. NG6: Bulw 3A 20
Woodley St. NG11: Rudd 6G 67
Wood Link NG6: Bulw 6E 19
Woodpecker Cl. NG3: Bing 6F 51
Woodpecker Hill DE7: D Ab 6E 39
Woodrow Av. NG8: Bilb 1G 43
Woodsend Cl. NG14: Bur J 3F 37
Woodsend Wharf NG7: Nott 6C 4 (6F 45)
Woodsford Gro. NG11: Clftn 3C 66
Woodside Av. NG12: Rad T 6H 49
NG16: Nuth 1B 30
Woodside Cres. DE7: Ilk 2H 27
NG10: Sand .5D 62
Woodside Dr. NG5: Arn 5H 21
Woodside Rd. NG9: Bee, Lent A 2F 55
NG9: Chil 1A 64
NG10: Sand .6C 52
NG12: Rad T .6H 49
NG14: Bur J 4D 36
Woods La. NG14: Calv 4G 11
Woodstock Av. NG7: Radf 3C 44
Woodstock Rd. NG9: Toton 2G 63
Woodstock St. NG15: Huck 5H 7
Woodstock St. W. NG15: Huck 4H 7
Woodston Wlk. NG5: Arn 3C 22
Wood St. DE7: Ilk 6B 28
NG5: Arn 5B 22
NG7: Radf 3A 4 (4E 45)
NG16: Eastw .3B 16
WOODTHORPE 2B 34
Woodthorpe Av. NG5: Woodt 3A 34
Woodthorpe Ct. NG5: Sher 4A 34
Woodthorpe Dr. NG3: Mapp 3A 34
NG5: Woodt .3H 33
Woodthorpe Gdns. NG5: Sher 4B 34
Woodthorpe Grange NG5: Woodt 4A 34
WOODTHORPE HOSPITAL
Nottingham 2H 33
Woodthorpe M. NG5: Woodt 3H 33
Woodthorpe Rd. NG3: Mapp 4B 34
Woodvale NG8: Woll 5B 42
Woodview NG12: Cotg 2G 71
NG12: Edwal .2D 68
Woodview Bus. Cen. NG5: Top V 4E 21
Woodview Ct. NG3: Nott 5E 46
Woodville Cl. NG9: Chil 5C 54
Woodville Dr. NG5: Sher 4G 33
Woodville Rd. NG5: Sher 5G 33
Woodward Av. NG9: Chil 3B 64
Woodward St. NG2: Nott 2H 57
Woodyard La. NG8: Woll 4G 43
(Coachmans Cft.)
NG8: Woll 4G 43
(Tom Blower Cl.)
Woolacombe Cl. NG3: Mapp 7F 35
Woolliscroft Cl. DE7: Ilk 5G 27
Woolmer Rd. NG2: Nott 2G 57
Woolpack La. NG1: Nott 4F 5 (5H 45)
Woolsington Cl. NG8: Stre 5D 30
Woolsthorpe Cl. NG8: Bilb 3F 43
Woolsthorpe Cres. DE7: Kirk H 5H 39
Wootton Cl. NG8: Bilb 2D 42
Worcester Gdns. NG5: Woodt 1A 34
Worcester Rd. NG5: Woodt 2A 34
Wordsworth Av. NG15: Huck 5D 6

Wordsworth Rd. NG12: West Br 5A **58**
  NG5: Arn 6H **21**
  NG7: Radf 3C **44**
  NG16: Aws 2E **29**
Worksop Rd. NG3: Nott 4B **46**
Worrall Av. NG5: Arn .6B **22**
  NG10: Long E 4G **63**
Worth St. NG4: Car 1G **47**
Worthy Row *NG5: Bestw* *2E 33*
                              (off Arnold Rd.)
Wortley Av. NG9: Trow 6F **41**
Wortley Cl. DE7: Ilk 1C **40**
Wortley Hall Cl. NG7: Nott 1A **56**
Worwood Dr. NG2: West Br 1G **67**
Woulds Fld. NG12: Cotg 4F **71**
Wragby Rd. NG7: Lent 4C **44**
Wray Cl. NG3: Nott 4A **46**
Wren Ct. NG10: Long E 3C **72**
Wren Dr. NG6: Bestw V 2C **20**
Wrenthorpe Va. NG11: Clftn 4C **66**
Wrights Orchard NG12: Key 5G **79**
Wright St. NG4: Neth 2A **48**
Wroughton Ct. NG16: Eastw 3C **16**
Wroxham Dr. NG8: Woll 6D **42**
Wychwood Dr. NG9: Trow 1F **53**
Wychwood Rd. NG13: Bing 5C **50**
Wycliffe Gro. NG3: Mapp 5A **34**
Wycliffe St. NG7: Bas .6D **32**
Wycombe Cl. NG11: Clftn 5B **66**
Wye Gdns. NG7: Radf .3B **44**
Wykeham Rd. NG5: Woodt 2C **34**
Wykes Av. NG4: Ged 5H **35**
Wymondham Cl. NG5: Arn 1C **34**

Wynbreck Dr. NG12: Key 4H **79**
Wyndale Dr. DE7: Kirk H 3G **39**
Wyndham Ct. NG9: Chil 1B **64**
Wyndham M. NG3: Mapp P 2F **45**
The Wyndings NG5: Woodt 3B **34**
Wynhill Ct. NG13: Bing 4C **50**
Wynndale Dr. NG5: Sher 4E **33**
Wynwood Cl. NG9: Toton 3B **64**
Wynwood Rd. NG9: Toton 3B **64**
Wynyard Cl. DE7: Ilk 4G **27**
Wyrale Dr. NG8: Stre 6E **31**
Wysall La. NG11: Bunny 6D **78**
  NG12: Key 6G **79**
Wyton Cl. NG5: Bestw .2E **33**
Wyvern Av. NG10: Long E 1F **73**
Wyvern Cl. NG16: Newth 5C **16**
Wyville Cl. NG7: Radf .4C **44**

Y

Yalding Dr. NG8: Woll .5C **42**
Yalding Gdns. NG8: Woll 5C **42**
The Yard *NG7: Hys G* *3D 44*
                            (off Sophie Rd.)
The Yard Gallery 6G **43**
Yarwell Cl. NG3: Nott .2E **47**
Yatesbury Cres. NG8: Stre 1E **43**
Yates Gdns. NG5: Top V 5E **21**
Ye Olde Trip To Jerusalem Inn *6D 4*
                            (off Castle Rd.)
Yeoman Av. NG6: Bestw V 1D **20**
Yeomans Pde. NG4: Car 2H **47**

Yewbarrow Cl. NG2: West Br 6E **59**
Yew Cl. NG5: Sher 5H **33**
Yewdale Cl. NG2: West Br 6E **59**
  NG11: Clftn 5B **66**
Yew Tree Av. NG5: Sher 6G **33**
Yew Tree Cl. DE75: Hea 5A **14**
  NG12: Rad T 6D **48**
Yew Tree Ct. NG5: Sher 6G **33**
  NG9: Bee 5G **55**
Yew Tree La. NG4: Ged 5A **36**
  NG11: Clftn 3A **66**
Yew Tree Rd. NG15: Huck 6H **7**
Yewtree Rd. NG12: Cotg 6G **61**
Yonge Cl. NG12: Rad T 1E **61**
  NG10: Sand 6C **52**
York Av. NG9: Bee 1F **65**
York Cl. NG4: Ged 5H **35**
York Dr. NG8: Stre 5D **30**
Yorke St. NG15: Huck 4G **7**
York M. NG5: Arn 5B **22**
York Rd. NG10: Long E 4E **63**
York St. NG1: Nott 1E **5** (3G **45**)
  NG4: Neth 2A **48**
Young Cl. NG6: Bulw 2F **31**
Yvonne Cres. NG4: Car 2H **47**

Z

The Zone NG1: Nott 3F **5**
Zouche Cl. DE75: Los .3A **14**
Zulla Rd. NG3: Mapp P 1G **45**
Zulu Rd. NG7: Bas 5D **32**

MIX
Paper from
responsible sources
FSC® C016201
www.fsc.org

SAFETY CAMERA INFORMATION

PocketGPSWorld.com's CamerAlert is a self-contained speed and red light camera warning system for SatNavs and Android or Apple iOS smartphones/tablets. Visit www.cameralert.com to download.

Safety camera locations are publicised by the Safer Roads Partnership which operates them in order to encourage drivers to comply with speed limits at these sites. It is the driver's absolute responsibility to be aware of and to adhere to speed limits at all times.

By showing this safety camera information it is the intention of Geographers' A-Z Map Company Ltd. to encourage safe driving and greater awareness of speed limits and vehicle speed. Data accurate at time of printing.